MODEL MACHINES

In the series *Asian American History and Culture*, edited by Cathy Schlund-Vials, Shelley Sang-Hee Lee, and Rick Bonus. Founding editor, Sucheng Chan; editors emeriti, David Palumbo-Liu, Michael Omi, K. Scott Wong, and Linda Trinh Võ.

A list of additional titles in this series appears at the back of this book.

LONG T. BUI

MODEL MACHINES

A History of the Asian as Automaton

TEMPLE UNIVERSITY PRESS
Philadelphia • *Rome* • *Tokyo*

TEMPLE UNIVERSITY PRESS
Philadelphia, Pennsylvania 19122
tupress.temple.edu

Library of Congress Cataloging-in-Publication Data

Names: Bui, Long T. author.
Title: Model machines : a history of the Asian as automaton / Long T. Bui.
Other titles: Asian American history and culture.
Description: Philadelphia : Temple University Press, 2022. | Series: Asian
  American history and culture | Includes bibliographical references and
  index. | Summary: "A study of the stereotype and representation of
  Asians as robotic machines through history"— Provided by publisher.
Identifiers: LCCN 2021046256 | ISBN 9781439922330 (cloth) | ISBN
  9781439922347 (paperback) | ISBN 9781439922354 (pdf)
Subjects: LCSH: Asian Americans—Ethnic identity. | Asian Americans—Social
  conditions. | Asian Americans—Public opinion. | Stereotypes (Social
  psychology)—United States. | Humanity.
Classification: LCC E184.A75 B85 2022 | DDC 305.895/073—dc23/eng/20211122
LC record available at https://lccn.loc.gov/2021046256

Printed in the United States of America

9 8 7 6 5 4 3 2 1

Contents

List of Images

Acknowledgments

This book was a product of love and labor inspired by a community of wonderful humans and some cool nonhumans. Funding for this book came from the Center for Asian Studies at UCI and the National Endowment of Humanities (NEH). First, I would thank Jerry Harris and the editors of the journal *Perspectives on Global Development and Technology* (Brill) for allowing me to republish my article "Asian Roboticism" as part of Chapter 5, "Global Machines." At Temple University Press, I would like to thank the incomparable editors Shaun Vigil and Vijay Shah, my stellar peer reviewers, copyeditor, and the entire editorial board of the Asian American History and Culture series. The humane Yen Le Espiritu will shape my thinking for all lifetimes; she really is my model. Much love to Evyn, Maya, Abe, Gabe, and Ms. Delia. Ross Frank's work on digital communities gave me the courage to enter technocultural studies with abandon. Denise Ferreira da Silva's love of science fiction and philosophy prompted the impulse to pursue eccentric projects like this study. I hope this book answers her question, "What happened to Man?" Lisa Lowe helped me flesh out burgeoning ideas about Asian/American and Orientalism. Ricardo Dominguez helped me to virtually hack into my cyborg imaginary and posthuman nanofuture. Thu-Huong Nguyen-Vo is my muse, while Paul Amar is my biggest advocate. Bishnupriya Ghosh is simply "iconic," as well as Phung Huynh and Anh-Thu Nguyen.

Peers I admire are Pronoy Rai, Ga-Young Chung, Julie Thi Underhill, Marimas Hosan Mostiller, Thao Ha, Lawrence Minh-Bui, and Mimi Khuc.

Davorn Sisavath is truly "peerless," much like Cathleen Kozen, Kyung-Hee Ha, Tomoko Tsuchiya, Ma Vang, and Kit Myers. Homegirl Yessica Hernandez is my *amiga* forever, while distant friend Ayako Sahara understands me too well (I value her for comments for my Japan chapter). Other folks I met at the University of California, San Diego, include Lisa Park, Andrew Jolivette, Daphne Taylor-Garcia, Simeon Man, Shaista Patel, Chien-Ting Lin, Leslie Quintanilla, Joo Ok Kim, Alvin Wong, Todd Henry, Amanda Solomon, Linh Nguyen, Victor Betts, Ash Kinney, Yumi Pak, Kalindi Vora, and Josen Diaz. Admirable colleagues outside this university include John Paul Catungal, Chris Eng, Jane Pak, May Xiong, and Mai See Thao. As my constant reviewer, Tim August is the man! The infatigable Robyn Rodriguez and Martin F. Manalansan are my professional goals.

Much respect goes to Wesley Attewell, Kale Fajardo, and the queen of robots, Margaret Rhee. Special recognition goes to Rashne Limki and Julie Hua for keeping me up-to-date on feminist technology readings. Mohamed Abuyame is a winner in my eyes, much like soul brother and clone Juvenal Caporale. Kudos to my academic little sis, Ly Thuy Nguyen, and big sis, Ofelia Cuevas, for all their successes and those to come. Ly is a creative genius, and Ofelia is a wonder woman. Gina Opinado, Maria "Tere" Cesenas, Monika Gosin, and Michelle Gutierrez are superwomen. Best of friends Stevie Ruiz makes me laugh and think all the time; and his thinking is as radical as the artificial/natural intelligence of Jeremy Yu. Stevie is simply the best collaborator and friend I can have, no less than my dear friend Martha Escobar. Jennifer Kim Anh Tran keeps the fire of inspiration alive. Other people of note are Van Pham, Daniel Olmos, Claudia Sandoval, Jude Paul Dizon, and Sam Samod. Those in my circle include Vinh Nguyen, Nguyen Tobias Dang, Khoa Le, Hien Huynh, Nam Phong Le, Huy Foster Nguyen, Alex Chien, Terry Thai Tran, Marvin "Bao" Trinh, Jay Tran, Ryley Dee, Viet Hoang, and Quan Nguyen. Nguyen Le has remained a main anchor for everything; I owe much to him. Christy Vosges is an angel put on earth, while Peter Keo is a leader that I am in awe of. Hy "Tim" Bui is an avid reader and thinking machine. Anika Santorelli is the best social companion, partying along with Ali. Joseph Allen Juanto-Ramirez brings magic and myth to everything he does. Bestie Carol Vu's friendship sustained me for ages. Besides the superhuman Viet Le, Tram Le and Wolfgang Shane as well shower me with sage advice for navigating this complex human world, alongside Ysa Le and Yvonne Tran. Louie Nguyen is one cool dude. I thank Tam Vo for all he did for me. Darlene Lee is a great observer of mortal behavior; she is the best.

Cathy Schlund-Vials remains someone I can always count on for everything. Mimi Nguyen's groundbreaking essay on queer Vietnamese mutant cyborgs sparked my earliest interest in feminist media; she showed me the magic behind the myth. Sandra Ruiz is like a sister to me much like Patricia

Nguyen. Fiona Ngo has taught me many things, and I appreciate her guidance. Jodi Kim read this manuscript with meticulous eyes and true care, and I thank her profusely. Julie Dowling has helped me in so many ways, along with Laura Castaneda and Alicia Rodriguez. Laura Kang offered key advice that allowed me to pursue this project with gusto. With Marisa Duarte, Arely Zimmerman is the kind of companion I need in the best and worst of times. Fantastic people I met while at University of Illinois Urbana-Champaign include Lisa Cacho, a key advisor on fashion and jobs. Others include Douglas Heintz, Naomi Paik, Soo Ah Kwon, Augusto Espiritu, Junaid Rana, Jeannie Shinozuka, Durell Callier, Xuxa Rodriguez, and Richard Gessert. Rehema Barber always keeps it real with me, as does Kieu Linh Valverde, Sarita See, and Catherine Nguyen. Yolanda Escamilla (and Beto) are just good people.

At Wesleyan University, I met the wonderful Krystal-Gayle O'Neill, Michael Meere, Roger Grant, Paula Park, Bo Conn, Tricia Hill, Indira Karamcheti, Cybele Moon, Jeannie He, Quan Tran, Olivia Drake, Abbie Boggs, Alton Wang, Marguerite Nguyen, Sunny Xiang, Joan Cho, Ying Jia Tan, and Takeshi Watanabe. Carlos Dimas brought out the true historian in me; I hope I make him proud. Much love to Karen Aldridge and Eddie Torres for keeping creativity alive during these times. At Vassar College, I met lovely people, such as Nancy Jo Pokrywka, Carlos Alamo, Wayne Soon, Leonard Nevarez, Seungsook Moon, Bill Hoynes, Erendira Rueda, Diane Harriford, Jose Perillan, Louis Romer, Li Kang, Pat Turner, Krista Brown, Maria Hoehn, Jaime del Razo, Pinar Batur, Leroy Cooper, and Jasmine Syedullah. Osman Nemli and Pauline Goul are comrades in the struggle for humanity. My pandemic peer Erin Malone keeps me sane in the world, besides Antonieta Mercado. At the University of California, Riverside, I met down-to-earth folks, such as Arifa Raza, Kehaulani Vaughn, Charlie Sepulveda, Angelica "Pickels" Pepino, Keith Miyake, Tammy Ho, and Emily Hue. Viet Nguyen and Lan Duong still inspire me to this day. My close coven still consists of Tessa Winkelman, Genevieve Clutario, Christine Peralta, and Shantel Martinez. Phi Su is my human doppelganger, while Victoria Reyes is my twin.

I would like to thank my current Department of Global and International Studies, especially its founders Eve Darian-Smith and Phil McCarty. At the University of California, Irvine, I found great colleagues in muses like Tiffany Willouby-Herard, Sal Zarate, Nasim Fekrat, Liz Rubio, Sharon Block, John Marquez, Annie Ro, Rocio Rosales, Jewel Quilaton, Sarah Whitt, Christopher Paul Harris, Tiara Na'Puti, Yatta Kiazolu, and the always unforgettable Ruth Goldstein who I miss dearly. Vibhuti Ramachandran is my colleague turned confidante, while Sarah Whitt has the best eye for all things Mamyrah Douge-Prosper and Felix Jean-Louis III are absolute joy. Thanks to Gustavo Oliveira and Li Zhang for all the tea and other snacks. What fine neighbors I have in Chelsea Schields and Yousuf Al-Bulushi, who always keep me entertained. Richard "Brian" Williams, Richard Cho, Daniel Tsang, and Christina Woo are the best research librarians ever. Jeanett Castellanos remains a core part of my academic *familia*, which includes the immortal Caesar Sereseres. My "besties" at UCI include Jessica Canas-Castaneda who remains for me a true believer in keeping it real, along with another passionate companion, Luis Fonseca. Jeffrey Wasserstrom mentored me in public scholarship; I look up to him, as well as "em" Diu-Huong Nguyen and "anh" Tuan Hoang. Linda Trinh Vo remains a trusted adviser in and outside the workplace, while Teresa Neighbors, Yara Maria Bojorquez, Ted Watson, and Jonathan Lui are key accomplices in diversity work. Glenda Flores is my anteater homie and lover of food. Anneeth Hundle and Sherine Hamdy are the best AI (amazing interlocutors) I can always count on. Judy Wu, Isabella Quintana, and Dorothy Fujita-Rony are great femtors with a human touch. Dorothy especially is my rock for all ages; she showed me the power of history and how it reaches forward to the future.

I look forward to seeing what wonderful things come from the students I have the privilege to closely mentor or befriend, from all the countless undergrads to the graduate students I got to know well: D. Alex Pina, Edward Kenneth Lazaro Nadurata, Gvantsa Gasviani, Trinh Dang, Pascal Dafinis, Katherine Funes, Quyen Nguyen-Le, Ann Thuy-Ling Tran, and Qianru Li. Others at Irvine that I find affinity with are Jonathan Lui, Edward "Ted" Watson, Alicia Marie Carroll, Samar Al-Bulushi, Yidong Gong, Roberto Tinoco, and Anita Casavantes-Bradford. Jerry Won Lee is literally my cyborg brother from another (alien)mother. Let me thank the UC Humanities Research Institute Fellowship (UCHRI) group I participated in called Artificial Humanity, where I culled even more creative ideas for the book, especially from Annie Mcclanahan and Renee Fox. Lastly, I thank my biological family, including my wonderful siblings (Thuy, Luan, Thoa), cousins (Hanh, Linh, Nhung), elders (Bac My and Co Ha), and future model minority machine nieces and nephews: Tiffany, Ethan, Danielle, Libby, Mason, and Simon. I am grateful to everyone in the extended family and friends around the world who make me remember my human side even when I feel sometimes like a model machine.

MODEL MACHINES

Introduction

The Model Machine Myth

In 2018, Albert Einstein's travel diaries to Asia were published to great fanfare. Documenting his personal voyages to far-off places like Japan, Ceylon (modern-day Sri Lanka), and Palestine, these personal items were never meant for public viewing. But upon their release, the private contents revealed a young man with troubling thoughts. Once denouncing racism as a "disease of white people," the most famous scientist of his time held fast to odious thoughts about Chinese people. In Hong Kong, the physicist remarked upon his encounters with "industrious, filthy, obtuse people. Houses very formulaic, balconies like beehive-cells, everything built close together and monotonous." He surmised that "it would be a pity if these Chinese supplant all other races . . . [and] noticed how little difference there is between men and women."[1] These normative claims about the people of Hong Kong found renewed expression in Shanghai and the mainland, where he chanced upon "a peculiar herd-like nation . . . often resembling automatons more than people."[2]

The Jewish American intellectual spun a lengthy yarn about the sorry state of the Chinese as beastly creatures of stupor—too loathsome to be taken seriously—and as dumb machines imperiling humankind. Einstein was not the only one who believed such things throughout history. Given this thick bias, how then do we take stock of these kinds of intrigue about foreign "machine people" and automaton races? In what ways does this casual stereotyping upend the sense of human progress epitomized by great men of science like Einstein? From his theories of (social) relativity, we can advance some queries of how modeling humanism casts a distorted picture of Asians as model machines.

In the contemporary Western imagination, Asian people are frequently described as automatons, a symbolic union that assumes they are (un)naturally fitted to the exacting demands of modern capitalism, while typifying a primitive form of economic life that is also precapitalist. So wedded are Asian minds and bodies to all things tech, they come to resemble robots, an opinion sketched by college admissions officers that typecast Asian Americans as "quasi-robots programmed by their parents to ace math and science."[3] Attributions of joylessness to work-focused Asians resonate with the model minority thesis of Asian Americans as bookish and smart but not necessarily intellectual or creative, ever so proficient in engineering, mathematics, and technical subjects lacking a "human touch." This popular myth abides by the general techno-Orientalist perception of Asia as a land soaked with superhuman laborers who only know work not play.

This concept of techno-Orientalism originally concerned the economic ascent of Japan in the late twentieth century and its economic threat against the West, while the model minority myth was born of the Cold War to explain away "race problems" in twentieth-century America. Neither framework is sufficient to explain how Asians and Asian Americans were figured as automata well over a century earlier or how this cultural meme spread to encompass multiple regions and time periods. Conflations of people from the East with "living machines" seem to originate from newfound fears of white Europeans being bypassed in the mechanical arts in the age of informatics and computers. But such thinking emerged much earlier at a time when the vocabulary of Asian automata was furnished to "coerce certain figures into nonbeing."[4]

Model Machines: A History of the Asian as Automaton follows the long career of a rather strange concept, one that assumes that Asians act and behave like numbed automata bereft of deep feeling, spontaneous thought, and human consciousness. Numerous scholars have deployed the general term *techno-Orientalism* to analyze the Asian machine trope. The working concept has been taken up by scholars of literary and cultural studies observing that the Asian body is "a form of expendable technology—a view that emerged in the discourse of early U.S. industrialization and continued to evolve in the twentieth century."[5] Despite their acute observations, there is not yet a full historiography that follows that body's idiosyncratic development and evolution over a long arc of time, factoring in such broad themes as colonialism, globalization, war, and labor or such paradigms of thought as race, gender and sexuality.[6]

Model Machines is the first work to offer a historical overview of the overlapping racialization of Asians and Asian Americans through their conflation with the robot-machine nexus. Such an offering gives ample space to think through what I have called "Asian roboticism" (how Asians are imputed robotic characteristics and vice versa) to signal major sociohistorical changes as well as technocultural shifts.[7] With figurations of Asians as automatons as my conceptual template, or "model," I make the case that this conflation worked to justify the ideological and material workings of U.S. empire. Extending the scholarly work on techno-Orientalism (the imagining of Asia and Asians as technologically advanced), I put forth "the model machine myth" as an analytic to outline, follow, and trace the mutable forms that this social entity—the Asian automaton—has assumed in an expansive U.S. techno-imperial imaginary. In laboring as essential workers for humanity, helping to develop the global economy and U.S. trade, Asians are rendered as superhumans and less-than-human threats, in both a domestic and foreign sense.

The model machine is central and complementary to the Asian American model minority and the unassimilable Asian foreigner. While occupying a unique category, the model machine is not necessarily a distinct variant of perpetual foreigner syndrome (alien outsider), racial formation (race as changing over time), and racial form (economically efficient).[8] It is this through line that braids all those things together. Yet the model machine thesis holds specific queries about personhood, citizenship, and rights in the transnational making of Asian/America.

This introduction explores the germ of this myth and the genesis of the man-machine metaphor in ancient times. It then proceeds to shift toward the colonial and modern eras. This origin story for the model machine myth segues to Chapter 1, on the first wave of Chinese laborers to North America, those "coolies" stamped as animal-like machines during the age of Asian exclusion. After middle chapters on Japan and the Cold War/Vietnam, the book delves into the late twenty-first century, when Asians are reimagined as model minority/machines in the virtual age of late capitalism. The final major chapter ends in the new millennium, where the global resurgence of China presages the "rise of the machines" and all the doomsday scenarios this might spell for humanity at large. Much of the research on the racialization of Asians finds that they were coveted as skilled cheap labor and dehumanized by dint of their perceived cultural foreignness. However, contrary to prevailing wisdom, I reveal that they did not always register as fully human in first place. Rather than assume that racial machinization involves more than a reduction or refusal of Asian humanity, it might be best to consider it as a revamping or refiguring of said humanity.

Under new technocultural logics of difference, where cultural meanings conjugate with technological ones, ancient myths about the Asian automaton took "on a racialized life of their own, and thus complicate modern anthropocentric discourses like Asian American history and subjectivity."[9] Centered on a moral value system that inferred Asians as the best kind of workers and the worst kind of enemy, the model machine thesis constructed a population, full of foibles, that could bear a life of struggle beyond human comprehension. A disdain or preference for Asian humanities supported the generalized associations of Asianness with degeneration (morality), drudgery (labor), and despotism (civilization). As laborers simply *doing* things with nary a sense of *joie de vivre* (exuberance of life), Asians posed a sizable danger to white human *being* and *making*. This paradox in thinking about Asians—harmful for being too handy—ensured that they would never be completely free agents. Despite being captive objects subjected to the dominant powers that sought to bind them, these branded machines always found ways to resist.

If techno-Orientalism describes modern Asia as an economic and civilizational threat, I indicate the model machine myth as a U.S.-specific (and perhaps older) version of techno-Orientalism with a focus on uncovering the historical contents of this myth. While techno-Orientalism might be an adequate term to entirely frame the Asian automaton, it does not capture the variegated, granular forms of mechanical embodiment. The model machine myth is more precise in its intervention with specific inquiry into the flattening of the Asian foreigner/minority distinction. As I demonstrate, the multiscalar myth served as a mechanism of U.S. imperialism, American corporatism, and white nationalism. My use of the model machine expressly riffs on the myth of Asian Americans as a model minority. In this way, it raises the close relationship between the contemporary post-1965 development of Asians as a hyperproductive model minority and the longer history of Asians as a racially coded model machine. The running power of this myth—Asians as superhuman minority/machine—stretches from the age of Asian exclusion to the present-day pivot toward what many have called the "Asian Century."[10]

Model Machines suggests that the means and methods by which Asians and Asian Americans acquired a mechanical appearance is essential to measuring growth for the United States, both as an emerging industrializing nation and as a maturing global empire. The model machine myth puts limits on who (or what) it can accept into the United States or integrate in its expansive orbit and biopower (political control of humans as a species and as individuals) as well as who it can violently incorporate or destroy under necropower, which refers to how colonized "populations are subjected to conditions of life conferring upon them the status of living dead."[11] As the United States came into more direct contact with Asia through trade and travel, the machine myth kept pace with the opinion of Asian people as shorn of any human qualities. As useful yet threatening robot figures, they are unable to act in a self-determined fashion and thus exist as mere machines without salvageable parts. Their social construction as such cordoned them off from the "human rights" that Western liberal democracies, such as the United States, supposedly embodied and promulgated.[12]

Moving out from an older colonial tradition of white Europeans siting Asia as a baffling continent of slavish lumbering masses, we find the model machine myth fully materializing out of an Anglo-American tradition in the United States. That tradition evangelized to the rest of the world a doctrine of fraternity among all people, even as it deemed certain races as inherently "unfit" for humane treatment. The controlling image of Asians as controllable cogs marks them as not empowered intellects but encumbered bodies, a nameless sludge that is easily imposed upon. This image factory shored up a mental image of Asians as opportunistic or calculating. Such a liberal/racial orientation fixes in place a professed belief that "all men are created equal" while holding up the tenet that others are somehow not "real" men (emphasis on men as a patriarchal priority). Attentive to dynamics of gender and sexuality, Asian American studies scholar Susan Koshy finds that America's "most cherished axioms of choice, equality, and autonomy . . . engage in 'human' terms the exclusion of the Asian from union."[13]

My study charts the model machine myth as a phenomenon credited foremost to the United States, a world leader and mainspring for casting the modern tenor about global democracy, human rights, and market fundamentalism. I found that this myth crystallized during the late U.S. modernist period, when the boundaries between Asia and America had begun to collide around the same time as the threshold between man and machine began to break down. Never achieving the status of a coherent ideology or full public discourse like "forever foreigner," "Yellow Peril," or even the "model minority," the model machine myth arises more from sporadic ruminations and random musings. It erupted in erratic fashion during times of panic related to major political turmoil and socioeconomic transition. The myth's disjointed global history owes much to the fact that human beings did not always know how to make sense of the technological-human dimensions that arose with the forces of American militarism, racial capitalism, and technoscientific modernity. Few did know what to do with the alien creatures who deviated from the modern "human condition" to stand in for technology par excellence.

Insofar as the Asian (as) automaton trope gave shape to and helped diagnose public anxieties around social issues concerning immigration, capitalism, race mixing, communism, sexuality, and labor, I document the historical record of a public persona that does not technically exist in "real life" but is very much imagined as real. As a fabricated "thing" and symptom of larger forces, the Asianized automaton reflects the surrealism of the modern technocultural imagination. While many might know of Chinese exclusion as a historic fact, few know that American politicians chose to occlude them on the reasoning that they were "not real people" and rather akin to machines. The spectacular myth of the Asian automaton operates as a primary site for making out modern-day freaks. Monster-machine myths color the attitudes toward those entities suspected to be not autonomous persons but instead automated nonpersons, blindly following their masters and heeding orders like a semisensate idiotic puppet.[14]

Model Machines takes a critical view of the Eurocentric conception of *Homo technologicus*, or "technological man," which says man's superiority is the product of his own physical stores of energy and pure mental reasoning.[15] Man, in his boundless mastery of nature through tools of work and art, opposes his enslavement to nature's mechanical functionality, but we must also come to grips with what happens when man becomes machine. The term *machine* refers to devices or appliances that perform a task, a person who acts deftly like a machine, or a superlative group of people doing repeated tasks like a political party.[16] A machine (automaton) is always part of *the* machine (capitalism).

Here, we may consider the various definitions of machine: (1) "an assemblage . . . of parts that transmit forces, motion, and energy one to another in a predetermined manner"; (2) "a living organism or one of its functional systems [that resembles a machine]"; (3) "a literary device or contrivance introduced for dramatic effect" (e.g., deus ex machina).[17] These definitions of machine introduce my critical engagement with the concept of the model machine as an assembly of material objects and technology, the resemblance of human beings and bodies to technology, and the cultural narratives used to dramatize the reality of human design.

The model machine myth thus concerns the making of a model (representation/discourse), machine (economy/system), and myth (ideology/imagination), revealing a glimpse into how things are seen, how they are produced, and how they shape thinking (see fig. I.1).

The machine concept hews closely to the automaton, insofar as the *human automaton* refers to mechanical beings confined to simple tasks, things shaped in the likeness of man. Synonyms for the word *automate* (besides *robotize* and *mechanize*) are *brutalize, barbarize,* and *dehumanize*. Automating thus means stripping the organic parts of something until it is bereft of authenticity.[18] Tagging people as alien automatons is thereby a conduit for vitiating their natural worth or authentic humanity with little thought given to that process. As literary theorist Catherine Liu writes, "The automaton is a monadic figure, who represents technological optimism and a demonic double, whose imagined inauthenticity allows for the indefinite deferral of a confrontation with thinking."[19] Sociologist Meltem Ahiska explains the

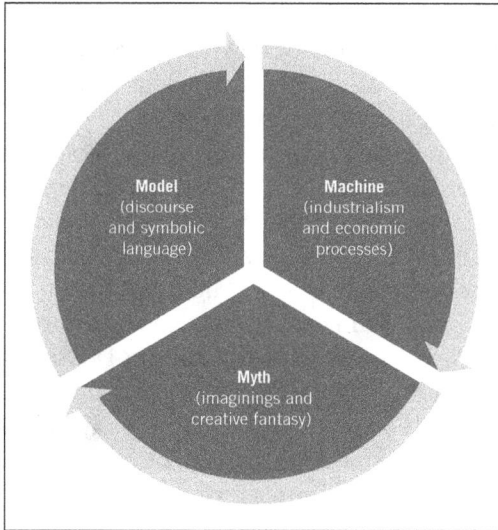

Figure I.1 The model machine myth as conceptual paradigm (Long T. Bui)

historical fantasy of mapping differences between the (Western) model and the (non-Western) copy. Even countries adjacent to Europe proper like Turkey are Orientalized as a facsimile of the "real" thing and always fall short.[20] Asia and America may be two sides of the same coin, but their relationship is asymmetrical. While white workers were sometimes described as automatons or machines, as was often done by labor advocates during the Industrial Revolution, it means something else when Asians are named so.

Likewise, the automaton and the machine are one and the same in that they often refer to one another. Machine means something more general, and automaton, more specific: machine points to a broad characterization of societies and cultures to suggest their operational efficiency, while automaton, and its more contemporary formulation the robot, brings that disciplinary arrangement home onto the corpus and character of the individual. This fusion of race and robot defines the modern Asian as a perfectible working machine, though morally imperfect. If it contains a brain, that working brain is never divorced from the natural calculations of the animal body (unlike the floating theories and traveling minds of white Europeans).[21]

A modern "machine-society" churns out "machine-men," says philosopher Michel Foucault, whether they be incarcerated prisoners, impressed soldiers, indentured workers, or inured prostitutes. In the eighteenth century, a new disciplinary power took root, one that was "no longer simply an art of distributing bodies. . . . but of composing forces in order to obtain an efficient machine."[22] The Asian machine stood apart from the white bodily subject, as colonial technologies spread across the surface of the planet, populations, and bodies.[23] The model machine stereotype fell into a modern global order of things by latching onto fungible ideas of race and/as technology. What is more, Asians were described as human technology with greater frequency as humanism found greater currency in the world.

Tensions abound in the effort to distinguish between those people who truly live and those "somewhat human" beings who do not really live or fake life. At what point does the mock-up ever become a model? Imagined divides built on mythic foundations are never stable, and tech-savvy copiers are occasionally better than their masters. In this vein, how does the model machine myth represent an unexplored dimension in Asian racialization, delineating new ways of exploring further techno-Orientalism? Do Asians ever truly surpass humanity, or will their Asian automaton-ness always be a failure of humanness? What does the roboticization of the Asian tell us about the history of the human? How do we make sense of the incongruencies between models of being free (man) and unfree (machine)?

We tend to think of being human as timeless and natural, but what does the Asian becoming (model) machine tell us about the history of the human, humanity, and inhumanity? As ethnic studies scholars Sau-Ling Wong and Rachel C. Lee observe, throughout the nineteenth and twentieth centuries, "Asians have been contradictorily imagined as, on the one hand, machine-like workers, accomplishing 'inhuman' feats of 'coolie' manual labor, and on the other, as brainiac competitors whose technological adeptness ranges from inventing gunpowder to being good with engineering and math."[24] Picking and taking apart this oxymoron of the human machine requires a working knowledge of race, technological culture, and economic labor that moves beyond the general techno-Orientalist imaginary of the Asian as foreign Other to delve into specific examples of machinelike Asian labor, whether low-tech or high-tech. If Asians are examples of lifelike robots, how and why did this myth take root in popular thinking?

The model machine and its many permutations twist the classic sense of *Homo automata* (man as machine) by separating out "those who dominate [and are] seen as subjects and those who are dominated objects."[25] As shown throughout these chapters, the Asian automaton body took many somatic forms, maturing alongside technological innovations like the steam engine, telecommunications, and the computer. The figure's evolution alongside the mutation of the model machine myth helps make sense of the "alienating" impact of industrial-technological processes upon human society (from thermodynamics to biotechnology) as it is displaced on to alien beings. This propensity of the machine myth—to freeze subjects in time and ossify them within a temporal narrative—gives us context for framing the diversification and sedimentation of technocultural myths across the horizon of humanity.

In this introduction, I discuss the ancient origins of the human automaton and its connection to the modern Asian automaton. I then probe the Asian automaton as it is figured within colonial mythology, the racial capitalist system, and the field of Asian American science and technology studies. The introduction finishes with an overview of the subsequent chapters, starting from an "American Century" and moving to an "Asian Century." What we find is that the history of the model machine flourishes, and continues to blossom, in conjunction with the ingrained conviction that non-white people are not free-thinking subjects but *Automaton asiaticus*. This myth justifies the real exclusion, exploitation, or extermination.

Artificial Men and Asian Automata

Before delving into the reasons Asians came to embody model machines within the U.S. technocultural mindset, it is crucial to first unpack how the man-as-machine schema enmeshes itself in modern history and when Asians first began to be noticed as automatons. The term *automaton* closely relates to *automatism*, meaning someone or something with mechanical involuntary action, especially as a form of unmediated art and practice. Ingenious machines called automata, which can take human form, hew closely to the hyperrealization of masterful men who play God in an artificial world wholly of their own making.[26] In the ancient world, the thinking around automata (from the Greek *automatos* meaning "moves on its own") dates to scientific efforts to build robots that could masquerade as real humans. Early forerunners were kindled in mystical Taoist parables of people with machine bodies hammered out in human likeness. From the Chinese female inventor Huang Yueying came the "artificer" presented to King Mu of Cho, who exclaimed, "Can it be that human skill is on a par with that of the great Author of Nature?"[27] As tributaries to immortal gods, inventors in Egypt hoped to build robotic sentient beings as undying slaves for their godlike rulers. During the golden age of Islamic science, the polymath Al-Jazari designed a servant girl that could endlessly serve drinks or fill water for toilets.[28] Historian Adrienne Mayor documents Greek and Indian legends that professed robots to be perfect soldiers or ideal servants that could never wear down. But once the Roman Empire fell to barbarian invaders and Christian medieval superstition set in, another worldview about robots took hold: "Associated with the exotic and the idea of an 'infidel' East, automata were viewed for some time with awe and suspicion."[29] Automata came to signify the inhumanity or gross human qualities of Asia.

From early scientific obsessions with building actual robots, the *principle* of the automaton as an uncanny double of the human came into full effect during the European Renaissance and the "great divergence" between a diminishing East and reinvigorated West. One of the main features of the European humanist project has always consisted in understanding what it means to "be human," foundational to unraveling the philosophical divide between self and Other(s).[30] Self-control, rationality, and autonomy have long defined what it meant to be human, as those qualities represented a break from nature (animals), religious tradition (God), and the divine rule of kings. The self-determination of a (European) man differs in kind and degree from the mechanical actions exercised by an automaton, a term derived from the Greek for self (*autos*) and self-willed or operating (*automatos*). Not all human automatons are thought of in the same way since race came to serve as a proxy for the machinic Other.

The seventeenth-century concept of Oriental automata combined the "unknown world" of self-operating things associated with the Orient, affirming medieval Christian theology, European sovereignty, and the view of Muslims as prostrating to a "mechanical world of gears."[31] In France, monks used the term *mechanicum* to describe Muslim sorcery, effectively purging Islam of any moral authority even as it retained the power of exotic mysticism.[32] The term *Mammets*, referring to followers of "Mahomet," or Muhammad, was used as a way to make fun of young women as behaving like mechanical marionettes and to combine the notion of human automata with the religion of technology and population control. As communications scholar Ayhan Aytes writes, "Oriental automata represent a crucial link in this two-handed engine: On one hand the automaton performs the docility for the Western subject in the image of the Oriental. On the other, it casts the Oriental subject outside of the norms of being human by subjecting them to the world of the machines."[33]

The Oriental automaton formed the early nucleus for the man-machine metaphor, lasting and lingering even as people's lives were raised by the Industrial Revolution. Great thinkers of the day bandied about confabulations of "machine-people" to describe the profound planetary changes wrought by such technologies as the Watt steam engine.[34] Scientists in eighteenth-century Europe switched from simple corpuscular analogies of biomechanical physiology to Romantic evaluations of personality by looking at the "automaton-man" as a flawed being who reflects the chaos of being a "living organic force in the universe, the state, and the body of man."[35] Calling someone a machine serves as a slander of character since it means "someone is stiff and monotonous in speech or movement, one who lacks imagination, emotion, spontaneity, or a sense of humor, a fanatical follower of rules or regulations, or a social or political conformist who is easily manipulated due to an inability to think critically and independently."[36]

Media theorist Bernard Dionysius Geoghegan considers this intellectual landscape a thought experiment in disability. In a brilliant historiography that connects medieval technology to the age of informatics, he professes the human automaton no longer denotes purely human impairment but rather "the unequal distribution of potentials in the broadest class of animated things."[37] He blames the fading of human, social, class, and labor distinctions within Europe and the United States to the hyper-representation of exotic Others as simulations without proper substance. Given themes of maimed laboring bodies in public debates about machines, he avers that the fundamental transformation in the nineteenth century was transposing the bodily aberrancy of the automaton to the ethnic sexual particularities of "the lower-class bodies that worked—and were worked over by—machines. . . . A new, threatening violence took up residence in the mechanism. The machine was not only exotic: often it was alien."[38]

The change from the classical man-machine trope toward a complex automaton-man came with the Enlightenment and the rise of a sentimental culture that rejected simple machine analogies, given their associations with authoritarianism. As European historian Minsoo Kang expounds, the "living machine" in the industrial age prefigured a whole new modality of life where technology was infused with human essence to seed dynamic life forms that stand contraposed to "natural man." My project contends that while Asians were (and continue to be) treated as artificial humanity, they have pushed against these kinds of transactions, resistant to colonial freedom/being/truth. They also offer other modes of being human obscured by the European overrepresentation of man.[39]

The wild postulation that humans could somehow be likened to machines drew on early theories of mechanistic physiology expounded by such French philosophers as René Descartes, who, in his 1633 "Treatise on Man," outlined a formalized vision of the human mind/body as an effective combination of automatized natural functions. Cartesianism maintained that humans possess divine souls and rational minds as "masters and possessors of nature," elevated over and above nonhuman animals as downgraded copies of "natural automata."[40] The 1739 invention of robotic humanlike servants and a bedazzling mechanical "digesting duck" in France by the same inventor of the mechanical loom set the course for conceiving the entire world picture through the automaton/animal.

Later, the classification of humans and animals into self-multiplying *automata mechanica* would inform Europeans' discernment of the natural world during their colonial expansion around the globe. The "lower races" they encountered were seen as animalistic automata, being so close as they were to nature. The *homme machine* of Descartes could upgrade itself, but other types of machines could not, as when Carolus Linnaeus (the creator of the Western taxonomic system) strangely put white people and orangutans into the *Homo sapiens* category, while placing Chinese, Indians, and

Hottentots from southern Africa in the separate category of *Homo monstrosus*.[41] That certain races could be classified as monsters revealed that racial ordering was based on the personal whim of its arbiters.

The human/animal/machine distinction stood center in Euro-American modernity and the formulation of race, nation, and citizenship.[42] The distinction took another direction under Julien Offray de La Mettrie, who, in his 1748 work *Man a Machine*, pushed against Descartes's basic doctrine of mechanical man. Insofar as all organisms vary in sophistication, humans and animals are complex machines.[43] Descartes looked upon the human "body as a machine made by the hand of God."[44] By contrast, La Mettrie propounded that even though man can be thought of as a machine, there are still unknown pleasures, moral instincts, and emotional intelligence beyond comprehension. This more sensuous, open approach toward the *machine man* did not accord with more determinist thinkers who saw the automaton as a rational model for a new mechanistic social order.

The school of thought called vitalism, which arose in popularity during the nineteenth century, sought to explain biological "living things" as containing a unique vital force separate from nonliving inanimate ones. French mathematician, inventor, and writer Blaise Pascal would argue that we are all automatons due to customs that influence a human mind to remain free and independent.[45] Robert Boyle, the father of modern chemistry, toed the line between mechanism and vitalism, agreeing with Descartes that nature was a great machine and that the human body was endowed with powers and qualities of God. Yet he countered that organic matter's "seminal" impressions and spirits are irreducible to mechanical quantities.[46] As director of the East India Company in India, Boyle believed in getting rid of all forms of deism and paganism to unite the human races under a West European contour of Christianity. Under the motion and energetic wheels of missionary colonial work, all men fell under the "grand and noble machine" of God.[47]

Despite such ecumenical efforts, the cleaving of man from his subservient machine complemented the detachment of Europe from Asia, apart from the contiguous geographic body of Eurasia. As historian of science Simon Kow formulates it, many of the top Western intellectuals could not conceive of the Oriental state in a positive hue due to this geopolitically determined partition of continents. In this light, Johann Gottfried von Herder considered the Chinese as imitative and industrious but not inventive, while Gottfried Wilhelm Leibniz took them as "natural automatons" in their customary rites (despite his view that all people are spiritual automatons with souls). Montesquieu, in his uniquely sarcastic way, found that "the constancy of the Japanese during torture might be due to the fact that physical suffering is perhaps not so great there, that the bodily machine is not so susceptible to pain there."[48]

The orientation toward Asian slavishness finds its earliest antecedent in Aristotle's formulation of man as a "rational animal" and those humans living in Europe as "full of spirit, but wanting in intelligence and skill . . . [with] no political organization, and are incapable for ruling over others. Whereas the natives of Asia are intelligent and inventive, but they are wanting in spirit, and therefore they are always in a state of subjection and slavery."[49] Aristotle believed, not without some uncertainty, that Asians were "slaves by nature," in spirit "creatures with no moral qualities, no capacity for independent judgement, but with brains enough to interpret their master's orders when required and brawn enough to carry them out."[50]

This classical sense of Asians as quick-witted yet slow-to-act peons—and Europeans as not-so-skilled yet rational civilized people lacking in political organization—would be slightly altered by colonialism. By the time a handful of European nations rose to global power through colonial conquest, it was believed that Asian societies consequently went into relative decline and fell from favor. For Georg Hegel, the civilizations of the Orient came to preside as archaic lands, where undifferentiated herds of humanity groaned under the weight of cruel tyrants without the rule of law.[51] In *The Philosophy of History*, he contends that the Chinese are blindly obedient, dwelling in communal lands where "subjective freedom is absent."[52] With new imperial organization and freedom of colonial travel, Europeans could now preside over this land of skilled yet spiritless serfs. As he put it, "The Chinese have as a general characteristic, a remarkable skill in imitation. . . . They are born only to drag the car of Imperial Power. . . . [This] testifies to no triumphant assertion of the worth of the inner man, but a servile consciousness."[53]

While Egypt, Arabia, Persia, India, Mesopotamia, Assyria, and China formed the cradles of human civilization, they now seemed past their prime. Beyond worshiping brute animal idols, Asian societies dwelled on reproducing rigid social castes and a classical education based on rote memorization, while Western Europe signified the zenith of economic development, state administration, and formal scientific experimentation. It was probable that Asians might catch up to Europeans someday, Hegel posited, given their ability to imitate, but they demonstrated a lack of true spirit of evolutionary change. Even if they would learn to industrialize or improve themselves economically, time's arrow would never redound back to Asia, since "Europe is the absolute end of history."[54] Whereas Africans, Oceanians, and Amerindians occupied an obtuse place in humanity's primordial past, the people of Asia assumed an ancillary, fugacious place in world history, one that could only partly and crudely rival an advanced Europe with its scientifically managed societies. Conversant with the Orientalism of Adam Smith, Max Weber, Karl Marx, and Karl Wittfogel, Hegel brought forward the grandiose schema that the planet's occupants could be parsed out into universal rational human beings and sedate unthinking automatons.[55]

Hegel was preceded by Thomas Hobbes, who wrote of the "Artificial Man" in *Leviathan* (1651) as a marvelous metaphor for the incipient social order under the modern state and its "body politic." This materialist philosophy shaped more modern thinking around the virtues of "civic humanism" and concerns of men becoming "feeling machines" under manufacturing economies—free-market subjects yoked to the mechanical reproduction of commodity culture.[56] Modern humanism, as an intellectual exploration of man's entire plane of existence, intermingled with not only capitalism but scientific findings about how the world works in the physical universe.

The myth of the automaton-man as a living thing was reignited by the theories of thermodynamics, or the science of motion from heat. In the mid-1800s, scientists like Ludwig Boltzmann drew parallels between the kinetic force of the human body and energy-converting machines.[57] The Newtonian order of fixed, stable natural forces and physical elements was reconstituted by a new paradigm trained intellectually on the chemistry between energy and entropy found within the "human motor."[58] Even as there occurred a popular shift toward discussions of technology by the twentieth century (technology is simply the "application of scientific knowledge for practical purposes"), the language of human machinery prevailed as a way of explaining the terror of galvanized monsters in our modern times, similar to the malevolent creation in Mary Shelley's *Frankenstein*.[59]

From these eclectic origins, the chimera of the racial robot and "robot races" was born. Pseudosciences like phrenology—measuring the human skull anatomy for intelligence—set the new anthropometric terms for fixing others in nature by carrying forth historical impressions of Oriental slavery, despotism, and barbarism into the age of human emancipation. Finding great popularity in the antebellum United States, French writer Arthur de Gobineau wrote, in his influential 1852 work *The Inequality of Human Races*, that the Negro was a "human machine, in whom it is so easy to arouse emotion, show, in face of suffering, either a monstrous indifference or a cowardice that seeks a voluntary refuge in death."[60] For this elite man of letters, the Black man possessed basic needs and instincts with no faculty of reason (racist notions corroborated by U.S. president Thomas Jefferson's *Notes on the State of Virginia*), while the "yellow man" displayed a machinic scale of operation that went beyond nature's biological utilitarianism. Gobineau construes that the Asiatic race "is practical, in the narrowest sense of the word. He does not dream or theorize; he invents little but can appreciate and take over what is useful to him."[61] The yellow man craves freedom, yet he remains a creature of utility, quicksilver inventiveness, and avarice. He is a "knock-off," or false copy, of the white man, ripping off the latter's gifts of courage, feelings for order, and reflective energy. While Gobineau thinks Black people possess "animal character" with a slight intellect (useful to a certain degree), he makes plain that every civilization should have yellow men as no modern capitalist society can be fully operational without them, the consummate copycats of the Westerner's nous. Despite the economic usefulness of Asian workers, Gobineau's final assessment is that the white man's life should never be debased or enervated by intermixing with the "formalism under which the Chinese are glad to vegetate."[62] Notwithstanding the great need for Chinese labor, there needs be excorporation of their dirty bodies lest whites too become subhuman in this unholy communion.

The visualization of Asians as embodied machines did not really take off until the advent of modern nation-states. The concept of the machine travels between individuals, groups, and communities through the various pathways in which nations are constructed, entangled, and imagined. These fictive ties bind people across swathes of space and time, and nations "are to be distinguished, not by their falsity/genuineness, but by the style in which they are imagined."[63] Insofar as the United States imagines itself as a nation that does not practice colonialism or imperialism (or even racism), we see this "nation among nations" marking out special territory from the world, as the "first" modern liberal constitutional democracy. To elaborate on this relationship between a "God-given" nation and its internal mechanisms, we must ask how the concept of the machine travels between nations in ways that are mutually reinforcing, as it circulates between the United States and other nations. The machine describes the modern political state and its citizens, as articulated by Hobbes. The democratic myth of the self-generating "American machine" contains the Hobbesian idea that man is an *artificer* and not a mere machine, capable of designing and making products for his own purposes, the mechanic who contrives machines through his artistry.[64]

The threat of the Asian automata and its array of stock characters (e.g., Chinese coolies, Korean pop singers, Vietnamese prostitutes, Japanese salarymen, Filipina maids) interfered with the "inalienable" rights promised by the new republic. The social contract forged by an upstart democracy would be tested by encounters with migrant populations that did not fit snugly within the founders' vision. These encounters with alien machines would force a revision of the unbreakable bond between (citizen) man and (state) machine to include those marked populations precluded from the general status of humanity. The possibility of equal inclusion for the Asian automaton has remained hampered by a mandate to demure and cater to a white master. This robotic call to serve a higher power withholds security from the colonized subject in terms of cultural legitimacy, political protection, and economic autonomy.[65] Fashioning powerful myths out of pure conjecture, the leap from thinking of Asians as simple human automata to complex model machines, is never straightforward, which is why a history of colonialism is sorely needed.

Colonial Myths and Modern Technoculture

In the shift from robot mythology in the ancient world to colonial settings, machine myths are generated through the modern culture of science and technology. Whereas science refers more to cultivation of the mind through exploration of the physical world, technology refers to material objects crafted and wielded by humans to shape nature. Modern technology is edified as perennially moving human culture forward, propelling it toward the future to leave behind old prejudices and outdated thinking.[66] Technology concerns how knowledge is aggregated through aesthetic dimensions rather than purely denoting its practical aspect, as the word is originally derived from the Greek word *techne*, meaning "art" and "skill," even though today it bears connotations with "mechanical-logical" aspects.[67] We could argue that human culture is always technological, given the import of both tools and art in shaping human perspectives and behavioral norms. When cultural discourses and contexts take on a tech-based appearance, it is apt to call it technoculture.

Modern technoculture is rooted in colonialism and its white mythologies. As the "barbarians" of Europe finally gained the upper hand over Asians in terms of war and industry during the eighteenth to nineteenth centuries, the human machine analogy turned up to describe the conditions of the colonized subject found under British rule. At a general meeting of Britain's Royal United Service Institute, scholars and other influential elites reflected on a hundred years of British rule in Ceylon (Sri Lanka). Tea planter and foreign market expert J. L. Shand took note of the human master-automaton slave dialectic operating in that colonial territory: "There is no country in the world where the relations between master and servant work so satisfactorily as in Ceylon. We have in the Tamil coolie a perfect machine for the cultivation of our tea, coffee, or other tropical produce."[68] Under the white man's rule, Asian and African conscript workers suffered negative ascriptions of them as the perfect ideal of human machines. As a scholarly observer astutely wrote in 1933, new colonies were acquired by conquest, and under Britain's expansive military empire, "African negroes and Chinese coolies . . . [were treated] merely as human machines for digging trenches, carrying loads and building base camps."[69] Conjoining the words "human" and "machine" did little to humanize the person or group labeled as human machine, as it alludes to them as not fully human by association with machinery.

The language of the human automaton found specific purpose in colonial settings and laboratories to substantiate white racial superiority. Protestant missionary Karl Friedrich August Gützlaff wrote extensively about Chinese manners, customs, history, and society to generate support for the spread of Christianity in East Asia. The Prussian-born explorer provided insight into the inculcation of Confucianism and this cultural system's firm hold on an unchanging race: "Faithful to ancient customs, they abhor nothing so much as change, even when it is for the better. Their etiquette is proverbial, and their affected politeness is subject to the strictest rules. Individuals of the higher classes are naturally more under this influence, presenting, on occasions of ceremony, living automatons."[70] Though not all Europeans thought this way, such cogitation remained popular with certain learned classes and enlivened mainstream discourse, percolating through various social circles and spheres of influence.

Human subjects and body parts were put on display as objects within colonial exhibits and museums, and this public staging encapsulated "various New World acquisitions in cabinets of curiosities and, indeed, of ethnographic objects from the 'savage' peripheries of Europe."[71] So broad in scope was the anthropological project that some colonial scholars used the term "Oriental machine" to describe the indentured servants of East Africa ruled by Germany and "Orientalized" Africans as tractable workers for building railroads in present-day Tanzania and Namibia.[72] This infantilizing description circulated in Egypt under British rule, where a colonial manager found the "lazy boy" mechanic similar to the work "fitting to address lazy, childlike, subject races."[73] Insofar as colonial political society and schedules were understood mechanically, nonwhites had been crafted as stagnant in the mind, patiently suffering, and wasteful of time; in short, they were automatons for temporary use. This colonial myth appeared self-evident to that British administrator, who claimed that once someone explains to an "Egyptian what he is to do . . . he will assimilate the idea rapidly. He is a good imitator, and will make a faithful, even sometimes a too servile copy of the work of his European teacher. . . . His movements will, it is true, be not infrequently those of an automaton, but a skillfully constructed automaton may do a great deal of useful work."[74]

Colonialism's imposition of technoscientific racial knowledge upon the capitalist world system forced a radical rethinking of the machine-man metaphor. Even when some European thinkers sounded sympathetic to the plight of the colonized, they still considered colonialism necessary to free *those* people of their automaton-like existence. Adherence to primitive lifestyles meant they did not maximize or utilize the ecological abundance of nature.[75]

The "machine" in English-language Victorian discourse generally meant the technology the British were importing to dissipate the entirety of India's well-established garment industries, while in the process of casting the myth of Indians as lazy or lethargic machines. In 1881, the British colonial governor of Bombay made the assertion that "the Hindus are not a mechanical race."[76] That is, they were not mechanical in the industrial sense but were still mechanical in their manners and affectation. British merchants bemoaned the slow importation of electric fans, owing to the popularity of "punkah-wallah," a low-caste servant that manually fanned colonialists in the hot tropics. Punkahs were considered natural substitutes for cooling machines, according to one British naval officer, as they were reportedly able to "go through three times as much fatigue . . . as would kill an Englishman outright."[77] The myth of the "self-acting punkah" bore the distinctive automated ability "of a small specimen of Asian humanity" able to inordinately work even while fast asleep—a talent "that was difficult for any machine to replicate."[78] Leaders in the British engineering industry found the punkah to be an inefficient worker, but "the same may be claimed of a very large number of human machines."[79] They admitted that mass electrification in the state of Bengal would take some time to replace the punkah coolie, since no machine could actuate the machinelike punkah.

Political economist Karl Marx commented on the practices of the Dutch East India Company in Java as setting the example of mercantilist domination as it "employed all the existing machinery of despotism to squeeze from the people . . . the last dregs of their labor, and thus aggravated the evils of a capricious and semi-barbarous Government."[80] The Western colonial project extended the European automaton metaphor from the core to the peripheries, as observed in the Netherlands' control over modern-day Indonesia. While the British were ruthless and vile in their plundering of India, Marx admits, their ill-gotten ways could be justified on the basis that Europeans propelled mankind's global destiny. The British spread mental freedom by wringing Asian Indians from their "vegetative" animal-worshipping state: "Whatever may have been the crimes of England she was the unconscious tool of history in bringing about that revolution."[81] Britain's colonial machine trumped the despotic Oriental machine as the revolutionary engine for humanity.

When measured against more "advanced" civilizations of Japan and China, the races of South and Southeast Asia occupied a lower tier with human variability, occupying a less-admirable status as performative machines of tedium. Milton Reed, an American travel writer, toured throughout the

Asia Pacific to compare the white man's active personality with the perfunc-
toriness and pusillanimity of "the passive Oriental character."[82] Reed found
the natives of the East Indies to be cognitively sterile, "without any spark or
potency of intellectual power."[83] Even touring Burma, he found the "Hindu
coolies" there to be the same sea foam of humanity he encountered back in
India. This prompted him to ask: "Who are they? What are they? Are they
realities? Do they have thoughts? Or are they only so many human automata?"[84] Unlike the quaint adaptive Japanese or the patiently industrious
Chinaman, he cringed at the work ethic of the Javanese, whose childish,
monotonous lives of toil justified over two centuries of colonization by the
Dutch. While initially objecting to the colonizers' cruel administration, the
observer felt at a basic level that the Indian coolies were "silent, somber,
cheerless . . . a ghostly procession of human automata; shadowy and grim."[85]
This is much different from the "human machines" referenced by Mahatma
Gandhi in arguing for Indian economic independence using the collective
autonomous power of villagers.[86]

Indigenous and autochthonous peoples from the Global South were
thereby considered primitive automatons who were unlike mechanical humans of the north. The Amerindians in British Guyana would celebrate hol-
idays with dance, but missionaries there would describe how their "unvar-
ied and regular movements of the hands and feet, together with the absence
of animated expression in their countenances," gave them the appearance
"rather of automata than human beings."[87] This statement was very similar
to generalizations made by German ethnologist Fedor Jagor in 1875 about
the "natives" in the Philippines. A paucity of natural "gaiety" characterized
the population living under Spanish rule, which he said could be ascribed
to the small development of their nervous system and wonderful ability to
bear pain.[88] Describing them as "eccentric" copycats of Western culture,
professional scientists like Jagor saw the people of the Philippines almost no
differently than religious envoys on civilizing missions. Jagor provided this
vignette about watching native actors moving in robotic fashion: "Their
countenances were entirely devoid of expression, and they spoke like automatons. If I had understood the words, the contrast between their meaning and the machine-like movements of the actors would probably have
been droll enough. . . . Both the theatrical performance and the whole festi-
val bore the impress of laziness, indifference, and mindless mimicry."[89]
These brown Asians are described as indolent rather flamboyant robotic
mimics. This portrayal departs from the industry and diligence attributed
to the Chinese or Japanese. As soon as the United States colonized the Philippines at the end of the nineteenth century, wresting it away from Spain, it
developed this myth about these islanders as affable animalistic automatons
that would reflexively follow colonial education and "ape" American cus-

toms. What it means to be an Asian automaton was worked out across the many transits and moments of U.S. empire.

As more Asian labor was needed for the United States' hungry empire, the importation of *orientalium machina* took on greater precedence, especially as the African slave trade came under assault. This heightened economic demand for coolies only reinforced workers' nonhuman status rather than encouraging their inclusion in the Western humanistic tradition. Historian Lewis Mumford proposes that great civilizations are the sine qua non of a "megamachine," built on powerful institutions in which humanity aspires toward building something big that could reach the heavens. Slaves in the megamachine did the bidding of kings and mass controllers as cogs in the machine. Their "mechanized human parts" held together an artificial social system built on worshipping powerful gods and towering totems of progress.[90]

If empires are structured as megamachines, says Mumford, then what about those human machines subjected to imperial rule? In *Myth of the Machine*, Mumford documents how since the fifteenth century, the thought of lifelike automata emerged alongside clocks and mills, while men gained mechanical attributes. Through (scientific) invention and (social) regimentation, we find a double movement: "Mechanization of human labor was, in effect, the first step toward humanization of the machine—humanization in the sense of giving the automaton some of the mechanical equivalents of life-likeness. The immediate effect of this division of process was a monstrous dehumanization."[91]

In the second of his two-part magnum opus on machine society (*Power of the Pentagon*), Mumford segues from the megamachine first originating in ancient Egypt to the American megamachine. He recognizes that the monsterization and mechanization of humanity—epitomized by the totality of American command control—was not the end product of human beings striving toward greater efficiency or civilization (technics). Rather, it posed a series of choices by political actors in pursuit of power, profit, publicity, and prestige. The humanization of the machine and the mechanization of human beings find their apogee in the ultimate machine society, the United States. While the Soviet Union under Stalin was a totalitarian megamachine premised on turning people into enslaved unfree robots, the United States relied on its myth-making powers to instantiate a machine system based on protecting freedom and humanizing other races, often through force.

This set of qualities also came to define new regimes of power centered on technologies for managing life and death. Complementing the anatomo-politics of thinking "the body as a machine," says philosopher Michel Foucault, is the biopolitics of the collective body of the "species" which aims to discipline population, morality, health, and longevity.[92] The automatized colonial subject-body disrupts these assumed social domains to announce another physical life-form and species-being, those racial specimens found beyond the normal purview of Western modernity. In *Machines as the Measure of Man*, historian Michael Adas observes how, by the early 1900s, many prominent Western thinkers thought of nonwhites as inferior humans.[93] With the "white magic" of industrial technology replacing Christianity as the marker of modern life, imperial civilizing projects legitimized "efforts to demonstrate the innate superiority" of the white race over other races through "the application of technology and scientific gauges of human potential."[94] With formal colonization operating on a global scale, Europeans no longer found themselves enthralled by the mighty Asiatic civilizations of yore. Former awe transmogrified into a sense of the darker societies as stunted and immutable, as it was now fair-skinned men who held the means to mold mankind's future. The superstition of myth shores up the might of the sword.

Myths provide a center of gravity for a national community and who belongs in its cosmology. Derived originally from *mythos* and the fables of old mythology, the word *myth* entered the English language in the nineteenth century to describe a product of the human *imaginaire* that conveys fabulist and magical elements of the nonhuman world, coming to life as expressions that are "'timeless' (permanent) or fundamental to periods or cultures."[95] Myth is the story of a people involving supernatural beings or events that suspend the belief in the fixity of human limits, a cognitive mapping that defies rational explanations, an exaggeration or distortion of truth, and a widely held tendentious belief about a person or fictitious thing. Myths come to define so many of the shibboleths that emblematize the uniqueness of the United States as a "nation among nations." They are baked into narratives of social mobility (the American Dream), religious calling (Manifest Destiny), and cultural distinctiveness (American exceptionalism).[96] Such myths, for all their glorification of the triumph of the American national spirit, gloss over much. Specifically concerning Asians, the model machine myth denies them human status due to their extraordinary ability to perform and function in ways that resemble the work of automatons, where the basic meaning of the word *automaton* is something or someone who can "act in a mechanical or unemotional way."[97]

Myths replicate themselves through stories where technological rationality/artifacts and cultural mores/practices converge. They compose the magical alchemy of that technocultural interaction. A historical explanation of the model machine myth brings much needed awareness to technoculture and the close relation "between technological reproduction and cultural displacement."[98] As literary scholar Despina Kakoudaki writes in

Anatomy of a Robot, the cultural work around artificial people is just as important as technological knowledge in constructing the human (and its nonhuman negation) for it recognizes the participation of fictional entities "in the larger negotiation of what it means to be a person at any given point in a society."[99]

Kakoudaki speaks to noncitizenship and slavery. Recognition of the robot as slave is instructive here for ideas about how automaton performances are not so different from the mechanism of slavery. Like slaves, robots can be humiliated (affected) when bought and sold or "honorably" brought into pressed labor (absorbed). The institution of slavery was and remains formative in the discourse of indentured servants and "the artificial human." While people of Asian extraction were never enslaved in the same manner as Black Africans were, the impressment of "coolies" into forced labor regimes collapsed into running "models of national cultures," which relied on myths produced from "post-slavery histories."[100] In that awkward dissonance, historian Lisa Yun explains how Asians were a "presence yet absence" placed in a "deep and lengthy process of disclosure, one of unfixing entrenched binaries."[101] Different machine imaginaries disclose binaries like visible and not visible, enslaved versus free.

In critical fashion, the model machine allows for discussion about all sorts of people who are both summarily extruded from the category of humanity. It must be remembered that this excision is nuanced, multidirectional, and contradictory. Within humanity are sliding scales of value and a spectrum of humanness. Humanity is a category of law with the capacity to make someone human, and its application can invariably also take away one's humanity. This polarized notion of humanity comes out of colonial history to measure distance between global populations. Under colonialism, for the first time, humanity itself needed to be performed, declared, grounded, and asserted as the ideal of the human, one in which imperial powers mobilize the full human against the "absent human" (women, colonial subjects).[102]

The almost-human Asian falls into those polarized spaces, which seem to align with the value consignment of "threatening" or "useful." Whether the discussion of the Asian automaton is about imperial expansion (war machine) or capitalist innovation (virtual machine), those things can encompass use and threat at the same time, but they still are about Asian exclusion from humanity writ large. Even if all figurations of the machine involve some form of threat and use value, the very utility of the Asian model machine means it can be both a capitalist worker and cultural threat. As an instrument of capital, the automaton-as-Asian depletes the human values of the United States and, by extension, Europe. On the other hand, when the machine is about brainless imitation (labor machine) or libidinal functionality (sex machine), there is a sort of subhuman or less than human use value to be co-opted by imperial states.

Philosophical questions of mechanical contrivance or machine-people must inevitably touch upon racial epistemologies, legal bureaucracies, gender regimes, political environments, religious institutions, and economic systems. All these facets are involved in giving an identity or name to a nonperson and the duties and responsibilities accorded therein. Thinking of the Asian as human technology throws a wrench in our commonsense definition of history as a mere record of human activity, since the "automaton is a figure of both repetition and allegory, of the radically discontinuous temporal relationship that cuts us off from the pre-origins of modernity."[103] That is, the racial automaton could perhaps operate as another form of human storytelling and mythology, but because it is fully born out of the framework of modernity, it cuts people off from the pure world of fantasy to make something unreal appear real.

Social critiques made from deconstructing the model machine myth offer a way out of what philosopher Denise Ferreira da Silva describes as the sociological documentation of how groups have been treated inhumanely in the past.[104] The post-Enlightenment constituted a global racial project that must be considered through the figure of (European) man as it oscillates vis-à-vis the "Others of Man."[105]

The self-determined subject of Western philosophical thought was always a white (hu)man. Cultural feminist Amber Jamilla Musser connects projections of opacity and robotic automaticity to brown and Black people; despite their perceived overt bodily sensuality, they appear to merely react, and do not feel or think. By virtue of their nonhumanity, these people are thought to have no human thoughts and lack interiority (reflection, contemplation, innovation, imagination). These social projections, of course, are founded and predicated on brutalizing machine myths.

While the machine provides an excellent lens through which race scholars can materially examine the depersonalization of Asians, myth focuses critically on the power of words. Myth, opines Roland Barthes, forms a type of speech derived from everyday discourse, where "everything can be a myth provided it is conveyed by a discourse."[106] The actual thing conveyed by a mythic sign is "arbitrary and natural ... [since] the meaning is always there to *present* the form; the form is always there to *outdistance* the meaning."[107] Because the model machine gives symbolic form to some meaning of informational content, the "myth is not defined by the object of its message, but by the way in which it utters this message."[108] Myth hides more than what it divulges, and certain myths proliferate enough in society in that they perpetuate the hegemonic interests of the ruling classes. Barthes refers to the tendency of myths to become so naturalized and unquestioned that they take on preternatural features. More than false truths, myths are forms of speech that imbue images and social constructs with enormous power. In a sense, myths give shape to abstract forms of knowing and behaving in modern societies, bringing nonhuman occult elements into the man-made world. Myths marry ancient beliefs in magical spirits to a modern cosmology where "the dead and the living, the invisible and the visible, the medium and the message—became one."[109]

Imperial myths veil certain incontrovertible truths and realities about race. Cultural theorist Wendy Chun suggests that *race as form of technology* reframes ethical questions of good and evil, right and wrong.[110] Recognizing that race, like technology, is constantly improvised, Chun contends that "race historically has been a tool of subjugation . . . through which the visible traces of the body are tied to allegedly innate invisible characteristics . . . rendering some mere objects to be exploited, enslaved, measured, demanded, and sometimes destroyed."[111] Chun asks whether the data-like Asian subject can be a site for creativity and insubordination. Chun's observation and suggestion calls into question our usual modes of "visualization and revelation . . . making possible new modes of agency and causality."[112] Framing race as technology splits up the neat coeval relationship between form and function, essence and artifice, the basic and the exemplary. Asians signify the machine even as they break the machine.

Scholars of American Studies like Leo Marx, David Nye, and John Kasson, known for their "myth and symbol" school of thought, attended to popular narratives of technology undergirding myths about the American frontier, progress, and heroism.[113] Technology becomes imagined as supernatural in the morality play of the United States, a country whose creed of "exceptional humanism" does not square with its ugly history of jingoism and special pedigree in racial chauvinism. This creed manifested in the pseudoscientific language of biometrics, which was developed most thoroughly in the United States. It was based on the "mismeasure of man," derived from the symbology around the "unlived" Other.[114] That form of computing humanity would guarantee that the "white living body" and the "mathematics of the unliving" would become the "measuring stick through which other bodies are calculated."[115] This biased knowledge economy held a strong current in history, as capitalism forcefully converged with race.

Racial Capitalism and Model Machines

Beyond the realm of colonial science and technoculture, the production of *modern* model machines occurred through the racial capitalist system broadly. Asians are a model for being/becoming machine, from the perspective of the person who construes them that way. When they are described as imitating humans, these Asians are supposedly modeling themselves on good or bad terms dictated by whites. We detect this claim when Asian Americans are given the moniker of "model minorities" or Asia is described as a model civilization for lesser ones. The racial modeling of Asians as hard workers or successful merchants falls into this dynamic, casting them as better than other people of color, but they are never as good as whites within the pecking ordering of humanity. As political scientist Claire Jean Kim notices, relative valorization (economic insiders) and civil ostracism (cultural outsiders) of Asians work in tandem with anti-Black racism and discourses in which Asians are "presented as so hard-driving and self-denying that they seem barely human."[116]

The balancing act between valorizing and ostracizing Asians changes with the time or place. My focus on labor, war, sex, the virtual, and global machines represent five main areas for examining the model machine myth, because they speak to different modalities for being almost machine and scarcely human. They reveal how the racialized technologization of the Asian functions in relation to new developments in U.S. racial capitalism. Moreover, they are interrelated: they all involve some form of (mis)recognition of Asian people as useful automatons for articulating labor needs and social threats within specific circumstances. What ties these historical chapters is a critical attention to the Asian automaton as a figuration of alternative/surrogate/artificial humanity. A deeper engagement with the cultural history of the Asian machine addresses how technological progress relies "upon rendering invisible those excluded."[117]

Racial capitalism emerges as a central concept for this project to draw out how the model machine flares up in history. It is based on critiques of the United States as an exclusionist nation, racial state, economic superpower, and imperializing force. In this vein, I ask what the machine myth does to Asian racialization and how it functions through global/American racial capitalism. Racial capitalism—as it has been articulated by political scientist Cedric Robinson and other critics—can be found in the middle ground between the racism of "liberal" apartheid regimes like the United States and an antiracist radical tradition arrogated by people of color. While acknowledging that national/social formations of race and class are specific and ever-changing, Robinson asserts that the racism and racialism that emerge from capitalism generally operate as a matter of *civilization*—namely, Western civilization as the acme of human civilization, one built on the very machinery of colonial expropriation and exploitation of "colored" labor. Quoting W. E. B. Dubois, he exposes the *permanence* of the systemic oppression of nonwhite people: "Out of the exploitation of the dark proletariat comes the Surplus Value filched from human breasts which, in cultured lands, the Machine and harnessed Power veil and conceal. The emancipation of man is the emancipation of labor and the emancipation of labor is the freeing of that basic majority of workers who are yellow, brown and black."[118] Similar to political theorist Tiffany Willouby-Herard, who posits the U.S. modes of racial capitalism as a centrifugal force for "global whiteness," geographer Yousuf Al-Bulushi unpacks and locates racial capitalism in the generative spaces and possibilities of imagining race and capital beyond the obviousness of state racism and political economy.[119] In this broader open sense of the system, U.S. racial capitalism works through global capitalism.

For Asians, racial capitalism plays out differently, if not separately, than for other groups. According to cultural studies scholar Iyko Day, Asians as alien capital/labor embody the social ills of capitalism that must be somehow integrated, if never really resolved, into the white colonial settler state.[120] Capitalism's destructive capacity is based on the rehearsal of Asia as a relatively "developed" site of heightened economic-labor exploitation, one intimately linked to Indigenous displacement and the treatment of First Peoples as nonhuman savages. Modern empires were able to meet greater demand for labor through the Asian coolie, whose place in colonial history forms a kind of absent presence.[121] New scientific demands for categorizing and sorting out racial difference (to justify racial subjection) churned out "unintelligible" forms of humanness that manifested within the "complicated anxieties regarding external and internal threats to the mutable coherence of the national body."[122] According to cultural theorist Lisa Lowe, Asians, rendered malleable, could embody all at once "the invading multitude, the lascivious seductress, the servile yet treacherous domestic, the automaton whose inhuman efficiency will supersede American ingenuity."[123]

Despite its liberal pretenses, the United States could never acknowledge the full humanity of nonwhite people, which distilled a central problem at the heart of American modernity and its ruse of liberty. While European powers scrambled to gobble up colonial territories with impunity, the United States advanced itself in the world in an imperial manner without the formal pretense of a colonial empire. As a token of Americanist imperial thinking, the myth of labor machines reached into academia to scientifically explain the sallowness of the yellow race. Take this "scientific" observation about the Chinese from ethnologist and historian Hubert Howe Bancroft, who in the early 1900s trumpeted U.S. global leadership in his masterwork *The New Pacific*: "As an economic factor, the Chinaman is the ideal human machine, the best intelligent and industrial animal that can be produced at the price. . . . Call him animal, vegetable, or mineral, he comes all the same, and proves indeed a worthy implement [of civilization]. . . . Not that he is altogether perfect. . . . He is less human than some others. First, his skin; it is off color; for so says the constitution of the United States, the Black and white shall inherit, but not the yellow."[124] This quote frames Chinese as animals and machines, but also as vegetation and minerals. The Chinaman is the barest of living organisms and is sometimes an inorganic element. The academic gave some thought to the Chinaman, a great liar and thief, similar to the Black man, concluding that "Negro Peril" and "Yellow Peril" are not comparable for the latter "is a machine; good only for work. . . . For American society and citizenship better material can be found."[125]

Despite suggesting America's "pure" racial stocks were diluted by the "non-advancing" Chinese race, educated scholars like Bancroft were self-avowed "enlightened" liberals who believed all people are equal. He berated slavery and argued that the United States was less imperialist than the French, Portuguese, Spanish, Dutch, and British. Yet Bancroft also recognized that "Nature" is not equal and does not give great potential to all. While the scholar was quick to indict the colonial domination of India, long suffering under the blows of England, Indian people were of such "low development," he said, they required "whitewashing" to enter the world historical movement toward rational freedom. Echoing philosophers like Hegel, this disparagement of Asian society went hand in hand with white men's exploitation of Asian labor. At the end of the day, Bancroft argued, the "New World" is determined "by American capital and Asiatic labor."[126] Whites can own foreign lands with the proviso they never stay permanently or else they "go native." We can spot the currents of this contradiction within U.S. popular thought—between economic liberalization and cultural racism, between domestic protection and expropriation of resources—running within iterations of the machine myth.

Throughout this book, I provide provocative ways of rethinking Asians and Asian Americans as machines. This rethinking is done through examples in which they are literally and figuratively called machines but also through a sustained rumination upon the wider stakes and repercussions of this trope in the development of U.S. society and global societies. Conceptually, I theorize the model machine in terms of what it is as a social construct or stereotype and what it does as a condition of subjugation or oppression. My creative play with language works through the model minority stereotype to give greater historical weight to something we might think or know as contemporary. In many ways, identifying the model machine in history helps us advance the discourse about the model minority, recognizing that this post-1965 social type bears an older lineage.

Within U.S. racial capitalism, racial difference marks the type of labor to be exploited to death. Arguments defending such labor exploitation were given life by unverified speculations, rumors, gossip, guesswork, hearsay, and conspiracies about the Asian machine. The machine's iterations—labor machine, war machine, sex machine, virtual machine, global machine—coalesce in the model minority myth, influencing and shaping it and bending its convoluted history. The machine myth takes present worries and themes related to Asian representation and marginalization and bounces them back to previous moments when Asians were thought of as not yet human. When presented in any discussion, the model machine recenters old-fangled discussions of the machine—industrial fantasy and colonial labor—within latter-day concerns with identity and social class. One cannot entirely talk about a model machine in the same way as a model minority, but their similarity is suggestive in warping our given sense of time.

Long before the model minority, the model machine myth foretold of Asians as the most perfect technical workers, an ingenious if stupid bunch of automatons—qualities that haunt today's model minorities. While the notion of the perpetual foreigner is still relevant as a concept, the model minority appears as the preeminent organizing principle and linchpin for racializing Asian Americans presently—an accident of history explained by historian Ellen Wu that demands more critical expectations for engaging the preconditions enabling the historic rise of the model minority myth.[127] Model machines are a symbolic precursor to model minorities, reaching across a long stretch of time to say we never abandoned the practice of indentured servitude, sexual slavery, and military conscription just because (certain) Asians are now considered good worker-subjects. Multiculturalism, masquerading as postracialism, cannot dent the colonial reminders of the history of dehumanization, or even mishumanization, as practiced over the course of centuries.

Plumbing the depths of model machine mythology does that work, reminding us of history's imprint upon our thought process, which is why lab workers today can be called "high-tech coolies" in an echoing of machine stereotypes from centuries ago. A factory worker employed, moreover, by an American subcontracted company in China is *not* a model minority since they are not found within the confines of a U.S. nation. Yet they "model" ideas about the docile capitalist racial subject in a globalized world, which collapses the distinction between the foreign Asian and the domestic Asian American. These "Americanized" workers in Asia are global subjects. As a machine, within a local-global spectrum, they exist uniquely within the dominion and extended "parts" of the United States.

The model machine myth jumps spatial scales but also loops through the historical "unthought" of history. Indeed, it is a series of not totally realized expressions about crisis and regeneration. Just as the robot's ancestor is the automaton, the (Asian American) model minority trope finds its predecessor in the (Asian) model machine myth, a rambunctious myth that cannot be confined to a singular history. As signaled by the multiple arcs of this myth, past humans were always obsessed with the horror or great splendor of a monster, and this speculative history changes form, ad infinitum, much like monster stories.

Machine myths can be considered one subset or offshoot of Orientalism in the way that Edward Said summarized that term as marking the "positional superiority" of white Europeans over non-Europeans. The slippery slope of talking about Asians as robot/automaton/machine gives way to the real issue of the Western "gaze," the way the Orient and Orientals are treated as inanimate objects to be taxonomized, grasped, and acted upon by outsiders.[128] At the same time, the Asian machine myth transcribed the particular technocultural inflections that Orientalism might take in places like the United States, which "likes to imagine [itself] a great nation whose citizens all conform to a single model and are directed by a single power."[129] This quote belongs to French diplomat Alexis de Tocqueville, who spoke of the young republic as paradigmatic of a dynamic state in contrast to the proper social order of China, which he calls the finest model of centralized administration "that exists in the universe."[130] Despite China's tranquility and harmony, he said, the Chinese trampled their own great civilization by losing the power of renewal, absorbed only in productive industry and formulaic imitative behavior.[131] Stasis of the kind seen in China is what could happen if liberal democracies like the United States do not improve and constantly evolve. Asian robotic conformity and the inertia it engenders cast a shadow over the United States' future.

While not addressing specifically Asians as model machines, Cathy Schlund-Vials's *Modelling Citizenship* is a useful study as it provides a path to understanding citizenship in the United States through modeling selfhood. She documents the unfairness of the 1790 Naturalization Act, in which the "free white person of moral character" clause provided the precondition for becoming a citizen. This racial prerequisite excluded unfree and unscrupulous aliens of color "through discourses of liberalism, rubrics of whiteness, and rhetorical omission."[132] Here, "naturalization" means more than legal or cultural Americanization; it means the natural ability to be human and be naturalized as human. The fictive space of U.S. liberalism masked a decidedly "racist citizenship matrix, replete with innate moral values and assessments of racial inferiority."[133]

The study of model citizenship helps us track the bumpy historical move from conceiving Asians as perpetual foreigners (forced exclusion) to model minorities (forced assimilation). The idea of "never white" as "never human" is important to Schlund-Vials, who discusses the "model minoritization" as the affective frame for utopian/dystopian rhetoric surrounding Asians in the United States. Asian Americans never made it out from the space of the nonhuman (or out of Asia), even when later designated as model minorities. The "break" between a dehumanizing brutal past and humanizing future is flummoxed by the spatiotemporal "crossings" between American human and Asian nonhuman. These zoonotic "species crossings" remain undeniably present in U.S. immigration policy as well as in racial characterizations of Asians. As I show, both the "positive" and negative characterizations of Asians as machines summon an antiquated dehumanizing past to bear upon a posthuman future where nothing is ever what it appears to be.

Taken together, the chapters of *Model Machines* serve to compensate for the scant attention paid by scholars to racial unintelligibility via robotic impressionability. The book provides a massive and sustained history on the topic of racial mechanization. There have been books and articles in the field of Asian American studies that, at times, examine how the Asian/American has been presented as cyborgs and robotic machines. Despite citing a wide array of scholars from various fields, my work and arguments are mostly posited in relation to and engage with contemporary thinkers or texts, such as David S. Roh, Betsy Huang, and Greta A. Niu's edited volume *Techno-Orientalism*, David Palumbo-Liu's *Asian/American*, and Kalindi Vora and Neda Atanasoski's *Surrogate Humanity*.

I take particular interest in intervening in the history of science and technology studies, ethnic and cultural studies, and global and international studies. In science and technology studies (STS), race has served as a new lens to think about the history of technology and rethink techne.[134] Within ethnic studies and cultural studies, Asian American specialists are seeking to discover posthuman ecologies, imagining otherwise the field as one without proper human subjects, now more concerned with analyzing *objects* of knowledge and the production of *difference* rather than starting with an assumed Asian human identity.[135] In global studies, there is a renewed push to reimaging the world through a continuum of space and time. In keeping with what global studies scholars Eve Darian-Smith and Philip McCarty laid out in *The Global Turn*, I seek to decenter Asian and American exceptionalism by thinking globally but also aim to recast the world imaginary by overcoming the "prevailing logics that put everything into hierarchies, ordered positions, center and periphery models, and developmental progressions."[136] Hence, the global encompasses the local, the regional, the national, the subnational, the supranational, the imperial, the colonial, the transnational, the postnational, and the international.

I put all these spaces into play when discussing the model machine myth—a global myth that moved with U.S. nationalism, imperialism, militarism, and capitalism, amid the circulation of scientific ideas and technology.

Asian American Science and Technology Studies

In a burgeoning field that I designate as Asian American science and technology studies, my book comments on how the machine trope has been approached by transdisciplinary studies scholars interested in transnational flows of militarism, migration, capitalism, and globalization as they shape the racialization of Asians. It offers a much-needed intervention into cultural critiques, which have not properly addressed the machinic typecasting of people as a unique form of racial subjection. Speaking to all these sites, *Model Machines* intervenes by *bridging* various intellectual areas of concern, *adding* temporal parameters and useful vocabulary for study, and *building* a conceptual scaffolding and stitching of bodies of thought into one cohesive project. Further, it aims toward *subverting* the idea that the Asian automaton was some weird fluke or minor footnote in the annals of history to assert that model machinerization remains a vector of transacting American racial capitalism and colonial modernity. This key symbology forms a root cause of current human (and nonhuman) oppression.

In *Surrogate Humanity: Race, Robots, and the Politics of Technological Futures*, feminist scholars Kalindi Vora and Neda Atanasoski identify the "surrogate" as a racialized gendered form of humanity elided under the common belief that technology is performing or doing the work of actual humans. The scholars aver that this surrogate effect appears as a fantasy in which the real humans are "removed from the degraded arenas of manual labor and killing, and instead nonhuman others populate warehouses and the field of war."[137] Following Vora and Atanasoski, I contend that Asians act as the surrogate humanity for white humanity. This surrogate, though, sits as a product of history that precedes the neoliberal contemporary moment. I explore this historical matter of freedom versus exploitation through my examination of the model machine myth (MMM) in terms of interior/exterior life (models), closed/open systems (machines), and new/old imaginaries (myths).

Media studies scholars like Chun and Beth Coleman have theorized the broad connections between race and technology. If race and technology can be considered almost the same yet distinct, according to Chun, how does that inform "an engagement of race as technology—specifically, Asians as robot-like"?[138] How do alternative readings in the rendering of Asians as robots help evacuate the hidden transcript of race behind technocultural discourse?

Parallel with Chun's task of making the unseen knowable, Coleman reflects on the invisible mastery found in the colonized voice: "In rendering *certain* people machines—dumb and mute ones, who have no proper voice—a structural position of mastery had been encoded in the machine itself. . . . This mistreatment set in motion a binary logic of master/slave, man/machine, or man/beast with deep and long consequences for Western culture as a whole and for the fate of people of color in particular."[139] Here, the social modeling of nonwhites as machines says more about Western civilization than it does about intrinsic qualities of people of color.

Methodical tracking of humans treated as machines helps rupture historical linearity and document how they are denied any self-determination of *will* and of *presence*. And to critique machineness as a lived social experience reveals the obfuscation of the obvious: people remain human in every single way, even when powers do not acknowledge this fact. Asian American critiques of science and technology bridge broader theories of race as well as the relationship of Asians and/as technology.[140] My contribution to the conversation is in saying that we must grasp the model machine as moored in specific historical moments and institutions. This intervention is necessary, even if model machine discourse seems to exceed or escape facile periodization, given an assumption that the "intelligent machine" is a thing of the future.

While techno-Orientalism as a framework is elastic and capacious enough for all kinds of rich analysis, it can also be too broad; the same criticism has been similarly leveled against Edward Said's definition of Orientalism. A working definition of techno-Orientalism, according to scholars David S. Roh, Betsy Huang, and Greta A. Niu, is "the phenomenon of imagining Asia and Asians in hypo- or hyper-technological terms in cultural productions and political discourse . . . infused with the languages and codes of the technological and the futuristic."[141] As literary historian Michelle Huang observes, the Asian robot's origins predate the techno-Orientalism of the 1980s and Japan Panic, but it provides a bridge to earlier historical moments: "Indeed, the 19th-century Chinese coolie [as] . . . the robotic worker thus serves as a hinge point between historical forms of Orientalism (railroad worker) and more futuristic iterations (cyborg)."[142] Given this temporal cycling of machine tropes, Huang recommends a posthumanist reading of history and speculative futures.

Asian American science and technology studies adapts to the long duration and future-thinking of U.S. liberal empire. With a numerical upsurge in naval clipper ships and steamships able to navigate across vast oceans, the pastoral myth of the republic as a yeomen Jeffersonian garden or Eden gave way to the halcyon myth of an "American machine" that could successfully extend much farther than prior European empires could.[143] Historian Leo Marx elaborates on how the unshakable faith in American exceptionalism grew stronger, accreting under U.S. technocultural imperialism: "The American machine has become a transcendent symbol: a physical object invested with political and metaphysical ideality. It rolls across Europe and Asia, liberating the oppressed people of the Old World—a signal, in fact, for the salvation of mankind."[144] Marx claims that the metaphysical machine—pivotal for Newton, Bacon, and Descartes studying the cosmos—was replaced by visual images of the biological world. A new scientific-philosophical rationalism emerged through the "appearance of the machine technology in the underdeveloped 'new world' [as the] . . . great central figurative conception of nineteenth-century American culture."[145] The nineteenth century that Thomas Carlyle proclaimed the "Age of Machinery" found a bold model of progress in the United States, blazing forth in the world with inventions like the cotton gin, phonograph, and electric light bulbs. The American machine supplied a beacon of hope to improve cultures and societies stuck in an animal/automaton state of nature. American science and technology brought "locomotives rushing and roaring, and the shrill steam-whistle, tying the Eastern to the Western sea."[146] During this transition in which the United States rose to become a global power and imperial machine, the myth of Asians as human machines took off as "preindustrial societies, less powerful governments, and people of color proved a powerful magnet to a maturing American technological base that at the same time was challenging the 'workshop of the world' within its own boundaries."[147]

The field of racial science and technology explains why this presupposition of people as machine gained traction over time. Beginning in the industrial age, the United States sought to affirm its superior humanity over and against alt-human others who appeared more mechanical in appearance. Hedging against the technological determinism that says man-made machines will chasten ignorance and bring enlightenment to all (freeing humans from toil), there is a need for scholars to deconstruct machines as just another feature of human culture. They must disassemble how discourses about human automatons become appropriated in conjunction with folk prejudices to generate the myths of the machine.[148] The human automaton is not simply a metaphor or misrecognition of Asians as actual human beings but serves a tangible product made from the dehumanizing mechanisms of race.

Despite profound changes to society wrought by human innovation, technology still functions as an imperializing tool of white mythology that affirms Euro-Americans as human subjects and world masters.[149] Race concerns more than intergroup differences, since automated racial bodies can stand in as "vectors for evidence" to stake out a mythological war against animals, monsters, the undead, and aliens in our midst.[150] Against the historical backdrop of technology as a vehicle of white supremacy, it is crucial then to outline the mechanized Asian corpus as part of "social relations of science and technology, including crucially the systems of myth and meanings structuring our imaginations."[151] Retrieving the genealogy of the model machine allows us free rein to co-imagine "what was" and what seems nearly impossible.

The machine is more than a system or a small unit of a system. In an essay titled "Machine and Structure," theorist Félix Guattari draws out the spatiotemporal dynamics of historicizing the machine: "The emergence of the machine marks a date, a change, different from a structural representation. The history of technology is dated by the existence at each stage of a particular type of machine. . . . Yesterday's machine, today's and tomorrow's, are [related] by a process of historical analysis, by reference to a signifying chain."[152] In other words, the model machine is a sign in a long chain of signs. Conceiving this machine, as of its time and beyond it, allows me to grasp the disparate effects of historical disruption, retroactive thinking, and futuristic orientations found in the model machine.

To bring up the outlandish idea of Asians as robotic raises both mental confusion and curiosity. It is a familiar yet bewildering idea that exceeds a clear frame of reference, supplying fleeting impressions and quick snapshots of time. This somewhat unbounded "subject" of history, the Asian automaton, lies somewhere in the psychic undercurrents of our public discourse. It haunts the edges of the social imagination, alongside demons, aliens, ghosts, witches, vampires, and zombies. Insofar as every version of the Asian machine resembles or copies previous models, a machine incorporates some aspect of the wider social machine and assimilates other terrifying figures. The machine time travels across a richly imagined panorama filled with infinite possibility. The model machine is a monster machine.

Let us attend nevertheless to specific times when people are designated as robotic machines or automatons and when they are imagined as such in relation to "Asian-looking" cyborgs. Even at moments when charges of roboticism are assigned to someone who appears to be a lackey or minion, a special resonance inheres when it is applied to Asians. There is an added racial layer of unease toward machinelike races, which goes beyond the "uncanny valley" or empathy/revulsion humans feel toward robots with an eerie resemblance to *Homo sapiens*.[153] The endowment of Asian bodies with machine meanings casts a mold (or model) of intelligence and a physicality that appears to defy the laws of mortal physics. This association of para-human qualities only serves to manifest and entrench the elements of Orientalism, which Said described as a Western intellectual enterprise that "shares with magic and with mythology the self-containing, self-reinforcing character of a closed system, in which objects are what they are *because* they are what are, for once, for all time."[154]

Despite Said's main emphasis on humanism as the answer to Orientalism, it might be best to think of Orientalism (or even techno-Orientalism) as an open pathway for unspooling the (de)humanization of Asians and, perhaps, the Asianization of technological objects.[155] As literary scholar Anne Cheng points out, Orientalism is not a one-way process of turning people into machines but turning machines into the likeness of people: "The history of Orientalism in the West is not just a history of objectification but also a history of personification: the making of personness out of things. This non-person, normally seen as outside of modernity and counter to organic human individualism, actually embodies a forgotten genealogy . . . [about] the modern understanding of humanness."[156] The long-running myth that Asians are technomarvels calibrates difference—where the affirmation of American life, liberty, and happiness is counterposed to Asian death, unfreedom, and misery. Ratios of humanism gained even more import in the transition from the American Century to the Asian Century.

From the American Century to the Asian Century

As there is no specific historical archive for my unique subject matter, *Model Machines* proceeds as a scholarly work of the imagination, building a unique collection of texts and gathering a wide range of sources that run the gamut. It is a historical project that reaches into literary and cultural studies, film and media studies, global and international studies, ethnic and American studies, and gender and sexuality studies. The book achieves all this range by following the roving figure of the Asian automaton as it manifests within newspapers, films, television shows, creative fiction, war propaganda, cultural ephemera, personal memoirs, legal court cases, and political discourse. From the outset, all these sites appear to bear no direct relation to one another but, when brought together, speak to the roboticized Asian as a constant fixture in the minds of prominent leaders (in academia, politics, or business), in the creative brains of artists, and in the *sensus populi* of everyday people.

The history of technology tends to be understudied when it comes to Asian racialization, which is interesting considering that representations of Asians are ineluctably connected to technological skills or artifice.[157] Charting this capricious myth of the model machine and how it is fostered and disseminated in history, this study bears important stakes in terms of raising queries about the ethics and ramifications of calling a whole race machines. Recognizing this sleight of hand as a point of contention follows David Palumbo-Liu's observation that American attitudes toward Asians have involved "shifting and often contradictory predications of 'Asia' onto and into the United States imaginary."[158] Through reckoning with the model machine myth, we can track the means by which actors in the United States and elsewhere contributed to "the eroding distinction between the human and the robot [as] an analogy for the slippery distinction between the American and Asian."[159]

One can spot this semantic slippage with the U.S. designation of Asians as "aliens ineligible for citizenship," a legal category of exclusion ironically cemented in the same year as the etymological birth of the robot.[160] In 1921, dramatist Karel Capek coined the term *robot*, a neologism he first brought to life in 1917, when he wrote about the existence of intelligent but stupefied mechanical people in his dramatic play *R. U. R.*, or *Rossum's Universal Robots*, which imagined a race war between differently colored robot workers in a factory that included Negro robots, Chinese robots, and Italian robots. Robot derives from the Czech word *robota* for "to work," in the vein of "forced labor" and compulsory service/hardship. It was invented to denote things that look human meant for use by their human creators, who still feared their mechanical slaves might overtake them.[161] In the very same years that Capek was developing the robot, the U.S. Congress passed two major racist immigration acts: the 1917 Asiatic Barred Zone Act and the 1921 Emergency Quota Law, barring almost all Asian immigration to the country, prompted by distress over an alien takeover. The correlations between enslaved robot and the indentured Asian worker coagulate in the labor machine myth, a distortion that also helps explain why Asians in Asia and Asians outside of Asia are often indistinguishable (as one and the same). As a trope for representing the dehumanizing of humans by other humans, robots are used "to express anxieties over annihilation . . . [and] convey an ongoing agitation about human domination over other humans."[162]

In its century-long westward expansion, the United States set its sights on Asia as the key site for expropriating cheap labor and natural resources. In the meantime, the United States buffeted its national borders to halt Asian immigration. Triggered by the Asian machine's threat to the country's "spirit of invention," the United States felt a need to legally exclude Asians while economically needing them, which displays the complex "modeling function the Asian plays and fulfills for the American psyche."[163] The dynamic started to change as modernized Asian nations like Japan and China began to brook serious challenges to the United States as the preeminent world power in the twentieth century, or what political commentator Walter Lippmann nicknamed the "American Century."[164] Also referred to as the "Technological Century," the period witnessed the birth and mass production of inventions developed in the United States, such as lasers, transistors, DNA decoders and recombination, nuclear weapons, airplanes, automobiles, mobile cellular phones, satellites, and computers. The last portion of my book takes place in this momentous time, concluding with what many today declare to be the Asian Century.

The timeline of this study will be recognizable to those readers familiar with Asian American history and the chronology of U.S.-Asia relations: the labor migration of coolies to the United States and the exclusion of Chinese workers (1840–1924); the U.S. conflagration with Japan and the internment of Japanese Americans during World War II (1907–1945); the U.S. embroilment in the Vietnam War and the Cold War conscription of Southeast Asian women into military sex/service work (1950–1980); the globalizing late-capitalist era that saw greater influence by Japanese corporations as well as immigration of Asian high-tech labor to the U.S. (1980–2000); the rise of global China and other Asian economies at the beginning of the new century (2000–present). I chose these case studies because they appear as defining moments, so examining them allows for closer study of recurrent ideas about model machines.

Model Machines considers the rise of the United States as a hegemonic and technocultural power, one forged in relation to the model machine myth and its unsettling history. I find that the myth popped up at moments of crisis for the United States but occasionally appeared in other places like Peru, South Africa, Australia, Canada, the United Kingdom, Mexico, and Japan. There is burgeoning work on Japanese people's views of automaton life that is well beyond the scope of this book, but the final chapter discusses how countries in Asia like Japan are renovating the notion that robotic people are characteristically "Asian."

While historical events are arranged in chronological order, I thoroughly explain how each periodic model machine type is produced by previous formulations or speaks to later ones. Starting with this introduction, I spot the ways Chinese coolies contracted by evil employers are the modernized retelling of Asians as slaves of despots. In modern times, however, the "emperors" exploiting the automaton masses are foreign countries and multinational companies. To synthesize a vast array of sources that span well over hundreds of years, I supply useful typologies, such as the "labor machine," to organize a vast body of scientific, legal, scholarly, cultural, and religious knowledge.

Given all the shapes or models that the machine assumes, this introduction begins to parse out when the Asian automaton presents a sign of innovation (innovating technology) and when it is a sign of a stripped human authenticity (regressive roboticism). It attends to the parallel moments when the machine trope was attributed to "more advanced" Asian states like South Korea as opposed to less wealthy countries like the Philippines. The individual chapters are productively worked out in thinking about the model machine in terms of what it means to fight, assemble, exploit, contain, and reconfigure the machines. Each chapter asks: What is the figure or model of machine being presented (automaton), what ideal exactly is being socially modeled (archetype), and what is the machine modeled or based upon (assumption)?

Chapter 1 commences in the early nineteenth century with the first arrival of Chinese coolies to the United States and how they arrived on the path to fame as the world's greatest "labor machines." This chapter irons out the distinctions between free white labor and indentured Asian servitude to describe various degrees of humanism found at the dawn of the so-called Second Industrial Age. It shines light on perceptions of the Chinese as demonized effigies of technology and how their mechanized gender-confusing bodies threatened the American national family, manhood, and civilization.

Chapter 2 moves from domestic concerns with migrant coolie labor machines to international issues with Japan as a "war machine," given the ascent of Japan as a military power. It examines the Japanese citizen-soldier as an incarnation of Japan's technocultural empire, one able to steal Western technology only to deploy it against the United States. The reimagining of human relations under this war machine trope puts up the Japanese—whether in the United States or in Japan—as a superhuman race perpetually on the warpath.

Chapter 3 provides an interregional geopolitical focus, remarking upon the mythic construction of Southeast Asian women as "sex machines" over the course of the Cold War, when demands for both assembly-line-style factory work and militarized prostitution exploded. In a period when the United States sought to turn foreign territories in into militarized "societies structured in domination," I identify the simulation of bionic women of color as slaves for men.[165]

Chapter 4 charts the late twentieth century as a moment of high-tech capitalism shot through with dystopic digital fantasies of "virtual machines" epitomized by Japanese corporatism and new Asian immigrant labor. The chapter synthesizes popular meanings about the Asian alien as alien cyborg in the twilight years of the American Century.

Chapter 5 explores a moment when Asian automatons are truly global, defined more and more by Asian cultural influences. In this global millennial era, Asians are still seen as machines, but this myth is no longer strictly an American worldview or intellectual province but one involving non-American nations and imaginaries.

While early historical examples of model machines distinguish national/ethnic types as different kinds of machines (Chinese as labor machines, Japanese as war machines) given the dominant discourse about the Asiatic threat, Cold War Orientalism brought a panoply of other Asians under the extensive fold of the U.S. model machine myth. Hence, the machine labor type of Vietnamese, Thai, and Korean women might reference the labor of Chinese coolies as its historical origins, even as Asian women were already thought of as sexual automatons long before the Cold War. And yet those machines reference the power to shape perception by the United States, engaged in a furtive "war on women" in the Global South.

My first three chapters take on particular pivots: Chinese coolies (labor machines) as a *national* concern for U.S. race wars and Japanese war machines operating within an *international* world war. The rest of the chapters take notice of the forms of labor (use) and war (threat) that can take shape. Asian woman (sex machines) caught up in a *supranational* Cold War are sexually threatening and economically useful to Americans. The last two chapters move to discuss Asia and Asian America more broadly in my take on *transnational* virtual machines and *postnational* global machines within a more deterritorialized setting. Attention to this *differential* sense of model machines—become crucial in (dis)articulating the alternating stipulation that Asians are excludable threat and exploitable labor. The posthuman is part and parcel of the imagining of the model machine, which is why I engage with this concept in the epilogue on Asian posthuman futures.

Model Machines acknowledges the economic and political incentives found in pegging certain races as machines and denying humanity to whole groups of people. Low-wage migrant workers from Mexico and Latin America are often accorded the status of "techno-braceros," appearing to signify *manual machines*, who simply provide the raw energy to power up major U.S. agrobusiness and service industries.[166] Native Americans were described by evolutionary naturalists like Comte de Buffon—one of the earliest inventors of modern racial categories based on anatomy and aesthetic appearance—as an inactive, feeble *primitive machine* or "a kind of weak automaton . . . incapable of correcting Nature" with "no control over either animals or elements."[167]

As both "low-tech" and "high-tech" workers, Asians are envisaged in a different register of automaton, especially given their "significant roles as developers, consumers, and manufacturers of technology."[168] Decoding the myths about Asians as model machines in connection to other automatons of color, I scrutinize how Black, Latine, and Indigenous people never quite moved from being monstrous "objects" of fear and fascination to proper minority "subjects." They remain unable to evade the skein of objectification or the process of thinging.[169]

The excessive framing of the Asian as real-life automata provokes many queries, chief among them: What does the language of model machinery do in terms of producing the Asian/American subject? What does the model machine myth tell us about the symbiosis between culture and technology, alienation and personhood, material reality and media representation?

What does the Asian as automaton reveal in redefining history as stories of human "objects" with voices which can and must be heard? As our world becomes more complicated with droids, cyborgs, and robots, it behooves all of us to center the perspectives of racialized automatons struggling to find their place in the white (hu)man's world.

1

Labor Machines

*Fighting the Mechanized Coolie in
the Age of Industrial Slavery*

This chapter analyzes key historical records and sources produced in the mid-nineteenth century to the turn of the twentieth century about Chinese laborers in the United States. Focusing on populist writings from prominent U.S. labor organizers, businessmen, and anti-immigrant groups, such as the Asian Exclusion League, it documents the suppositions of Chinese workers as mechanized coolies, at a time when the country moved from a factory-centered agricultural economy to a consumer-oriented Fordist society. In doing so, it sheds light on coolies as a sign of an emerging Asian modernity that took on mythical status and conferred the title of *labor machines*, whose fine-tuned industrial bodies threatened to erode U.S. technological superiority and chip away at the roots of Western civilization, American nationalism, and white manhood. The myth of the labor machine, as I call it, revolved around vexing questions about immigrants (culture), work (labor), citizenship (nation), civilization (race), biology (nature), and humanity (species). As will be uncovered, the phantasm of the indefatigable coolie that works and reproduces endlessly formed a primary role in framing the bumpy transition from indentured servitude to modern-day "industrial slavery."[1]

Conflicting opinions over the coolie's mechanical method of labor induced further thinking within the public referendum on the place of Chinese in diaspora. The coolie problem not only reflects economic worries about foreign laborers but also denotes the threat of automaton workers. This robot was deemed by anti-immigrant activists to be antithetical to

Western civilization, the essence of which was thought to have been inherited from the ancient Greeks and Romans. In 1922, American lawyer R. F. Pettigrew argued for the modern Anglo-Saxon to eschew Asian automatons like the Romans did: "When he came into competition with the Asiatic races, people of low vitality and with a great tenacity of life—human machines who could subsist upon the least food and perform the most work—the Roman farmer was destroyed, the foundation of power was shattered and the Roman Empire passed away."[2]

An impressive amount of scholarly work exists on the history of Chinese coolie labor and anti-Asian racism.[3] Building upon this wealth of knowledge, the chapter probes these queries: How does the figuration of the coolie as a laboring machine add another dimension of racialization to the Chinese as hyperproductive (exploitable), degenerate (low-class), animalistic (primitive), monstrous (frightening), and alien (outside)? These categories' interrelationship, I discovered, form the bedrock for dehumanizing the Chinese. How then does the coolie not only provide a shorthand reference for experiences of wage work under industrialization but offer the signature of "alternative" life-forms under racial capitalism? This chapter regards the labor machine myth to be a vested site for resuscitating the mythology of an Anglo-Saxon nation of laws and civility and China as a godless place of mechanical monstrosity and animality. Whereas the coolie's body historically served as a place to narrate the imaginative horizons of American society, this techno-body gives new "image schemas" that affirm whites as the titular human and the Chinese as effectively not human.[4]

From this contest of wills, there emerged a competitive match between the older "machine civilization" of China, represented by the coolie, and the power of America's young "machine society," buoyed by the white male industrial worker. Through technocultural myths about the physical makeup and profligacy of the coolie, we can almost locate a theory of (alien) labor value tied to the Asian model machine, one that extends outward into areas of law, immigration, and political economy. In this manner, the Chinese alien worker endangers a maturing America that imagined itself as a national family and insular consumer market. This fallacy of thinking, based on tirades about morality and humanism, comes up short in capturing the lives of nonwhite populations under U.S. racial capitalism. Across this chapter and others, we find a deep connection between the embodiments of *a* machine (automaton) as it connects to *the* machine, a term that can refer to a worker, a factory, the military, political parties, and the capitalist system.

Whenever new foreign workers appear on the scene and manage to outwork regular laborers, once-secure ideas of the human are up for debate. In this chapter, the model or figure for the machine is the coolie. The coolie conveys a model of racialized *labor* that works efficiently but cheaply. Such a labor machine is modeled on the notion of Chinese as feudalistic (communal) and semicivilized (barbaric). I dwell on the specific association of the Chinese with labor machines, displacing white workers and filling a void of Black workers. This association shaped what the ideal capitalist laborer looked like. The chapter ends with Fordism and the progressive mission of paying white workers a living wage—human workers who are not machines but make machines as opposed to the regressive Chinese. If Chinese are machines, they are not real workers nor fully human ones. Socially undesirable, they remained ideal workers for a racial capitalist society that needs what can be extraordinarily generated from their mechanized bodies.

This sharp contradiction in ideals—between a "national" culture that excludes particular racial groups and a capitalist culture that will exploit and absorb almost anyone—was pointed out by the economist Gunnar Myrdal among others. African American scholar W. E. B. Dubois finds instead a historical shift (and re-sorting) in ideals of free and unfree labor under U.S. racial capitalism. By the early twentieth century, anti-Chinese exclusion provided the stepladder for white Progressives eager to move beyond these racial class divisions. Yet they only moved from early religious intolerance (Chinese paganism) and biological racism (Chinese as diseased) toward cultural racism based on intelligence, morality, and other traits (Chinese as incompetent or deficient). Confined to the social category of labor machine, the coolie marks the eventual transition point between the denial of people from humanity based purely on their cultural foreignness to testing their inherent moral "fitness" for cultural citizenship.[5] That historical move is anchored in the human question and, ultimately, what makes coolies not so human and, perhaps, too human.

The Human Question in a Time of Coolies

This section considers the meaning of the coolie or Asian indentured worker within the United States at a time when African chattel slavery was still practiced. Coolie—a slur translated as "bitter strength" in Chinese and introduced into the English language by the British Raj—means cheap outsourced labor. The term found popularity in the United States during the introduction of Chinese indentured servants in the U.S. West, beginning in the eighteenth century, often recruited from the poorest parts of southern China, for the purposes of gold mining, farming, cotton picking, and digging war trenches for European colonial powers. The conflation of coolie labor with machinery first came about when a deluge of new factory-made, labor-saving machines burst onto the scene. Mass industrialization coincided with American capitalists seeking to reap the benefits of importing Chinese labor as cheap mechanical substitutes for European immigrant or

Black domestic workers. As something that signified industrial processes and products on a global scale, coolies were "stamped out on a production line like so many millions of pins."[6] Coolie mythology and the myth of Chinese invasion made everything modern appear circumspect, driving anxieties about the manufacturing-oriented future and the "transformation of the field of work and capital into a transnational economy dominated by automatons and machines."[7]

Coolieism was controversial as imported contract labor deviated from burgeoning liberal views of free labor, citizenship, and human rights in the Western Hemisphere. Historian Jason Oliver Chang documents the colonial history of Mexico and how industrial periodicals referred to Chinese coolies as *motores de sangre* (engines of blood), a disposable labor force comparable to draft animals.[8] To Euro-American observers, the coolies in Peruvian haciendas were treated by local capitalists "as a machine out of which the greatest amount of work possible is to be got."[9] One encyclopedia conflates the despotic states of the Americas with those in Asia: "In Peru, as in China, the most trifling and insignificant affair of life was made the business of the state, rendering the mass of the people to a condition of human automata."[10]

During British parliamentary debates over Chinese immigration in 1908, then undersecretary of state for the colonies, Winston Churchill, made the argument that coolies were found living in appalling conditions in South Africa, brought in after the decimation of local Black populations due to the Boer Wars. Churchill convinced the Liberal Party to ban further recruitment of coolies for this reason: "He is required to act as nearly as possible as a human machine. His function is to extract gold for his employer, and when his utility is finished he is to be cast aside as a creature with whom it is filthy to come into contact. . . . His ability to commit offences is the only thing that distinguishes him from a machine."[11] Churchill is essentially saying the Chinese are human machines and what separates them from pure machine is their criminal behavior. They are bad (active) machines compared to the inert good machines that can be used at will like wheat mills. Even when British liberal types advocate for the Chinese in South Africa, like Lord Houghton, they use the animal-automaton metaphor to make their case: "The coolie, having got to South Africa, is taken more or less as a prisoner. . . . He is not a citizen of the country; he is a human automaton, with no more distinct rights than a beast of burden."[12]

Following British leaders who moved toward banning coolieism throughout the colonies, Canadian officials considered excluding Chinese workers for a different reason. In one notable Canadian Supreme Court case in 1885, one judge ruled that the Chinese in British Columbia should not be juxtaposed with Westerners. They should be approached as "living machines, differing from artificial and inanimate machinery."[13] The main appeal of accepting the coolie was that he was easily terrorized by authority, displaying natural docility, and those useful qualities were needed to supply an economic base for Canada's settler colonial society. These living machines were not popular with the white workers, who routinely harassed the Asian immigrants with mob violence and who pushed successfully for the government to levy a prohibitive head tax on this human technology.

An obdurate, more widespread view of the Chinese as labor machines really took off in the United States, which experienced a tidal wave of social change due to mass immigration as well as grand diffusion of technology. Sweeping changes were wrought by the explosive number of time-saving devices generated from the Second Industrial Revolution, a period running from 1870 to 1914. This revolution bore witness to a rapid change in the production speed and economies of scale related to agriculture, transportation, communication, and medicine.[14] While the first Industrial Revolution in England depended on iron and textile production based around the cotton spinning loom, this revolution in the United States was centered on innovations in steel, railroads, mass electrification, the internal combustion engine, metal alloys and chemicals, the telegraph, and radio.

Beginning after the collapse of Radical Reconstruction, this new industrial age of "wage slavery" provided the context for sowing and searing the image of the Chinese as a foreign cog in the North American factory system of interchangeable parts, where hired hands were as replaceable as metal parts. Chinese became synonymous with machines, as immortalized by the Iron Chink, an automated processing machine made by Victoria Machinery Depot, which revolutionized the salmon cannery industry, named after the way Chinese handled and cut seafood so effortlessly.[15] Chinese processing crews inspired Edmund A. Smith to name his patented mechanized fish-butchering machine in 1904 the Iron Chink, reflecting public attitudes held toward the Chinese as adulterated machines, and early advertisers promised that the Iron Chink would ironically free canneries from their dependence upon Chinese foreign workers. As historian Patrick O' Bannon says, "The name evoked images of a machine as smoothly efficient as the butchers but requiring neither rest nor pay."[16]

This equating of machines with Chineseness began half a century earlier. In 1851, the U.S. inventor William Kelly, with a strong knowledge of metallurgy and chemistry, discovered a process of turning iron into steel through combustion, giving rise to an inexpensive method for the mass production of steel from molten pig iron (the cast or wrought pig iron of the time was brittle and too hard). Prior to this invention, steel was too expensive to make and was used primarily in swords and armor. Working in tandem with British inventor Henry Bessemer, Kelly was reportedly the first importer of Chinese labor, hoping to replace African-descended people in his foundries, even though Kelly construed these sojourners as willing to stay only temporarily. Kelly hired Chinese ironworkers to help him refine the decarbonization-oxidation process to remove metal impurities from iron. This process of blowing air into its molten form (natural oxygen tamps down the carbon content)—instead of raising the boiling temperature and wasting biofuel—had existed in China in a milder form since the eleventh century. What Kelly learned from his Chinese engineers laid the ground-work for U.S. mass production of steel from iron, pushing forward a new industrial "American system" that would become the source for steel sky-scrapers and other edifices of U.S. techno-modernity.[17]

The Kelly system later found great commercial application in the fast assembly of firearms, sewing machines, and reaper industries in the 1880s, resulting in substantial increases in industrial productivity and propelling scientific management systems like Fordism. As U.S. historian Howard Zinn writes: "Between the Civil War and 1900, steam and electricity re-placed human muscle, iron replaced wood, and steel replaced iron quickly through the Bessemer [and Kelly] process. Machines drove steel tools and steam engines, oil-lubricated machines and the telephone, and sewing ma-chines, the typewriter and adding machine speeded up work."[18] Steel mills relied on machine jigs for guiding fixtures into proper holding and gauge blocks to check the fit of parts, and the replaceable parts method contrib-uted to the rise of the aircraft, automobile, and electric power industries.[19] Technological revolutions brought by the Chinese concretized novel modes of specialization. This innovation ran up the modern assembly line, a U.S. style of manufacturing allowing North America to quickly surpass England as the world's industrial hub. Despite the major contributions of Chinese engineers to Kelly, they lived in the shadows of a U.S. inventor and the my-thology and genius of the "lone" human scientist.

The human is defined as having the attributes of man as "opposed to animals, divine beings, or machines."[20] The sudden appearance of large numbers of Chinese immigrant labor, huddled in crowded ships and work huts like animals, signaled and hastened the death spiral of the human, as it was customarily believed the Chinese were held in slave-like conditions against their volition or worked to death in conditions that were simply inhuman. Literary scholar Lisa Lowe discusses the centrality of the coolie in the production of "modern humanism" and a "racialized division of labor," where unfree labor economically benefited those who espoused hu-manist precepts of free personhood.[21] She finds that "the social inequalities of our time are a legacy of this definition of the 'human' and the discourses that have placed particular subjects and geographies at a distance from 'the human.'"[22] In the Romantic period, stretching from the 1800 to the 1850s, humanism came to define autonomy in terms of economic freedom through labor and market exchange and through bourgeois notions of family and respectability—moral values consolidated in the post–Civil War period and dwelt upon as conditions for national economic renewal.

An expanding U.S. humanism overlapped with new forms of wage slavery brewing under advanced racial capitalism. The postwar afterlives of chattel slavery (reconfigured as forced penal labor) and actualities of indentured servitude (revamped into contract work) hinged upon this new sense that nonwhites were not fully human and thus subject to annihilation, displacement, or captivity. Here, the labor machine myth served as a corollary to the "race question" in shaping the United States of America into a "conglomeration of racial imaginings."[23] African American writers and activists, for their part, never outright called Asians machines, even if they made casual references to the "patient, drudging, machine-like industry of China" and how the country had become "dead weight" due to stolid overpopulation over the centuries.[24] They still regarded the Chinese as human.

It is at this juncture that Asian immigration and the coolie machine's continued presence threw into crisis the white Progressives' push for more freedom and rights for the domestic population. Fears over the replacement of Anglo-Americans by yellow machines revolved around the Chinese population in the U.S. West, where most Chinese were concentrated. In the postbellum American South, the coolie posited an opportunity for "technological" advancement for a devastated postwar region that lacked industrialization due to decades of dependency on slave labor and plantation economies. As historian Matthew Guterl notes, insofar as the South lacked "the modern *ingenio*, it could at least import human 'technologies' who worked liked slaves, only cheaper and more efficiently."[25] In New Orleans, coolies imported from China and California worked as "regular as an automaton," whose superior "machinelike" workmanship was best paired with the "tropic brute strength of the bestial African slave."[26] Yet Guterl finds that turning the fantasy of the coolie automaton into a reality was a lost cause, since the incredible "mix of man and machine" sought by, for example, U.S. sugar companies could not be well placed in a devastated region lacking modern capitalist infrastructure.[27]

The Chinese labor machine myth had been deployed to displace Alaskan Natives and Native Hawaiians. In Alaska, it was noted by the state's governor, Ted Hinckley, that salmon cannery operators preferred "China automatons" over the Indigenous Tlingit people, who were found too leisurely and lacking in the white man's skills.[28] In short, the Chinese were convenient proxies for the white laborer. In 1881, U.S. secretary of state James Blaine wrote to the minister of the Kingdom of Hawaii, saying there was always a need for a "purely American form of colonization" since white settlers were "not like the coolies, practically enslaved, not as human machines, but as thinking, intelligent, working factors in the advancement of the material interest of the islands."[29] Questions arose concerning the heavy cost of importing this convenient form of mechanical labor. Soon, the United States moved closer to completely excluding and banning those machines from its shores.

Beasts of Burden or Tools of Convenience?

This section considers the arguments for Chinese exclusion and how the angles of vision or political philosophy that animated them relate to the labor machine myth. Despite regional differences in attitudes toward Chinese immigration, they proved such a threat in California that the legislature passed a law in 1858 making it illegal for any person "of the Chinese or Mongolian races" to enter the state. Justification for a nationwide ban was advanced in the 1878 state report by the Special Committee on Chinese Immigration. It directed this message to the U.S. president: "They can be hired in masses; they can be managed and controlled like unthinking slaves. But our laborer has an individual life, cannot be controlled as a slave by brutal masters, and this individuality has been required of him by the genius of our institutions."[30] The statement conveyed a sentiment that was just as present in public debates about individuality, rights, morality, control, genius, citizenship, life, and mastery.

Not all Americans were unreceptive toward Chinese workers and immigrants. For the celebrated satirist Mark Twain, the Chinese were a harmless, decent race subject to the cruelest insults and injuries commonly meted out to dogs. He argued that the gentle Chinese were never found slacking, and they could teach indolent Americans a thing or two about productivity. Such well-disposed people did not complain about work, yet they could be stoned to death by disorderly racist "scum." In his 1872 semiautobiographic travel book *Roughing It*, Twain described the Chinese as a great convenience to all, even to the worst class of white men, since "they are quiet, peaceable, tractable. . . . They are as industrious as the day is long."[31] While visiting Chinatown, he recounts being personally impressed with the genius of a Chinese bookkeeper that "figured his accounts on a machine . . . with incredible rapidity . . . as fast as a musical professor's fingers travel over the keys of a piano."[32] Regardless of the writer's earnest sincerity and affinity for the Chinese, we find some of the earliest models or stereotype of Asians as accountants and piano prodigies. Despite their incredible labor value, and the protestations by famous men like Twain, the general feeling toward the Chinese as public menaces to society impelled the U.S. government to pass the 1882 Chinese Exclusion Act—the first and only immigration law targeting one ethnic group or nationality.

Figure 1.1 "What Shall We Do with Our Boys?" cartoon from *The Wasp*, March 3, 1882 (Sourced from Oakland Museum of California/Wikipedia)

The same year the U.S. Congress passed the Chinese Exclusion Act, banning all low-wage Chinese labor migrants, a political cartoon was published in *The Wasp* entitled *What Shall We Do with Our Boys?* The cartoon (see fig. 1.1) depicts a gargantuan Chinese man armed with a dozen arms making shoes, washing clothes, laying bricks, and collecting and counting money to be placed in a rickshaw to export "For China." The "boys" mentioned in the cartoon refer to the indigent men looking for jobs as hired hands after an economic recession began that same year. Along with the reference to the power of foreign companies, a plank labeled "Chinese trade monopolies," the visual reference to Chinese freneticism with "windmill-like hands" boasts the vigorous thrust of labor quantity (multiple arms) and promptness that reflects the modern lithography by which this mass image was produced.[33] It explains away Chinese men as an exploited labor caste comprising unique individuals, promoting instead a singular mythic factotum taking over a range of practices and professions once dominated by working-class whites. This portrait of the multiarmed coolie works in tandem with other animalist cartoons of the time caricaturing Chinese immigrants as a giant octopus with tentacles invading the West.[34] These visual forms relay bitter feelings of threat by Americans piqued by "the shaking of their paradigm of racial superiority, a worldview that saw Anglo-Saxons as the world's most skilled people."[35]

The cartoon underscores the coolie's mythic ability to make a serious dent or "chink" in the armor of white supremacy.[36] While depicting an existential struggle over labor and life purpose, the cartoon also reflects the mechanical work of new print technologies at the time in newspaper publishing, accelerated by the lithographic rotary printing press. These mass-produced ink prints led to the dispersion of racist images that imbued "authenticity" to the optic of Chinese as mechanical curios.[37] Standardization in the imagery of the Chinese churned out a media product of mythic proportions, while also turning the Chinese into scapegoats for loss of economic power by the white working class. The *Wasp* cartoon shows immobilized white humans standing outside, watching as their work is being taken away by greedy, tricky laboring Asiatic machines. The pictoralization adds a mechanical dimension to the racial doctrine of the time, social Darwinism (a misapplication of Charles Darwin's evolutionary theory), which holds that certain races are less developed, as they are closer to animals and nature.

In its verisimilitude with economic-material processes, the Chinese labor machine signals the takeover of industrial automation, where a moving mechanical device imitates a human being and performs a function according to a set of coded instructions or rules.[38] It points to a factory-style system of manufacturing that came to replace the cottage style of textile handiwork and its singular, freestanding human-operated inventions, like the loom. Coolies, with their mechanically optimized bodies, frighteningly corroborated the process by which the "discrete machine was being replaced . . . by a new kind of socio-technological system."[39] Their alien presence announced what would happen if the capitalist machine ever took over civil society, and the Chinese were the model of that new scaling.

In the U.S. context, the registering of the Chinese as not-quite-human labor machines meant they did not *become* nonhuman through dehumanizing industrial practices. They appeared already as such, given the ways Chinese workers sparked a technological sublime "eruption of feeling that briefly overwhelms reason."[40] Ethnic studies historian Ronald Takaki recognized that the Chinese minimalist, no-nonsense way of working jeopardized Protestant forms of labor based on personal thrift, higher learning, and self-cultivation. This Asian labor form buttressed the snapshot of a "yellow proletariat" and "industrial menace."[41] Though the Chinese helped build the Transcontinental Railroad, their precarious position amid a growing corps of aggrieved mostly Irish and Italian American workers asking for better pay and quality of life made them highly unpopular and unwanted. These automatons invited rage against the machine.

The political vitriol levied at the Chinese morphed into moral crusades against them. This overlay can be found in the words of such statesmen as Henry George, a major architect of anti-Chinese ideology, who wrote about these foreigners' "peculiar" adaptation for machine-based production given their biological makeup for manual dexterity and patience. In his essay "The Chinese Question," George acceded that the Chinese were excellent workers, but too many of them would lead to the same stagnation in the country as seen in dynastic Qing China.[42] In response to the warnings of respected public statesmen like George, public distress over the "heathen Chinee" took on acute fears that "bodies—yellow ones—could undermine the ascendancy of machinery and mind . . . [and] retard but also subvert the very genius of the age—American technology."[43] Their physical appearance was rendered such that back then even the strange-looking pointy shoes worn by coolies were described as "huge machines."[44]

The labor machine myth extends "Western imaginations of the universal human" in which China constitutes a "paradigmatic site of the inhuman, the subhuman, and the humanly unthinkable."[45] Whereas economic elites perceived the Chinese as prime industrious workers, their equal characterization as a "race apart" led some business leaders and the American public to see the Chinese as a problem. They posed a problem for the country domestically as an extension of China, which had been an advanced civilization for centuries ahead of Europe. But a long period of economic "stagnation" slowed China's progress and gave whites the impression that Europeans were now the center of the world, which now saw few contributions from the Chinese. At this time, Euro-Americans still did not know much about this place or its people, but the old mythology of a great Chinese civilization full of strange curiosities fell in favor of the new myth of China as a place of enslaved machines laboring for monarchal despots. Unbowed to progress, they refused to concede to the human gifts bestowed by the European Enlightenment, an intellectual movement that, despite its philosophical influences from China, emphasized modern reason, science, and economic progress. Early theories of labor value argued that the term rightly only exists for free men or human subjects contractually selling their abilities in a free market exchange. An alien race from an alien society, the Chinese did not exist in the proper sense as "alienated" labor, since they appeared more as alien labor machines.

Occultist elements could be found in Marxist capital as "dead labor," grinding manual laborers into the toiling undead. Workers are synthesized as animals (beasts of burden) and machines (tools of use) through capitalist modes of production, which Karl Marx said would move toward automation. Factories transformed into "mechanical monsters" with an undead body consisting of giant limbs, moving parts, and numerous organs with workers "a living appendage of the machine."[46] Capitalism worked like a big machine with the human machine working within factories, learning to adapt his movements to the uniformity of automatons. The instrumentalization of labor left out the intelligence of the worker and converted his use value into surplus value as "a live monster that is fruitful and multiplies."[47] While Marx considers industrial machines as dead capital, we can only guess what this means for the surplus (alien) value generated from Asian laborers, who are not valued as human beings in the same way as whites. These monster machines are at once superhuman workers, subhuman races, and nonhuman things.

The German intellectual was often panned by critics for failing to account for nonwhites, those who do not properly occupy the category of "class-conscious" proletariat and the main agent of world history.[48] Whenever Marx did mention Asians, it was problematic, like when he concluded that only the Englishman with his "mighty automaton" worker could create proper capital, at variance with the Chinaman's spinning wheel, a repetitive talent reflective of the "unchangeableness of Asiatic societies."[49] Asians fit awkwardly within Marx's humanist focus on class struggle and man's "species-being." He wrote of Oriental despotism and the necessity of the British colonizing India to waken and foment mental reform in people who worshipped nature and animals, bearing no sense of destiny.[50] Believing that "Hindoos" held "great industrial energy" and remarkable "mathematical" talent, Marx would assume a separation between Asia roboticism and European humanism.[51] Asiatic modes of production and labor machines never quite registered properly into this human calculus, which calls for all the world's proletariat to work together to undo the shackles of capitalism. For Marx and other Western thinkers, Asians could only join the capitalist world system as an ideal type, the colonized automaton.[52]

As U.S. capitalist society developed further, the humanoid cog in the bureaucratic machine came to stand in for the social anomie that arose with rational management and maximum efficiency.[53] Despite the "disenchantment of the world" under the steel-hard casing of modernization, as social theorist Max Weber put it, there remained other forms of magical thinking within the industrialized world. Even as economic science sought to dispel feudal beliefs, the coolie automaton laid bare the sacralization and sorcery of Asiatic modes of production. In India and China, Weber finds Asian religious society's rigid subjection of the individual to be at odds with the secular reorganization of Protestant-influenced Euro-American society and an ascetic culture where humans are "subsumed under the total process of the machinery itself."[54] The modern culture of machine capitalism showed up best in the United States, where as "aliens ineligible for citizenship," Chinese contract workers not only lacked basic social citizenship and labor rights but also bore the brunt of indignities as *automatons ineligible for personhood.*[55]

During a high point of Jim Crow racism, the radiating fear of the Chinese labor machine came to define who is a person within a narrow sphere of citizenship. In 1890, Judge Lorenzo Sawyer of the U.S. Ninth Circuit Court voiced his dissent against the Supreme Court case *Chew Heong v. United States* (1884), which denied reentry to Chinese immigrants who were overseas while the Chinese Exclusion Act came into effect. Judge Sawyer compared the Chinese to Black people:

> The Chinese are vastly superior to the negro, but they are a race entirely different from ours and never can assimilate and I don't think it desirable that they should, and for that reason I don't think it desirable that they should come here. . . . *We are much further advanced in many of our industries than we should be, had it not been for the Chinese; but the cheap labor is no feature that concerns me at all. The steam engine is nothing but cheap labor and you might as well cry out against that on that account as against the Chinese.*[56]

Sawyer shared gratitude for the Chinese in making the United States more industrious, but he fumed against them as cheap machines that cannot be racially digested. Such a comparison yields some insight into the enslaved African person as an early alternative prototype of the Asian labor machine myth, one originating out of the colonial optics toward Black people as savages in a natural state "dominated by their bodies rather than their minds, by their sensations rather than their reflections."[57] In the United States, as in other parts of the Americas, the Black bondservant was thought of as a "mere machine" connected to animal livestock and other plantation devices like the cotton gin.[58]

The pseudoscientific construction of Black people as "pure bodies"—not able to "feel" emotional pain, psychic trauma, or mental abuse—validated their commodification as the property of white masters.[59] The white slave fantasy of Black people as *brutish machines* set the pretext for the labor machine myth applied to the Chinese, though both groups experienced the effects of racial power differently. Writings from anti-Asian nationalist groups often compared the Chinese to Black people in terms of their economic usefulness and low racial status but frequently made mention that the United States did not need such a semicivilized alien race to complicate domestic racial matters. The "Chinese question" gained poignancy after the change in the legal status of enslaved African people from machinelike property to nominally "free" citizen-subjects, despite a lack of real rights.[60]

Judge Sawyer's contention that coolies are useful machines of industry, not unlike steam engines, might appear as a compliment, as the leading innovative technology of the time was the steam engine, but Sawyer's comments are nothing short of negative. He made use of the coolie-machine analogy, propagating gendered myths of Chinese men as sexually inept wimps (who can be also hyperfertile) and Chinese women as mere sexual props or rejuvenating aids to men. As exemplars of desexualization/hypersexualization, the Chinese are nothing more than mechanized breeds unaffected by romance or felicity. Their high fecundity and capacity for biological reproduction, in all its animal crudeness, make them not quite the same as a steam engine, which cannot reproduce itself.[61] And yet they are quite barren as engines.

Despite worries over Chinese mass reproduction in the United States, most Chinese women had been effectively prohibited from immigrating under the 1875 Page Act on the false premise that they were all to be sold as potential sex slaves. In the gender construction of the Chinese woman as whore and the effete Chinaman as not "man enough," we find the former weighed down more by the corporal logics of sex. This is because prostitution or any female-associated service is not considered labor, which stands as an exclusively male domain. Chinese women were pure sex machines. Perceptions of Chinese men as *the* labor machines stood on this paradox: they could be either asexual (eunuch-like domestics) and hypersexual (opium-seducing rapists). In any case, they were not "real" men having normal conjugal relations. What Sawyer dreads most is the change in status of Chinese from "perpetual sojourners" and transient migrants to permanent settlers:

> So far as the mere labor is concerned it is a great advantage to the Country. What we complain of, what the public complain [*sic*] of is really a virtue, their industry their economy their frugality and perseverance. *If they would never bring their women here and never multiply and we would never have more than we can make useful, their presence would always be an advantage to the State.* It enables thousands to employ labor who would otherwise have to do their own work. It lifts a very large class to a position superior to what they would otherwise be able to attain, and so long as the Chinese don't come here to stay, their labor is highly beneficial to the whole community.
>
> They will begin to multiply here and that is where the danger lies in my opinion. When the Chinaman comes here and don't [*sic*] bring his wife here, sooner or later he dies like a worn-out steam engine; he is simply a machine, and don't [*sic*] leave two or three or half dozen children to fill his place.[62]

The lone specter of the permanently settled Chinaman, forced to work without sexual gratification or family (and dying out like a steam engine), dovetailed with the scary thought of the Chinaman mass producing children who would become cheap laborers like him. Spurious arguments for Chinese exclusion located the Chinese as gender-ambiguous robotic subjects that lacked a solid sexual profile. The portrayal of "sameness" for the Chinese follows the science of eugenics at the time, claiming that the downfall of the white race came from "better breeding" and little intermixing with Asian bodies. By that logic, the Chinese's lack of moral decency would lead to a type of profligate biological reproduction, one that does not advance humanity but takes it to a decrepit level.[63] What kept white Americans fully human was the organic nature of their families—something beyond the reach of Chinese with their frail opium smokers, polygamous families, bee-like large clans, rampant prostitution, and femaleless "bachelor societies."[64]

Yet Chinese as laboring machines were deemed too culturally inassimilable to be succinctly absorbed by U.S. racial capitalism. In an 1881 congressional debate, California's Senator John Miller stipulated a twenty-year ban on Chinese immigration to the United States. He proclaimed that "forty centuries of Chinese life" made them "machine-like . . . of obtuse nerve, but little affected by heat or cold, wiry, sinewy, with muscles of iron; they are automatic engines of flesh and blood . . . patient, stolid, unemotional, and persistent, with such a marvelous frame . . . of obtuse nerve . . . [that] herd together like beasts."[65] In 1877, a few years earlier, U.S. congressman Edwin Ruthven Meade echoed this peroration:

> The Chinaman comes here as a laborer. He personifies the character in his absolutely menial aspect—what the operation of fifty centuries of paganism, poverty, and oppression have made him—mere animal machine, performing the duties in his accepted sphere, punctually and patiently, but utterly incapable of any improvement. . . . The qualities of coolie labor mentioned, and the fact that it can be secured in any desired amount, and discharged without controversy, renders it especially attractive to capitalists and contractors. African slave labor presented to some extent the same features, but in a marked degree coolie labor is cheaper, and therefore competitive with white labor.[66]

Such convincing arguments led to the 1882 Chinese Exclusion Act to prevail as the law of the land, soon after the granting of Black American citizenship. People of color, as labor machines, were perceived as built for serfdom in the familiar racist language. During debates on whether to allow free Black migration (and access for monopolies) to California, one opponent rebuffed the proposal: "The capitalists will fill the land with these living laboring machines, with all their attendant evils."[67] In the period from the 1870s to the 1900s, the United States experienced rapid industrialization and attendant problems of economic inequality. This widening gap led to the question of how "lowly" and "depraved" labor machines existed in relation to a growing white pro-labor movement.

Free White Human Labor versus Unfree Asian Machine Labor

While the mechanical Chinaman promised to steamroll industrial progress by sheer dint of his mechanized cheap labor, there was still the hope that if American labor could not beat or drive out these foreigners, then American technology could do the job. In the same year as the *Wasp* cartoon displayed the image of the multiarmed coolie, there appeared another image that gave hope to Americans aching to find ways to stand up against Chinese incursion. A trade union card for the Missouri Steam Washer depicts a steam washer machine chasing away the coolie back to China for stealing from American companies (see fig. 1.2). This anthropomorphism of technology does not necessarily suggest that all Americans are now empty-headed machines. Rather, it signals the power of Western technology to protect U.S. interests, even if it is the Chinaman that looks more human in form. Recycling the terms of anti-Chinese vigilante violence by white mobs, the cartoon depicts a coolie worker clutching his washing board, fleeing from a machine with the nativist refrain "The Chinese Must Go" inked under it. Another advertising trade card with the same motto drew a clothes wringer grinding up a Chinaman, inferring the destruction of unmanly coolie machines by man-made machines or the replacement of human automatons by man-made automation.[68]

Gender historian Rosanne Currarino notes discourses about white labor in the late nineteenth century began to stray from working conditions and wages toward consumption and how much a man can provide for his family. She notes the Chinese alien's presence ran afoul of white domesticity by introducing a form of nonconsuming output labor that did not buy or really produce anything. The Chinese simply toiled, contributing nothing to the market or the bourgeois family, because they were viewed as "tireless (and sexless) drones."[69] They did not enjoy work for what it can give in terms of creating prosperity and a higher standard of living, though they had given so much to industry since, according to Currarino, "no European immigrant group filled this role of a machine."[70]

James Whitney, an American lawyer, who inveighed against Chinese immigrants, surmised that the average Chinese did not need to purchase machinery because he worked "as an automaton . . . endowed with consciousness."[71] Whitney gauged the mindless work habits of a Chinaman making

Figure 1.2 "The Chinese Must Go!" trade card from Missouri Steam Washer Company of St. Louis, Missouri, 1883 (Sourced from www.worthpoint.com)

cigars: "Tawny fingers moved as if directed by the regular stroke of steam, and with an accuracy that no mechanism could have surpassed."[72] The Chinese lived in a manner not natural to man, always working, never pausing, and remaining indifferent to onlookers—a creature of habit bearing a dull comportment with an "animalized visage peculiar to his race" and manpower honed through forty centuries of labor.[73] Whitman believed Black people were more human than the Chinese, even if both were close in nature to animals.

Ho Yow, the Chinese imperial consul general to the United States, felt a need to respond. Particularly attuned to overblown fearmongering, he issued an acerbic public statement to disabuse people of any illusions about the Chinese. In it, he reposed the fears of the labor unionist and out-of-work white laborer with the plenty and products obtained from letting imported machines do the dirty work. It is included at length here:

Suppose that the Orient, instead of being full of human laborers, should be full of inorganic laborers, to wit, machines. And suppose these machines should be brought here and set up, and that they should be so finely devised that they would entirely abolish and do away with human labor, and that henceforth there would be work for no one.

Press a button or turn a knob, and all of material service or commodities the human heart desires would be forthcoming in overwhelming abundance . . . *inexorable Asiatic machines*, turning out produce so cheaply and of such exquisite finish that no hand could compete with it! . . . Released from the drudgery of menial toil, your laborer would aspire to higher things? Learning, art, science, the aspirations of the soul and the pleasures of the mind. He would rise above drudgery, cease to be a slave, and become a fully rounded and noble man.[74]

Yow presses the paradox of Americans wanting an industrialized life of abundant luxury and conspicuous consumption, but only through the soul-crushing drudgery of so-called Asiatic machines toward which these lazy Americans felt revulsion. With Chinese taking up the bulk of arduous wage labor, he foresees the end of hardship for the average U.S. worker, elevating him beyond concern for basic material needs to higher aspirations, thus becoming more human and less animal/machine.

All told, the diplomat is quick to point out that the *real* machines doing harm are not these imaginary Chinese labor machines but those factory-made machines produced by Westerners. Yow quips, "This imaginary machine is not a mere figment of my thought. . . . You say the Chinaman labors cheaply; he does not labor as cheaply as a machine. . . . His opponents in combating his coming overlook the prime consideration, that he is a laborer, that he is a producer, a creator of wealth in the fullness of which they share."[75] Yow's conclusion redeems Chinese workers as fellow contributors to American wealth and bounty, regular people, not simply machines.

Such an eloquent rebuttal by a Chinese diplomat faced a rejoinder in "Why the Chinese Should Be Excluded," by James Phelan, then mayor of San Francisco, who dismissively responded to Yow:

In an American sense, we cannot regard a laborer, as does Ho Yow, as a human machine. . . . He argues that if the Chinese, on account of their number and the little fuel which they require to keep them going, are in a sense perfect machines, they should be admitted. *But there is a limit even to the capacity of a machine.* It must have a man behind it. That man is a unit in the government of a free country; and we must insist, in a *patriotic* sense, as well as in the best economic sense, that his status as an intelligent human being, endowed by his Creator with inalienable rights, shall be preserved.[76]

Phelan then speaks of the enormous productiveness of labor-saving devices, which are only supplementary to human skill. But the Chinese, knowing nothing but ceaseless and unremitting toil, would remain a part of the mechanism of control and be content as another cog in the machine. Phelan takes the sarcastic language by Yow at a literal level, saying Americans cannot brood over human laborers as insensate automatons. But then he goes on to say that even *if* the Chinese were automatons, those animated machines still need a real man to operate and run them as a reflection of skilled human intelligence.

With Chinese imitating Western man so well through their potent wizardry, Phelan believes there is reason they might someday come to overtake the country. Those (Asian) machines made to service (white) man will slip from the latter's rein to control him instead. Joining a chorus of speakers at a convention in San Francisco in 1901 to discuss the permanent enactment of the Chinese Exclusion Act, Phelan points to the gradual Chinese takeover of factories as machine operators. In short, the little labor machines were taking over the big machine.

Mayor Phelan shares the belief that the Chinese are good workers but not good *citizens*; since they are found to be "laboring incessantly, and subsisting on practically nothing for food and clothes, a contingency to which they have been inured for centuries, they enter the lists against men who have been brought up by our civilization to family life and civic duty."[77] Working under inhuman conditions, the Chinaman in the United States cannot socially assimilate into the American body politic:

> This is not a mere labor question, nor a race question. It is an American question, impacting the perpetuity of our institutions and the standard of our civilization. . . . *As mere laborers, there is little to complain of in them*; but for all purposes of citizenship their usefulness ends with their day's work; and whatever they are paid, they are paid too much, because they make no contribution by service or citizenship or family life to the permanent interests of the country. *The Chinese are to the last degree imitative. They have taken up the skilled work of our white population, and mechanically duplicate it.*[78]

Phelan goes on to describe how Chinese workers are not just makers of cigars, shoes, and clothing and discusses how they have acquired technical skill in a variety of industries, like dentistry, photography, journalism, commercial electricity, and watchmaking. They moreover acquired vocational skills in painting, bricklaying, carpentry, and the culinary arts, excelling to the point of supplanting whites. What is interesting is how Phelan claimed he was *not* making this issue about labor or race but what he called an "American question" regarding the "standard of our civilization." He worried about the economics of Chinese taking up, duplicating, and copying white skills in fields like masonry, and butchery. His observation of them as reprobates implied a lack of aptitude in familial domesticity and social reproduction—two values that must be defended in the new Progressive Era.

Automated Coolies in the Progressive Era

Given the frequent comparisons between Black and Chinese male laborers, it is vital here to briefly pivot from the sexual confusion presented by Chinese men—working without women or like women—to comment on the tropes of Black men as mechanical brutes (with Black women as baby-making machines).[79] Following Benjamin Franklin, who believed slavery reduced men to animal machines, abolitionist Frederick Douglass wrote that slavery degraded the Black man into "a brute—a mere living automaton, that is not permitted in any degree to act for himself."[80]

In the Jim Crow era, the forced conscription of incarcerated Black Americans into chain gangs was justified by the romanticized tall tale of John Henry. In this epic American myth, Henry races against a steam-powered railroad hammer, a competition he wins only to perish tragically in the process. This folk legend showcased the physical endurance and virility of Black maleness as much as it conjured up the new status of the indebted freedman, who could easily be pressed into hard labor in the mold of what feminist writer Alice Walker calls "pieces of machinery . . . machinery that could be mutilated, raped, killed, if the desire arose. Machinery that could be cheated, cheerfully, without a trace of guilt."[81] This American hero myth processes reenslaved Black male bodies as "a complex machine . . . a finely tuned instrument that a manufactured steam drill could not match."[82] The negation of Black humanity operates "through brutal acts of racist violence designed to actualize psychic and embodied alienation."[83]

The 1915 U.S. military invasion of Haiti inspired Black machine myths abroad. Building off the harsh penal rule of the island's dictators, the occupiers concentrated on the nonhuman qualities of Haitian people to deflect attention from their dehumanization under vagabondage. According to one American writer invited to observe American sugar plantations operating there, "The supposed zombies continued dumbly at work. They were plodding like brutes, like automatons."[84] Myths of zombified "walking dead men" and "black magic" eased white mental panic over free Black people by reinscribing the colonial image of subjectable African automatons. The neocolonial exploitation of "undead" labor allowed forms of corvée to exist and endure during a more forward-thinking era.

The turn of the twentieth century saw the ascendancy of the Progressive Era (1890s to 1920s), a period concerned with advancing social welfare through universal suffrage, fair wages, worker protection, better living conditions, and social benefits for all people simply because they were human. The racial impurities of the Asiatic automaton, broadly construed, promised to lead to a regressed American society and humanity. Progressives were avid modernizers, asserting the good of eugenics (i.e., the racial pseudoscience of better breeding) and fully employing the new doctrine of human betterment as it worked in tandem with the scientific management of lowly "undesirable" populations.[85] In the field of education, the strong national push for liberal arts over vocational tracks swayed Pennsylvania superintendents to place "value that comes from the *human element*" and affirm that "here in America the *expression* of individuality stands in strong contrast to the *subjection* of individuality in the Orient."[86] Free thought and action in the West are ideals set against the benumbing organization of Asian work and learning styles, with their "fossilizing influence, producing a human automaton."[87]

Despite the culling of Chinese workers under the Chinese Exclusion Act, Chinese immigrants still faced accusations of taking away good factory jobs from U.S. nationals.[88] This claim of labor machines operating manufacturing machines was not accurate. By 1910, most Chinese men in the country were not found in well-paid male-dominant manufacturing jobs but rather "feminine" service work, like restaurant cooking and domestic help, due to labor discrimination.[89] Anglo-American romance writers constructed prose about their edifying impressions of Chinese laundries. Here, they encountered "yellow-visaged pig-tailed automata in blue cotton [who] slaved, mysterious, sinister."[90]

Calling Chinese machinic automata enshrouds the work of the American political machine, a machine based on artifice, fabrication, and conceit. California Democrats like Phelan expressed the racist rhetoric of the national Democratic Party, which relied on the labor machine myth to oppose the Republicans' hypocrisy of promoting U.S. industry while importing coolies to the detriment of American workers. One Democrat, an elected official of New York, cried out in a similar tone to Phelan: "I see them advocating protection and at the same time importing labor machines free of duty. . . . Liberty and equal rights are liberty and equal rights of men, not slaves, not of coolies. The freedom of an eating, drinking, opium smoking, working automaton is not the freedom which our citizens enjoy. The rights of a well-worked machine are not their rights."[91] This usage of "the machine" to describe both a coolie and a political party would appear within California's legislature in 1909 over a contested bill to regulate rates for railroads (ironically, the national transportation system that Chinese helped construct in the country but for which they did not receive much credit). A partisan war broke out between the congressional "machine" held by corporate interests and "anti-machine" Progressive forces that wanted public ownership of public utilities. In the heated fight, a reform-minded reporter said it was best for public officials never to become a "machine coolie" or slave to government.[92] The coolie machine figure always conjured despotism within the demos, the base thing standing in the way of progress.

Despite the explosion of technology during the twentieth century, the U.S. industrial system still relied heavily on cheap foreign labor, which caused great consternation among xenophobes. Chester H. Rowell, a prominent newspaper editor and progressive, employed the terminology of the labor machine to oppose the importation of Asian migrant workers. He raised concerns about animalistic coolies, when the federal government considered lifting the Chinese Exclusion Act to complete major engineering projects abroad, such as the Panama Canal. In an official publication for the United Garment Workers of America, he stretches the truth: "If the ideal laborer . . . is merely a worker who obeys and works like a machine, then let us get trained baboons and keep them in cages and feed them on grass. Next to the baboon is the Chinese coolie. You can get more food out of the land by making California a province of China. If you want only money and food, then import Chinese."[93]

This animal-machine characteristic played a most crucial role in discussions about the importation of Chinese immigrants in colonies of the white man's world. Medical journals published editorials about the Chinese threat to Black and white populations in South Africa, the United States, and Europe. The *Cincinnati Lancet-Clinic* published a 1903 correspondence from Paris about the Chinese producing children "like rabbits" since that is "their principal industry," insofar as they have "animated motors; they use their arms and feet to till the soil, dig up minerals and to transport their merchandise. These human machines need no coal. . . . The Chinese working machine is run on rice, and they are sustained thermo-dynamically by virtue of their industry."[94]

In a 1909 *Fresno Republican* essay entitled "Chinese and Japanese Immigrants: A Comparison," Rowell made his case against the Japanese who were coming to replace the Chinese, elevating the latter above the former as the "ideal industrial machine" highly valuable to U.S. business owners, even if they were also a moral hazard to American civilization.[95] He elaborated: "The Chinese coolie is the *ideal industrial machine, the perfect human ox.* He will transform less food into more work, with less administrative friction, than any other creature. They are patient, docile, industrious, and above all 'honest' in the business sense that they keep their contracts. Also, they cost nothing but money. Any other sort of labor costs human effort and worry, in addition to the money. *But Chinese labor can be bought like any other commodity, at so much a dozen or a hundred.*"[96]

Beyond the issue of manual workers, Rowell zeroed in on the Chinese economical method for contracting or hiring labor, devoid as it was of human qualities: "The Chinese contractor delivers the agreed number of men, at the agreed time and place, for the agreed price, and if anyone should drop out he finds another in his place. The men board and lodge themselves, and when the work is done, they disappear from the employer's den until again needed. . . . *This elimination of the human element* reduces the labor problem to something the employer can understand. The Chinese *labor-machine*, from his standpoint, is perfect."[97] As a primitive beast of burden (animal) and tool of production (machine), the labor machine is one defined by the reproducibility of its nonindividualized body and collective groupthink. Though Rowell finds the Chinese an honest people compared to the duplicitous Japanese, he believes there should be a buffer against the rising tide of Asiatics if the white race is to survive.[98]

Despite the winnowing of Japanese migration to the U.S. under the 1907 Gentlemen's Agreement between Japan and the United States, preoccupation with Asian labor machines failed to dissipate as migrant workers from India, the Philippines, and Korea came, mounting greater turmoil over other Asian corporalities. The fear that many would come and stay permanently remained ever present regarding migrant workers from the American colony of the Philippines, who already came with U.S. nationality. Subjected to the maximization of their labor, the Filipino men were described by their employers as having "machine-like bodies" able to harvest crops around the clock.[99] But their racial designation as less civilized brown "Malays" rather than yellow "Mongoloids" led to their debasement as clever "brown monkeys" who could work the machine too or at least ape the Americans. The American Federation of Labor (AFL) hoped companies would replace the Chinese with Filipino blacksmiths and ironworkers in making car parts, since they believed the latter worked just as hard but for cheaper, even if the Chinese were admittedly more skillful.[100] The differentiation between various Asian nationalities circled around the endless ways that they can be hailed as machine workers and as another "species" in the animal kingdom.[101] Despite the influx of Filipino workers, Chinese still held status as *the* most threatening labor machines.

Trade unions leaders seized upon the argot of Progressivism to advocate for the protection of white labor as something of utmost importance. Billed as the world's first industrial statesman, the head of the AFL, Samuel Gompers, launched a broadside against the Chinese, touting how the influx of so many coolies impinged upon American workers' rights to living wages and opportunities for betterment, derailing them from a higher position. He called his labor organization a "living, sentient thing" spreading freedom, as the American labor movement "cannot be handled or computed as material quantities" in the way coolie labor can.[102] Gompers and his allies effectively mobilized anti-Asian racism to effect an immigration ban on *all* Asian

workers, a law patterned after Chinese exclusion. Observing the rising political influence of Chinese and Japanese union workers in Hawaii and California, Gompers envisioned a type of future industrial war that would dic-
tate which "type of human species" would dominate the world.[103] While
Gompers conceded Asian laborers aided in expanding global trade for
American goods, he believed Asians and whites could not coexist because
the former was another species of man.

In Gomper's eyes, the Chinaman was a "cheap man," a mere simulation
of real people. By associating with cheap Chinamen, white lives were demeaned to the point of ceasing to be recognizably human.[104] Speaking before Congress in 1902, when the Chinese Exclusion Act was up for renewal,
the labor leader testified to the breathtaking ability of "John Chinaman" to
endure toxic miasmatic fumes of sewers and factories that would normally
kill people.[105] Like many Progressive thinkers at this time, Gompers was care-
ful not to appear overtly racist, although he harbored a trenchant dislike of
Asians. Gompers advocated for a better quality of life, a philosophy operating under the assumption that the Chinese were too mechanically driven by
money (though he avoided using the term automaton) to ever live a life of
love, joy, and passion.[106] To that end, Gompers authored the pamphlet "Meat
versus Rice," which sought to measure the survival of American manhood
against Asiatic coolieism.[107] This perception of machines powered by rice
was affirmed by editors of *Harpers Weekly* who called the Chinese pagan
"human machines" that worked every day of the week, even on the Sabbath,
surviving on nothing but rice and vegetables.[108]

Many of the Progressive antimonopoly lobbying efforts in the United
States took on a decidedly racist tinge. Animus toward Chinese labor machines exacerbated mounting concerns with the loss of animal husbandry
and traditional farming, arousing antagonism toward immigrants and mass
industrialization. Throughout the nineteenth century, the United States
speedily transformed from an agricultural society into an urbanizing nation defined by monopoly capitalism. Under a plutocracy, vast social inequalities between rich and poor threatened to tear the country apart. A
strident labor movement grew out of landless workers and rising numbers
of proletariat laborers in the states. Spurning Chinese labor meant checking
the power of greedy corporations to exploit Chinese labor.[109]

The labor movement's push against all Asian immigration found its
greatest success in the 1917 and 1924 Immigration Acts barring entry to the
United States. With exception of the Philippines, a colony of the United
States, the federal laws made verboten low-wage laborers and migrants from
Asia. The humans, it appeared, found a momentary victory or reprieve against
labor machines. With a reduction in Asian immigration, American artists
would begin to mythologize the fading presence of the Chinese automaton.

Fictional storytellers at the time romanticized coolies, who toiled to build levees to protect crops along California's San Joaquin River—even while calling them machines. In one short story "An Episode of the Float Lands," which was published in 1907, a young American girl comes upon a riverbank where "groups of imperturbable Chinamen labored unceasingly . . . every yellow-faced automaton doing his appointed part with the established rhythm of Chinese concerted movement."[110] She is inquisitive about the men but maintains a safe distance away. The coming-of-age story ends with the river's high-tide water sweeping away the painstaking work of the men and their bodies to the horror of the narrator, who comments negatively on the vigilant white male overseers that patrol the "coolies." The Chinese coolie labor machine myth had become part of the American pastoral and Western frontier myth. Yellow automatons were assimilated into moral tales of human welfare but as sad wretches.

By the turn of the twentieth century, labor machine myths persisted even as coolieism as an economic practice began to die out and scientific management styles came into the picture. No less a figure than Henry Ford believed coolie machines were impediments to this technological revolution. At this moment, Ford's vertically integrated assembly-line method of automated car production paved the way for a more refined system of U.S. manufacturing, one without the need for time-consuming handmade products or skilled craftsmanship. It was hoped that a more modern, enlightened citizenry would prevail from all this, but this egalitarian vision of a smooth-running American consumer society was overshadowed by the labor machine myth. In his 1926 essay, *Today and Tomorrow*, Ford writes that improved training affords the worker purchasing power "so that he may earn more and have more and live more comfortably. The Chinese coolie working through long hours for a few cents a day is not happier than the American workman with his own home and automobile. This one is a slave, the other is a free man."[111] Fordism as a social engineering project, which paid workers a living wage so they could buy modern commodities like cars, excluded the nonconsumptive Chinese, who carried the specter of indentured slavery into an era of industrial science. For the innovator, the poorest white would never be as poor as the Chinese, who did not know how to make or buy anything of real value.

In the Fordist era, Chinese mechanized bodies personified technology run amok. In a 1901 speech presented as an annual address at the American Academy of Political and Social Science, the sociologist Andrew Ross spoke of the ominous and "extraordinary power of accommodation" of "the Mongolians," blaming centuries of Chinese idolatry, poverty, and oppressive tradition for making Chinese people move like machines blessed with technical proficiency but no mental improvement.[112] Ross believed human rationality could not be accessed by the Chinese as they were ignorant of laws and science and technology. Though he found the Chinese people formidable leaders of trade and commerce, Ross cast moral aspersions on the Chinese. To him, they appeared to lack both self-control and an inability to forsake "cravings" or "temptations" in favor of higher reason. With a machinic body and animalistic nature, the Chinaman was driven by the "sensori-motor" rather the "ideo-motor" way of thinking.[113] In imitating Westerners, the Chinese, as a lower stage of humanity, bore the potential to usurp the mighty West, and Ross predicted an industrial world war where the Chinese might prevail. Despite their feeble brains, they would grow stronger, aided by the machines and scientific inventions taken from whites: "There is no reason why that *mediocre and intellectually sterile race* may not yet defeat us industrially by the aid of machines and processes conceived in the fertile brains of our Edisons and Marconis . . . each race must, in the long run, produce from its own loins; but in the industrial Armageddon to come it may be that the laurels will be won by a mediocre type of humanity, *equipped with the science and the appliances of the more brilliant and brain-fertile peoples.*"[114]

For Ross, the great discoveries of great white men are exploited and appropriated by mediocre types of humanity who are building their own mini-empire. The Chinese fare best in this regard, he avers, given their facility in appropriating Western technology and growing unchecked in number with lower living standards. The Malthusian fear of populations multiplying beyond sustainable means and stampeding any means of "acceptable living" refracts the labor machine, mass producing and just automating its form of cheap degrading life. As Ross goes on to write, a true scientific revolution must begin in China if Westerners can turn the Chinese into "assimilable elements" for the West to use and, ergo, prevail. Otherwise, this situation would result in the silent replacement of Anglos by Asiatics, resulting in "race suicide." Here, Ross appropriates the "survival-of-the-fittest" evolutionary language of natural selection for animals and applies it to human competition:

> The silent replacement of Americans by Asiatics go on unopposed until the latter monopolize all industrial occupations, and the Americans shrink to a superior caste able perhaps by virtue of its genius, its organization, and its vantage of position to retain for a while its hold on government, education, finance, and the direction of industry, but hopelessly beaten and displaced as a race. In other words, the American farm hand, mechanic, and operative might wither away before the heavy influx of a prolific race from the Orient. . . . For a case like this I can find no words so apt as "race suicide."[115]

With deepening loss of jobs for the American farmworker and mechanical operator, Ross intones the power of "prolific" Orientals, raising alarm for a white race that can still lose out to the former, despite being an inherently superior and smarter race. Despite his cynicism, Ross concludes his essay by valorizing the American capacity for overcoming natural adversity, where the individualizing "struggle with the wilderness has developed in us what it would of body, brain, and character" so much so that Americans are "destined to play a brilliant and leading role on the stage of history."[116] This preeminent role turned real with World War II, a watershed moment in which the United States found itself allied with China against the Axis powers and arrayed against an up-and-coming Asian superpower able to adopt Western technology and use it even more effectively against the West: Japan.

Conclusion

Like the Chinese, other Asian immigrant groups started to come to North America as workers, such as Punjabi Sikhs from India. These "Hindu coolies" experienced similar linguistic comparisons to Chinese coolies in terms of alien labor, even if they had a different reception as "machines." Asian Indians were not called human machines with the same frequency as seen with the Chinese, due perhaps to their more ambiguous racial character, but they were treated as labor machines nonetheless.[117]

The imperial-capitalist machine's ability to incorporate the Asian automaton is evident in a bluster from the agent general representing the British colonies' interest to the Crown. Alongside importing newly freed Black labor from Virginia in the United States, colonial lawyer E. Buck proposed in the late 1870s bringing Indian "coolies" to New Zealand to level up profit in tobacco farming. Substituting costly labor-saving industrial machines with Black freedmen and Indian coolies, he believed, New Zealand could grow economically prosperous without detriment to the white settler, so long as governments were prudent to understand the necessary temporary value of *all* labor. He believed the commonwealth should not object to importing some coolies simply based on bigotry, since Asians could be civilized and domesticated. Buck writes, "Favorable circumstances will enable the industry to be continued with white labor, mainly, if not exclusively. Nor would I object to the coolie if he became more than a laboring machine. I have no objection to the denizen of any country if he can be civilized, and if he will harmonize himself with the institutions of the country in which he lives."[118] Buck's comments are the early inklings of Progressive gospel, which were rooted in the absorptive totality of white settler colonial thinking.

My attempt to label the Chinese as labor machines in this chapter is not meant to replicate the imitative machine racial branding laid out by men like Buck. The intent is not to mark them out as pure labor and separate them out from other Asians or even African Americans. Instead, I provide a working point of reference for dissecting the overlapping imaginaries of the automaton. In *Farm Worker Futurism*, American studies scholar Curtis Marez documents how Asians, African Americans, and Mexican immigrants were lumped together under the category of "farm worker," which doubled as machine worker.[119] It was nearly impossible to imagine machine workers at this time in a singular way, when racial labor of all kinds was placed within the catalog of human technology. However, I argue that Asians and specifically groups like the Chinese occupy a special place as model machines.

Counterdiscourses to the narrative of labor automatons came from all corners. They emphasized the humanity of Asians and never invoked machine vocabulary to make their point. Believing the Chinese were more egalitarian than Westerners, one white American in a literary op-ed piece claimed that, no matter a man's class or reduction to physical labor, the Chinese properly recognized the democratic potential of "every man the right to the fruit of his labor and intelligence."[120] Ta Chen, a fellow at Columbia University, wrote about the changing social roles of Chinese women, while laboring in the industries that powered the new democratic Chinese republic. The sociologist found that Chinese female workers were willing to strike and organize against business owners. Chen warns that the employer "cannot ruthlessly enslave the employee, for the temperament of the Chinese social composition is strongly antagonistic to capitalist exploitation at the expense of the 'human machine.'"[121] Other intellectuals found that everyday Chinese engaged in protest against their exploitation as machines. In southern China, Hakka women pushed against societal gender norms, foot binding, and marriage, raising a furor over becoming a "human machine of propagation."[122] This challenges the sex machine typology, which can be found in a quote from Orientalist scholar Sir Monier-Williams, commenting on the subjection of women in India, where a "general feeling is that they are the necessary machines for producing children."[123]

A general belief in Asian people as productive labor machines, and Asian women specifically as reproductive labor machines, withered under mounting criticisms—despite their rarity in mainstream presses. In laying out the history of Asians and Asian Americans being called or treated as automatons, I also acknowledge the need for testimonies of microresistance. In her book *The Coolie Speaks*, Lisa Yun works arduously to assemble a "coolie narrative" through a vast trove of documents to speak truth to power.[124] Locating these scattered, interlaced human voices can be a challenge, but Yun uncovers the cloaking device of a globalizing legal regime that justified a "new slavery." It is through this document and other archival forms that we can hear forgotten historical subjects speak.

The technocultural meanings and myths attached to the coolie body paper over these voices in history. As scholar Eric Hayot explains, the "obscene ventriloquism" of the coolie body was the scaffold for peddling mistruths by American missionaries, who described the Chinese as having a "calm endurance," an "absence of nerves," and "staying qualities," with a capacity to endure much pain without complaint.[125] Hayot writes that "the coolie's biologically impossible body was the displaced ground for an awareness of the transformation of the laboring body into a machine. . . . His ability to endure (in work and in life) permitted him without succumbing to exhaustion."[126] In terms of mental capacity, it was believed the coolie "could no more awaken to his own privation or boredom than an animal could to human language."[127] This comparison to animals brings us back to Asians as close to nature, even if they appear superhuman in ability. To the extent that the male coolie was used to pump up the economy of Pax Americana, his sojourn across the colonized world posed a civilizational threat in terms of presenting "the possibility of a new human era marked specifically by its Chinese-ness."[128]

In the U.S. context, the mechanized body of the coolie testified to what literary historian Colleen Lye calls "a biological impossibility and a numerical abstraction" that promised the evanescence of the "robust American body."[129] Tied to low-wage labor, the coolie's physical superpower is a product of popular lore, which offers a road map to studying what Lye calls Asiatic "racial form." Dislodging the Asian body as something real or natural, Lye avers the generative power of speaking about the *form* that race takes on as it "always points to the presence of something not shown."[130] Beyond the speculative qualities of racial form, we discover in racialized work patterns the material expression of the "actual unfreedom of free wage labor" and the "industrial modernity of race."[131] The labor machine offers a way to consider how "the coolie signifies a different kind of monstrous presence."[132]

The labor machine myth therefore denotes the *impossible humanity* of those servile coolies so well adapted to the accelerated rhythms of industrial capitalism, an adaptation born out of centuries of abasement to emperors and one that cannot be tempered by simply abolishing coolieism. The model machine myth, as it is attached to the coolie's body, collapsed—even while it reified—the divide between master and slave, citizen and alien. It muddled the once clear separation between technological means and ends, free will and forced labor, economic scarcity and plenitude. As a modern sign of Asian slavery, the long-gestating myth of the labor machine disrupts the general Progressive push for human development and progress. We find evidence of this in the twenty-first century, when Chinese factory workers are labeled coolies and machines. As a thing of economic utility and cultural threat, the labor machine falls outside the known bounds of *Homo economicus* (economic man) and *Homo faber* (working man).[133] One cannot be those things without first being a *Homo sapien*, a term that means "knowing man" in Latin. But in the minds of racists, animal-like Asiatic machines shall never serve a higher purpose than lowly work.

In time, Chinese labor machines shall become more utility maximizing under European tutelage but will never advance. Animals and machines traditionally represent the servants of man, and human civilization has been built on cultivating natural resources, harnessing technology, and engaging in animal husbandry. But this progressive human civilization develops and stalls due to the introduction of monstrous coolies full of unbridled reproductive activity, who cannot be controlled so easily. Despite the United States' economic need for their labor, the mere presence of the Chinese was menacing enough.

The labor machine myth anatomizes the coolie body as symbolic of the aggregate forms of life (and nonlife), which are set against the whole of white humanity. Hysteria over alien machine societies would inflate into greater paranoia over "war machines" from modernized Asian societies like Japan. As the American Century wore on, Chinese labor machines would continue to agitate for recognition, rights, and respect under the shadow of U.S. empire, while the Japanese would reshape the modern human world in its own bid for empire.

2

War Machines

Assembling the Robotic Japanese Soldier
under the Shadow of Empire

After the Sino-Japanese War of 1895, China lost its vaunted position as Asia's foremost power to the empire of the rising sun. From this high-water mark of battle, Japan loomed large on the horizon as a formidable threat to Euro-American imperial stakes in the Asian continent. The Russo-Japanese War of 1907 cemented the status of Japan as a major player in the world, who would not bow easily to Westerners. By 1941, Japan emerged as an outright threat to the United States, after assailing the Pearl Harbor military base located in the U.S. colony of Hawaii. In response to the dispiriting sight of powerful Western machines capsized and turned to ashes by small foreign attack planes, the image of the Japanese as stealthy enemies and pure agents of war etched itself indelibly in the U.S. technocultural imagination. Americans, ignoring their own faults, looked on in horror at the Japanese, buoyed by the popular myth of an advanced martial ethnorace able to pilfer and improve upon the white man's industrial secrets. Whereas the Chinese coolie engendered the problem of low-grade labor machines displacing the white civilization of the United States, the Japanese problem revolved around them being higher-end mimetic militants, appropriating Western scientific and fighting know-how to dastardly ends.

This chapter attends to perceptions of the Japanese as war machines in the run-up to World War II, tracing this trope during the conflict and beyond. Tracking the public gaze toward what I call the war machine, I show how imperial Japan was presented as a technological "empire of signs," one that betrayed an American penchant for fantasizing about Japan's warrior

culture as it converged with more modern impressions of Japanese as imperial aggressors.[1] This example sheds light on the Japanese state and Japanese
people as they morphed into bona fide machines of war. This war machine
myth is important to study comparatively, especially when Japan's efforts to
colonize other nations clashed with those of the United States', also vying
for power in the strategic Pacific region. This period of pressurized military
buildup fed into the creation of legendary tales about Japanese super soldiers that held an unflinching determination to win and die for their country. This war machine added another entry into the U.S. canon of the model
machine myth, but it likewise shored up Japan's own technocratic imperium
and mythology of greatness.

This myth of the war machine corresponds with the labor machine myth
since the armament of Japan turned on the conversion of everyday workers
into military personnel. This pulsating sense of Japan as a war machine
shielded criticism of the United States' own incubating war machine, which
was much bigger in scale. Even though the United States as a militarized nation had been engaged in bloody wars against "foreign" nations from its very
inception, this country's military power expanded tremendously when its
naval forces became more determined to hold ground against international
threats like Japan.

During World War II, Japanese Americans would be recruited in the U.S.
war effort against Japan, and their status as loyal Americans and as armed
actors would be put to the test. In this chapter, we move from talking about
machine societies or civilizations to consider imperial machines and machine empires. The creation of a modern war machine in both Japan and the
United States tapped into new military capabilities and logistics, which suggest that the Asian automaton lives not exclusively as a floating figure of capitalist labor but as primed myth-symbol for competing technocultural sov-
ereignties.

Summing up the work of the war machine myth goes beyond the simple
imaging of Asians as automatons to direct attention to the imperial assemblage of citizen-subjects for military conquest. The term *assemblage* means
"a collection or gathering of things or people, a machine or object made of
pieces fitted together, some vast assemblage of gears and cogs."[2] This word
aptly describes how the United States perceived Japanese society as one of
harsh social rules and duty-bound assembled subjects, culturally static and
rigid in their fealty to the emperor. If Japan was a modern nation, it was not
yet modern like the United States, with its supposedly free democratic elections and freedom-loving citizens. Like Nazi Germany and fascist Italy, imperial Japan was seen largely at the time as a machine society—a taciturn,
cold society with no human pleasure or freedom. But unlike white-majority
European countries, Japan was a nonwhite Asian society that brought a more

alien racial element to international relations by assembling its own distinct war machine. We discover this in the writings of American author Jack London, whose fictional and nonfictional stories captured the almost "unreal" qualities of the Japanese.

This war machine mythos of Japan remained true in the post–World War II period. Despite being a U.S. ally during the Cold War, Japan presented an *economic* war machine primed for trade wars with the West in the late twentieth century. Before we can reach this point, it is first necessary to understand how in the eyes of Americans the Japanese transitioned from being fierce medieval warriors to becoming ferocious war machines.

From Samurai Warriors to War Machines

The striking imagery of the war machine was not historically unique to Japan, as it applies to all Asian societies that were earlier "Orientalized." This myth of a purely violent foreign Other had been ironed out through centuries of bloody showdowns between Europeans and invading foreign tribes from the east, such as those led by the Mongol conqueror Genghis Khan. Manichean struggles between a humanistic Western civilization and semicivilized Asiatic hordes are propagated in narratives of epic encounters between Greeks and Persians, Romans and Huns, Christian Crusaders and Muslim infidels. More to the point, the atavistic mythos surrounding Asian war machines remains the thick grounds for drawing on a whole repertoire of ideas about cruel emperors and warrior societies.[3] A mental picture of Asian enemies with primal rage merged with animal technology to portray them as machines of death. As historian Geraldine Heng notes in her study of race during the Middle Ages: "With horses that seem half human and human that seem half horse, a Mongol rider's inseparability from his animal, we might say, is the thirteenth century's equivalent of the posthuman as a fighting unit in a war machine."[4] Animality would always mark the Asian war machine, even when he learned more modern fighting techniques from the West.

The West developed its own war machines after the Napoleonic Wars dissolved the boundaries between peaceful societies and "nations at arms." The call to protect the war machine at all costs marshaled all economic and human resources in service to the post-Westphalian nation-state system. The warfare state's torpor downplayed the fact that the goal of war could never be fixed as a stable ideal. Arguing that military states were irreducible to mechanical systems, Prussian general Carl Von Clausewitz in his 1832 classic *On War* denunciated the training of soldiers as "automata, designed to discharge their activity like pieces of clockwork set off by command."[5] Going beyond the general logic of war to make mechanical soldiers, we can ponder further the fictive separation between European autonomy and Asian automaticity as a result of war's technocultural imaginary. John Mill's 1876 publication "The Ottomans in Europe" highlighted such distinctions in his observation of the "eastern question" in relation to Slavic nations that do not distinguish between human autonomy and human automaton: "So far as the claims of Russia are concerned it would be better to use the noun instead of the verb, and call the thing an automaton, 'an image moved by springs' . . . [autonomy as automaton] means that the State should follow the example of the church and the school and become Russianized—a machine of which the Czar kept the key."[6]

Justifying western Europe's intervention in bordering states that do no respect treaties and rights, Mills pontificates on pan-Slavic "secret societies," Turkish colonial militias, and Russian socialists armed with assassins everywhere, spreading savagery and disorder.[7] This Eurocentric sense of "the East," a geography that sometimes includes eastern Europe or western Asia, served up this vast area as slow to reform and beyond the pale of civilization. An Orientalist militarized sense of this East would persist after the Ottoman Empire fell and as other Asian societies accommodated the gunboat diplomacy of the West—a category that came to awkwardly include rising military powers like Japan, with "an army of intelligent automatons, fighting with machines."[8]

One even finds this comparison of Japanese with war machines in contrast to other Asian automatons even in the literature of commercial science. As reported by a 1914 cereal industry handbook: "[Rice] is the chief diet of the wonderful Japanese soldier, whose strength compels the admiration and wonder of the world. It is eaten almost exclusively by the coolies of India and China, those human machines who can carry all day, under a burning sun, a load that would stagger an American or European."[9] Such generalizations sustained the lore of Japanese soldiers' power in contrast to Chinese/Indian coolie workers. Both these machine groups were powered by rice—a food staple that had been invoked before by labor union leaders like Samuel Gompers to mark out Asiatic coolies from "real" American men who mostly consumed a meat-based diet.

Throughout this chapter and the book, I recognize a tension between the study of the United States at a certain moment in time and the world historical perspective that includes other powerful nations like Japan. Discussions of non-U.S. imperial imaginaries are somewhat essential to the construction of American history, so while my analysis is mostly about the U.S. nation-building project, it recognizes that other parts of the world also racialized Asians, even if they did not call or perceive them as machinic automatons to the same extent as the United States. As global historians have shown, the United States set a precedence for laws that banned Asian migration in white settler colonies like Canada, Australia, New Zealand, and South Africa. The United States was not responsible for all anti-Asian racism in the world, but it acted as a main driver for the articulation of the "global color line" and the ontological line separating humanity from everything else.

The French have formed a legacy of Chinoiserie and long-time fascination with Asia but tried to distinguish itself from the more overt Orientalism or racism of the United States.[10] Like Anglo-Americans, the French recognized that the Japanese posed a grave threat to European empire building. Japan's threat was made patently clear in a 1907 publication from the French Asia committee of parliament, which observed colonial activity in the United States two years after the Russo-Japanese War. A speaker from the committee, Louis Aubert, found the domestic economy of the U.S. colony of Hawaii strained by the growing presence of Japanese immigrants. Finding them insufferable compared to the Chinese, the French emissary to the United States considered the Japanese as overly ambitious in their willingness to adopt Western ways, wear cool gadgets like watches, and dress vainly like Americans. But despite their taste for Western manners, these Japanese migrants appeared like robotic subjects waiting eagerly for a command from the Mikado. Unlike the Chinese, who married native women and settled in other countries to develop business skills away from their emperor, the Japanese brought wives from Japan to settle and colonize new lands on behalf of their distant master. While the Chinaman remained lost sojourners from a decaying civilization, Aubert claims, the Japanese man was an imperial loyalist "in relations with his country and does not settle definitively abroad."[11] As a danger to the whole island community of Hawaii, Japanese expats were known to be difficult to lead. They were childish and insolent but succeeded as jacks-of-all-trades able to acquire new professions easily. Working harder (and harsher) than the Chinese, Japanese people's ambition for constant improvement made them not easily controllable by the Portuguese foreman, the French attaché argued, especially when they were unwilling to live in crammed chicken-coop huts like the Chinese. With a state proposal to import Chinese workers again, Aubert made this remark against naysayers: "The Chinese on the contrary is a perfect automaton that goes slowly, surely, without spurts, so it appears as the best antidote against Japanese supersaturation."[12] For some white people, the Japanese were no less than war machines, as they proved their mettle in the economic and military battlefields against the Allied forces.[13]

That machine had long been waiting to prove itself. Starting from the mid-nineteenth century, the Japanese imperial state set forth on establishing an insulated technocracy, sharpening its skills in preparation for wrangling with outside invaders. While China was sluggish in setting up a sophisticated military force, leaving it vulnerable to onslaught by Europeans,

Japan went to great lengths to learn military science and applications procured from the West. It sent advisers and cadets abroad to Europe and the United States to attend foreign military schools. Beginning in 1868, under Emperor Meiji, Japan became the first Asian country to fully industrialize, turning into a "modern" nation in a rather short time.[14] Tokugawa shoguns of the Edo period, ruling for centuries from 1600 to 1868, were implacable in their steely resolve to move from a chaotic feudalist system ruled by warlords to one that reinstated a powerful emperor. Samurai clans submitted to the new central authority. Forcing the hand of parliamentary moderates, rural soldiers found work in the imperial army, consolidating their right-wing militaristic spirit into a national ethos built around modern warcraft and imperialism.

By the time U.S. envoy Commodore Perry arrived in Japan in 1853 with coal-fueled steamships, pushing for trade between the island nation and the United States, it was clear to the Japanese nationalists that they should embark on the road to military preparedness against potential incursion. This nationalizing project included modern docking ports, Western-style gunnery (like muskets with locks), and other artifacts of war.[15] Iron—viewed as the building block of civilization—came into high demand, requiring the importation of arsenals and machines from outside. Steel soon replaced iron in Japan, which was slowly ratcheting up to match the levels used by European nations that fought in World War I.[16] Hermetically sealed Japan became a garrison island state with a hard metallic shell.

Japanese military actions during the Russo-Japanese War would make an impact on the social construction of Japanese in the United States. My view of the hypermasculinity of the Japanese war machine draws on previous concerns with the gendered industrial threat of coolie labor machines. Perceptual threats to white American masculinity and domesticity anchor both stereotypes, despite China's military alliance with the United States against Japan. In the United States, ethnic studies historian Amy Sueyoshi writes how "explorations of ideal manhood among middle-class whites would be projected on both Chinese and Japanese men. On the eve of the twentieth of the century, Chinese symbolized a degraded savage masculinity and Japanese embodied feminine civility. . . . Within five years, however, the representations would switch. . . . The Japanese became oppressive fighting automatons."[17] The rapid switch can be attributed to Japan's military victory against Russia.

In this chapter, the model for the machine is the imperial soldier, and what is being modeled is the war machine. This machine type is modeled upon a totalizing sense that all citizens of a nation are potential human technology for the imperial war economy and that nations themselves are powerful machines. The Ottoman Empire and Russian Empire had presented beguiling forms of Oriental imperialism on the European continent that frazzled West/East boundaries. As international studies scholar Patrick Porter wrote in *Military Orientalism: Eastern War through Western Eyes*, the cultural hybridity of Eurasian societies means they are almost white but not entirely. With a mix of fascination, admiration, and dread—the British and Americans perceived the Japanese differently from the Russians or other Eurasians. Japan was Westernized in a sense, but they were most definitely not white and geographically not close to Europe. Japan was the antipode of the West.

The homogenous picture of the Japanese Other belied the political complexity of Japan. After the rebellion of samurais against central authority had been put down and the emperor restored to power, government propagandists set out to claim ancestral virtues like respect for elders as the reason for samurai submission. Turning the former reverence for samurai feudal life into a new state ideology, the myth of Japanese continuity intensified in 1882 via an imperial proclamation by the newly empowered emperor to all sailors and soldiers demanding their complete obedience.

The antiauthority mentality of samurai warriors transformed, and the Japanese nation by this time appeared to "have wrapped up the future, hemmed it in, taken control of it."[18] Under a British-Japanese alliance in 1902, a counterweight to the Kremlin's threat to Europe, Japanese military professionals studied and trained under English advisers. Perceiving Japanese soldiers as simply the mechanical arms and legs of the imperial state (and the emperor as the head), British military elites took the martial rule of Japan to be the inverse of European liberalism based on "this concept of an almost automaton military, divorced from politics and obedient to the state," an idea congruent with the "theme of a nobler chivalric world annihilated by mechanized butchery."[19] Porter finds the malleable cultures that surround the modern security state still rooted in preconceptions of the past, despite the rapidity of changes to their surroundings due to global trade and diplomatic exchange. Meanwhile, Japan's own imperial mythmaking machine and war machine allowed for a relational discussion of imperialisms. Japan had imperialist designs, which were directed to the United States and other nations.

Japan appeared as a menacing war machine even while enjoined to the side of "good." During World War I, it had been made (by force of treaty) to find common cause with the Entente powers (a coalition led by the British, Russians, and French) against the Germans and Ottomans who were part of the Central powers. As a somewhat minor player, Japan used the war as an opportunity to dominate China and seize areas in Siberia and the South Pacific—colonial appropriations protested by Britain and the United States. The Japanese were hungry for glory like their European counterparts and, in time, would move to parry against its former allies in the next great world war.

After World War I, it became abundantly clear that Japan's imperial machine was on the march. While Japan took the top position in Asia, the United States was fast becoming the successor to Europe as the new seat of Western power, armed with sonar, radio, bombs, airplanes, and steamboats. World War I was a watershed moment in military history, as it introduced mass production in all types of war technology in the form of barbed wire, wireless radio, aerial balloons, and media propaganda. With these new technologies in tow, the Americans obtained the means to make the world in their image just as the Europeans had done before, but with a more "humanistic" liberal bent. As historian Merritt Roe Smith observes, U.S. "liberal empire" occurred through "benevolent assimilation" and a "civilizing mission" of spreading democracy, technology, and science. In this respect, those imperial ends "not only became the great panacea for everyday problems; they also stood for values at the core of American life."[20] Such globalizing values stood endangered when staring down an enemy who seemingly did not respect those ideals; and so the myth of the war machine arose to describe a race of robots that only knew death dealing. This U.S. myth corresponded to *nihonjinron*, the new religion of racial superiority that formed the "cultural essence" for Japan's military projects.

For Japan, national security meant funneling all its human capital into an expansionist "vision of a systematized society rooted in the energies of the people . . . creating a more efficient social machine for wartime mobilization and empire."[21] When Japan invaded Manchuria, magazines featured stories of "robotic war machines and robot soldiers" that solidified the notion of *Robo sapiens japanicus*.[22] In 1931, a "mechanical human" was displayed in a Tokyo department store for the first time, sparking a national love of mechanical bots, while the first Miss Nippon beauty pageant made its debut with female participants described by newspapers as beautiful soldiers for the nation. Forced to conform to new bodily standards about good hygiene, human breeding, racial purity, and physical athleticism, Japanese women (and men) were socially engineered by the state to become citizen-cyborgs "programmed to function with machine-like precision as a corporate unit . . . incorporated into the machinery of imperialism."[23] In the Japanese imperial army, defense officers viewed the body politic as an "electronic fortress," with radar technologies as the state's eyes and remote-controlled systems as the mechanical arms of the sovereign.[24] Adopting defense strategies against outside threats by conducting preemptive strikes, Japan charted a course to become a fully weaponized nation, making effective use of Western-made cannons and steam-powered warships to ramp up its military capabilities.

All of this produced mixed results for Japanese society. To maintain cultural purity in the face of Westernization, Japan's ideologues extolled the virtues of the Meiji slogan *wakon yosai*, meaning Japanese spirit with Western knowledge and technologies, a catchphrase that popularized as a war motto (and a motto for Japanese business takeovers in the late twentieth century). Japan's war machine harnessed the industrial practices of Euro-Americans, modifying them in accordance with Japanese cultural standards, and so the country modernized its economy without sacrificing its core identity, leaving firmly intact an inherent belief in the mythological power of Japaneseness. Japanese intellectuals advanced this thesis, declaring that it was the spirit that allowed its people to utilize "barbarian" technology and leapfrog over feudalism.[25] Per war historian John Dower, the country was "modernizing internally and competing internationally with extraordinary speed and skill . . . [producing a] system being geared to the mass production of obedient subjects who absorbed what they were told like sponges."[26]

The myth of the Japanese nation as war machine thus owes as much to Japan's own self-aggrandizement as it did to U.S. racial views of Japan's robotic citizenry and the state's adroit duplication of Western weapons, like the machine guns, torpedo crafts, and electric mines.[27] Imperial Japan succeeded in its "techno-military mimicry" of the Euro-Americans and built a unique national mythology.[28] From the 1910s onward, Japan grew even more strident, able to play the white man's game of war but on its own terms. Moving from what Japanese war historian Janis Mimura calls *technodiplomacy* in the nineteenth century to *technoimperialism* in the early twentieth century, Japan's bureaucrats lurched toward *technofascism* in the 1930s, where the ironclad rule of military agencies fused with state authoritarianism.[29] If imperialism is the highest form of capitalism according to Lenin, and capitalism for Karl Marx serves as a rapacious "machine for demolishing limits,"[30] Japan's rapacious economic/war machine entrusted a special imperial apparatus, one that could inject what Marx called the "Asiatic mode of production" into the modern theater of war.[31] The United States' hope for territorial expansion was complicated by Japan's ascension into the elite circle of imperial nations powered by lethal killing machines.

Interwar Fictions about the Japanese Robotic Mindset

Before Japan came to blows with the United States in World War II, there were concerns with Japan's expansionism, especially after the outgunning of China in the Sino-Japanese War, which tipped the scales of power in Asia. Before then, it was largely the Chinese seen as the greatest machine threat to the United States due to its huge labor population, growing manufacturing economy, and army of millions. An opinion piece written in 1890 for the monthly magazine *Public Opinion* aptly describes this threat: "The Chinese, getting rifles, may overwhelm Europe under showers of bullets poured upon her from human machines. . . . The white man will successfully call on science to hurl back his yellow adversary."[32] The U.S. minister to Siam (currently Thailand) observed more competition from China due to the country's population and size: "Chinese laborers going in and out of these mills at shifting hours. Nothing that human beings do more resembles the action of bees in a hive . . . the supreme lack of ambition among the masses, whose plodding nature, it would seem, all the electricity in the world could not cause to experience the slightest twinge."[33]

Japan's machine civilization began to come into sharper view as it quickly industrialized. This acuity trod into earlier first-person accounts made by Westerners who had traveled there. Watching peasants working at coal bunkers at a dock, a Christian missionary in Nagasaki in the 1920s made this observation: "I saw nine men and women on a scaffold, hand coal up the twenty-five feet in this manner at the rate of four seconds per basket, including dumping it in the bunker. I saw nine women consume only three seconds with the same operation. . . . An American woman looking over the railing of our ship down on to the human machines under us, exclaimed, 'Again I am glad I am an American woman!'"[34] The *China Monthly Review*, a pro-Chinese journal started by the first U.S. political adviser to the Chinese republic, described the misdeeds of Japanese people and their strange ways of eating, living, and working, which did not accord with "modern" American standards. Two years before Japan invaded Manchuria, the editorial commented: "Wide kimono sleeves are looped back in tending the [milling] machines. Then scuff, back go the industrial automatons to squat on their mats of their wooden home whose rents are about one-fifth of those paid by a family of factory workers in the United States. And all wanting more comforts and wishing they could have some meat instead of so much fish!"[35] The Shanghai-based English language journal goes on to warn of Japanese cotton mills underselling the British in China, India, and other territories or outright buying out English mills. Intersecting concerns with meat eating (manliness) and family (domesticity) and worker-consumer processes (Fordism) previously linked to Chinese coolies are extended to the Japanese who, despite their economic advances, are nothing more than basic automatons on the death march.

During the Russo-Japanese War, which ran from 1904 to 1905, Japan claimed victory in the first great modern war of the twentieth century. Japan's win over czarist Russia sent shock waves in the West by torpedoing the myth of white supremacy and jolting Europeans out of their sense of indomitability. Decades later, Japan's militarized economy built on Western technology proved to be a decisive factor for why it was willing to wage a fight with the United States in the Pacific basin. Preceding Japan's full-scale attack on Naval Station Pearl Harbor and before getting on a collision course with the United States, the interwar period was already freighted by the myth of the Japanese war machine.

One of the seeds for this myth of Japanese as malefic war machines was formulated by Jack London, a celebrated American writer who was also a journalist, essayist, news correspondent, and photographer. London often commentated on international affairs in the Far East, though he was never a government official or statesmen. Known for the naturalistic literary masterpieces *Call of the Wild* (1903) and *White Fang* (1906), London made a name for himself as an Asian expert at a time when few Americans knew much about Asia or Asians.[36] Watching the Russo-Japanese War with keen interest, London professed in his 1904 essay "The Yellow Peril" a belief that Japan was a warrior nation of fighters most effective in rallying other Asians to fight. Unlike the Chinese, who tended toward modernity slowly, the writer respected the country of Japan as it was able to fast rebut what he considered the imperial overtures of Europeans in Asia. With a penchant for bellicosity borne out of centuries of medieval shogun culture, combined with a new love for white technology, London found the Japanese to be "a race of mastery and power, a fighting race through all its history, a race that has always despised commerce and exalted fighting. Today, equipped with the finest machines and systems of destruction the Caucasian mind has devised, handling machines and systems with remarkable and deadly accuracy, this rejuvenescent Japanese race has embarked on a course of conquest the goal of which no man knows. . . . And to this dream the Japanese clings and will cling with bull-dog tenacity."[37] While respecting their tight machinelike military discipline, the famous writer reduced the Japanese to animal by commenting on their display of doggish ferocity as well as beelike social organization.[38] Despite their human prodigiousness, this animal dimension captures the tincture of species inferiority associated with the Japanese.

The rapid buildup of Japan's war machine was attributed to the unique cultural bearings of the Japanese, group-oriented resilient types believed to be drilled in the art of war as well as the cult of the emperor. London describes the Japanese soldier:

> He is not interested in his own moral welfare except in so far as it is the welfare of the State. The honor of the individual, per se, does not exist. . . . He does not look upon himself as a free agent, working out his own personal salvation. Spiritual agonizing is unknown to him. He has a sense of calm trust in fate, a quiet submission to the inevitable, a stoic composure in sight of danger or calamity, a disdain of

life and friendliness with death. He relates himself to the State as, amongst bees, the worker is related to the hive; himself nothing, the State everything; his reasons for existence the exaltation and glorification of the State. . . . The patriotism of the Japanese is blind and unswerving loyalty to what is practically an absolutism.[39]

Though London admired the Japanese in thwarting Western imperial aspirations in East Asia, he felt convulsed with worry about their zeal to sacrifice human morality for military victory. This mindset resonated with British economists at the time, who noted the reflexive "action of a Japanese [soldier] who throws himself upon the Russian bayonets at the word of command."[40] This essentialization of the Japanese nature seemed as informative as it was speculative. London's writings cast the Japanese as "Buddhas in the machine."[41]

As an influential writer with huge impact on culture, London's "machine anxiety" exerted a powerful hold over the public's imagination with his diehard journalism and creative writing. In this mixed literary mode, he combined fictional tales with journalistic yellow press writings about the Japanese. His "evidence" of them as "marvelous imitators" was often based on sensationalism. In doing so, he perfectly captured the general U.S. admiration for and horror of the Japanese as "dread engines" with a "superhuman, robotic control of emotions and pain, a seamless 'clocklike precision' in military organization, and a serene 'Japanese calm' with which they greeted war news."[42] Sightings of "human bullet attacks" during the Russo-Japanese War paralleled articles in the United States about the clandestine Japanese troops presumed to be hiding under the guise of "coolie" gardeners. Alas, the Japanese could be coolie workers too like the Chinese, but those Japanese coolies could be activated into action at any moment as soldiers of war.

With literary flair and poetic license, London wagered in a 1909 essay called "If Japan Wakens China" that China's power would be actualized through Japan's militaristic and technocultural influence.[43] While London contemplates the white races as stuck in their own bubble dreams of imperial racial superiority, he sensed that Japan would soon burst those dreams as it was the one Asiatic nation "able to borrow from us and equip herself with all our material achievement. Our machinery of warfare, of commerce, of industry, she has made hers."[44] While the popular writer believed that the Japanese could not duplicate the "spiritual" power behind white technology and could only duplicate Western machines in material terms, he fulminated against the presumption that the Japanese possessed no soul due to their dreams of conquest. He contemplated that we should never assume what the Japanese were thinking, asking instead what would happen when the "Asiatic dream [clashed] with ours." In an age of scientific management that reduced everything to "intelligent design," London's commentaries on the guile of the Japanese mindset—observable but not fully knowable—supplied fodder for his apocalyptic visions about the future of modern wars, similar to H. G. Wells's novel *The War in the Air* (1908), which featured a story of Japanese samurais taking down German airplanes with whirling swords.[45] In London's novel *Iron Heel*, published the same year, he imagined a grim scenario in the late twentieth century whereby the Japanese led an all-out war against a wobbly and weakened United States now run by a tyrannical oligarchy. While gobsmacked by Japan's ability to expand its war machine to the United States, he describes the internal conflict back home in Japan between lower-caste workers and soldiers loyal to the emperor:

> The cry in all Asia was, "Asia for the Asiatics!" And behind this cry was Japan, ever urging and aiding the yellow and brown races against the white. And while Japan dreamed of continental empire and strove to realize the dream, she suppressed her own proletarian revolution. It was a simple war of the castes, Coolie versus Samurai, and the coolie socialists were executed by the tens of thousands. Forty thousand were killed in the street-fighting of Tokio and in the futile assault on the Mikado's palace. Kobe was in shambles; the slaughter of the cotton operatives by machine-guns became a classic as the most terrific execution ever achieved by modern war machines.[46]

This passage described "socialist" workers murdered by marauding samurais loyal to the emperor; coolie labor was replaced by Japan's most ardent fighters. Despite no such massacre happening, London's fictional words are a symbolic processing of a moment in which science fiction offers no less than an alternative historiography to explain the sublime qualities of militarized capitalism. This "war to end all war" had a big impact on London and succeeding generations of Americans, serving as a prelude to bigger confrontations between Allied forces and their enemies in World War II. (French wartime postcards drew the head of the Japanese emperor on the tip of a torpedo, conflating Japanese bodies and the state with technology.)[47]

London's prophesies of the war machine were complementary to estimations by politicians like James D. Phelan. In 1914, the California Democratic candidate for the U.S. Senate suggested more tact with the rising Asian power, given its imperial ambitions at the time, and to take care when dealing with Japanese immigrants in the United States, as he considered them "efficient human machines" who were a "menace to our prosperity and happiness."[48] One finds similar qualifications in the 1914 short story by London "The Unparalleled Invasion," written as a kind of historical essay or report. In the plot, Japan's military helps rouse and egg on China to modernize, something that Euro-Americans tries to do to little avail, since the Chinese are "mental aliens" while the Japanese are the "freak and paradox among Eastern peoples" with their "peculiar openness" to Western material achievement and the ability to translate Western technoculture to those of fellow Mongol stock.[49]

It was common for Americans to compare Japan and China, given these two major Asian powers at the time. American pathologist William Henry Welch, who played a major role in the establishment of modern medical practice and education, wrote about medical care and training in China. Welch held slim hopes for the Chinese to improve under Japanese and American tutelage: "They have very little aneurism—which is surprising on account of the amount of work done by the human machine in China, where it is cheaper to feed the human machine with rice than to lighten its labor. I do not know what would happen if machinery were introduced into China: it would probably disrupt the whole nation."[50] China's equilibrium based on the drudging labor of coolie machines formed a barrier to proper mechanization/modernization. Progressive American writer and Asia expert Victor Murdock still referred to modern China as a mysterious and marvelous nation. In this change-resistant Oriental republic, he argued, "the Chinaman, as a human machine, is equipped" like other national subjects in fighting abilities, but he lacks offensive action. Unlike the Japanese, who finally awoke to imperial modernity and adopted modern devices, and now led the teeming millions of Asia into machine production, the Chinese republic's isolation in thinking and dedication to democracy rather than imperialism led to its demise.[51]

As a speculative writer who eerily could peer into the future, London sounded the alarm about Japan's harbored wish and yearning to invade Manchuria, in China. If Japan could harness China's highly disciplined machinists and miners, this "would make Japan a truly great world power."[52] In contrast to the Japanese or Koreans, who were the "perfect type of inefficiency—of utter worthlessness," the Chinese were efficient labor machines: "The Chinese is the perfect type of industry. For sheer work no worker in the world can compare with him. Work is the breath of his nostrils. . . . To till the soil and labor interminably was all he asked of life and the powers that be. Work is what he desires above all things, and he will work at anything for anybody. . . . The awakening of China had given . . . access to the highest and most scientific machine-means of toil."[53]

London located the big threat of Japan in its engineers, who were building factories, telephones, telegraphs, railroads, and canals in China. With Japan pulling the latter out of lethargy, China "awoke and inaugurated the machine civilization, her productive power enormously increased [by] working at her machines and growing."[54] The Japanese war machine acted as the prime mover and comptroller of China's development, spurring advances in a dormant machine civilization and its imperial army: "Japan's officers reorganized the Chinese army. . . . Her drill-sergeants made over the medieval warriors into twentieth century soldiers, accustomed to all the modern machinery of war and with a higher average marksmanship than the soldiers of any Western nation."[55]

In this fantasy tale, the Chinese, formerly at the beck and call of the Japanese, would throw off the yoke of foreign domination to build up its own great war machine. Japan mutates into a peaceful nation, devoting itself to creations of art and beauty for the world. Uninterested in conquering others, China "went on consummating her machine civilization," until other paranoid nations of the world came to the conclusion that the Chinese had to be eradicated, waging a united campaign of chemical genocide and wiping out the entire Chinese population.[56] As a "history lesson from the future," this story of Western powers prevailing over Asian aggressors served as a prescription of racial genocide.[57] London's prediction that Japan's war machine would try to mobilize all Asian nations to unite against European colonizers proved eerily true later during World War II.

As a socialist, London lobbed his barbs at Western capitalist greed, but this master storyteller presented mixed racist messages about Asians and Asian societies.[58] London's observations about Korea were corroborated by American businessman and scientist Percival Lowell, who wrote about his impressions of Koreans while serving on a special U.S. diplomatic mission to the peninsula. In an unknown land under Japan's sphere of influence, Lowell sketched out this outline of his fast-moving Korean guides: "To be lost going into a strange country would have been perhaps pardonable, but to be lost coming out was preposterous; and all because the coolie was a first-class automaton, over which I had little or no control."[59] Koreans' "far Oriental nature" prevented them from passing into a more "attractive state where the body is recognized as something better than a mere automaton."[60] As an Asian country with Western features, Japan would retain this mechanical impersonality and move into an unattractive automaton state, exploiting its own people while trying to turn Koreans, Chinese, and other Asians into machines.

London's image of a militaristic Japan turned peaceful nation proved to be false. Passing away before Japan's formal entry into the Axis powers, he nevertheless bore witness to the growing reality that "the machine age is something quite different from a heroic age," since modern wars no longer followed former ideals of bravery but concentrated on systematic ideals of control.[61] London knew Japan would never be satisfied with colonizing Korea, as it might try to poach Manchuria with its larger pool of workers and deposits of coal and iron, to amass more resources for its hungry war machine.[62] Perceptions of a hostile foreign takeover obfuscated some suspicions, at the time, that it was American planes sold to the Japanese, who then used this technology to down the USS *Panay*, a gunboat stationed in China in 1937. The surprise attack turned U.S. public opinion against the Japanese, since the United States was not officially at war with Japan at the time.[63]

Soon, the Japanese replaced the Chinese as the Asian enemy/Other for the United States. Says the *San Francisco Chronicle*, "They may tell you that the Japanese will copy our Occidental dress, will imitate our modes of warfare and copy our war ships, and so may China, but that is as far as they will go. They will have none of our morals."[64] In the literary serial The World's Work: A History of Our Time, editors commented on the new "Japanese problem." A chief lesson gained from the Supreme Court's decision in 1923 to uphold California's Alien Land Law (barring Japanese from owning land) was that the United States had enough factory machines to fare well without the labor input of Asian machines. Despite some adverse effects on California's agricultural sector due to the ban, there was no need to import inassimilable labor machines: "The United States possesses abundant machinery to protect itself against the influx of an unassimilable alienism.... Manufacturers in certain sections demand practically unrestricted immigration so that they may obtain a large supply of inexpensive unskilled labor. *The need of human machines to meet their peak manufacturing necessities has seemed to them the main consideration in the immigration question....* The only question at all important in our immigration policy is the necessity of peopling the United States with the racial stocks out of which a nation can be built."[65]

The editors conclude that "Mongolians" and Americans should never intermarry or mix to deter the rise of a "Pacific civilization" that was half white and half Asian. While the United States considered the "less-developed" people of the Philippines, Hawaii, Guam, or Samoa to be the "white man's burden," the Japanese were an outright threat to Anglo-Americans because they were modern and powerful but not yet white/human. Per racial psychologists, the Japanese were better at conserving their cultural strength since the handicap of Westerners was "the humanitarian impulse," while the Japanese lacked empathy for the weak and lame.[66] Ironically, this perception of nonempathetic Japanese would justify American violence against Japanese people during World War II. In the psychologists' view, American industry was the "inheritor of all the fruits of the effort and wisdom of the Western mind," and Japanese would "use effectively the weapons of our own modern industrial and business competition."[67] They advocated for the exclusion of Japanese immigrants to avert the foreign takeover of American industries, since "it is always aggravating to be beaten at one's own game by those we consider our imitators."[68]

Reservations toward the Japanese and their machine mimicry were related to mass contamination by pesticide residue in modern American industrial food production, which were linked to "invasive species." Early Japanese immigrants to the United States were forced to overcome the roadblocks of racism and warlike descriptions of them as "human bullets" penetrating the national landscape.[69] While agriculture became increasingly mechanized in the 1920s and 1930s, still more common was the demand for immigrant farm labor, which intensified. Of interest was the Japanese worker who embodied both the "alienating" effects of mechanization and immigration with its "unstoppable economically efficient, mechanized Asiatic body."[70]

Decimating local crops, the pestilent nonnative Japanese beetle came to be synonymous with American children born to Japanese parents, construed as the spawn of and miniature soldiers for the Japanese emperor. This heightened alertness around a racial-mechanical-biological threat set the pretext for the placement of almost all Japanese Americans in concentration camps during World War II. Two-thirds of those interned were U.S.-born children; with little knowledge of Japan, they were believed to be born with some built-in robotic loyalty to Japan's god-emperor. The concentration camps served as quarantines for containing the ballistic bodies of alien machines. By the early 1940s, public concerns about the Japanese had reached a tipping point, and anti-Japanese war propaganda went into overdrive when the United States formally declared war against Japan.

Robot Soldiers and the Propaganda Machine

The surprise assault on Pearl Harbor shocked Americans as it soon became apparent that the nice little Japanese, "whom they associated only with cherry blossoms and geisha, could really build up such a machine," admitted the chief of the U.S. Department's Division of Japanese Affairs.[71] Still reeling from the global depression of the 1930s, Japan's own lack of economic/national security meant a desperate scramble for natural resources to support its rampaging war machine. The imperial government began to build garrisons, forts, ports, and airfields on nearby islands, turning natural land masses into giant "unsinkable aircraft carriers."[72] Its navy seemed bent on devouring smaller territories in the South Pacific, turning whole islands into coaling stations for steam-powered warships. Even so, Japan justified its imperialist actions in other nations as installing a "modern industrial machine as well as a defense force which could ward off invasion from the West."[73] The reach of Japan's war machine was regional and international.

As it pressed on in Southeast Asia, Japan advanced carnage by torturing prisoners of wars, who were beaten and beheaded (with swords). This style of execution reinforced the chivalrous military code of Bushido, meaning the "way of the warrior," which says a samurai is willing to die for his mission and lord at any time. Says two prominent Japanese military historians, "The Japanese war machine had many facets. Tanks, small arms, ships, planes, and artillery were its tools. The warrior spirit of medieval Japan was its engine."[74] Endowed with a natural instinct for killing, Japan's "mimic modernity" of the West meant it was also "a not-quite-modern nation."[75] Japan combined the best of an old, venerable feudal spirit with the innovative machine culture to perfect its military death drive. Here, the samurai warrior cum war machine presented only a modernized Oriental state of war rather than a modern state of laws, diplomacy, and forms of engagement associated with the "superior force of European minds."[76]

Displaying the ugliest aspects of industrialized warfare, the Japanese war machine epitomized the horrors of hypermilitarization. Here, the Americans fended off a highly organized enemy and ethnic foe rallying around war propaganda, produced ad nauseum to boost public morale and the war effort. News mogul Henry Luce considered the Japanese soldiers cockroaches, while his magazines conferred on them the title of "automatons in uniform."[77] American media put its spin machine into maximum drive, avidly affirming Uncle Sam as the human hero and Hirohito as a war machine who totally controlled his people. An editorial piece in the U.S. Army's *Infantry Journal* warned American soldiers not to underestimate the average Japanese as some comical buck-toothed simian creature but to think of them as a sneaky "robot-like creature."[78] This ascription was reinforced in Japan, where propagandists regularly described the country's population of "100 million people as one bullet."[79]

The U.S. Department of Defense produced many propagandic war films, and one portrayed the Japanese particularly as war machines. The major production was entitled *Know Your Enemy* (1945). Directed by famed auteur Frank Capra, it depicted Japanese men as clones who act and look the same, claiming that scrappy Japanese boys are raised from birth to be "as much alike as photographs off the same negative." The film drew on myths about the Japanese, which affirmed modern battlefield as more than hand-to-hand physical combat; it included the visual field of perception where "the war machine appears to the military commander as an instrument of representation, comparable to the painter's palette and brush."[80] *Know Your Enemy* was the culmination of many efforts by Capra who, after Pearl Harbor, sought to produce documentaries for troops to learn about the foreign enemy, though those films were eventually shown to the wider public.[81]

Despite the Pentagon's disapproval of the film for portraying the Japanese too sympathetically, the final product managed to be a satisfyingly enough product for the public to consume. It taps into the dominant thinking of the time by recounting the greatness of Euro-American scientific ingenuity by exalting Benjamin Franklin, Thomas Jefferson, and Louis Pasteur and remarking upon the telegraph and steam engine as part of the technological contributions made by white men to the world.[82] The film shifts to provide an overview of Japan's history, recounting the myth-history of a once isolated nation that fell to military pressure from Commodore Perry to belatedly wake up to modernity. As discovered in the film, Japan quickly learned to appropriate inventions as the "hairy white barbarian had machines and weapons that made him powerful." The exercise in military mythmaking took the Japanese as a gestalt, a total sum of parts, organized more by what sociologist Emile Durkheim had called the "mechanical solidarity" of interdependent communities that share the same beliefs and work ethic. This mechanical solidarity is weighed against the "organic solidarity" of modern industrialized societies like the United States, shaped by human-oriented values and a complex division of labor.[83] The U.S. response of "total war" and "military orientalism" was predicated on the sense that "Japan was a nation without individuals, full of conformist robots brainwashed by ruthless militarists out to take over the world."[84]

Fixating on Japanese people's "natural" docility toward authority deflected from the Japanese imperial state's systemic efforts to dragoon citizens into becoming robot soldiers for empire. The human comfort of the masses was of little concern to Japan's modernizing elites, "whose eyes were fixed on overseas conquest."[85] *Know Your Enemy* took liberties with exaggerating Japan's cultural backwardness by discussing the millions of rural Japanese women sold to factories and brothels, and people treated as little more than rice-cultivating "human machines" as the film blithely puts it— an off-putting description that made Japan look devoid of any real humans.[86]

War machine myths fed into the eye-witness accounts of the Japanese as main culprits of military violence on the frontlines. Exaggerated historical portrayals ordained them as "alternately irrational and slavishly conforming, a group of human automatons who, beneath their programmed politeness, harbor proclivities for lurid sex and violence."[87] In the Philippines, Filipino soldiers were bombarded and besieged by Japanese forces, and the foreign soldier "used to living on nothing," but this perception was complicated by the Japanese soldier's survival skills in the wild: "Part of our wishful thinking about the Japanese Army was that it was composed of human automatons. We learned better. Every Japanese soldier was capable of planning and fighting on his own initiative, living alone in the forest for days."[88] Machinic metaphors were applied even to Asian U.S. allies like the Chinese. While the U.S. military was overseas teaching Chinese soldiers how to fight Japan, the Chinese were described by their American trainers as "efficient human machines," always "eager to learn" with an "expert eye for detail."[89] As weaponized coolies, the Chinese were winnowed down to "those human machines who can carry a load all day."[90]

It did not matter if one was an ally and citizen of the United States, being Asian was enough to be construed as a militarized machine. Seen as natural extensions of Japanese society, Japanese Americans were painted as little war machines for Japan, thereby requiring security measures to control them. Liberal congressperson John Coffee voiced opposition to the removal of all Americans of Japanese descent from their homes, and he claimed they were victims of the American war machine as much as "victims of a Japanese war machine."[91] The United States consequently imprisoned over 130,000 Americans of Japanese descent under the presumption one could not read their motives and thoughts; their facial inscrutability meant they did not exhibit regular human behavior. Historian Brian Hayashi observes that with lie detector machines and intelligence data, "these army officials felt confident they could ferret out the 'disloyal' and potentially dangerous."[92] Insofar as the Japanese ethnic makeup suggested they were potential subversives, government scientists leveraged new screening technology to smelt the iron core of "citizen Japan." Intelligence operatives attempted to pierce their stony-faced demeanors to discern craven intentions lurking beneath robotic stoicism. This pseudoscientific assessment was affirmed in a 1934 book by the missionary Albert Palmer entitled *Orientals in American Life*, where he merged the metaphor of the inscrutable Asian "mask" with the aloof visage and hard veneer of the automaton. Describing not only Japanese but people from China and the Philippines, he claimed, "To the Western mind the Oriental seems to wear a mask. There is something inscrutable about him—his face, which seems so unresponsive, his eyes which tell no certain meaning . . . [Asians] seem to look alike. They do not have those variations of hair or coloring or even of features which make it so easy to tell us Occidentals apart; and this uniformity, because of its very strangeness, sometimes seems ominous—a kind of uncanny, depersonalized, robot-like regimentation which is not quite human, and might prove sinister in crisis. What's behind the Oriental mask?"[93]

Modern biometric practices were employed on a mass scale against Asian American populations, contributing to the normalization of new body technologies widely used today.[94] Such technologies unleashed the FBI's automated process of screening civil servants onto average citizens for the first time, part of an intensifying techno-security regime based on fingerprint collection, computerized tabulating machines, and instruments of surveillance. All deemed necessary because the ascetic Japanese war machine possessed a foreign face and mind that could not be deciphered by regular human screening. To breach the thick integument of this iron-clad mask required a new technology of biopower.

While the Japanese military was secretly experimenting on prisoners of war, removing body parts and injecting toxic chemicals to inflict sadistic cruelty, the U.S. military unleashed mustard gas and other chemical agents on soldiers of color to create the perfect superhuman soldier.[95] One Japanese American soldier who endured this experiment recounts: "They were interested in seeing if chemical weapons would have the same effect on Japanese as they did on white people. . . . They were contemplating having to use them on the Japanese."[96] Buoyed by scientific racism and conjecture about physiological differences between whites and nonwhites, the U.S. Army reveled in the dogma that people of color experienced pain differently. This racial hypothesis justified the use of humans for experiments, whose results could help take down a bloodthirsty diabolical species believed to be devoid of human sensation.[97]

Meanwhile, Japanese American men were recruited to fight for the U.S. military to prove their humanity. Many answered this national call, but their demonstrated valor did little to stop the government from restricting these soldiers from possessing radios, cameras, or guns, lest they use them to turn on their white commanding officers.[98] These model/minority veterans were ironically prohibited from using technology, even as their bodies presented a form of technology that needed to be reined in and deployed.[99] Occupying a *conditio inhumana* and state of rightlessness, the Asian automaton need to either be vaporized like the Japanese imperial soldier or humanized in the case of the "volunteer" Japanese American GI who enlisted under duress.[100] Given the way race works, distinctions between domestic and foreign machine soldiers were not always clear.

On the physical battlefield, there was a need to distinguish between Japanese soldiers from Japan and those mobilized to fight on behalf of the United States against Japan. Staff Sergeant Edgar Laytha wrote about his experience fighting alongside Japanese American comrades in the China-Burma-India theater during World War II: "Nisei grow about two inches taller and are far better built than their relatives in Japan. . . . The Jap is the son of an undernourished nation and looks it. The uncanny discipline and self-negation . . . [made him] more of a human automaton than a human being. But this all vanishes under the American sun."[101] The Japanese American soldier blossomed into a full human being under the rising sun of American empire. His strong physical body differed from the sickly emaciated warrior from Japan, feeding only on a maniacal devotion to murder and sacrifice for his impoverished master. This overlords' empire hinged on not only an unquenchable lust for power but also a fatalistic love for *kokutai*, translated as the community or essence that makes up the cultural content of Japanese sovereignty. A unique political concept imbued with religious connotations, kokutai held sway as the identity of the people and the state were fused into a technocultural totality.[102] During World War II, the theocratic model of kokutai was tweaked considerably to mean military units in Japan's naval aviation services; in passing, the term went beyond the dispensation of Japan's defense army and imperial optics and later described the magical power of Japan's postwar economic empire and its army of salarymen.

Despite its military bravado, Japan soon realized by the mid-1940s it would not win against a well-assembled military like that of the United States, so strategies were designed to strike the opposition hard and fast. One stratagem included banzai attacks or charging toward the enemy on the ground with samurai swords in a last resort to overwhelm the enemy. In a modern war that lacked much close contact, Japan deployed human torpedoes called *kaitens*, suicide submarines manned by an individual or a few persons loaded with tons of explosives. Akin to this were *okas*, which were but empty gliders strapped to warheads "with humans as targeting computers."[103] Despite sacrificing many lives and much energy, Japan could not fend off the output of the American war machine, and the quality of Japanese-made weapons worsened, clearly outmatched by the strength of U.S. inventions like the semiautomatic M1 Garands and Thompson machine guns. The Japanese were still handling lighter firearms developed earlier, such as the self-revolving Type 94 Nambu 8 mm Pistol, modeled after classic Western gun brands like Smith and Wesson.[104] That the Japanese were willing to fight to the death—literally turning their men into weapons—made it seem that these mad machines did not put value on human life as white people did, an idea that would carry over into the Cold War.

As Allied forces pressed forward in the Pacific and the war reached a fever pitch, the Japanese deployed new human technology like the high-flying kamikaze "death squads" composed of frenzied pilots ready to die for the emperor. These floating suicide vehicles were loaded up with explosives meant to fatally damage and wreak havoc on enemy fleets, repurposing old planes as a phallic technology of a flagging war machine.[105] Popularizing the Orientalist myth that Asian people value collectivity and suicidal death over preserving individualism and human life, Japanese kamikaze pilots were thought of as cannon fodder for Japan's artillery, inseparable from the warplanes they piloted. Yet those special attack forces expressed desperation by a Japan that saw no alternative to losing, after facing material shortages in aviation fuel, oil, steel, and scrap iron. Japan's impressive imperial assemblage rested on shaky structural foundations. For this reason, fighter pilots had to be turned into human cudgels.[106] Fortified by the mythical powers of the kamikaze, the faltering Japanese military government gave itself over to obsessions with breeding the perfect soldier that could withstand pain and never fear death. A belief in the insuperable facility of its self-sacrificing soldiers conveyed the idealism and instrumentalism of empire. The Japanese self-modelled war machine played into the viewpoint of the Japanese as "possessed of uncanny discipline and fighting skills. Subhuman, inhuman, less human, superhuman—all that was lacking in the perception of the Japanese enemy was a human like oneself."[107]

Some American commanders were terrified by the might of a seemingly dissolute enemy that did not know human limits or constraints—the Japanese "superman" promoted by journalists and spin doctors. By 1942, many U.S. military experts became "almost morbidly obsessed by the specter of a seemingly invincible foe, capable of undreamed-of military feats."[108] The armature of the Zero—the best fighter plane in Asia manned by skilled pilots—led Allied forces to scope a "new creature [that] roamed the fertile fields of the Anglo-American imagination."[109] In response to the Japanese superman, the American comic book character Superman was commissioned to fight Japanese spies sneaking around factories and trying to blow up planes. The antagonist of this wartime story line tapped into conspiracy theories about secret Japanese plans for industrial sabotage.[110]

This villain got another face and name when the Douglas Aircraft Company commissioned a series of posters to muster support for U.S. home defense against the "fighting Jap." They featured a grimacing cartoon figure named the Tokio Kid, a buffoonish infantilized caricature of Hideki Tojo, Japan's prime minister and general of the Japanese imperial army. The "Kid" was sponsored as part of the company's campaign to mitigate the waste of factory products and conserve national resources. One image pictured the protofeminist wartime icon, Rosie the Riveter, in the factory at a cog wheel, oblivious to a gargoyle-like changeling with big oversized canines, claws, squinty bespectacled eyes, and dark skin slinking around her factory. Here, the Japanese war machine myth had a perverse side to it, as it clarified an urgent need to protect innocent white women from violation.[111] The caption beneath the image says, "Tokio Kid say—Rivets on floor gone to scrap making victory in bag for Jap. Thank you." Other catchphrases are just as striking: "Broke up tools waste for scrap just like bullets make for Jap" or "Bombers not building may win war for Japan." Such visual productions were persuasive in beseeching Americans to save their metal and rubber scraps for recycling into munitions and other war objects. If Americans left work early, it was insinuated, the Japanese used that as a leg up to build their war machine.

The Tokio Kid brought alive the Japanese foreign threat within the United States' domestic sphere. Complementing the open-kill tactics of brazen Japanese combatants, this undercover agent plotted to reverse the terms of U.S. industry from within, tampering with its operations. With the doggerel of Orientalist fortune-cookie lettering (and the staccato manner of aliens speaking English), one poster had the kid brandishing a sword and making bullets. His sword symbolized the time-honored fighting style of Asian war-

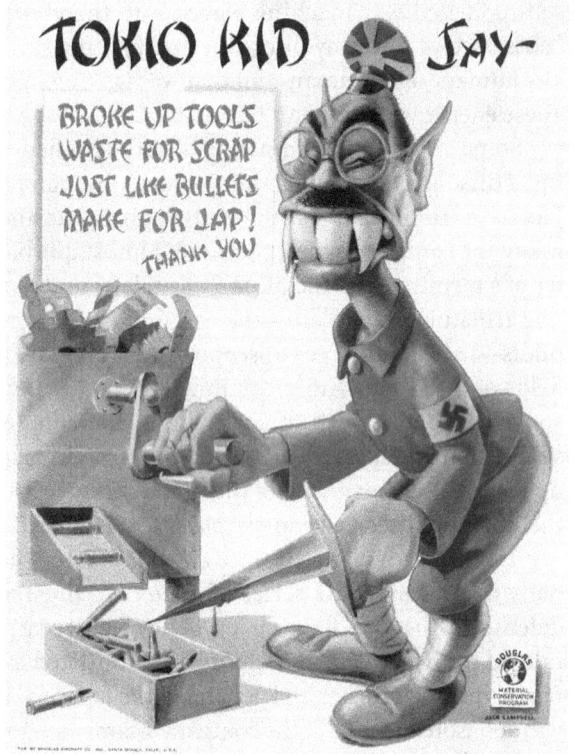

Figure 2.1 "Tokio Kid Say—Broke Up Tools Waste for Scrap Just Like Bullet Make for Jap" poster from the Douglas Aircraft Company, 1943 (U.S. National Archives)

rior machines, while bullets presented the weaponry of a modern killing machine, one able to repurpose the enemy's scrap metal and industrial waste to good use. The poster bore the warning "Tokio Kid say—broke up tools waste for scrap just like bullet make for Jap" (see fig. 2.1). Douglas suppliers sent these posters for use by other firms, including Chrysler, Remington, Westinghouse, and Carnegie Steel. The U.S. Treasury even used the Tokio Kid to sell war bonds.[112] More than a popular stereotype, the war machine myth was a major state-backed public campaign.

In another war poster, the Kid brandished a bloody knife like a murderous assassin. The pointed ears and sharp fangs piled on the sense of nonhuman menace with rodent-like features, adding an animal element to squinted eyes, enlarged buckteeth, and drooling that inferred a dopey quality to the unrelatable Japanese. Poised and perched to seize American power from any angle, the war machine thus can mean both an entire system and its constitutive elements, the component parts (kamikaze or spies) of a bigger whole (military-industrial complex). Tokio Kid epitomized that complex assemblage indeed.

Propaganda like this masked the real operations behind myth. For example, Japan's war industry could not withstand the energetic momentum of the United States' sectorial organization of war production.[113] The Tokio Kid presented the Japanese maven in a style at odds with America's "machinery of government."[114] But this stereotype overstated Japan's industrial threat as it did not reflect the fact that Hirohito's war administration did not nationalize his country's economy in the same extensive way that President Franklin Roosevelt did.[115] By 1943, the bottom fell out. Japan's war machine suffered battle fatigue, stunted by a tapering supply of raw materials and a labor shortage. On the other hand, the American war machine came into its own as a full-blown enterprise as there was no aspect of civil life that did not go untouched by the wartime command economy.

As consequence, Japan finally capitulated to the United States, who ended the war by dropping on Japan two atomic bombs—the ultimate symbol of the age of mass destruction.[116] When Japan surrendered to General MacArthur's army, it was reported that the victors found no humans with remorse or sadness. Instead, they discovered human automatons accepting death and defeat with a "resignation and stoic appearance that surprised their enemies."[117] Dr. Michihiko Hachiya, a Hiroshima physician who survived the atomic blast, described this scenario in his diary differently, opting to write from the perspective of those afflicted by the atomic bombing in Hiroshima. "They were so broken and confused that they moved and behaved like automatons. . . . The outsiders could not grasp the fact that they were witnessing the exodus of a people who walked in the realm of dreams. . . . Why was everyone so quiet? . . . It was as though I walked through a gloomy, silent motion picture."[118] This doctor captured the eerie dreamscape of human survivors after a nuclear attack. This narrative stands apart from the image of unfeeling war machines vividly painted in American military accounts and Hollywood-produced propaganda films. Foreign perception of the Japanese as machinic automatons, and not human targets, seemed to justify the use of nukes, but the people of Japan learned this tragedy as a lesson for all of humanity.

After the dropping of the atomic bombs, the U.S. government became inclined to redeem itself of atrocious crimes against humanity through the "Hiroshima maidens," Japanese women scarred by atomic bomb radiation who were selected to undergo reconstructive surgery in the United States.[119] This project remade the image of the United States by turning the women into technologically enhanced cyborgs, their rehabilitated bodies the perfect analog to a Japan that needed to be humanized. After 1945, however, the United States would become the largest arms dealer and military power in the world, one bent on girding its geopolitical interests with the onset of the Cold War. Meanwhile, a defeated and "reformed" Japan found more economical ways to reassert its dormant war machine.

Economic War Machines

With the conclusion of World War II, the U.S. mandated a new constitution for occupied Japan, barring national rearmament and a large standing military force. With the United States promising to protect Japan, this security pact set the latter up to become the "Workshop of the American Lake," playing a key assistive role in U.S. military and economic expansion throughout much of Asia. American journalists writing at the end of the war gave purchase to the U.S. government retaining the seat of the Emperor Hirohito to utilize the "ready-made machine consisting of the two million or so Japanese citizen in government employ, from top-rank ambassadors to village postmen."[120] Forced to renounce war, Japan and its cookie-cutter citizens soon plugged into the U.S. Cold War machine, supplying technical and financial support.[121] Subordinated to the American war machine as a "contemporary manifestation of U.S. neo-imperial hegemony," Japan discovered other ways to enhance its global standing in what many call the "second machine age" by producing technology like cars, video cameras, and robotics.[122] Though U.S. popular media remained fervent and consistent in its techno-Orientalist characterization of Japan as machine-like cybersociety, the Japanese responded with a techno-Occidentalism that painted a "dehumanizing picture of the West," criticizing it for its love of violence, cold scientificism, and "machine civilization."[123]

Japan's love of robots can be interpreted as cultural adherence to spiritual traditions like animism, holding that the sacred world inhabits everything, that all objects and creatures bear a consciousness or soul.[124] A robot could achieve human qualities, a far cry from the customary belief of American science fiction gurus like Isaac Asimov who envisioned robots mostly as servants to humans. This difference in perspective is spelled out in Japanese anime characters, such as Astro Boy, a little boy robot with a nuclear reactor heart, computer brain, and rocket feet. This boy spends his time fighting monsters and bandits in the name of peace, living comfortably among humans in Japan's "robot kingdom." Astro Boy personifies a resurgent Japan ready to fight the United States again.[125] Creator Osamu Tezuka hatched a story in 1987 involving Astro Boy going back in time to stop U.S. servicemen from bombing Vietnamese villages during the Second Indochina War.[126] The robot boy warrior gave pacified Japan a popular small replica of its former war machine, one that could scale back the bloodbath of American Cold War mayhem in the form of a "nearly perfect robot who strove to become human."[127]

Other war machine figures helped imagine the might of a revitalized Japan, which contrasted with the U.S. war machine. In his 1963 comic book premiere, Iron Man appeared as a cocky, rich American weapons manufacturer who hunts down Asian communist agents using a metal armor powered by an electromagnetic reactor heart.[128] *Iron Man* serialized the way playboy industrialists could use a well-crafted metallic fighting suit against enemies of the United States. This thoroughly human-machine hybrid was similar in design to Mitsuteru Yokoyama's 1956 Japanese Ironman creation, even though the latter was almost entirely machine.[129] Japan's Ultraman was another war machine of import, but the main character Hayata transformed completely into an alien to save the earth from monsters. Unlike the U.S.-originated Iron Man, the man-machine bonds in Japanese characters seemed more complete; the Japanese cyborg body here is tightly fused with intergalactic technology in a complex union of man/machine/alien.

Robot anime cinched a new popular fixation. The visuality of Japanese robots brought machine imaginaries ever closer to industrial robotics, a field that found a strong niche in Japan.[130] Robot mania was brought to the foreground by *Robotech*, a first major Japanese anime broadcast in the United States, whose success spawned a merchandising industry in robots. Offering a view of earthly residents who "actually took elaborate robots and their narratives seriously," *Robotech* told the story of technologies found in an alien spaceship. This technology was later developed into "mechas" by humans to head off outerplanet invaders.[131] To appreciate the Japanese word *meka* (mecha) is to recognize that it is an abbreviation of human automatons in Japanese, referring to robots controlled by humans from the inside with human-machine body parts acting in unison. This amalgam figures humans as "merged with pieces of technology in order to 'give birth' to new creatures."[132]

Before the 1980s, Japan was known for producing shoddy low-quality consumer products and cheap things, such as tinplate car toys, as the country sought to catch up with the West after the war. When it finally reached economic superpower status and started to make real cars, this manufacturing shift prompted U.S. industrialists to accuse the Japanese of "reverse engineering," poaching American machines and taking them apart only to reconstruct them into Asian products. This was sometimes the case in the machine-tool-making business and the production of "mother machines" that make other machines. Soon, Japan owned twenty to fifty of the world's flexible manufacturing systems, leading the world in just-in-time, quality-control lean production systems.[133] Responding to U.S.-imposed rule, Japan rebooted the technological capabilities of its former imperial government. Despite the United States' effort to subordinate Japan as a junior partner in the Cold War, Japan's wish to return to the top of the global chain remained ever present, especially when the same military elites who built the country's military apparatus were the primary agents responsible for funding and greasing the machinery of Japan's postwar economic "miracle."

After World War II, the myth of the Japanese war machine took on another guise within global political economy. Japan's quick postwar recovery made it once again a moral hazard to the United States, and globalization did little to diminish Japan's past associations with imperialism. In fact, the myth of the war machine came roaring back under Japan's "aggressive" business practices and takeover of U.S. companies, such as when Sony bought Columbia Pictures, which was a response to Hollywood blocking the use of Japanese video recorders. As a noted scholar of Japan writes: "In light of its dramatic economic recovery since the war, Japan has been popularly viewed through the bifocals of admiration and jealousy as the super-efficient, globetrotting businessmen purveying Japanese-built television sets and automobiles with the missionary zeal of atonement for prior war crimes."[134] Japanese quietly appeared to work hard as a possible sign of guilt or indemnity for their reign of military terror during World War II, and yet their very economic efficiency betrays a hint of the zeal that justified past crimes against humanity.

The bifocals mentioned in this quote seems to evoke the memory of the bespectacled Tokio Kid, but now the kid had grown up, working as a salaryman for Japanese businesses, versed in the subtle art of trade war. Eventually, Japan's preeminence in consumer technology incited the Reagan administration to impose protectionist policies aimed at fortifying vulnerable U.S. industries from Japan's economic machine.[135] Americans opposed to globalism could not stand to see the Japanese war machine resurrected again, exploiting the laziness and weakness of the United States. In the neoliberal era, market performance speaks as much as arms stockpiles. As the second largest economy in the world, Japan was criticized for launching their own secret kamikaze-style attacks against free trade by manipulating foreign currency exchange. It was not unlike a giant Godzilla stomping on Wall Street buildings. These accusations came forcefully, when Japan's government promoted state-backed corporations like Toyota, a mercantilist practice that seemed unfair to private U.S. businesses. The country's remarkable ability to recoup from defeat, rising from the ashes of war and marching onto the economic field of battle, fed into the "myth of the voracious Japanese economic machine that plays by unfair rules, consume anything in its path and gives nothing back in return."[136]

This post–World War II myth of the economic war machine sowed panic over Japan's growing robot empire, but U.S. manufacturers hurt themselves by opposing the early introduction of robots for automating factory work. Too busy vilifying Asian automaton society, they had overlooked the actual

merits and benefits of automation. That delay gave the Japanese a compara-
tive advantage in the global tech economy as two-thirds of all industrial robots were by the end of the century found in Japan. With uniformed robots
directing traffic or greeting customers in stores, Japan saw fit the need for
robots of all types for powering a "gizmo nation" where "machines stand for
humans" and "human-machines stand for the nation."[137] The country soon
led the world in research on "biomechantronics," a field of study devoted to
integrating human parts and gadgets to create *techno sapiens*. Japan built
cyberware and humanlike androids to produce a "startling victory over the
United States in the automotive and electronics wars."[138]

In achieving global economic success, the Japanese appeared nonhuman once again as reflected in U.S. popular images of unsmiling robotic
throngs of pedestrians crossing busy city streets in perfect unison. It is personified most in the cold sterility of the Japanese salarymen. Within performance reviews of international companies, American economists would
describe Japan using strange descriptors like the "fatherland of the unfeeling, robotic salaryman."[139] With newspapers and politicians naming Japan
as the United States' enemy number one, the myth of Japan as a capitalist
machine virtually "at war" with the West—supported by salaryman-sol-
diers who were carbon copies of one another—glossed over U.S. military
and foreign aid to Japan, thus enabling it to invest more into technological
research and development. This neocolonial relationship of mutual security
obscured how Japan was a recession-prone nation wobbling under an asset
bubble that would later burst. Despite these structural issues, Japan and
other emerging Asian economies like Singapore, Taiwan, and South Korea
collectively signified a "yellow future," one that threatened to "abolish the
authenticity and legitimacy of American culture."[140]

Within the United States, the changing public perception of Japanese
Americans as good citizen-subjects provoked academics and media pundits
to advance a stereotype of Asians as model minorities. Asian American
scholars have called this a myth as it does not reflect any sort of reality. In
the face of Asian America's economic stratification, Asians in the United
States are saddled with the totalization of them as apolitical robotic subjects
and hyperintelligent workaholics with family-oriented beings, a typology
that functioned to chastise "nonmodel" minorities like African Americans.
The model minority as portrayed by sociologists like William Peterson held
great public influence with its simplistic portrayal of Asian drones. In a famous published account of the Japanese American "success story," he described the American of Japanese descent as simultaneously peaceful and
warlike by studying engineering and other technological fields in a dogged
pursuit of success "conducted like a military campaign."[141] Even international
students from Japan were perceived as foreign aggressors. Like their coun-

terparts in Japan, Japanese American students appeared to have a secret insidious plan to conquer the United States, burrowing deep inside the country's bosom like alien viruses and computer bugs. This time, though, they were using test scores instead of kamikaze air raids to win in an arms race of another kind.

Conclusion

Japan's leading role in industrializing Asia fostered other machine myths as the Cold War heated up. A year after China fell to communism in 1959, the Association of United States Army published in its journal one military officer's counter to his leaders' opinion that the "human factor" is less important to develop than the military machine; a war machine cannot turn "soldiers into robots without revolutionary initiative."[142] He quoted from General Lin Piao, pointing to the revolutionary imperative of Maoism to transform China's rural population into an automaton army. Bowing to McCarthyism and its goal of exposing "commies," the U.S. Senate Committee on Foreign Relations pivoted against totalitarian regimes such as Maoist China, which was "destroying all human values" and turning people "into mere robots serviceable to the state."[143] For Taiwan's ambassador to the United States, these subjugated mainlanders acted like "faceless robots" for Beijing's booming war industries.[144] Despite his own imposition of martial law in Taiwan, President Chiang Kai-shek called the People's Republic of China a deplorable machine-state, converting human beings "into robots by a series of shameful indoctrination."[145] Recognizing China's threat to U.S. allies like Japan and Taiwan, the assistant secretary for Far Eastern affairs made similar comments about the grave threat of China, one where a "nation of robots [are] responsive only to that regime's dictates."[146]

This kind of language contributed to the expansion of the war machine myth beyond Japan to reflect a pan-Asian assemblage with many regional parts. In the 1962 Sino-Indian War between China and India, American reporters published these comments from an Indian senior officer: "You must remember that an Indian soldier is an individual. Give him the proper weapons and he can outfight the Chinese any time. The Chinese are automatons."[147] One can sense gradations within the treatment of Asians; those allied with the United States can be individualized and humanized, but those malefactors that stand in the way are automatonized and massified.

Alongside the economic threat of Japan and its industrial robots, the threat of "red" robots in Asia proved too great to shrug off in the decades following the end of World War II. Ferment over Asian war machines developed into mania about Japanese corporatism and later Chinese communism and the creeping ability of new postcolonial nations, such as Laos and

North Korea, in making Cold War automatons out of their people. Here, the war machine myth transitioned from modern-presenting Asian nations like Japan to developing ones. Throughout the Cold War, the U.S. government worried about cold-hearted "killing machines," such as the Khmer Rouge in Cambodia or the Viet Minh in North Vietnam. These international threats to humanity required a much bigger security apparatus. But when the U.S. military command pushed further into the Global South, other human machines came onto the scene—namely, female workers and prostitutes as fetishized "sex machines." The establishment of new U.S. military bases throughout Asia's Pacific Rim did not create more spaces of humanitarianism. Instead, these sites retrenched and advanced myths of the model machine.

3

Sex Machines

*Exploiting the Bionic Woman of Color for
the Cold War Economy*

In the 2017 satirical guidebook to sex tourism titled *Sex, Lies and Bar Girls: The ABC's of Bar Fines and Short Times*, James Bamber enumerates the exotic places where a customer can pick up an ASM ("Asian Sex Machine"). At these locales, one could meet a "yellow or brown Asian female heathen, ready and available for timed commercial sex in Southeast Asia, Korea, Japan, Taiwan, Okinawa, China, and anywhere else you can buy a ladies drink and a short time (see LBFM)."[1] These sex spots happen to be found in places with military bases established by the United States, eroticized contact zones that have cheap Northeast Asian (yellow) and Southeast Asian / Pacific Islander (brown) women available for sex, the latter derogatorily classified as "Little Brown Fucking Machine" (LBFM). Painted in broad strokes, women (of color) are assumed as hardwired and programmed to serve.[2] This chapter brings attention to the mythologized image of women in the Asian Pacific Rim as "sex machines" during a time of major geopolitical upheaval and global economic restructuring. It demonstrates how the "hot" figure of the ASM circulated in a Cold War economy that stretched across many jurisdictions, one riveted to hardening diplomatic tensions and solidifying thoughts of "Third World" women as robotic handmaidens of capitalist military expansion.

My present concern with the Cold War sex machine follows on the previous one, the Japanese war machine during World War II. It recognizes that Japanese women registered as an anomalous sort of automaton in postwar Japan and its economic machine. Accompanying and entertaining the postwar Japanese salaryman was the "hostess," whom one feminist writer describes as playing a particular role in consumer society:

> It would be easy to construct a blueprint for an ideal hostess. Indeed, if the Japanese economy ever needs a boost, Sony might contemplate putting them into mass production. The blueprint would provide for: a large pair of breasts, with which to comfort and delight the clients; one dexterous, well-manicured hand for pouring their drinks, lighting their cigarettes and popping forkfuls of food into their mouths; a concealed tape-recording of cheerful laughter, to sustain the illusion that the girls themselves are having a good time. . . . The hostess—the computerized playmate—may conceivably be an illustration of the fact that Japan is just the same as everywhere else, only more so; perhaps she is indeed the universal male notion of the perfect woman.[3]

As the international blueprint for female comfort and entertainment, the computerized hostess appears to customers to always have a "good time." Her enhanced breasts and dexterous hands are well-made body parts that offer both sex and other kinds of service. As an updated version of the geisha stereotype, the mechanical hostess registers as a sexist illusion: the perfect woman created for the pleasure of men and the companies for which they work.

Alongside Japan's globalized corporate culture, the expansive machinery of American warfare answered the riddle of how to mass produce such perfect doting women. Warmongering, on such a big scale as never before seen, established a military-supported sex/service industry that pushed the myth of the Asian woman as having an inexhaustible body. This myth is locally embodied, whether in the figure of the military prostitute or the factory worker. One cannot discuss Cold War history without touching upon gender/sex themes, where robotic soldiers find their fictive counterpart in bionic women of color who serve as functionaries of men. The myth of the sex machine induces critical thinking about other dualisms like human/automaton, woman/man, and slave/worker. Insofar as the sex machine is posed as a kind of labor machine, this figure helps expand upon prior discussion of how workers are used to fuel military industries.

This chapter delves into the patriarchal model (the prostitute / factory worker) of the machine. What is being modeled (sex machine) depends on what the machine is modeled upon—the myth that Asian women are easily dominated by men and thus serviceable for growing military economies. The examples brought up allow us to think of imperialism relationally and how the model machine myth ties to empire building across borders. First,

I address Japan's enslavement of women as a wartime "renovation" of sex slavery, which became in part a model for the subsequent U.S. Cold War myth of the Asian sex machine. I then delve into Hollywood's creation myth of Asian women as sexy robots with hearts of gold. From this section, my analysis then transitions to Southeast Asia to discuss "Little Brown Fucking Machines," and this concern ends with commentary on female factory workers in low-cost market economies.

Using what I call the sex machine myth as a guide for analysis, I zoom into the "larger picture of the complicated histories and the many other bodies that have determined the meeting of woman with machinery."[4] The myth of Oriental sexual prowess has been around for a long time, ever since European travelers like Marco Polo made up licentious tall tales of foreign "Oriental" women versed in decadence as matter of their promiscuous cultural upbringing. But the reformatting of erotic natives into sex machines happened precipitously after World War II, when the United States began to gain a more permanent military presence in Asia and pushed forward a sex trade to match its lust for extraterritoriality.

In this heated geopolitical context, sexual automatons became central to economic ventures and gender projects propelled by large-scale military ventures, simultaneously prized as meek laboring bodies and pliable love toys in a new international system where they were designated as "machines in the service of that uncontrollable male lust for sex and power."[5] The global circumnavigation of the sex machine myth partially undercuts claims to human rights and women's rights, construing certain subjects as not real people but as living dolls. But as we shall see, there is still room for resistance by so-called dolls.

Manufacturing and Militarizing the "Living Doll"

Men have always imagined themselves building their own sex machine, but this male fantasy project of "giving life" to female automatons always carried subversive potential as the woman robot performs, malfunctions, and goes awry in ways that work against her vilification as whore and monster.[6] The mechanistic male framing of female desire leaves out much in terms of women's political agency, especially when the feminine automaton has become a well-hashed figure in science fiction stories in which men build customized sexual companions since they find "real women" unsatisfactory.[7] The modern myth of the machine-woman hearkens back to Greek mythology, but the more modern narrative of female invention involves male manipulation aligned with the cold science and moral insouciance of industrial capitalism. In the eighteenth and nineteenth centuries, Minsoo Kang says, rather than emanating from pure magic or divine intervention, the building of the sex machine took on supernatural qualities that reflected a world affronted with all sorts of "technology."

The fashioning of Asian women and girls into sexual technology in the twentieth century found roots in European obsession with all things Oriental. Early fascination with "foreign" automata turned on the pleasure of discovering, watching, and playing with new wondrous toys—human and otherwise. This obsession with small exotic toys matched the fixation with small Asian corporalities with respect to "their exotic features, the color of their complexions, their enigmatic smiles, their indolent gestures, and sensual poses."[8] That bodily fetishism hinged centrally on foreign men's long desire to extend control over women's bodies. As a result, Asian women ceased to be flesh-and-blood humans, acting instead as a prosthetic and decorative piece for the built world of powerful white men. As literary theorist Anne Cheng tells us, "Asian femininity has always been prosthetic. The dream of the yellow woman subsumes a dream about the inorganic . . . embroiled with the inhuman well before the threat of the modern machine."[9] "Orientalism as ornamentalism" conjured an exotic "toy-world."[10]

Ornamentalization of Asian women took a bigger turn with a greater U.S.-Japan cultural exchange of friendship dolls, beginning in the nineteenth century. The dolls signified the diminutiveness of the Japanese island and its people, who were perceived as "living dolls" by the taller Americans that encountered them.[11] After Japan turned on the United States during World War II, Americans soon were revolted by and averse to those quaint little toy people in Japan. The men took on the ugly facade of war machines, but Japanese women presented a nonthreatening sexual commodity to be bought or sold; and this explains why, even during and after the war, Americans remained obsessed with Japan's doll-like women.

The dollification of Asian women as life-sized playthings took precedence in commercial public spaces as Japan morphed into a consumer hub. Young women were hired to greet and bow at department store customers; they were even trained by company robots to bow at the right angle, while speaking in a small squeaking voice. One Japanese female interpreter looked askance at these "unbaked automatons" and thought to herself, "These girls are trained to be robots. With the elevator girls, you don't see a person but a doll."[12] Anthropologist Laura Miller described how working women, dressed in similar manner with assigned greeters, managed to adopt a veil for the public in which being "denigrated as doll-like or robot-like becomes instead a suit of armor."[13] This veil of polite deference and quiet fortitude was a psychological coping mechanism in Japan's tight labor market, one dominated by men, with low female integration.

Asian women reduced to serving automatons updated the geisha stereotype. The popular motif of Asian woman as a toy servant traces back to the early exchanges in robotic automata, during the seventeenth and eighteen centuries, when Jesuit missionaries gifted to the Japanese emperor tea-carrier figurines that resembled geishas. Under the Western male gaze, Japanese geishas began to be regarded as prostitutes, though the term refers to an artful professional entertainer.[14] In the postfeudal context, when the sex trade was made official and more widely available in Japan, the geisha was sometimes thought interchangeable with the indentured sex worker (*yujo*), but women of all classes were "treated as mere objects, not as human beings or persons with human dignity."[15] The good dutiful wife was an asexual birthing machine and the geisha/prostitute served as "tools of pleasure for men."[16]

Such treatment of women never abated after Japan's military defeat and the U.S. reformed Japanese civil society. While living in U.S.-occupied Japan, American writer Lucy Herndon Crockette commented on the country's desperation to hold onto geisha traditions, "which for centuries have existed solely [to treat women] as decorative automatons to delight the male."[17] She observed how this patriarchal institution cracked beneath the Allied forces and their attempts to shape Japan into a modern constitutional democracy that respects women's rights. The United States' liberalizing influence would ironically involve easier access for American men to local women.

Considerations of Asian women as a sex machine found greater mutation and distinction after World War II. The prior treatment of Korean women as sex machines at the hands of Japanese soldiers bled into their objectification as such for American GIs in the Korean War. Women's romantic or conjugal relations with U.S. military servicemen appeared to legitimate the former adulation of Asian women as living dolls.[18] With the rapid development of South Korea's economy under U.S. foreign aid and Japanese-style management, the sexy machine founds its analog in the "cute" living doll, who came to sharply define the statuesque childlike look that characterizes contemporary Korean (and Japanese) beauty culture. Doll culture attenuated the socioeconomic mobility of South Korean women within modified Asian patriarchal orders that both put little value on female work. Customization of women's bodies was subverted by professional women, who disliked their zoomorphic transformation into inanimate things. Professional Asian women at turns voiced their opposition to sex machine stereotypes by confounding the boundaries between being an "anthropomorphic artifact and the biological human."[19] This contest took physical form, such as adopting an androgynous or "plastic" style of beauty that flummoxed gender boundaries as well as the human-object continuum. Their challenges were directed against the industrial "masculinization" of the female workforce and the concomitant pressure for them to always be "dolled-up" for men. As South Korea got wealthier, it tolerated the biggest gender pay gap of any developed nation, owing in part to the economic subordination of women.

While buttressing Japan's and South Korea's economies as a bulwark against communism in Asia, the United States pushed further into other parts of the continent due to its divine sense as a liberator protecting the "developing" world from the "red menace." Its deep military-economic investments abroad inspired the production of urban myths like the sex machine, which treated Asian women as commodities to be traded like fungible goods within a global imperium of exchange. It is important here to note that the modern sex machine myth did not begin with the Cold War. In his travels to "the Oriental," the early nineteenth-century French writer Gustave Flaubert met a famous Egyptian dancer and courtesan, who ended up being the prototype of "learned" sensuality and "mindless coarseness" in the novelist's work.[20] After sleeping with the woman, he wrote to a friend and described her as "no more than a machine: she makes no distinction between one man and another."[21] The Asian woman under the male colonial gaze was many things, but she was "at once sexual enchantress, productive machine, and racial inferior."[22] She stood for an inferior that obeys, an enchantress that seduces, and a machine that produces for the master.

The mechanical-sexual oppression of Asian women confounded Western feminists who did not know what to do with their more "oppressed" counterparts. Wealthy Scottish women like Constance Frederica Gordon-Cumming wandered around the world sightseeing, and when the globe-trotter reached China, she could not help but comment on the strange gender customs there. In Canton, she encountered women with crushed, bounded feet, bowing and servicing men at any given time. Without a cultural interpreter, she could only make a rough impression of these "ladies [that] stood utterly irresponsive, like mute automatons."[23] In the 1907 book *Women in All Ages and in All Countries: Oriental Women*, professor Edward Pollard considered the social status of women as an "index of civilization." He compared the deified status of women in Semitic myths and Christian scripture to the "loose morals" and cruelty of Hindu and Muslim societies. More cosmopolitan feminists, such as Jane Addams, however, felt women of Asia should do away with copying the highly mechanized lifestyle of the United States in favor of a more "personal" one, an alternate view premised on the belief that the "entire Pacific" was based on a more "basic culture." For Addams, "eastern civilization held within it the capacity to lead world civilization into a more human and humane" world because it was closer to nature.[24]

Even for white feminists like Addams, Asia's atavism and the mechanizing Asian female formed the symbolic grounds for articulating and humanizing an "ultimately Western, global future."[25]

Notions of Asian women's subservience fed into the U.S. Cold War orientation toward Asia as an alterable space for molding and modeling. As a byproduct of the Cold War, the sex machine myth set the pretext for discovering the mechanisms behind what Asian American studies scholar Fiona Ngo calls "militarized Orientalisms."[26] Mammoth demands for "sex" work generated under military operations found remediation through the Asiatic woman able to assemble manufacturing parts and engage in sex endlessly. Machine myths of a sexual nature displaced the real focus on militarized misogyny and the myth of invincible American manhood, where an ordinary man recruited into the world's mightiest army could aspire to be a globe-trotting stud with "an inexhaustible penis," roaming around the world as a "sex machine who could have sex whenever and where he wants, and with whomever he wishes."[27] This myth of military manhood gave men free license to act out carnally, while the sex machine myth would lead us to believe Asian women ravenously throw themselves at these men's feet. The female sex machine is rendered as the automaton with less agency, under the gendered frames of war and "intimate empire."[28]

Within the microphysics of war, women's "bionic" bodies—anatomies enhanced with artificial parts or appendages—serve as the repository or vessel for channeling sexual technologies of conquest. As Asian studies scholar Carol Fisher Sorgenfrei writes, "Female sexuality, once the mythic heart of Japanese national identity, was officially (if not privately) submerged. . . . Military prostitutes were transformed to faceless sex machines, enslaved and conscripted as 'comfort women' whose function was not to provide pleasure or fantasy, but to aid the war effort by permitting the release of physical tension."[29] Under Japanese wartime occupations of Asian nations, close to a quarter of a million women throughout Asia were kidnapped and forced to satisfy the voracious appetites of Japanese soldiers.[30] The personal effects of automated "sex" induced on a mass scale was evidence by one former Korean comfort woman recounting her nightmarish ordeal in serving twenty to thirty men per day in an assembly line: "Can you imagine what it was like that you are lying there and serving so many soldiers day and night, making me a sex machine, and I grew up in the society where chastity is more precious than the life itself? Can you imagine it? . . . And that pain came to me like electricity."[31]

Instead of a gynoid with no mind or voice, as we commonly find in sexist science fiction, what we find here is a woman able to speak her mind and clearly recall the trauma of rape. Her painful memories of sexual violence flash like a shocking voltage in a psychic and bodily return of the repressed.

Another Korean woman echoed this statement: "When they were on top of us, shamelessly exploding like animals, we were simply imprisoned sex machines."[32] It is noteworthy that the men are spoken of as sex-crazed animals, and women are positioned as captive sex machines, a distinction that disturbs the animal-machine connection. Framed in this way, the sex machine myth seemed more than a simple stereotype of anodyne bionic women; it was a semantic contested space (and rhetorical device) for addressing postwar memory and ethics. The speakers' words testified to the fact that there was more going on than the pure reduction of women to fetishized automata. Women's personal fight for recognition as something other than sex machines resonates with first-person accounts of South Korean female factory union workers after the war, when South Korea's hyperindustrialization was yoked to militarized nationalism. One woman reported having "no dignity, no identity. I was treated as though I were not human at all, but a 'thing.' There was no difference between me as a person and the sewing machine that I was attached to."[33] The stock and trade of women workers as attached parts of the military state are exposed by harrowing personal stories of how one is rent of humanness.

All these examples prove that war is as much about storytelling and mythmaking as it is about physical combat or political economy. They are crucial to decoding the American response to Soviets building an army of citizen-soldiers perceived as "mechanized rather than made of flesh and blood."[34] The United States' main task was "no longer just to defend freedom against communism but to defend humanity and life itself."[35] Since the Cold War was not only a time of calculated geostrategizing but also a watershed moment for new imperial fantasy production, Asian women took on the mythic appearance of sex machines precisely because they were fully enveloped within the ambit of governmental designs to stratify occupation and "join sexuality and labor in one unconscious, rhythmic automatism."[36] While the Japanese government continues to this day to deny its role in sexual slavery, its wartime activities provided the beachhead for an expanding global sex trade later picked up by the United States, which utilized a conquered Japan as an industrial base for penetrating the "virgin" markets of Asia.[37]

The sex machine myth rose to prominence through the speedy transformation of this vital strategic region and its women into targets of geopolitical capitalist interest. While the myth of the prodigious Asian woman manifests differently in various locales, it crops up as a transnational phenomenon through the "mass production of prostitutes."[38] It is within this dense translocal setting that the Asian female sex machine comes into sight as someone that needs to be liberated by the American (hu)man. But as it turned out, this sexy robot was one who could not be toyed with.

Cold War Productions and Hollywood's Sexy Robots

The Cold War witnessed the budding powers of the Hollywood motion picture industry as a driving force in socializing movie watchers into sex machine myths. More than a matter of pure entertainment, American cinema glorified mythical stories about cowboys and warriors (and their rescued damsels), obscuring the actual history and volatility of modern warfare, which "respects neither the prerogatives of gender nor the integrity of myth."[39] Films routinely depicted Asian women as automatic participants in their own sexual exploitation, though audiences were left to interpret the narrative. In films like the 1960 drama *The World of Suzie Wong*, a white expat Robert Lomax from the United States has relocated to Hong Kong for a year to work. While living there, he falls for Mee Ling, a formerly high-class woman who turns out to be a prostitute and the stuff of legend. The popular film cemented and solidified the perception of Asian prostitution and made Chinese women like Suzie into "dispensable playthings with a backward culture."[40] Forced into sex work as a child but wanting to escape, Suzie Wong's indentured labor reiterates the Orientalist script of a young Asian woman needing an older foreign man to save her and use her as a blank canvas on which to draw his desires (the male protagonist is a painter). The other prostitutes in this movie are depicted as "cute, giggling, dancing sex machines with hearts of gold."[41]

For writer Jessica Hagedorn, the main character, like Suzie, is reduced to "a sex machine, unfettered by any domestic inclination" and motivated only by the "mechanical sex act."[42] The character of Robert is depicted as all too human while Suzie Wong becomes relegated to playing the part of the "object-*to-be*-looked-at," a female thing in waiting for male direction to breathe "life" into, like an automaton.[43] In subsequent interviews, Nancy Kwan, the actress who played Suzie Wong, disregarded the accusation she was perpetuating sexual stereotypes by saying that she played the role as she wanted it. Viewed another way, the meaning of the title, *The World of Suzie Wong*, can slip from signaling an insulated harem to indicating a world that belongs to Wong. It is her name in the spotlight, not the man's. As a kind of global icon, Suzie and her body become a "moving technology capable of unlocking totalizing systems."[44]

At the same time, we must contend with the overwrought cliché about Asian women, which gathered pace. In the heyday of the Cold War, the newly invented labels of "Yankee whore," "war brides," "bar girls," or "foreign 'girl-friends'" shifted the portrayal of Asian women as pure lotus blossoms toward puerile nymphomaniacs that were "childlike, submissive, silent, and eager for sex."[45] Rather than interpret these penned accounts by soldiers and war observers simply as the testament of men's (wish for) mastery over the other sex, we can discover how they carry mutinous potential. It is prudent to never regard women as entirely denigrated bodies or "objects" of war, since they can refuse to accede to being made into things.

At best, the sex machine trope afforded a way of interpreting a range of subversive desires and acts. Considering the film's lack of explanation on the military context behind local prostitution (Hong Kong, a neutral zone, was an early stopover for U.S. troops heading to Vietnam), the audience must work to decipher the power dynamics of sex work. But as evidenced in the film, the main character engages in her own war games and battle of the sexes by displaying a strong willfulness, frustrating her boyfriend's attempts to possess and get to know her. If Suzie Wong is a sex machine hypothetically, she is not one easily acquired or subdued by anyone. By turns and degrees, this "machine" passionately plays with the stiff, hapless (hu)man in the film.

Whereas *Suzie Wong*, on its face, reduced Chinese women to tempestuous robots with the capacity to love, Hollywood films depicted Vietnamese women as sexbots without any emotions. The cult classic *Full Metal Jacket* (1987, dir. Stanley Kubrick) has been immortalized by way of one scene in which an unnamed sex worker propositions two U.S. soldiers on the street. She asks, "You got girlfriend Vietnam?" To which one replies, "Not just this minute." The prostitute then repeats in rapid succession these catchy lines: "Me so horny," "Me sucky sucky," and "Me love you long time," sauntering before the men with alacrity. These coarse phrases became part of American popular culture as sexual idioms targeted toward all Asian women, suggesting that they are all potential "hookers." In this now infamous scene, the promise of "long time" does not denote the timeless devotion of a Japanese geisha in Puccini's famous opera *Madame Butterfly*, waiting eternally for her distant Western male consort. The Vietnamese prostitute's repetitious come-ons (and the customer's use of "minute" to convey "time") bloviate a scripted form of sexualized economic exchange. This address by a woman of color appears not as a moment of women's liberation and makes her stand apart from her white American counterparts (a disjuncture made implicit with the U.S. feminist anthem "These Boots Are Made for Walking" playing in the scene's background).

Full Metal Jacket popularized the stereotype of a sex machine that has no name or story. It rendered Vietnamese women as automatons, springing into action at any given moment, spouting lines like a broken record.[46] Male soldiers are depicted with the elastic volition of sexual choice that bumps up against "the erotic force of the myth of Asian femininity."[47] The Vietnamese female cyborg is afforded full erotic revelation by showing "*too much body— too much sex, too much skin, too much history.*"[48] One-dimensional dialogue can obfuscate the sexual agency of women, and so the audience must take pains to consider a walking stereotype that aimed to qualify myths of female sexual prowess. Beyond the cinematic male gaze and a flesh market induced by heavy U.S. military presence in Asia, we have the actual voice of the "sex machine." Papillon Soo, the actor who played the prostitute, put a sex-positive spin on her notorious role, exclaiming that work on the film "was like a 24-hour orgasm."[49] Even if the film tried to deny pleasure for her as an inarticulate, fulsome sex object, Soo's sustaining of a long-lasting orgasm provides an alternate interpretation of racial hypersexuality by centering the powerful mechanism of female self-gratification. Soo acts as a self-fulfilled agent of desire who can please herself anytime and address her audience forthright over a mechanical beat (Soo released her own ribald rap song poking fun at her infamous film lines). As literary scholar Amy Tang writes, "Rather than approaching repetition as a way to produce conclusive narratives of triumph or defeat, resistance or victimization, we might see it as reflecting the circumscribed sphere of action made available."[50]

Beyond displays of female self-empowerment, sex as a domain of power remained murky terrain, especially when the Asian female sex machine met the Black male sex machine. Later in *Full Metal Jacket*, another Vietnamese sex worker rejects an African American customer saying, "No boom boom with soul brother . . . Black man too beaucoup," or too "big," referencing the myth of the big black penis (the prostitute finally agrees to take the Black customer once he flashes his penis to her and proves the myth wrong). Though the film takes place in Vietnam, these minor lines of dialogue are the only ones given to characters of color, reducing them to sexual beings different than the white feminist protagonist of the late 1970s U.S. television show *The Bionic Woman*, which popularized the term *fembot*. The myth of virile and sexually potent African American men reiterated the tropes of Black hypersexuality in ways that intersected, if not overlapped, with images of the bionic Asian sex machine. Artists like James Brown (whose musical album *Sex Machine* filled American airwaves during the war) and Papillon Soo have adapted and appropriated the seductive mirage of the sex machine on their own terms.[51]

With a critical bent, Kubrick's gritty film tried hard to obviate the military's modus operandi of turning soldiers into "a working cog in a well-oiled machine" whose self is enveloped by a "full metal jacket."[52] In basic training, Private Joker quips, "The Marine Corps does not want robots. The Marine Corps wants killers. The Marine Corps wants to build indestructible men, men without fear."[53] That American male war machine without fear ultimately met its match in the fearsome Asian female sex machine. Despite exposing the insanity of war, *Full Metal Jacket* glorified masculine violence toward women.[54] Produced a decade after the Vietnam War, *Full Metal Jack-*

et communicated the crisis of Anglo-American masculinity as it followed white male soldiers as the main protagonists despite their foibles, while Vietnamese women were reduced to dehumanized machines with less than one minute of speaking dialogue.

The climactic scene involves the male protagonists cornering a sniper that has downed so many of their brothers. The killer turns out to be a lone woman and the men riddle her slim body with a hail of bullets in a phallic gesture of male homosocial bonding. Once fallen, the woman blankly verbalizes in robotic fashion, "Shoot me . . . shoot me . . . shoot me." With a body strapped with munitions, this single-woman army faces off against foot soldiers of the U.S. military and could be considered a sort of cyborg due to her ethnicity. To quote from Mimi Thi Nguyen, "She is a cyborg *because* she is Vietnamese."[55] With the demise of this cyborg assassin, the hero myth of the American GI is affirmed as "mythologies of murderous robots like the mythologies of violent and oversexed slaves are put in the imaginations of the populace to stabilize that which has never been stable, humanity."[56]

Despite the reality of female militants, U.S. servicemen rarely visualized Vietnamese women in uniform and armed with weapons. Most political cartoons about the war at the time depicted women in provocative though traditional attire. Threat of emasculation/death by a female sniper was subdued by love for the brown woman's sexual technology. With enhanced bionic bodies that concealed small grenades, these weaponized women needed to be pacified and probed. In a recreational book written for soldiers called *Sorry 'Bout That!* (1966), the sex machine qua war machine was fully revealed after being stripped by soldiers as shown in this limerick: "A bar girl wore 38 D's / Rather much for a Vietnamese / So they searched her, with pleasure / And discovered this treasure / One grenade, one plastique, two punjis."[57] The accompanying drawing only shows the side profile of a woman's chest, which is enlarged due to her hidden weapons.

As an "impossible" subject of war, the VSW (or Vietnamese Sniper Woman) and her "military equipment seemed un-representable as anything other than a tool for/of white male sexual fantasy."[58] That sexual fantasy operated on more than an interpersonal level, as it cropped up in many other realms.

The LBFM Myth in Southeast Asia

In extralegal proxy wars where military prostitution is tolerated and rape can be considered "standard operating procedure," local women's treatment as sex machines inserted the dispensation of "human rights" on an international scene governed by Cold War military logics.[59] Modern war involves "the controlled insertion of bodies into the machinery of production and the adjustment of the phenomena of population to economic processes."[60] With sexuality as a technology, we can decipher the meteoric spurt of the military-industrial-sexual complex, which included the United States taking control of Japan's military-run brothels. By 1938, the United States ran fourteen military bases outside its continental borders, but this grew to thirty thousand installations in approximately one hundred countries, consolidated into seven hundred bases abroad with countless sex camps around those bases.[61] By contrast, the USSR established a few dozen installations based in strategic locations. After the collapse of the Soviet Union and the pullout of the Americans from Vietnam, there continued a craving for sex machines that never abated.

The beginnings of the global sexual economy can be traced to large-scale military enterprises during the Cold War.[62] During that war, the myth of the sex machine morphed into something even worse under the establishment of red light districts around U.S. military bases throughout Southeast Asia, outposts moonlighting as R&R (rest and recreation/recuperation) zones. Modeled after Japanese "comfort stations," these recreational zones were set up by the U.S. government in places like Thailand for weary troops fighting throughout Indochina.[63] These extracurricular zones of "nonmilitary-related" sexual activity informed the growing perception of Southeast Asian women as cheap serviceable objects able to match the libidinal demands of military tourism and its economies of desire. As film scholar Elena Tajima Creef captures it, low-income women in these places are paid to entertain camera-shooting tourists, "perform[ing] onstage like sexual automatons. . . . [And their] body technologies include the ability to shoot bananas, ping pong balls, and entire bottles of Coca Cola out of their vaginas."[64]

Over time, the sex machine myth waxed and waned only to lead into the coarser myth of the "Little Brown Fucking Machine" (LBFM). Feminist scholar Chung Hyun Kyung explains why the fucking machine framework emerged to dominate the lives of Asian women: "Why Are We a *Fucking Machine*? We became a *fucking machine* because we never have been a subject for the soldiers, capitalists, and colonialists. We have been made a machine for them."[65] She elaborates, "When Western men made the whole earth into a battlefield and became brutally violent warriors as hunters of the world, they began to mechanize the whole world, including us. And people who lose subjectivity (the right to act as subjects) become mechanized."[66] Kyung opines how the social subjugation of women acts as an extension of men's technological domination and how Southeast Asian women bear the brunt:

> Subjugated women were not used to symbolize the land figuratively, they were literally treated as part of nature—as beasts and cattle.

Although white women have been regarded symbolically and philosophically as close to nature, in modern times they have never been thought to be other than human. . . . During the Second World War, as many as two hundred thousand Korean, Chinese, and other Southeast Asian women were drafted or kidnapped for sexual servicing of Japanese soldiers throughout the Asian Pacific region. . . . Many yellow women are reduced to sex machines in the sex industry, which turns Southeast Asia into the "brothel of the world."[67]

Kyung rails against the animal-like nature attributed to forced sex workers, reflecting on the collective struggle among them to "communicate with one another" and voice their anticolonial struggle for liberation. While Kyung lumps all East Asian women together as "yellow," many Southeast Asian women are perceived as "brown," with all the semantic meanings of poverty that color carries with it in hegemonic racial discourses. Not all blame can be put on white men, as the scholar explains, "Asian men objectify. . . . making Asian women into the prostitutes of the world. . . . We Asian women are not robots Asian men switch on and off according to their convenience. We are persons of integrity."[68]

Theologian Pui-Lan Kwok blamed the Japanese military's conscription of Asian women into prostitution for the sex machine myth's popularity. Kwok also recognized that the United States expanded this process by contributing to economic poverty as a byproduct of warmongering, something that induced thousands of Asian women into sex work. While South Korea developed into a major economic power, Southeast Asia remains regarded as full of pauperized "developing countries." The myth of southern Asian women as an inferior fucking machine thus took root in the brutalities of "savage developmentalism."[69] Filmmaker Celine Shimizu comments on the Vietnam War–era designation of "little brown fucking machines powered by rice," tying the phrase "powered by rice" to the (under)development of nations like Vietnam, Cambodia, Malaysia, and the Philippines: "Her insatiability, an objectified assignation linked to her colonial subjection, constructs her as non-discerning sexual performer. In the deployment of this description, the women love fucking so much they exhibit an energetic and excessive sexual drive that is machine-like."[70] A sexual empire of myth was built on the economic shellshock of war.

Sometime after World War II, U.S. servicemen and sailors began wearing offensive T-shirts with the letters "LBSM," meaning "Little Brown Sex Machine."[71] These initials soon appeared in public places throughout Japan, embossed on posters and plastered as graffiti on buildings, starting in Okinawa, a colony of Japan that harbors its major American military base. Okinawans are the original peoples of the land upon which the base is built, and historically they are viewed as brown inferiors to the "whiter" Japanese. But the brown referenced here also meant the Filipina and Thai women who constituted most of the prostitutes brought to Okinawa.[72] Brown also meant the Aboriginal women trafficked into prostitution in Taiwan and other places.

Around the 1970s and 1980s, the term spread and morphed into the slogan "Little Brown Fucking Machines Powered by Rice," which popped up on other U.S. military bases, particularly in Olongapo, Philippines. The slogan distinguished between Japanese women and other Asian women. The former were desired as genuflecting sex machines with the capacity to love, while the latter existed as demeaned farming machines needing nothing more than rice to live. Where much consumer technology was made or sold at the time from Japan, most rice exports in the world began to be shipped from Southeast Asia's agricultural fields. The operative term "little" not only referred to the diminution of Southeast Asian women's bodies but also relayed the lesser value of low-income tropical countries in the Global South. Their brownness qualified them as uncivilized types, whose Asian machinery did not compare to the Asian mystique of their fairer counterparts in the north. The impressions of one foreigner's "colored" perception of Indonesian women at a bar are revealing in their racialized class dimensions: "A host of girls . . . ranging in color from toffee brown to a balsa wood beige. Regardless of skin tone, Bryn was dismissive of them, referring to them all as LBFMs—Little Brown Fucking Machines. They were rent girls . . . to be taken home and banged silly."[73] The phrase "banged silly" qualifies the woman as cheap items to abuse. The LBFM myth has nested itself in the "desiring machine" of neocolonial exploitation by privileged tourists and superpowers.[74]

To avoid equating imperialisms in such a way as to flatten important differences, I draw on the work of feminists who have critiqued American and Japanese imperialisms. Some sources have found that Asian women—Korean, Chinese, and Filipina—used by the Japanese imperial army were in turn used by U.S. occupation troops after Japan's defeat in World War II. With Japanese businessmen leading the way, the booming male service market went beyond prostitution to include massage parlors, dance entertainment, and the like. This booming erotic service market would later encompass "robot doll brothels," which began popping up in Japan, Korea, and Hong Kong for customers to have sex with actual robots.

The visualization of Asian women as half human and half machine hid the work of nations allied with the United States and seeking favor with Japan. Bound up to the girdle of complicit nationalisms, sex machines enabled diplomatic "sex among allies," who worked as "partners of prostitution."[75] Under the influence of the United States' liberal empire and Japan's economic sub-empire, South Korea's government "sold" Korean prostitutes as "personal ambassadors" to the world. Through Visiting Forces Agreements (VFA), governments like the Republic of Korea and Thailand agreed with the United States to set up R&R zones. These government-to-government pacts were criticized by international feminists. The stereotype of not-so-human subjects without human rights was contested also from within. A U.S. Army chaplain, horrified by what he saw on the bases, spoke of how his compatriots would fall for "tall tales" of glamorous Thai and Korean women. He admonished the men's lust and said the combination of racism and sexism would make the women "property, things, slaves . . . things to be thrown away."[76] As war spoilage, the female property/thing/slave was tossed aside.

While feminist media scholars focus on the iconography of sex machines in pornography, my historical analysis of the machine extends this critique into the crucible of war. As the engine for the global arms race, the war economy generated a new array of security defense weapons that resulted in such commonly used consumer products as GPS satellites, space travel, bar codes, plastics, the internet, and computers, all of which came out of the broader development of biological weapons, cruise missiles, and electronic reconnaissance.[77] This "technologization of life" under the pall of nuclear destruction and desiccation turned every facet of life on its head. With oil supplies in crisis due to geopolitical tempests in the Persian Gulf, humanoid machines in overpopulated East Asia were the only truly renewable "natural resource" to exploit. Differentiated spaces of control for "machine sovereignty" took shape in Southeast Asia, the locus of major techno-cultural wars.

As much a high-tech war involving intelligent machines as one involving guerrilla battles fought in the thick jungles, the Vietnam War was one installment in a series of high-tech proxy wars. The United States legitimated its machine-style warfare by mapping enemy territory as "inhuman geographies [that] are necessary for the continued affirmation of Euro-American values and humanitarian values."[78] International studies scholar Gordon Lee writes, "In the eyes of the United States military, it didn't matter if you were Vietnamese or Chinese, Cambodian or Laotian, you were a 'gook,' and therefore sub-human."[79] This perception is spoofed by a line from a Marine colonel in *Full Metal Jacket*, when he says the Vietnamese are merely targets to shoot for fun. This thought was reproduced by U.S. generals in real-life.[80]

Casting Asian life as "cheap" and predisposed to the condition of death allowed for all kinds of atrocities and massacres. Alongside F-4 fighter bombers, new statistical computer models devised by corporations like IBM through radar and remote consoles constructed enemy combatants as graphic representation. Visualizing them as pixilated data points on a computer screen, one military programmer observed: "The people of villages have gone from being 'gooks' . . . to being grid-coordinates, blips on scan screens. . . . The machine functions. The radar blip disappears. No village is destroyed. No humans die. For none existed."[81] While the U.S. military sought to change "hearts and minds" in Southeast Asia, the occupying force would not always attribute human organs to the local people. This virtualization and vanishing of bodies under the full throttle of the American war machine corroborates the hidden wish for a "thing-oriented" society, where "machines and computers, profit motives and property rights are considered more important than people."[82]

Previous historical examples of Asians as automatons distinguished different national/ethnic types of machines (the Chinese as labor machines and Japanese as war machines). But given the Cold War discourse about the threat of communism throughout all of Asia, a panoply of other groups fell under the umbrage of the model machine myth. Hence, the machinic labor of Vietnamese, Thai, and Korean women might refer historically to the labor machine archetype of Chinese coolies as its origins (even though Asian women were mostly thought of as sexual automatons).

In a sense, Asian sex machines are also war machines since they are both part of the military apparatus. The labor power of Asian female machines revved up economies and military presence in almost every corner of the world. A mighty empire like the United States was no longer fighting an immigrant menace or warring with another empire but engaged in a furtive assault on women of color. This war performs a "magic trick," turning an "open secret" like military prostitution into the myth of the LBFM. Such a crude sexual myth carries historic significance regarding women of color's treatment in the United States. As literary critic Hortense Spillers indicates, enslaved Black women did not have the same legal rights or recourse to bodily autonomy as white women as rape "victims" or domestic "labor," since they were simply human property. This framing ensures "the principal point of passage between the human and the non-human world . . . as the route by which the dominant male decided the distinction between humanity and 'other.'"[83] In the humanitarian discourse on sex trafficking and "modern sex slavery" in Asia, we can see how the human/Other axis "conjured up during slavery is still with us today."[84] Forms of slavery are not easily identified given the sexy allure of Asian women as the ultimate cyborgs.

Women's Bodies as the Engine of Globalization

Specialized systems of military control loop back into gendered techniques for labor management. In the global economy, sex does not only mean copulation or libidinal acts but the categorization of females as a "sex" quite apart from men in all spheres of life. The myth of the sex machine not only denotes prostitution but designates *sex-specific* forms of labor, such as microchip assembly or garment piecework, predicated on the myth that women are just better at these types of jobs. In the throes of the Cold War, the United States had a hand in the exploitation of Asian women, the racialized feminization of labor and the uneven development between countries that exploits poor women of color as an "accumulation strategy" of transnational capital.[85] According to political scientist Thu-Huong Nguyen-Vo, the crooked path of Vietnam's modernization first under the aegis of American anticommunism and later under globalization spurred a silent war on local women, turning them into the "collateral damage" of military-assisted market ventures.[86] The long march of militarism abetted the implacable advance of global capitalism and its lust for labor by "locating new sources of cheap labor to become the new producers of surplus value."[87] Surplus value turned on the merits of laborers' use value as machines with particular sex traits.

Globalization itself can be viewed as a phallocentric "sex machine" that hardens women's bodies to be durable for work, while increasing service demands for feminine "soft skills."[88] Asian women, along with other women of color, enter the high-tech industry as data-making human "computers" or "wetware," as they are referred to by their superiors, since they provide the biological material needed for operating the men's "hardware." In this location, women are "reduced to machine components whose claim upon an essential personhood is reduced to their sexuality; that is, their otherness to the electronic machine lies in their sexual function."[89] This sexual function is not always recognizable given the technical facet of their work. Such sex-determined digital work does not mean only women handling metal objects like microchips, since it also applies to the garment industry as evidenced by a 1971 American handbook on needlework and crafts: "In speaking of some far eastern workers one feels like saying 'rule of eye.' These embroiders are such by inheritance. No improvements are introduced among their tools—they themselves are human machines."[90] In this handbook, the knitting work of Asian men became evaluated as superior and more human derived than those performed by Asian women, given the latter's mechanical anatomy and work in a gendered economy of things.

In the 1970s, the falling rate of profit for commodities in many developed nations spurred the outsourcing of manufacturing, thus leading to the a "high-tech underclass," designed to finish putting touches on textiles, semiconductors, and microtechnology, such as silicone chips. To make these chips, workers strenuously place fine gold wires onto small data planes, peering through a tiny microscope all day, for all the new consumer electronics on the market: computers, laser videos, calculators, tape recorders, portable radios, televisions, and watches. U.S. companies dominated world production of integrated circuits in 1976, manufacturing 71 percent of them.[91] By the early 1980s, close to 90 percent of U.S. semiconductor assembly factories were found in Asia.[92] Chip bonding by American high-tech firms and Japanese competitors like Hitachi and Toshiba moved to cheap-labor countries such as Indonesia to avoid higher expenditures in more developed Asian nations like Taiwan, Singapore, and Hong Kong. They sought to find the "cheapest" female workers around.[93] By 1980, the electronics industry had become the largest employer of Asian women in the world.[94]

Economic competition between the United States and Japan and Europe brokered the rise of Asian women as the optimal form of labor for the global conveyer belt. Beginning in the 1970s, shortages in cheap domestic workers in North America and intensifying market competition led U.S. and Japanese multinational firms to transfer their base of operations. Many went to Southeast Asia, given real wage differentials between host countries and exporting nations. A lack of a real transfer of technology from Global North to Global South fed into an international technological barrier, making South and Southeast Asian women stand-ins or proxies for the robots or machines predicted to automate work and replace human labor.[95] Manufacturing companies mostly hire men as supervisors, which further ingrains the social construct of women as unthinking slaves and men as organized human planners. Special export-processing zones and supply chains reproduce patriarchal forms of authority by marrying Taylorism with its stringent motion techniques and systematized timed work to the treatment of female "workers as appendages of the machine."[96]

This gendered workplace schema plays out in production systems full of human risk. Multinational American companies like Nike hire subcontractors in places like Bangladesh, where corrupt factory owners put mostly women garment workers in hazardous buildings that end up killing thousands of them. With no regard for their humanity, and valued for their mechanized labor, Bangladeshi women are "turned into sewing machines," and men "turn on" the machines.[97] As objects of male conservatorship, the bionic woman (of color) signified the best breed of workers under global labor regimes that made little attempt to "humanize not-yet-modern others" and sought instead to "reaffirm Euro-American humanity."[98] The sex machine trope appeared beyond the factory space to include migrant female workers from former U.S. colonies like the Philippines, who came to be seen as "maid-machines" and "domestic technologies," in a neocolonial war to be human and independent.[99] Per feminist theorist Neferti X. Tadiar, the "equivalence of the Oriental woman and a sexual machine" emerged from the development of colonies into political appendages and economic dependents of developing nations. Their laborers "now operate as sexual machines for their developed 'master.'"[100]

Crucial to maintaining the scattered hegemonies of patriarchal capital, the sex machine myth has served as a critical site for construing the lives of so many toiling women around the world as not just dehumanized machines but also as hybridized cyborgs.[101] The labor-intensive facet of global manufacturing from South Korea and Japan incorporated other parts of the world beyond Asia, such that women in countries like Mexico and Latin America came to be seen as "cyborgs" within parts-assembly plants that globalize/Orientalize the local brown female workers.[102] Insofar as Asian export-processing techniques have spread to parts of Latin America, the management style of Japanese and South Korean multinationals are expanding the global myth of the sex machine.[103] For Asians specifically, there is a historical switch from being basic automatons to being complex cyborgs.

Cyborg is a postmodern concept for imagining a new social identity made from an amalgam of human and machine parts. As higher-grade machines, cyborgs are an improvement over the bionic human since it suggests more of a complete fusion of man and machine, describing an enhanced human with some inorganic parts. But as media studies scholar Jennifer Gonzalez writes, one must examine the social *form* of this composite subject position as "the cyborg thus is not necessarily more likely to exist free of the social constraints which apply to humans and machines already."[104] In other words, a cyborg may be a cooler updated version of the automaton-machine robot, but it comes with all the same trappings. As social theorist Mimi Nguyen points out, we must excavate "the technological imaginary" to rend the untrammeled form of domination that "manifests across free trade zones and troublesome histories of colonial fantasy."[105] The myth of the sex machine camouflaged the exploitation of female workers even if it simultaneously extended the practice of treating women as "throwaway cyborgs, used as servants, laborers, or toys."[106] The enduring impact of the Cold War on poor women of color problematized the utopian wish for a body politic "divorced from assigned or ascribed characteristics or social location."[107] Cyborg subject formation puts a spotlight on views of "the body as a kind of private satisfaction- and utility-maximizing machine."[108] The ties between sexuality and machinery remain close, even in the world of cyborgs.

Scrutiny of this sexual myth is pivotal given the all-too-convenient lure and trap of thinking of women of color as the ultimate cyborgs. In a 1985 influential essay entitled "A Cyborg Manifesto," theorist Donna Haraway popularized the concept of the cyborg, envisioning it as a new feminist mythology.[109] She writes that female reproductive labor is central to "high-tech myth systems structuring our imaginations of person and social possibility" and cites the Southeast Asian female worker as "real-life cyborgs." Haraway later apologized for her imperializing remarks, admitting a failure to recognize the human experience behind those "cyborg women making chips in Asia."[110]

The relationship between women and the machines is complicated, if also simplified, by cyborgization. While companies promote beauty contests like "Miss Motorola" and "Miss National Semiconductor," confusing consumer objects with women's bodies, one assembly worker in Hong Kong named Mae-fun said: "We girls are cheaper than machines. A machine costs over $2000 and would replace only two of us. And then they would have to hire a machine tender, for $120 a month."[111] Despite predictions since the 1960s of an automated robotic future, one can sense the tension found in mechanized workers who operate as a cheaper substitute and supplement to expensive factory machines. The Malaysian government even advertised the mechanized labor of Malay women to foreign companies: "The manual dexterity of the Oriental female is famous the world over. Her hands are small, and she works fast with extreme care. Who, therefore, could be better qualified by nature and inheritance to contribute to the efficiency of a bench-assembly production line than the Oriental girl?"[112] Automated industrial production enabled one worker to produce ten times as much as before, but this scaled-up productivity did not always entail a move to other high-paying quality jobs. Local human machines were considered sometimes more expedient than the real machines.

Long before the development of modern Asian economies, the Asian female's legendary dexterity was cited a century earlier by Thomas Ewbank, U.S. commissioner of patents. From 1849 to 1852, he discussed the Oriental woman's body as a form of mechanized labor able to balance heavy pots on her head to transport public water. Her sturdy anatomy was fashioned in such a way as to produce an "adhesion to ancient customs which forms so prominent a feature in Asiatic character."[113] By patenting Asian women as property, the commissioner engages women of color as property, not intellectual creators.[114]

When Asian nations later industrialized similarly to the United States and Europe, this mythological sense of Asian women as superbeings that can do so many incredible things with their bodies continued. The exploitation of women by developing nations was almost tantamount to "pimping," a form of state prostitution that enabled capitalist patriarchy on a global scale.[115] That Filipino women are now trafficked into Korea, despite official prohibition on the practice, suggests a form of commodification that cannot be explained simply through misogyny but also must take into account model machinery.

Researching women's local experiences and "the practice of humanity" on the ground, anthropologist Aihwa Ong described the ingenious ways Malaysian factory workers would subvert corporatized work schedules with hidden acts of subversion that include foot-dragging of work, jamming of machines, and feigning ignorance of tools, all of which conveyed a reprisal to male management.[116] Squelching the myth of deferential automatons, women broke down on factory floors, claiming possession by irate spirits, which introduced an otherworldly dimension into "rational" industrial systems. These revolutionary acts were not an example of "mechanical failure" but evidenced the ways women were unwilling to serve as good specimens of labor performance (robot) and postmodern life (cyborg).

These challenges run counter to organizational practices that persist as a form of "industrial sexuality" for "mechanizing women" and "manufacturing the docile worker."[117] A critique of the acquiescent sex machine requires recognizing the sociohistorical conditions that give rise to its mythic aura of the sex machine, one always upended by bold acts of breakage by women.

Conclusion

Today, the sex machine myth still manages to inspire X-rated material, including mail-order websites featuring ethnic women as mechanical toys "interchangeable in appearance and name."[118] A pornographic website with the initials LBFM as its domain name goes so far as to open its main page with a history lesson: "During the Vietnam War, Little Brown Fucking Machines was the nickname given by the military personnel serving on active duty to the thousands of amateur hookers working in the region. This appellation is still used by veterans, visitors or residents of these wonderful Southeast Asian countries."[119] This development suggests a possible expansion of sex tourism and its machine imaginaries.[120] In escort service ads, one can find solicitations like the following: "U can call me Cinta. I can be rent [sic] for $150/hour. Made in Indonesia. I am more fun than your XBOX or Play Station games very petite easy to lift around. Human friendly."[121] This "sexbot" may be a scam, but it perpetuates the machine myth of brown Asian women as sex toys. In a different register, Japanese and Hong Kong media depict gay men and male prostitutes as a "hyper-masculine sex machine, interested in sex, not romance, and moving in an exclusive homosocial world in which women are invisible."[122] The pervasiveness and motility of the sex machine myth means it moves across genders and sexualities. Sex machines do come in a wide assortment, especially if exploitation and exotification are the standard mechanisms of control.

Top airlines churned out Asian flight attendants like photo copies. For decades, Singapore, Eva, Qatar, China, and Asiana Airlines strictly employed mostly attractive, thin, young female flight attendants and put them in alluring clothing. Although they are less likely now to fire women when they age, marry, or become pregnant, the airline companies still treat women like living dolls. Flight attendants, however, rebelled against their tantalizing image as "playmates in the sky," something that overlaid with the overtone of the "flying geisha girl." The trope is ripped from written impressions by Pan Am Airline's president, who wanted a service-oriented "Japanese in every jet."[123] Many of these sexist practices fizzled in the United States back after harassment and sex-discrimination court battles, but they continue unabated in Asia, with its long lines of all-female crew members bowing in unison, like the kind employed by Malaysia-based AirAsia, described as "eager to please automatons in red uniforms."[124]

We spot pushback against such corporate framings of the female sex through the work of nonprofit groups like AIDS Intervention for Asian Pacific Islanders (APAIT), which in the early 1990s put out an informational poster in the first social-marketing campaign to target the trans API population (see fig. 3.1). Dressed in sexy evening wear, the model's anatomy is graphed in terms of plastic/reconstructive surgery. Even if the descriptive labeling is not so politically correct by today's standards, it reflects a public obsession with the sex-reassignment procedures of transgender people. The tongue-in-cheek poster directs attention to the expensive price of creating the perfect woman. Presented not as a sex machine to be abused or bought, this Asian's worked-over body is deemed "precious" and must be protected at all costs. By exposing the technologies of the sexed body, these kinds of public media projects present a "model for girls, in order to point to the artificiality of the cultural fantasy of perfect womanhood."[125]

One might have a hard time finding any sort of female empowerment in the import car scene that developed in the early 1990s, where Asian women often appeared as mere props or appendages to male-driven automobiles. Per Asian American studies scholars Robyn Rodriguez and Vernadette Gonzalez, "The import model's body as (sex) machine is an apt metaphor [since] like the car, she is modified, improved, and disciplined . . . circulated as a marker of cultural capital," while the Asian boys "are their masters."[126] Popular Japanese cars laid the foundation for the "rice rocket" subculture forged from the customization of "samurai warrior mythos with futuristic fantasy technology."[127] Tinkering with serviceable parts and adding new state-of-the-art designs and turbo chargers, the car racing industry gave rise to consumer culture, where Asian male drivers are enshrined as new "robot warriors," whose spruced-up foreign cars stage new alien technocultural encounters against classic American cars like the Ford, Cadillac, and Mus-

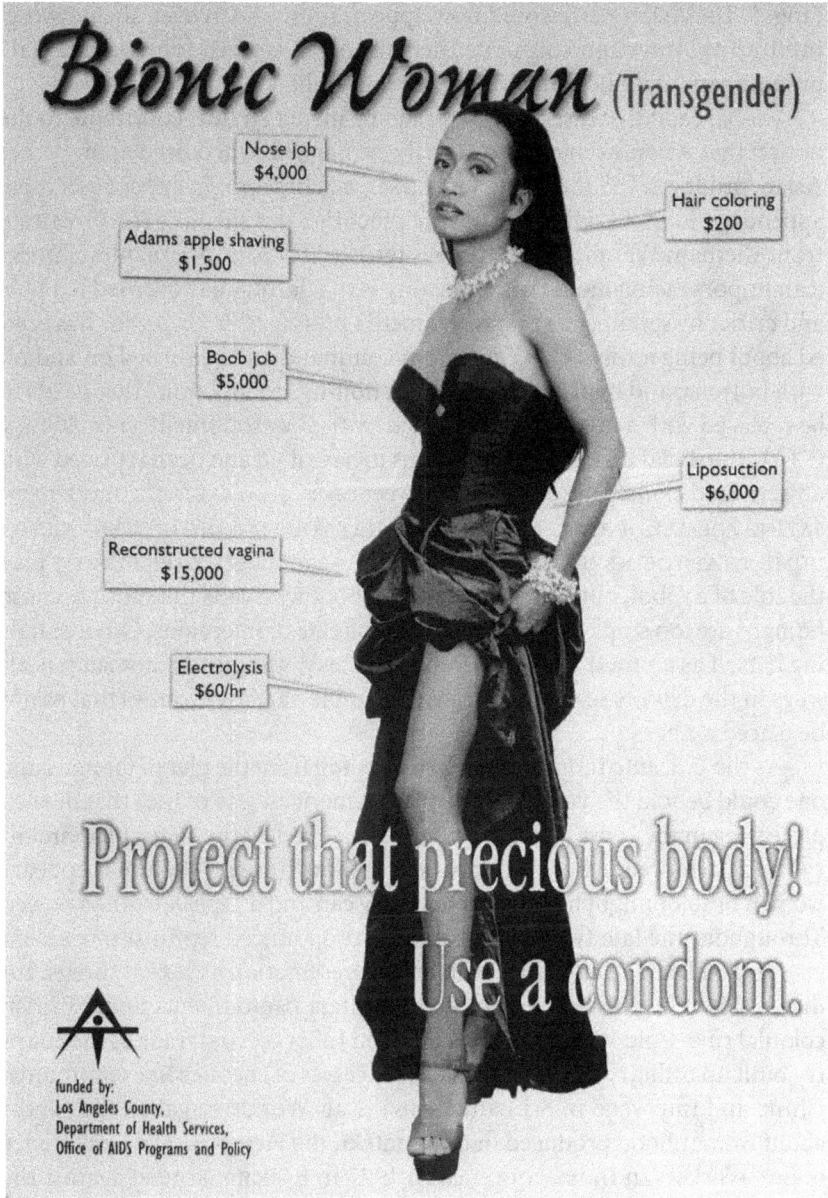

Figure 3.1 "Protect that precious body! Use a condom" poster from Asian Pacific AIDS Intervention Team, 1993 (Los Angeles County Department of Public Health, Office of AIDS Programs and Policy)

tang.[128] The Asian nerd would now appear as an undercover alien cyborg, infiltrating American corporate life, and Asian women took on "virtual" properties as a public thing hiding in plain sight.

Global capitalist discourses overlaid by media circuits contribute to the notion that Asian women are as "easily exchanged or acquired as any other Asian 'products.'"[129] The Asian female sex machine might appear as a mere appendage to the Asian male phallic machine, but she, like the prostitute from Vietnam War movies, never hesitates to talk back. Vietnamese American import racing model turned reality star Tila Tequila confused her fans and critics by sending cryptic social media messages. In them, she has talked about being a robot that can cry on command and be turned on and off with buttons, and one having a malfunctioning "robot brain" that needs to be replaced with a microchip implanted by the Central Intelligence Agency (CIA). The social influencer even claims to have died and been replaced with an activated clone. One provocative tweet says: "I AM SAYING & HAVE BEEN SAYING FOR ALL OF MY CLONED LIFE IS THAT YOU FUCKING HUMANS ARE SO DUMB THAT YOU NEVER KNOW!"[130] This message suggests Tequila may play the role of a robot, but it is the celebrity cyborg who calls the shots, because humans are too stupid to know her real thoughts or intentions. Often parading herself as a proud white neo-Nazi, this sexy, unhinged automaton is always in the driver's seat, controlling the simple narrative frames that might be placed on her.

As the U.S. auto industry faced a thumping from the glut of foreign cars, one could behold the vast changes in an "American way of life" that needed protecting in the "post" Cold War era, one defined by the "muscular circuitry" and "armored cyborg" of Japanese technoculture.[131] While it appears women of color might have no agency, they can and do speak truth to power. Throughout the late twentieth century, a pronounced feminist movement emerged in India to challenge women's representation as sexual things. India's modern brothels can be traced to military cantonments under British colonial rule. Cold War capitalism enlarged India's sexual trade as the country built up military forces to check the excesses of enemies like communist China and intervene in Sri Lanka's civil war. Working against the myths about womanhood produced in this context, the First National Conference of Sex Workers in India, convened in 1997 in Kolkata, argued against the dichotomy of "chaste" desexed wife and "immoral" oversexed prostitute. In their manifesto, they recuperated the stigmatized figure of the fallen woman who exists as "a sex machine, unfettered by any domestic inclination or 'feminine' emotion."[132] By knitting together struggles of women from different social classes and castes, this conference put value on all female labor and delegitimated a patriarchal system that puts them down as machines.

The movement to protect woman against the sex machine myth continued to grow in the following decades. The answer might not be more "human" rights, if it is connected to the idea of "acceptable" women. As we have seen, artists and activists engaged in raunchy erotics to contest the politics of respectability, while others smashed the patriarchal machine through what sexuality studies scholar Yessica Garcia Hernandez calls "pedagogies of deviance."[133] The 2016 short film *I Am Not a Sex Machine* from India talks about the torture and abuse faced by women like Nusrat Singh, who was raped and murdered in 2015. Connecting the familial pressures of being a daughter and mother to the potential victimization of all women by sexual violence, the film's narrator asks, "She's just a sex machine? Why can he use me as he pleases? Why does my freedom have to come with a cost? Am I even a person . . . [with] my own will?"[134] Affirming the right of all women to live on their own terms, the film questions the legitimacy of the sex machine myth across the spectrum of society and class. This critical line of questioning is one that must be always remembered, when we approach a more "virtual" stage in capitalism where sources of power and resistance can flow from almost anywhere in the world.

4

Virtual Machines

Containing the Alien Cyborg during
the Era of Late Capitalism

Aflashpoint for grasping what it meant to be an Asian American near the end of the twentieth century revolved around a major hate crime. In 1982, two white auto workers killed an American of Chinese descent named Vincent Chin, excoriating "Japs" like him for the demise of the U.S. auto industry. They blamed the decline on competition from more popular foreign car makers from Japan. Racial lumping sutured Asians in the United States to those people in Asia in an era of transnational cultural flows, commodity markets, and flexible labor regimes. The compounding effects of massive manufacturing layoffs in the United States, a deluge of Asian imports to North America, and the spike in the number of immigrants from the Third World to the United States—all contributed to the prevailing sense that everything in the country had seriously gone downhill.

Potential foreign takeover of American businesses and jobs impelled the murderers to bludgeon Chin to death with a baseball bat to the point of disfigurement, a measure to contain the pulsing embodied (yet hidden) menace of "foreign" capital and alien labor carrying "non-biological" substance. From this vantage of what cannot be fully represented, one could interpret the men as "striking down the automatons that had been sent in to replace them . . . rendering him [Chin] as not only a racialized Other, but a factory machine that had to be dismantled."[1] As a revanchist corrective to globalization, Chin's murder coincided with swelling anti-Japanese sentiment, culminating in televised bashes where ordinary citizens laid waste to Toyotas with bats in mob-like displays of cathartic amusement. Working as an industrial draftsman for an automotive supplier, Chin's battered corpus tragically served as a proxy for the hyper-efficient body of the foreign vehicle.

Despite the brutality of their attack, the assailants escaped doing hard time as the trial judge exculpated the men, reasoning they were not the kind of people that would typically commit such heinous acts.[2] In sanitizing the perpetrators as "real" men from good families, the trial judge validated views of Chin as a worthless expendable object or "cheap man," while safeguarding the natural "inalienable" rights of free white men of supposedly good moral character. The foreclosure of Chin's human and civil rights was the spark in mobilizing communities across the country around a "panethnic" Asian American political movement.[3] It also underscored the risk that comes when the United States' enduring possessive investment in whiteness confronts "model minority machine-ness."[4] Meeting their victim at a "gentlemen's club" and accusing him of mistreating a stripper, the killers' masochistic annihilation of Chin reduced him to an unmasculine drone, a common stereotype of Asian American men. Chin symbolized at once Japan's corporate threat, the Chinese communist state, the Vietnamese gook, and an Asian American model minority. As cultural historian Robert Lee writes in *Orientals*, "America's defeat in Southeast Asia was brought about by a faceless and invisible Asian enemy. . . . The rapid growth of the Asian American population and its apparent success render the model minority, like the now-mythic Viet Cong, everywhere invisible and powerful. . . . In the dystopic narrative of national decline, the model minority resembles the replicants in the science fiction book and film *Blade Runner*—a cyborg, perfectly efficient but inauthentically human, the perfect gook."[5]

The film's alien cyborg allegory captured white America's refusal to absorb an Asian humanity, despite the opportunities afforded by greater cultural and technological integration under globalization. Despite nativists' efforts to keep the different races apart, Asian automatons could no longer be sealed off completely from the United States' machine society. More and more Americans were buying cars and other products from Japan, while more Asians than ever were immigrating to the United States and naturalizing as citizens. These clever "foreign-made" alien cyborgs could now virtually pass as American.

Only two days after Chin's death, the cult classic *Blade Runner* (1982) opened in movie theaters nationwide. Depicting a dystopic Los Angeles illuminated by the neon signs of geishas, the science fiction film revolves around a white male protagonist who is hired to track artificially engineered synthetic humanoids, called replicants, manufactured by an omnipotent multinational corporation. Declared illegal on Earth, these humanoid cyborgs are used for menial work in distant off-world colonies, but any alien replicant that comes to the planet is immediately hunted by special operatives and mowed down. The problem comes from not knowing who are replicants as they have blended in with the rest of the human population. The movie supplied filmic language for the wave of illegal "aliens" from the communist world. Taken as a real-life "illegal" replicant, Vincent Chin and other Asians took form as virtual machines assumed to have penetrated the bodily integrity of the nation.

This chapter on the virtual machine immediately follows the previous one on the sex machine. Here, I recognize the gendered flows of transnational capital, which require a new breed of Asian cyborgs. The gender fluidity of Asian/American alien cyborgs followed the stereotypes of Asians as angry war machines during World War II and as eroticized sex machines at the height of the Cold War. The crossing over of "aliens" into once pristine domestic spaces blurred that line between the foreign and familiar. While Chin was a blue-collar machine operator, many Americans in the 1980s had begun to view Asian American men as mostly white-collar nerds, sexually impotent and perverted, perhaps not so dissimilar to the sex-starved Japanese salaryman that was coming to do business in the United States and other countries. This contradiction of being a use/threat was produced from Asian labor's overall value for the information economy, not to mention its association with the threat of Asian capitalism and communism. In this multimodal framework, we must ask who deserves to work or live in the post-Fordist economy. This chapter takes a transnational focus that follows on the heels of previous chapters on the emergence of Asian automatons inside an industrializing nation, between warring empires, and within militarizing superpowers.

Under emergent technocultural influences that supposedly turn all human beings into would-be cyborgs, we can track subtleties in the insinuation that somehow "all cyborgs are Asian."[6] A portent of digital times, the racially alien cyborg is produced under new virtual modes of capitalism or virtual capitalism defined by telematics, computer broadband, and cable news. As the embodied figure of the virtual machine myth, the alien cyborg calls up age-old fears of a secret invasion by Asian robots. This time, however, those racial fears operate within a context defined by the "computerization of society," one symbolized less by the hard appearance of computers and closed systems than the synergy of open source networks, computer software, and diffuse commodity circuits.[7] The myth of the virtual machine and the alien cyborg figure motion toward a postnationalist era ruled by the "proliferation of difference," where difference cannot be easily pinpointed or hemmed in, much less contained, at a time when popular images, migratory bodies, and information circulate rapidly and widely.[8]

This chapter considers a particular model of the machine: new Asian capitalists and new Asian migrants. The thing being modeled is the cybernetic alien, a virtual machine modeled upon the sense that Asian labor/capital is now more globally diffuse. This chapter discusses how the foreign Asian automaton became a transnational Asian/American cyborg. Along this course, I address the popularization of the model minority myth in the 1980s but how, despite this stereotype, the thinning boundary between Asia and America was maintained and renewed through Asian value-threat dichotomization. This chapter seeks to grasp the hybrid melding of the postmodern cyborg with the foreign alien. Let us now turn to the ways that the alien became entwined with the cyborg.

When Alien Meets Cyborg in Asia/America

Since the 1970s, the Asian went from being only seen as a completely alien being and machine to being represented as alien cyborgs. Insofar as cyborg describes the hybrid fusion of man and machine, the portmanteau of alien cyborg reflects a recycling of the historical notation of Asians as model machines. Media scholar Takeo Rivera wrote about Asian Americans becoming both machine and a "model minority." Rivera indicates these two processes "all converge in a mirror world of sorts, the virtual world."[9] My analysis builds on Rivera's concerns with the machine minority and "minority model" to identify the virtual figuration of cyborg alien. My sense of the virtual emerges out of the electronic world but also the virtual condition by which Asians are known (or not known) in modern U.S. discourse. The model minority myth, for example, produced in the vortex of changes wrought by late-capitalist America render Asians as silent and culturally irrelevant subjects— *even while* they are visibly produced as threats or workers. When the model minority myth slipped into the older myth of model machines, this further "virtualized" the Asian/American subject—virtual being a shorthand for technological integration and social invisibility.

Virtual can also describe the move from thinking about simple robots and human automatons to sophisticated cyborgs. In the first half of the twentieth century, the word *robot* increased in popular use to describe the increasing mechanization of factory work, and slowly it came to supplant the older term *automaton*, which still referred to manual labor in the most rudimentary sense. By the second half of the twentieth century, the term *cyborg* came into vogue to convey a technologically enhanced human. The term *cyborg* gained popularity to better describe the rewiring of human experience under the feedback loop of scientific-material production and complex technological systems. Two U.S. scientists coined the term *cyborg* to describe technologically enhanced human beings able to survive in outer space, but it then came into wider usage in the 1980s to describe the accelerated embrace of human-technological interaction. It soon became common by technologists to say that all human beings were becoming cyborgs, since our bodies could no longer be separated from technology.

I contend that the older view of Asians as alien machines haunt this contemporary cyborg myth. It is hard to avoid mention of augmented cybernetic humans without Asia, especially when this cyborg discourse arose at the same time as Japan and other Asian economies began to produce anxieties in the West around globalization and its "condition of potentially productive asymmetry and identification" with the East.[10] In his classic treatise *Orientalism*, Edward Said states: "If the world has become immediately accessible to a Western citizen living in the electronic age, the Orient too has drawn near to him, and is now less a myth perhaps than a place crisscrossed by Western, especially American interests."[11] Despite the lessening overt power of myth, the Asian Orient endures as a mythological place and racial wonderland in the tech economy insofar as "techno-Orientalist speculations of an Asianized future have become ever more prevalent in the wake of neoliberal trade policies that enabled greater flow of information and capital between the East and the West."[12] Despite all this spatial crisscrossing, Asian racial difference is reinforced and recoded through the alien cyborg. As Rachel Lee and Sau-ling Wong suggest, "Cyborgs. . . . are often construed as wholly alien figures—a race apart. When Asian Americans are imagined as cyborgs, it is their Asianness. . . . that helps create the association within the Western imaginary of cyborgs as a race apart."[13]

In the age of fiberoptics, the newfangled fiction of Asians as cyborgs builds upon the older take on them as aliens with infectious or imperceptible bodies. Robert Lee explains, "Aliens are always a source of pollution. . . . 'Alien' describes things that are immediate and present yet have a foreign nature or allegiance. The difference is political. . . . Only when the foreign is present does it become alien. The alien is always out of place, therefore disturbing and dangerous."[14] Lee documents the popular Orientalist images that formed in specific periods, delineating these images as cyclical. But the historical approach to representing Asians as pollutants, coolies, deviants, yellow perils, model minorities, and gooks are mashed up today into a kind of pastiche, one that I name as the *alien cyborg*.

Where the United States looked to Japan as the main source of economic and technocultural competition in the 1980s, other fast-growing alien societies in Asia constituted another point of concern. Exacerbating the problem of a U.S. recession at the outset of the decade, the growing wealth of the NICs (newly industrialized countries) of Thailand, Singapore, Taiwan, and South Korea made the American economy look worse, despite a financial crisis hitting much of Asia in 1997. Whereas globalization connotes the amplification of international cooperation and exchange, it also corresponds to a new spatiotemporal awareness engendered by the merger of human geographies, a convergence derived from the "Americanization of Asia" and the "Asianization of America."[15]

In this virtual context, we can think about what capitalist globalization does to the historical notion of Asians as model machines. In the main, I believe it augurs the shift from localized (and Westernized) modes of industrial production to global patterns of distribution, and yet nationalism reigns as a yoke for organizing technocultural life and discourses. Scholars in global studies argue that globalization as a decentering of circulation of capital, goods, information, and people remains bound up with the differentiation of national cultures.[16] Insofar as this argument is valid, we can equally recognize how nationalized cultures are always already mongrelized. The myth of Asians as cyborgs who remain alien communicates the message that they inhabit the U.S. globalizing nation as subversive communist spies, invading migrants, dissembling model minorities, duplicitous cyberhackers, and perfidious business capitalists. Alien cyborg, a composite figure borrowing elements from all these social categories, aligns with what Asian American studies scholars have written about. Drawing on what cultural scholar Stephen Sohn terms the alien/Asian and what literary theorist Greta Niu calls the Asian/cyborg, I zoom in to Asians and Asian Americans as complex figures of economic/technological integration as well as cultural/national exclusion. When the alien fuses with the cyborg, the hybrid provides an added dimension to the "the manufactured equivalent of a human [that] has reflected the particular perceptions of the alien that is characteristic of Europe-derived societies."[17]

Before they became cyborgs, though, Asians were aliens. Since the late nineteenth century, the most popular image of the alien from outer space has been one bearing a humanlike appearance that is "Mongoloid." Before then, aliens were depicted as giant bug-eyed monsters. Intergalactic aliens bore a frightful appearance based on theories about life on other worlds with the first telescopic observation of water-shaped canals on the planet Mars. This idea that space creatures could look like us became mainstream with the writings of H. G. Wells, especially in his *The War of the Worlds* (1897).[18] Extraterrestrials who looked slightly human truly came into view the same time as the arrival of "aliens" to the West. Early images of the Chinese in the United States depicted them as vermin-like creatures with non-human qualities. The earliest novels about space aliens were all written at the height of anti-Chinese prejudice, and this synchronicity underlined the mass hallucination of Asian migration as an "alien invasion" in the broadest sense.[19] As a foil to real life, media studies scholar Wendy Chun says, "Science fiction often addresses questions of race indirectly through stories of aliens and other implausible physical differences."[20]

I argue that the Chinese could be compared to the Gray Aliens of popular culture, given their stereotypical squat hairless bodies, neonatal flat faces, slender glabrous limbs, black almond-shaped eyes, inscrutable minds, vacuous expressions, and high-pitched, choppy singsong manner of speaking reminiscent of tonal Sinic languages. Coolie laborers from southern China bore shaven foreheads to signal obedience to the ruling Manchu dynasty; and this sign of fealty might have inspired the appearance of aliens with round "hairless" big heads like the Gray Alien. In the media, the Gray Alien is typically drawn colored in a drab yellowish gray, conveying a lethargic, deadened personality and lack of vigor evocative of the historical portraits of the Chinese opium addict.

Prognostications that human society could fall prey to a swarm of Asian-looking aliens were the fodder for science fiction.[21] Between World War I and World War II, in the golden age of this genre, space aliens acquired familiar racial characteristics, as science fiction historian John Cheng notes: "Oriental Asians were the only actual 'aliens' in interwar science fiction. . . . Many creatures in science fiction assumed the roles that Oriental Asians played. . . . They became alien by association with Asians and only later, in the Cold War period, became aliens by themselves."[22] Insofar as the basic definition of alien is a foreigner who is not a citizen of a country *and* an extraterrestrial from another planet, the foreign spaces outside a country are often inseparable from the alien spaces in other galaxies.[23] To be an "alien" is to be treated as nonhuman, hence the often inhumane treatment accorded to migrants, or those termed "illegal aliens."

U.S. engagements with alien cyborgs can be taken metaphorically as close encounters of the Third (World) kind. As the United States worked to send space crews into orbit, the great leap into intergalactic space worked in step with strides to break into formerly remote international spaces, which explains why the popularity of film series like *Star Wars*—an intergalactic space opera about a republic fighting a totalitarian empire with a droid army—occurred around the same time as Hollywood films with Mandarin-looking villains like Emperor Ming from *Flash Gordon* (1980), a space alien who turns human captives into mindless zombies with his dehumanizing machines. Science fiction once expressed a strict division between humans and nonliving aliens, but beginning in the 1980s, writers began to think about doomsday scenarios and devise new "life forms" with interchangeable elements.[24] Through the historical prism of Asians legally treated as "aliens ineligible for citizenship," we can zero in on the "alien at the core of the nation, and indeed at the core of the human."[25]

What I identify as the alien cyborg can be spotted in popular American films like those of James Cameron, the director of the killer robot *Terminator* film series and the intergalactic alien *Avatar* movies. Cameron admitted that he found inspiration for the story of his 1986 hit film *Aliens* from the Vietnam War, where the narrative is shaped by a conflict between technologically superior human forces and a subhuman cybernetic alien species that can be read as "analogous to the inability of superior American firepower to conquer the unseen enemy in Vietnam."[26] *Aliens* follows the story of U.S. Colonial Marines sent out to protect business interests, but the dark-skinned aliens show up to kill the crew, ripping apart their ideals of human supremacy. In Vietnam, the mightiest empire in modern history faced defeat by a supposedly inferior race that used old Russian rifles and booby traps against American B-52 bombers and Huey helicopters. That Cameron could equate American Vietnam vets with his human characters and the Vietnamese with aliens can be construed as racist, but it can also be interpreted as sensitizing Western audiences to how Asians are symbolized as alien machines needing to be extinguished like unwelcome space invaders. In Cameron's film, the aliens are a warrior race of drone xenomorphs with a metallic insect-like appearance that makes them look primitive yet futuristic. The cybernetic aliens are hell-bent on propagating their predatory species by impregnating human bodies, and this parasitic function is reminiscent of Vietcong communist forces influencing impressionable people. Insofar as the Cold War marked the beginning of the space race between the United States and the Soviet Union, the American endeavor to gain victory in outer space stakes "out a border to be defended against both the nonhuman (alien) and the non-American (alien) [and] builds on the fear of the passing-as-human cyborg seeking to gain entry and colonize human spaces."[27]

In *Aliens*, the horror of alien creatures impregnating the female human body attests to the horrors of interracial/interspecies mixing. During the cinematic run of the *Alien* trilogy, there was a huge influx of postwar refugees from Southeast Asian nations like Cambodia, Laos, and Vietnam, which made it seem as though the enemy that the United States had tried to "contain" overseas had come over to seed the country with their alien offspring. In the process of multiplying, they develop into virtually invisible parasites within the host country, eating away at state welfare programs. As ethnic studies scholar Yen Le Espiritu contends, they are assumed to have nonassimilating qualities by working low-wage jobs, such as electronics technicians, apparently due to their patient nature and ability to master boring, monotonous tasks that require quick memorization.[28] Polls at the time showed that most Americans did not want the post–Vietnam War refugees to resettle in the United States out of fear that some were communist spies, but the "invasion" had already begun, along with the flood of alien migrants from Latin American, African, and Caribbean nations. Though most refugees were trying to escape communist terror, they and their U.S.-born brood were regarded as virtual machines in ways not so dissimilar to Cameron's cinematic monsters.

By the late 1970s, the term *virtual* found wider dissemination, meaning "being in essence or effect though not formally recognized or admitted."[29] The term related well to highly interactive environments produced from the simulation of a computer network, such as virtual cockpits and flight experiences of "virtual reality" produced from such technology.[30] Additionally, the virtual is also *viral* in the same era that saw the beginning of the HIV/AIDS pandemic and saw human "bodies break down and/or refuse prescribed paths."[31] As a composite figure of the postmodern technocultural imagination, the Asian (American) alien cyborg stood out as "a technology, a screen, a projected image . . . a contaminated body, a deadly body, a techno-body."[32]

Despite this strange new virtual reality, remnants of the past float up in the ether of public consciousness. Hostile reaction to the Asian in Reagan's America hearkened back to an earlier "bodily discourse that led the anti-immigrant, anti-immigration legislation of the late nineteenth and early twentieth centuries . . . [and] constructed the 'national body' as an organism that must be protected from contamination or infection by the contagion."[33] Such aversion pointed to the virtual presence of an "Other from an Orient which is no longer faraway or 'out there,' but one that is 'here' and yet 'not-quite-annexed.'"[34] In the closing decades of the twentieth century, we find the United States defending itself against a whole host of intruders that promised to wreak havoc on the national genome. Even as Asian American groups like Indians, Koreans, Japanese, and Chinese became less often seen as low-tech model machines and more often as high-tech model machines, the hidden diseases "evoked by these clean machines are 'no more' than the minuscule coding changes of an antigen."[35]

Apart from the sense of the high-tech found in the virtual, religious studies scholar Jane Iwamura suggested the term *virtual Orientalism* to locate Asians as an "absent presence," something there but not fully there.[36] Tied to spiritual traditions of foregone ages, Asians, for all their superhuman qualities, appear foreclosed from technological modernity.[37] Mechanical forms of visual reproduction like the photographic camera were partially to blame for this elision. Chinese laborers were not invited to the final photographic shoot that signaled completion of the U.S. Transcontinental Railroad, which they helped to build. The American machine virtually excluded these labor machines. In the last half of the twentieth century, the model machine myth has "become so condensed that it no longer needs to be told. . . . One is able to discern the ideological impetus or underlying 'social use' of the myth."[38]

Virtualized Asianness poses as much an age-old question about immigration and labor as it does about extraterrestrial life. President Ronald Reagan worried about illegal aliens as much as communist meddling and built a satellite defense project that reporters jokingly called "Star Wars."[39] On the domestic front, Asian Americans have turned up in the news as model minorities, but their alienage as a super-minority casts suspicion over what masters they serve. Their cultural foreignness has been made to "travel under the logic of an expanded Orient."[40] Literary scholar Sohn believes that this stereotype of superhuman Asians codifies their "mechanized humanity" even as it tinkers with the "very inhuman qualities projected onto Asian bodies," so while Asians "conduct themselves with superb technological efficiency and capitalist enterprise, their affectual absence resonates as an undeveloped or, worse still, a retrograde humanism."[41] In other words, Asians represent a degraded or backward mode of being human because their racial bodies are virtually inseparable from the machine.

The racialized concept of alien is closely aligned with the cyborg.[42] Coined in 1960, the term *cyborg* refers to an enhanced human being who can survive extraterrestrial environments. The cyborg's promise for humanity is entangled with fear about what happens when humans occupy spaces that nature did not intend for them. *Cyborg* derives from *cybernetics*, a field its founder Norbert Wiener defined as the science of control and a branch of communication, which he says extends the traditional study of "automata, whether in the metal or in the flesh" by exploring the "flow of impressions."[43] As a study of both animal and machine automata, Wiener believes cybernetics involves a "racial" learning about self-reproducing machines, animals "capable of being transformed by its past environment into a different being . . . an animal that multiplies [and is] able to create other animals in its own likeness."[44] During the earliest wartime research on cybernetics, the Japanese were visualized in terms of an animalistic "enemy Other." This nonhuman status is contradistinguished from the semi-human "cybernetic Other" of the German solider, which the United States hoped to incorporate into its war machine. By this reckoning, the machine status embodied by Nazi (white) bodies could never be placed in the same category as Asians, who were in the first instance alien machines.[45] In the many years since Wiener's groundbreaking work, Asians (particularly the Japanese) have become a cybernetic Other that retain their historical alienness.

Cybernetic aliens are generated in new systems of control and communication that are always prone to being contaminated. Contamination can be related to the ingress of educated immigrants coming to the United States after the 1965 Immigration Act, which gave preference to skilled professionals, and attracted many Asian scientists and students. Some of these migrant workers constituted a class of "high-tech coolies" and "techno-migrants" within American research labs and start-up companies.[46] Relegated to behind-the-scenes office work, these alien automatons did computer coding, script reading, service training, and workplace maintenance due to the belief that they were better at "preprogrammed" routines and that they lacked executive decision-making. Too often denied leadership positions and promotions, "Asian immigrants are viewed to be mimetic rather than original and are taken to be suited for carrying out people's orders and ideas. In other words, they should not be bosses, but bossed."[47] When they cannot be bossed, they must be expelled.

It was in this heated political moment that the figure of the Asian nerd or geek merged with the communist Borg. This suspicion of Asians as "useful threat" coincided with the ambivalent reception of Japanese capital, insofar as Americans did not know whether to welcome or disavow the technological wonders of Japan. Through the propulsions of globalization, Asians in the United States assumed a virtual presence, as alien cyborgs who remained hidden from view but who also presented a corporate yellowface for a Japanized America.

The Corporate Yellowface of a Japanized America

There was a sense in the early 1980s that Americans were themselves becoming alien(ated) cyborgs under Japan's global business model and corporate hive. Scholars today employ the concept of techno-Orientalism to tease out the "use of Asia as a marker for advanced technology . . . [that] ignores the history and constructions of relationships between Asian people and technology."[48] The nomenclature was first developed by communication scholars David Morley and Kevin Robin to frame the ways technology and images of the future are "Japanized." This second reckoning with Japan's power forced many in the United States to ask, what are "Japanese technologies doing to us?"[49] While applicable to other Asians, the authors formulate "techno-Orientalism" to specify racist images of Japanese people as "economic animals" and "unfeeling aliens . . . cyborgs and replicants" who disturb "the political and cultural unconscious of the West" and the "image of capitalist progress."[50] Despite the muddling of economic borders due to trade, there cohered an abiding sense of the leader of the Western world, the United States, as quintessentially modern (rational), while Japan was caught in a double temporal displacement: concurrently traditional (stuck in the past) and futuristic (ahead of its time).[51] A new "techno-mythology" was thereby spun to foretell the mutation of human experience under the spell of "the greatest machine-loving nation of the world," where people were "imagined as mutating into machines."[52] While the U.S. appeared diverse and individualistic, Japan came to be positioned as a monolith, harboring a "robot-like dedication" to world domination. It appeared to achieve this assimilative goal, fusing technological innovation and economic rationality through karaoke machines, computer games, and robotics to exert a "new domain of artificial reality."[53] Though Japanese were "laborious artificers" and "lesser men" never to be trusted, they could be used as models for American economic revival.[54] To blunt their nation's downward spiral, Americans needed to copy the copycats and mimic the model machines.

The late 1970s had witnessed the making of a new artificial reality created by Japanese companies like Sony, which pioneered landmark digital technologies, such as mobile phones, compact disc players, digital cameras, computer memory chips, quartz watches, machine learning, and high-definition screens. It was nearly impossible at the time to find high-quality consumer technology that was not of Japanese design. The rise of "Japan Inc." cast the Japanese as members of a "cold, impersonal and machine-like, and authoritarian culture lacking emotional connection to the rest of the world" and exacerbated the sense that Americans would soon adopt that culture, the effect being "the barbarians have now become robots."[55] Japan's increasing usage of robots in everyday life meant it was moving from a "Robot Kingdom" to the "First Cyborg Nation."[56]

This characterization of Japan as an alien cyborg society with global technocultural influence accords with statements by media theorist Marshall McLuhan, who argued that the mere act of watching the television—an electronic medium American in origin but Asianized in production and development—"Orientalized" the average American child.[57] McLuhan's prognosis of a Japanizing America found evidence with the VHS recorder made by the Victor Company of Japan (JVC) in 1977 and the debut of Nintendo's Gameboy handheld video-game console in 1989. Alongside the global export of popular anime cartoons (Japanese animation), Japan brought Asian technology into the American home and expanded file sharing across the world. The first mass-produced laptops produced by Toshiba in 1985 and LCD screens finely wrought by Sharp bred this sense of dread: that modern people were essentially turning into alien(ated) cyborgs who no longer talked or socially interacted like normal humans but sat glued to the screen like zoned-out *otaku*, reclusive geeky youth who sat at home hiding away from the world to play video games all day.

Observations of this Japanese televisual revolution came as early as 1971, when *Time* displayed a cover with the title "How to Cope with Japan's Business Invasion." It features the American icon Uncle Sam gripping a television stamped with the words "Made in Japan" (see fig. 4.1). Sam holds the Japanese-made television set in his hands, but there is a subtly conveyed message that we do not know what ticking timebomb is in possession. It might be a mother box to communicate with alien world invaders. The property is stamped with the logo of a Japanese corporation and contains the yellow-tinted face of Sony's head, Akio Morita, on a yellow screen in a re-

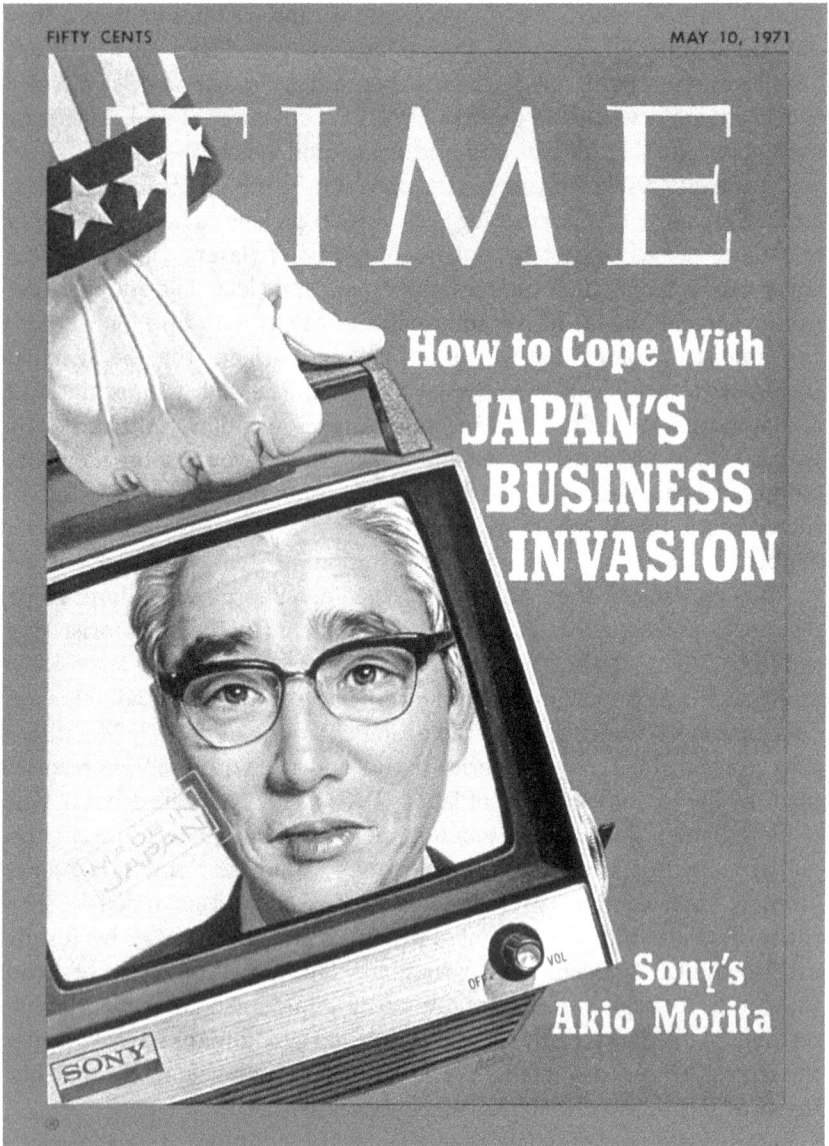

Figure 4.1 *TIME* magazine cover, May 10, 1971 (TIME. © 1971 TIME USA LLC. All rights reserved. Used under license)

print of the Yellow Peril cultural stereotype. Insofar as the television is a decidedly American invention, the Japanese have made that technology foreign by presenting the alien visage of an Asian cyborg on the screen of a television box that "we" are holding. The model machine is telescoped to adults and children, who cannot avoid mind control and who cannot help to look away from the ubiquitous Asian face. This was the new yellowface of America's future.

Sony's virtualizing process of turning American domestic citizens into Japanized alien cyborgs went beyond the televisual realm to encompass sound audio equipment. In 1979, Americans saw for the time the portable Sony Walkman, a small hand-held audio device designed for easy assembly by robots, which played a person's favorite records from a recorded cassette tape through a headphone jack. This more personalized, private way of consuming recorded music allowed for the delivery of sounds directly to the ears of the listeners, who no longer needed to hear sounds traveling through the air from radio or loudspeakers. The Walkman could give humans space to listen to music on a crowded bus commute or exercising in the street, perhaps turning Americans into socially awkward people who do not talk or make eye contact with strangers on the streets, much like the Japanese. By grafting technology literally onto human anatomies, substituting real human needs with false consumer ones, "we become, in our mind's eye, typical 'Walk-men'"—mentally subject to Japan's products.[58] The Walkman and its form of "Japanese-ness" was hungrily devoured by buyers, and the creeping oversaturation of Japanese electronics inspired campaigns to "buy American."[59] Sony's introduction of laser compact discs, a byproduct of the microcomputer, seemed as revolutionary as U.S. war technologies created around the same time like precision guided munitions (PGMs) or smart bombs reliant on laser guidance systems. Japanese just-in-time style of manufacturing made it appear that a pacified Japan virtually won vengeance for losing World War II, making "robot toys" that took the world by storm and displacing American technological supremacy.[60]

With the complete takeover of Japanese alien technology, there manifested the possibility of "turning Japanese," according to the name of a 1980 hit song by British rock band The Vapors. One benefit of turning Japanese was the possibility of jumping headlong into an advanced technological future and embracing capitalism completely, but there was a negative aspect as well. The easiest visual marker of loss in turning Japanese can be located in the "dull but dutifully conformist men who accept scripted roles as salarymen."[61] The *New York Times* observed this sad, tired white-collar worker as an internationally recognized automaton "who will work like a robot until retirement."[62] Echoing this opinion in more militaristic terms, a 1987 *Washington Post* editorial titled "Japan's White-Collar Clones" describes how the overworked "salaryman is mass-produced" to become an "industrial warrior."[63] American business owners visited Japan to observe Japanese management and experienced culture shock. They immediately reacted to "the image of the Japanese salaryman as a human automaton programmed to work steadily and unremittingly for his company until his useful lifetime has ended . . . [in] a system of employment grounded in centuries of Japanese tradition."[64] As a cog in a punishing cubicle culture, the Japanese salaryman was indistinguishable from the machine civilization that produced him.

The salaryman presented a new soldier for an emasculated robot nation. In *Notes from Toyota-Land*, an American engineer in Japan provides interviews with real-life salarymen lamenting their long office hours. When asked about fighting his corporate bosses and a paternalistic demanding work culture, one man replies, "Japanese unions are weak, we cannot strike, we are all robots."[65] Articulated in this way, the salaryman is not a static figure of the U.S. robot imagination but a real person with real needs and wants. This personal struggle to be seen as more than a stony-faced worker machine contrasts with speculations made in the 1983 book *Behind the Mask*, a kind of "exposé" by Dutch American writer Ian Buruma, who claims that beyond the programmed politeness of these human machines are lurid sexual proclivities. Behind the professional and industrial exactitude of the Japanese salaryman lay perversion and debauchery.

Ever after Japan rose to transform into a global economic power, Americans never stopped to wonder what was behind the Japanese "mask," what terrible thoughts existed in the minds of those mute automatons. Worries that American white-collar workers might become feckless salarymen in virtual, if not entirely real, terms are evident in the electronic synth-pop music of the rock band Styx and its chart-topping song "Mr. Roboto" (1983).[66] In the chorus—"Domo arigoto, Mr. Roboto"—the band's lead singer profusely thanks a Mr. Roboto, a machine mannequin "with parts made in Japan." Media expert Ken McCleod argues that, despite the song's use of U.S. technology like Oberheim OB-XA and PPG Wave synthesizers, what stands out in the video is the cryptic sight of band members wearing masks with bucktoothed puzzling grins and drawn slanted eyes that one music critic says would not be "out of place in American World War II anti-Japanese propaganda."[67] Part and parcel of the MTV cable television revolution, the rock song spoke less to Japanese culture than to the "machines that represent America on television screens of the world."[68] Roboto represented a new social "makeup," which Dennis DeYoung of Styx cries out as "hiding under my skin . . . [where] my heart is human, my blood is boiling, my brain IBM."[69] DeYoung apologizes for the excesses of the American man, no longer a hero or savior for the world, one whose global quest for power became out of hand while it appears the Japanese in their lean factory style of manufacture have found the right amount of total control and humility. The song projects an alien cyborg figure, where Mr. Robot makes mechanical parts for "us" Westerners, but "we" are also becoming more robotic like him.

In the post–World War II period, it came to be widely acknowledged the indispensability of Japanese robots to the world's economic development, something evident in Styx's album liner notes: "The present . . . is a future where Japanese manufactured robots, designed to work cheaply and end-lessly. . . . 'Mr. Robotos' are everywhere, as factory robots and as manual laborers in jobs that were once held by humans." The prospect of human jobs being taken away by automation and automatons matched the uproar over the United States becoming too much like Japan, the latter a "highly-conformist" society with stilted nonintimate manners and "mechanically repetitive assembly-line labor."[70] Becoming Mr. Roboto is "plain to see" given that there is "too much technology" in our lives; we therefore need "machines to save our lives" even if "machines dehumanize" as the song's lyrics go.[71] Mr. Roboto never ever says anything in the video and sends the message of noncommunicative laughter. This yellowface character reveals the gap in cross-cultural knowledge and his mythic status as a silent model machine.[72]

Given the increasing reach of Japanning, "Mr. Roboto" easily lent itself to a new alien cyborg identity that was already racially coded.[73] "Mr. Ro-boto" joined songs like "Industrial Disease" (1982) from British bands like Dire Straits singing about countries trying to "have a war to keep us buying Japanese" or Pink Floyd's satirical "Not Now John" (1983) lashing out at how "we gotta compete with the wily Japanese." While these songs were racist toward Japanese, they also give gratitude to the Japanese for "doing the jobs that nobody wants to." They cathected a range of ambivalent feelings and pathos around a coming "Japanamerica."

Fears over this merging of American technoculture with Japanese ele-ments contrasted with Japan's lack of worry over Westernization. This pro-cess of being Westernized has been going on since the 1860s, and the Japa-nese embraced foreign-made machines (despite contempt for foreigners) out of practicality, without feeling they were sacrificing their soul.[74] For the United States, any form of Asianization or Japanization was tantamount to death. Movies like *Gung-Ho* (1986) make believable the notion that Japanese corporate masters are coming to teach their U.S. workers about hard work and quality control, while the latter try to humanize their Japanese overlords.

Most U.S. media coverage of the Japanese corporate model felt sour. Starting in 1980, Japanese steel mills had given technical advice to the U.S. industry about new Japanese technology like continuous and direct casting. But the exchange took a different turn as conglomerates such as Mitsubishi sought to buy Ford steel-making factories and American tire companies (Firestone), while U.S. firms such as Motorola sold new technology like the beeper ("pocket bells") to Japanese corporations despite a ban on all foreign procurement.[75] With the Japanese use of new financial instruments to re-convert American dollars back to yen for profit, it was believed that the United States' former enemies were now devising an "economic Pearl Har-bor."[76] The systemic effects of this new attack would not happen suddenly but creep up on the country until it was too late. By then, the U.S. economy would be essentially backed by foreign securities and flooded with Japanese gadgets, while U.S. citizens would lose themselves in "the wealth of the postwar Japan Inc. machine."[77]

Marching under the banner of Japanese neo-imperial capitalism, an Asian automaton army came out in force. It comprised workers, students, business owners, and financiers, whose labor products matched the global output of new technological machines. The last two decades of the twentieth century witnessed a slew of inventions that changed modern life: portable video games, recordable videocassette tape, the personal computer, medical synthetic skin, high-temperature superconductors, cellular phones, genetic engineering, cloning, stem cell research, and genetically engineered human growth hormones. The United States was going through structural reorganization, centralized on mounting an information-based society of codes and specialized algorithms characteristic of software or telecommunications with nodes, servers, and signals. The speedy move from handy industrial tools toward "intelligent machines" led to an altered sense of human social experience, setting the course for what computer programmer Jaron Lanier predicted when he coined the term *virtual reality* in 1983.

Hastening the virtual shift from analog to digital, Japan's dominance in consumer goods (represented by hand-held cameras, compact discs, and laser discs) did little to change views of this country as an evil empire. Though cyberspace appears to emancipate us from territoriality and our physical bodies, it carries "corporeal logics" that underwrite the national public sphere.[78] A new "recombinant" subject is formed based on "anarchic affairs between automaton and autonomy," sanctioning a new cyborg citizen.[79] In late capitalist America, the myth of the virtual machine punctured utopian dreams of "democratic transhumanism."[80] The myth appeared at a time when millions of Asian business owners, migrant workers, international students, refugees, and immigrants resettled in the United States to pursue the American Dream. In the face of Asian cultural appropriations of that national ethos, what gave safe harbor to the dream and its "amorphousness of mythic time and space" was the mythos of Japanese and Asians as alien cyborgs.[81]

While escalating its use of internet communication technology (ICT), Japan's own technocultural identity also found itself in turmoil. In an essay titled "Aliens R Us," film director Toshiya Ueno observes, "If the Orient was invented by the West, then the techno-Orient has been invented to define the images and modes of information capitalism and the information society."[82] While Asia exists primarily as a geographic place, the Orient still stands as a fantasy space. Its reinvention under techno-Oriental discourse floats the view of the Japanese as the "automated Other," produced in the two-way mirror in which Japan misunderstands itself through the eyes of the West. Per Ueno, the Japanese unconsciously replicate a stockpile of "Japanoid" images made by foreigners about them. Here, the Japanese custom of bowing plays out like a robot-like gesture. Information creates new epistemologies.

Information capitalism makes people into alien cyborgs without them fully knowing it. But rather than extrapolate cyborgness to all Asians, technoculture studies scholar Wendy Chun interprets techno-Orientalism to mean Japanese *high-tech* Orientalism since it is a higher grade of technology that we associate with Japan. As she observes, the Japanese are the definitive "mechanical mimics," and their alien labor presents a "privileged example of the virtual."[83] High-tech Japan stimulates new virtual cyberspaces for the "alienation" of the U.S. under the "fetishization of the Orient as a signifier of the future."[84] Cyberpunk writer William Gibson cast Japan as the futuristic dystopian backdrop to muddle through high-tech Orientalist fantasies. In his 1984 novel *Neuromancer* (which gave us the term *cyberspace*), the Japanese and other racialized groups inhabit a social matrix of data, one that a white male computer hacker navigates. This sci-fi novel was often read as a product of 1980s America, its plotline allegorizing the need to protect whiteness against the "high-technology assault" of Japan. This ostensible yet virtual assault warranted Walter F. Mondale, the former vice president and 1984 Democratic Party presidential nominee, to ask a group of American electrical workers: "What are our kids supposed to do? Sweep up around the Japanese computers?"[85] This quote evokes the "What shall we do with our boys?" cartoon created by the *Wasp* publication in 1882 to speak to the mechanized threat of Chinese coolies. The neoliberal call for free-market enterprise exacerbated the United States' trade imbalance with its junior partner Japan and with other Asian allies, the so-called Asian Tigers: South Korea, Taiwan, and Hong Kong. As the political boundary between friend and enemy reshuffled, so too did the line that separated the distinct parts of Asia from the United States.

Unease with new technology takes on a globalized register when it concerns Asian cyborgs who embody such technology. A spurt in transnational Asian professionals, recruited into Silicon Valley and other tech industries, served as the promise and peril of "smart machines" or AI. If so-called (Asian) machines became too self-aware and began to think for themselves, what would happen to white/human supremacy? To approach that line of thinking of Asian/artificial intelligence, one that can suck humanity into its vortex like the Borg, I turn now to analyze how the Asian nerd instills fear of communism and alien races.

Asian American Nerds and the Chinese Communist Borg

With communist China on the fast track to become the United States' next great adversary, this new Cold War set the stage for the myth of Chinese American scientists as virtual spies. Starting in 1986, the Federal Bureau of Investigation (FBI) began arresting American scientists of Chinese descent based on accusations that they were deceptive agents sending top secrets to China, wresting precious information from tech companies, and hacking into national security infrastructures in an unremitting Borg-like assault. Asian scientists working and living in the United States—such as the wrongly accused Taiwanese American scientist Wen Ho Lee—were assumed to be following the orders of their communist overlords, downloading encrypted material from U.S. servers and passing on confidential information. Arrested in 1999, Lee was the American nightmare of Asian-heritage scientists fleecing protected government data, flagging the immigrant professional as an "un-American" automaton. Seen in this manner, Asians at home and abroad "are linked—for better or worse . . . to each other."[86]

Despite the multicultural rhetoric of the 1990s to respect cultural differences, the racialized language of foreign invasion and contamination continued to mark Asians as nonhuman creatures without true "lived experience." Communications expert Lisa Nakamura demonstrated that many early online forum users and chat room participants chose graphic identities (such as Japanese ninjas) that fetishized Asian culture.[87] These "Asian-passing" race-bending characters alienated real people of color, who were dismayed by the pervasiveness of racism in the virtual world. Media studies scholar Irene Chien studied the rise of martial arts and dancing games popularized by Japanese game consoles. She found that gamers often took on Orientalist avatars for characters that were entirely controllable with "programmed moves."[88] In the games, she found a symbiotic conjunction between Asian techno-capitalism and Asian American nerdiness that was epitomized in the character Data in 1985 film *The Goonies*. This Chinese American kid named Data has a cyborg body with a smorgasbord of gadgets, while his all-white friends are just "normal" humans. In this contrast of opposites, Data is more than a cyborg; he is an alien cyborg.

Wariness toward alien cyborgs reached a peak in 1996, when the popular television show *Star Trek: The Next Generation* premiered one of its most famous villains: the Borg.[89] Complementing villains like Khan and Ming the Merciless that had long populated the show's cosmology, the Borg is a cybernetic alien species made up of hideous organic and artificial parts striving to control, enhance, and incorporate other living species into their "hive mind" via nanoprobes and microbes—all with the intended goal of achieving perfectibility. Put simply, the Borg desired only to be "perfect," a trait consonant with the goal of many Asians to look perfect for the family and achieve perfect test scores. In this *Star Trek* story line, the aliens are not trying to assimilate into general humanity. Rather, they seek to assimilate the humans into an alien culture.

In this space opera, assimilation figures more than a one-way process of foreign migratory aliens seeking to have close contact with *Homo sapiens* and enter their space. The cybernetic aliens wished to co-opt all those they encounter. The Borg contrasted the sleek, black-haired, tan Cardassians introduced in 1991 as a highly disciplined militaristic "Japanese-like" race of aliens born with perfect memories who love to drink hot fish juice and conduct sneak attacks on the USS *Enterprise* with their "Hideki" ships. The Borg represents a clannish analog of China's totalitarian, overpopulated, godless society. As the most dominant race in the universe—similar to the Han Chinese as the largest ethnic group on Earth—this monstrous blob holds strong to a philosophy for enveloping all life, a goal best symbolized when the Borg hails the Starfleet to surrender in a dry monotone voice: "We are the Borg. We will add your biological and technological distinctiveness to our own. Your culture will adapt to service ours. Resistance is futile." With their mind-control technology, the Borg seizes control of the human occupants on the USS *Enterprise*, morphing them into the Borg's self-improving image and automated message: "You will be assimilated." Finding that the Borg is interested in capturing humans' life forms and not just their technology, Starfleet's members try to stall the Borg's imperative to adapt to their defense mechanisms and collectivist ethos. In a thinly veiled reference to the United States and its global leadership, Captain Picard objects to this act of aggression against the "United Federation of Planets." As the leader of the strongest Starfleet ship, Picard is asked to stand in as the main human communicator for the Borg, to which he responds, "My culture is based on freedom and self-determination." This contact sets off a dialogue about freedom and authority between the two sides:

> The Borg: Freedom is irrelevant. Self-determination is irrelevant. You must comply.
> Capt. Picard: We would rather die.
> The Borg: Death is irrelevant. Your archaic cultures are authority-driven. To facilitate our introduction into your societies, it has been decided that a human voice will speak for us in all communications. You have been chosen to be that voice.

This alien cyborg species injects a probe into Captain Picard, and he mutates into a depersonalized appendage of the Borg. Unbeknownst to his fellows, Picard now commands his subordinates to "service us." The coolie's penchant for an awe-inspiring amount of work now translates into the seamless mechanical organization of the Chinese communist Borg. The visual imaging of the Borg with its metallic tentacles reaching into every planet is redolent of the well-reproduced cartoons in the nineteenth century, which portrayed the Chinese as a giant octopus with appendages in every corner of the earth. As scholar Sohn observes, "Racism's literal displacement onto the alien body consequently . . . imagines a racialized future beyond the dualism that posits the West against the East, and even more specifically destabilizes Asia as the primary site for projected anxieties."[90] In *Star Trek*, the Borg can be interpreted as a racial metaphor for the Chinese, but this figurative example takes place beyond the planet's known boundaries. Through the Borg, we have a vision of automaton anxieties and alien futures, which are richly imagined. In this vision, humans now must confront the chicanery of some omnipresent alien presence against what the Starfleet symbolizes: individualism, freedom, democracy, emotionality, heroism, and scientific innovation. Just as die-hard fans of *Star Wars* debate the show's hidden racist aspects, passionate devotees of *Star Trek* on online forums hypothesize whether the Borg is a reference to the Chinese and if the warrior Romulans are North Koreans.[91]

Beset by the dual economic threats of immigration and globalization, American audiences considered *Star Trek* a form of "universal commonsense" based on a defensive cultural nationalism.[92] In 1999, a *Weekly Standard* article discussed a "new China" as the "next century's superpower," commenting on its youthful population who are "Borg-like in their unified loathing of our flag."[93] The Chinese Borg story line appeared at a time when Japan was experiencing an economic slowdown as an outgrowth of a bursting asset bubble and high stagflation. This slump enabled the People's Republic of China to leap into the American mind as the next Asian juggernaut.

One can find a similar cultural scripting in realms that conflate Asian nerdiness with Borg-like collectivity. These scripts appeared whenever there was mention of Asians as super-efficient engineers, brainy technological wunderkinds, in-sync gymnasts, regimented students, and number-crunching accountants. In the 1980s, an influx of Asian American mostly female newscasters suggested a newly scripted sexual automaton that reflected a social pollution of white-dominant media spaces. Even though star reporters like Connie Chung were accused of appearing "robotic" by viewers, they were also reported to have overly strong personalities. When these public personalities would short out or short-circuit, as when Chung fought with her male co-anchors, this behavior justified them being fired from their jobs. Despite the prominence of Asian American women like Chung, the internalized hatred from anti-Asian jokes led many Chinese American women to fear the stereotype threat of Asians as "passive robots who like tedious work and are not much fun."[94] Those robots, though, are never really passive. When Chinese American reporter Julie Chen got called "Chenbot" by online trolls, she took ownership of that joke by promising to copyright that label.

Besides media journalism, the rarefied world of the arts also experienced an alien invasion. As the number of classical musicians of Asian descent increased in Western concert halls, there was some sense by white composers that these artists had nothing creative to offer. The spectral density of the virtual machine—both inside and outside—is evidenced by this observation: "Asians have the technique, Westerners have the heart, the soul. The image of Asians as automatons, robots . . . [stand] in as an effigy conjured up by the Western resentment of Asia's growing prosperity."[95] The model machine myth reemerged in the 1980s in the press to explain the clandestine takeover of Asian "whiz kids" who played piano and got perfect grades. Those whiz kids were not always celebrated, since "the image of the diligent, well-rounded Asian American student devolves into that of the asocial, robotic, Asian American nerd who studies incessantly."[96] Under an American education system founded on myths of meritocracy, these "academic machines" promised to beat out true Americans, bringing forth a Borg-like social order full of "narrow mathematical paragons."[97]

Before 1965, Asians only made up a million people, or less than 1 percent of the U.S. population, due to four decades of Asian exclusion, but that number nearly tripled by the 1990s. A big wave of migration by Asian educated migrants occurred under a preference for a professional category drafted in the 1950s as "aliens of distinguished merit and ability." Despite the desegregation of immigration laws, the historical figuration of the Asian as alien automatons merged with the newfound myth of Asians as model minorities in the post–1965 era. As literary scholar Michelle Huang observes, the "robot and model minority myth have risen together to create a modernized world seemingly full of automation and non-white peoples, often coextensively."[98]

The cybernetic alien takes root in this new virtual setting that depicts Asian people as "nerdy but not flawless machine-like workers" with diminished emotional lives—an expression that needed to be "demythologized."[99] Starting in the 1990s and continuing into the new century, American universities were facing an explosive enrollment of Asian American students in concert with a spurt in Asian international students. News magazines churned out stories of Asians outperforming everybody, due to their high intelligence quotient and college exam scores, even if they were not so great at human activities like interpersonal communication. Above all, Asian nerds are made laughable because they are "socially inept, better equipped for cerebral encounters than social ones. . . . [They are] sexually inexperienced and unsophisticated."[100] The Asian nerd supplies fodder for endless ridicule.

The intense spotlight on the "Asian invasion" of American colleges bolstered the myth of the "standardized-test machine."[101] As potential national security threats, their academic success attracted government investigations that plots the Asian student as threat within the necropolitics of higher education.[102] A model minority/machine myth underlines this media framing of Asians college applicants, while white candidates are consistently rated as having more human qualities like courage, relatability, and likeability.[103] Insofar as whites possessed "deep expressive emotional selves," Asians appeared as nonindividuated sex-deprived bodies with flat "surface selves."[104] The underlying subtext was that Asians went too far in their academic pursuits, radically altering the normal state of learning and overturning the humanistic values of a Western liberal arts education based on human discovery, curiosity, and passion.

Economic jealousy does not entirely explain the antipathy toward the Asian nerd. For example, Asian Americans are often compared with Jews as model minorities based on their class status, but there is a slight difference. In the Jewish online magazine *Jewcy*, cultural critic Benjamin Nugent identified the steady replacement of the Jewish nerd with Asians in U.S. popular culture, but he found that Asians occupied a special place within a continuum that runs from "really sensual" animals to "not sensual" machines. He explained the scale this way: "Animals, then Africans, then Europeans, then Asians, then machines . . . If nerds are people who have been sucked into the orbit of the machine and sapped of human emotion, then Asians—who are perceived as industrious, asexual, machinelike—are the nerdiest of ethnic groups."[105] Modern anti-Semitism varied so much that he finds it very burdensome to locate Jews on the human-animal-machine scale. Even though Jewish people occupy the same role as the Asians as progenitors of the contemporary ethnic nerd trope, the latter practice more machine learning.

In Australia, many locals reacted harshly to "over-schooled robots" from Asia, who tore asunder the country's meritocratic educational system.[106] While Asian men are typically imagined as nerds, Asian women are sometimes implicated. In the Australian context, writer Jessica Yu notices a distinction made between the Asian and white women in the girl nerd stereotype of the late 1990s and early 2000s. Representing the democratic freedoms and rebellion of Western culture, white females are assumed to be intellectually original, urbane, and charismatic. They, however, individually must overcome the call to cultural conformity relayed by an army of "smart" Asian women. Yu finds this "automaton army" stereotype reminiscent of the stereotype printer, the repetitious machine used for mass-produced print media. Fabricated within an oppressive social structure, Asian women lack an inner life; they are unoriginal cultural robots, the opposite of "genuinely human" white women. No matter how smart they are, Asian girls remain a virtual machine, an abject cog within the conservative "family of Asian automatons, dull, intact, same-same, patriarchal, disciplined."[107] Without a mind of their own, Asian women are pure bodies, and "their bodies lack originality and vitality. . . . They are motionless bodies and motionless people, who might well be upwardly mobile but are unable to think slantwise downwards, sideways."[108]

Machine-like stereotypes influence the general perception of Northeast Asians. Confucian societies are already seen as unsociable and strait-laced, due to cultural norms that involve little to no direct eye contact, reduced physical touching, speaking or acting in ways that do not attract attention, listening to and obeying authority, never complaining, following rules, and adapting to social circumstances rather than asserting individualism. The model machine myth takes advantage of the racial constitution and cultural "fiber" of Asians, to justify cruelty toward them as "stifled, repressed, abused, conformist quasi-robots who simply do not matter, socially or culturally."[109] According to cultural pundit Wesley Yang, that stereotype of robotic minorities is written on his "reptilian" face, which causes self-loathing. With this visual marker of animality, Asian subjects must go to inhuman lengths to show or prove their humanity to others. Apparently, the robot stereotype remains so pervasive that it is internalized by Asian descendants themselves.

That burden to prove one is truly human remains a challenge. Throughout the 1990s and 2000s, conservative Chinese American organizations, in their vocal opposition to affirmative action, worked against the myth of "test-acing machines" by pointing to Asian innovation in the arts and sciences.[110] Beyond these "humanizing" efforts, Asian American bloggers homed in on "tiger parents'" as the primer of success for the super-minority. Journalist Jeff Yang says as much in an opinion piece entitled, "Asian Parents: Your Kids Are Not Robots." Despite the microaggressions associated with the "interchangeable Asian," he says Asians are sometimes to blame for this damaging grouping: "We're robots who can only copy and clone and grub and grind. . . . As much as we may publicly bristle at the notion that Asians are 'boring academic robots,' it's tough to cast this image off when loud segments of our community are doing their best to reinforce it."[111] From this vantage, literary scholars Lee and Wong say, "The Asian (American) cyborg is not solely the construct of the West, but also a self-invention that takes on model minority dimensions."[112]

One spots this self-invention and cultural reinforcement in Amy Chua's controversial memoir *Battle Hymn of the Tiger Mother*. In the book, the law professor hypes up the superiority of Chinese parenting over the Western style in her, where she wished one of her daughters to "benefit from the best aspects of American society," even if this stalwart parenting style denies them many American freedoms. This overparenting is not couched as harsh when compared to social rearing in Asia: "I did not want her to end up like one of those weird Asian automatons who feel so much pressure from their parents that they kill themselves after coming in second on the national civil service exam."[113] This tiger mother forced her progeny to brush off gym, theater arts, and playmates while taking piano lessons on top of getting the best grades. Despite the family's racially mixed identity, Chua believes in the Asian/American distinction. Her stated intent of not making her Jewish Asian American children like the pure automatons in Asia (who are totally robbed of life) resulted in "sweeping comparisons between Asian roboticism and American ingenuity."[114]

Sweeping stereotypes of Asians as quasi-robots entered as legal evidence. In lawsuits brought by some Asian groups against elite schools, the dean of admissions at the Massachusetts Institute of Technology was found to have described a top Asian American applicant as "yet another texture-less math grind."[115] For this administrator, Asians gave the appearance of overcoached model machines rather than helpless "model victims" of racial quotas. These simple-minded stereotypes played out in other legal arenas.

In the case of *State v. Chu* (2002), a teenager named Dale Chu was found party to a crime, committing arson of property with the intent to defraud an insurer for a dry-cleaning building that his parents owned. The minor contended his rights had been violated when he "was subjected to racial stereotyping suggesting that Korean sons are automatons who blindly carry out the orders even when the orders involve criminal activity."[116] In the writ of cert (brief) where his conviction was appealed based upon wrongful judgment, the boy confessed he resented the prosecutor's portrayal of him as a mindless robot—a bias that produced a negative impact on the boy's case. The state claimed race could be injected into the deliberation of a case with the caveat that it allows the jury to make "quick and easy decisions." While opposed to gratuitous racial references, the state court admitted in its appellate brief to using racial examples, claiming they were "relevant" to determining Chu's "interior" motive; it finally argued those robotic assumptions "were not improper racial stereotypes."

Unlike cases in which subtle stereotyping is hard to pinpoint, the prosecutorial agent in this case blatantly argued to the jury that Korean sons would never try to talk back to their parents and always did as they were told. In eyes of the law, Chu and other minors lacked legal personhood. As more or less ciphers, these virtual (nonlegible) subjects are caught up in the tableau of an alien family culture that squashed individual thought and a U.S. legal system that regards that culture as deserving of judicial scrutiny.

This racist loyalty test to gauge the Asian robotic mind echoes the psychological examinations set upon interned children during World War II, when the state assessed young Japanese Americans' undying "automatic" bonds to their ancestral homeland of Japan. The framing of a real American hovers around the query of who is a real human, a litmus test that Asian American children seem to contest but always fail.

If the adage that life imitates art is true, then the world of science fiction opens a window for noticing the conditions of present society, as much as it is colored by spectacular visions of the future. As a metaphor for Asian communalism, the Borg from *Star Trek* is an artifact of sci-fi myth that reveals how the polis of humanity can be readily absorbed by an alien blob. This tension came to a head in 1996, the same year the Democratic Party indiscriminately investigated donors with Asian-sounding last names for influencing the outcome of the 1996 presidential elections. In that year, California voters passed a proposition to end affirmative action policies, which advocates of the ban claimed hurt the Asian student-majority population at the prestigious University of California. That same year, political cartoonist Gary Trudeau drew a series of vignettes in his famous *Doonesbury* comic strip, poking fun at the scholastic achievements of Asian Americans. In one strip, an Asian student talks to another and says this line in a deadpan tone, "Take me to your leader." This line is commonly associated with aliens in old Hollywood movies, but in this example, it marks Asians as "being mechanical, robotic, relentless—seeming almost alien and out of this world—in their pursuit of academic success."[117] The aliens, it seemed, have not only arrived on planet Earth, but they also found a pathway into the United States' elite universities and cherished political institutions.

Understanding the divide between human insiders and alien outsiders is of the essence when persons are impugned. A case in point was Arthur Chu, who attained multiple wins on the popular American television trivia game show *Jeopardy!*. Chu irked die-hard audiences by refusing to play by the unspoken rules of the game and picking questions in random order. This bedeviling savant attracted the ire of online critics, who considered the player an antisocial and rude robot. A former champion of the show said, "Arthur is a machine," while an entertainment writer remarked on the "emotional distress this machine has inflicted on viewers . . . [with plans to] build an army of bespectacled robots that are programmed to irritate random strangers. Or maybe use the money to run for public office so he can pass a law against smiling."[118] This quip captured the wariness toward alien cyborgs weaseling their way into the American electorate. The insinuation here was that a whip-smart Asian machine had not only deflated an American intellectual pastime but corrupted the country's political machine with "yellow money."[119] By rigging the democratic process, this alien cyborg could virtually turn all Americans into lugubrious robot slaves. This wild postulation conferred power to the Korean War–era myth posited in *The Manchurian Candidate*, which suggested U.S. politicians are easily brainwashed by red states like China. Chinese Americans like Chu—for all their success and intelligence—constitute an extension of the socialist Borg.

There were real troubles underlying Arthur's "mechanical" performance and "failure" to display human character. It was later revealed that this Chu was earning money to pay medical bills for an ill wife suffering from cancer. As anthropologist Lila Abu-Lughod explains, people of color live "not as robots programmed with 'cultural' rules, but as people going through life agonizing over decisions, making mistakes, trying to make themselves look good, enduring tragedies and personal losses, enjoying others, and finding moments of happiness."[120] The fact that Chu was hot-tempered and often harangued the show's host, throwing around sarcastic barbs, was not enough to dispel impressions of him as a spineless nose-to-the-grindstone nerd. For disgruntled folks in the educated *Jeopardy!* crowd, Chu was another foreign robot, bringing computerlike cunning to American civil society. As an acculturated alien machine, this cyborg spoke perfect "unaccented" English and had a white wife. Chu's emasculation as an Asian American male is interpolated through the struggles of actors like John Cho, striving to "play human" to land romantic leading-man roles in a racist film industry: "That really is the Asian American conundrum, being thought of as not human. Sometimes you're superhuman like a computer, 'Oh, you're so smart,' or subhuman in the sense . . . The thing is not so much to play romance or to get the girl but to play human . . . to achieve equal status in the humanity department."[121] Though some might consider the model minority myth a "positive" stereotype, there is a sinister side to that racist trope, one that suggests foreigners are influencing U.S. politics and that "Asian Americans are machine-like drones, fearful competitors who have unbalanced lives."[122] The varieties of public discrimination and emotional turmoil Asians face tell us that there is more going on below the surface of the inscrutable Asian crypto-body. They hint at very personal battles waged on a public stage.

Conclusion

Near the tail end of the American Century, the issue of technocultural alienation and (inter)national borders continues to be important despite the impact of globalization. Social critic Keith Aoki inquires, "What happens when the others are now 'here,' and 'we' are actually over 'there'?"[123] Ultimately, the virtual apparition of Asians as a Borg-like cyberforce—a machine that is everywhere and nowhere—deflects from the ideological "machinery of whiteness" and the use of borders to define national existence. This technology of control flexes a "portal to be opened or tightened, racialized or deracialized according to the economic and cultural requirements of the moment."[124] That is, the operations of whiteness change according to and depending on necessity.

The virtualization of Asian bodies leaves unremarked the invisible power of whiteness and Western hegemony. Artificial intelligence doubled as the distorted mirror of Asian intelligence. The question "Can Asians think?" posed by Singaporean diplomat Kishore Mahbubani in the 1990s recalls the Turing test for early AI: "Can machines think?" The horrors of smart machines and smart Asians infer the problems of objectivity within human- and machine-made decisions.

This chapter presents the enactment of the virtual machine myth through the figure of the alien cyborg. It fleshes out this myth by observing both the boundary maintenance and virtual dissolution of boundaries between Asia and America as these constructs relay fears of foreign Asian labor, capital, and technology. Within the tension between new spheres of consumer trade and the presupposed grounds of national domesticity, we find the communist Borg, the Japanese corporate salaryman, and the Asian American nerd. Here, the virtual machine myth helps decipher the racial elements mired within the age of information. It teases out anxieties over an alien *creature* festering inside the belly of the national body.[125] The breakdown of boundaries between alien/citizen, analog/digital, and human/machine flags the slow disintegration of national binaries even if there remains opposition between a domestic inside and foreign outside. Technocultural logics of exclusion can be found in the nativist backlash against Indian call-center workers, even when these technical support assistants are no more than "virtual migrants" that seldom get to leave their homeland.[126]

We find many virtual machines infringing upon U.S. national security through a limitless range of technologically enabled avenues. This virtual machine myth corroborates Roland Barthes's remark that myth is a form of meta-speech, where certain meanings can be drawn out from what is *not* shown as much as what is made visible. The myth can be related to the terrorist attacks by radicalized Muslim extremists on the World Trade Center on September 11, 2001. After the attacks, the mythic figure of the Asian automaton took on other virtual guises. It was evident in all the conspiracy theories about Jihadist terrorist cells exploiting invisible networks to hijack planes. It was perceptible in the intensifying U.S. rivalry with China, the latter accused of not only undercutting U.S. businesses but launching cyberattacks against national agencies. Such examples call up (post)national crises that construct "alternative frames of reference" for the model machine.[127] That alien machine appeared in the personified form of serial killers like Seung-Hui Cho, a "resident alien" from South Korea who conducted the deadliest school shooting in U.S. history. In 2007, Cho produced a video manifesto rant before his murder spree, which went viral, announcing in a Borg-like monotone voice that "space aliens have replaced my brain with a remote transmitter and have made me into a robot."[128] With weapons strapped to his cyborg body, Cho was no simple robot, as he hunted his victims down like a video game. To a horrified public, this was an alien predator engaged in a high-tech proxy war. The robotic nerd was now a "domestic terrorist."

In the twenty first century, the foreboding danger of Asian machines would take on an enlarged dimension with the global influence of China, a sea change that warned the United States could either cede ground to or mitigate those machines. In 2017, a month before President Donald Trump was inaugurated on an antiglobalist platform of China bashing, white nationalism, and immigration restriction—the sequel to the film *Blade Runner* came out, called *Blade Runner 2049*. This new story involves K, a replicant officer employed by the Los Angeles Police Department, who goes around stamping out older models. He does his job well until discovering that his own species of bioengineered cyborgs has now reproduced with pure biological humans. This leads to a moral quandary for the protagonist: How or why destroy alien replicants if they have genetically blended with humans?

Insofar as fictional tales of slayed alien replicants are coterminous with real-life events like Vincent Chin's murder, where does one find the traces of humanity? According to Helen Zia, the activist and lawyer who handled Chin's legal case, said, "We have the good, the bad, and the ugly. We're not models. We should be seen in our full humanity."[129] It remains to be seen to what extent that aspiration is nurtured or tenable with the continued hunting of model machines in an impending Asian Century.

5

Global Machines

*Reconfiguring the Roboticized Asian within
the New Millennium*

At the dawn of what futurists dubbed "the Asian Century," we are witnessing a reorientation of global activity from the West toward the East. The move foreshadows a zeitgeist that operates like an integrated machine in terms of "distributed parts and patterns of circulation."[1] This chapter links the growing influence of robotics in the twenty-first century as it overlaps with the steadfast treatment and tenacious perception of Asians as robotic machines. Such correlations draw from a model machine framing of people from the East as animatronic blanks who merely mimic, copy, and toil relentlessly. This global reframing causes "racial recalibrations" in what media studies scholar Margaret Rhee calls the human/machine/animal triangulation.[2] From Chinese factory workers and Korean pop singers, the profundity of Asian roboticism, or Asian people acting or existing like robots, and the U.S. myth of Asians as model machines coheres within a global technoculture ever defined by Asian actors and interests.

This chapter assesses whether the automation of global work complicates or exacerbates the racial archetype of Asians as a robot-like population within global public culture. It addresses the following question: What does it mean now to be not simply a technocultural Other for the United States but a hybridized *global machine* shaped by different value systems? This globalism recognizes a multipolar world without a singular dominant power, even if the United States remains a hegemonic power for the time being. It can be detected in examples involving technological labor extracted from the former American colony of the Philippines or in Taiwanese subcontractors working with U.S. multinational companies in China.

This chapter on the global machine follows the last one about the virtual machine. My analysis recognizes that the result of "virtualizing" globalization processes is an acknowledgment of the complexification and globality of racial capitalism. The global, in many ways, becomes the natural end point to conceptualizing a history of (foreign) labor migration, (international) war, (geopolitical) militarism, and (transnational) economy. But global means something else when Asians themselves induce big changes in once-dominant Western paradigms like the model machine. Questions of nationality/citizenship, labor/class, and sexuality/identity that animated previous examples of the Asian automaton now take on a supercharged sensibility. In a world of interconnectivity, we start to encounter all types of Asianized automata. This chapter's models of the machine are Asian laborers put to work in the global factory or on the international stage. What is being modeled is a global machine premised upon Asian labor as the prime component to enhance capital on a planetary scale.

Tarrying with this myth of Asians as machines of the world builds on the old U.S. myth of Asian coolies as labor machines. It recognizes their use value in a global moment determined more and more by Asian modes of production. In the course of my dissection of Asian labor in the new century, I dismantle millennial discourses that articulate Asia's global takeover of the world and the ever-precarious status of low-wage Asian workers in the globalized economy—two factors that merged with and maintained U.S. technocultural hegemony in the twenty-first century.

Stepping away from the big question of what will happen to human beings in the age of smart robots, we can ask what it means to be an "automated Asian" in a postmillennial milieu increasingly run by the Asian machine. What does *robot* mean in a global context or a specific moment? For example, an academic in Singapore criticizes his country's narrow focus on grades and how students are pressed into service as "learning machines," drilled in the art of test taking with the unblinking piety of automata: "You're stifling someone's ability to think for themselves. You're like robots."[3] This admission of Asian roboticism by a Singaporean merges with the simple view of Asian countries as having a robotic army of overtested students. But with Singapore's promotion of "Asian cultural values" as reason for economic success over the West, Asian countries bear responsibility for those model machine discourses. By examining the myth and rhetoric behind media hype, new organizational practices, and state discourses, I contend that the conflation of Asians with robotic qualities—in personhood and in work style—persists even in Asian environments. A global fluency in the model machine myth affects and effects a variety of programmable "automaton-like" populations.

Through key examples around the world, I examine the globalization of this myth and what this dynamic means for notions of freedom, equality, and oppression today. Such critical work eschews any easy explanations of the robot-human interface to delve deeper into the global production of race, gender, nation, and class. Signifiers of human difference become transmitted through a topography in which it is hard to distinguish between the human "us" and alt-human "them." In the following, I first discuss the confluence of Asian robotics and roboticism in the new century, beginning with Japan. In the following section, I examine the rise of China as a metaphoric rise of the machines. I end with a discussion of Korea's famous fembots, diving into the South Korean pop-music industry and North Korea's female robot army. I connect South Korea's robotic economy to outsourced laborers, digital and manual, from the Philippines.

Moving across the world, this chapter considers how the automation of work also transforms the humanistic question of who we are as human beings. What has been missing from this important conversation about humanity's future are the social meanings surrounding how Asians are still being rendered as "robotic" subjects. Through the firmament of Asian workers as global machines exploitable by anyone and everyone, I assess whether the automation of work will lessen, complicate, or exacerbate this modern archetype. By looking at popular sites worldwide, I suggest that the Asian automaton figure will not simply evaporate in the new millennium but continues to inform and affect how particular human subjects are construed as exploitable/threatening automatons.

Robots and Robotics in the Asian Century

In this section, we can make sense of the Asian automaton figure as a mobile sign and signifier of change that circulates broadly and can be appropriated by even Asians themselves. We go from thinking of Asians and Asian Americans as model machines from a mostly Western perspective to consider Asian roboticism in its manifold and multilateral dimensions. There is still a modeling function at play here, but this function has stretched tremendously to the point that it little resembles what we have known in the past. My critical trajectory moves forward from the acute observations made by Asian studies expert Artur Lozano-Méndez that techno-Orientalist images of Asia are diversified and have been projected on such Asian societies as Taiwan, Singapore, South Korea, and China. While Lozano-Méndez focuses mostly on Japan and its development of robotics, he notes how the features of the "Oriental Other" in one country can be adapted in another to "epitomize a hyper-technified, dehumanized and materialist society."[4] Across a wide sweep, this chapter adds to the work of Lozano-Méndez and media scholars like Jane Park who are interested in the construction of "technological others" that are "racially coded Asian."[5] A specific aim here is to grasp the ways Asian roboticism and machine myth might work as a knotted form of difference making across regional scales—where various technocultural forms and conditions play into the creation of "new" model machine types. This critique pays attention to the subtle codes, hidden cues, and pluralistic sensibilities emerging not under one singular geographic "Asia" but the structural and linguistic incoherence of what literary scholars Tina Chen and Jerry Won Lee have described in terms of "global Asias."[6]

The start of the Asian Century does not necessarily mean the end of the American Century. Through the stretched command of political sovereignty and corporate controls, U.S. hegemonic power has now reached influence in the form of a global empire that is "spatial but also mechanical in the sense that the subject is transformed into . . . the machine."[7] According to political philosopher Michael Hardt and sociologist Antonio Negri, we are producing "new virtualities" that reach beyond what I described in terms of virtual machines in late capitalism: "The hybridization of humans and machines is no longer defined by the linear path it followed throughout the modern period. . . . The hybridizations and machinic metamorphoses can now be overturned . . . the political struggle over the definition of machinic virtuality, or really over the different alternatives of the passage between the virtual and the real, is a central terrain of struggle."[8] In this global terrain of power, we can imagine the role Asian automatons might play. Let us investigate what machinic metamorphoses might look like for those who exist outside the abstract collectivity of what Hardt and Negri call the "multitude."

In the United States, Northeast Asians have been usually viewed as robot-like beings, as embodied by the factory worker and all those who not only run the machine but remain machine. This primarily U.S. invention remains a main point of departure for scholars who work in the growing subfield of techno-Orientalism.[9] Beyond U.S. techno-Orientalism, we can reflect more broadly about technoculture beyond the Westernized definition presented to us by media scholar Constance Penley and social analyst Andrew Ross, who defined it as "actually existing technoculture in Western society, where the new cultural technologies have penetrated deepest, and where the environments they have created seem almost second nature to us."[10] In a global era when the Western "us" has been deeply penetrated by Asian technocultural products, we might focus on the myriad ways certain technocultures are not just Western or even Eastern but global in the sense that all kinds of actors are simultaneously and collectively refashioning

Asian roboticism. They are all altering the conjunctural means by which "Asian and Asian American subjects and objects are inextricably bound to feared and out-lawed technologies."[11]

In 2019, India swore in its first robot police officer, named KP-Bot. Though limited to salutes and greeting visitors to the department, this robocop does not yet include facial-recognition software or bomb-detecting capabilities, but plans are in place for those features in the future. A curious fact that it is a woman (with lipstick no less) says as much as what it hides: "Women empowerment and gender equality were kept in mind while deciding on the gender of the first robot," decreed the police chief. "The fact that most front office jobs are managed by women was considered."[12] We must think about how robotics takes on gendered terms and what it means for inanimate (though also animated) objects to be coded as female. How do these technocultural inflections reinforce gender norms even as they seek to support the coming robot revolution.

Lifelike androids that can talk and walk had been first conceived since the 1960s in Japan. But in 2000, ASIMO, a humanoid astronaut robot created by Honda, found fame as "the world's most humanoid robot," one which spotlighted the "racialized capital of technology."[13] When newspapers declare "the human population is shrinking . . . and robots are on the rise," this statement has special resonance for Japan, the "oldest" country in the world with a plummeting birth rate and a rising elderly population that needed care. With restriction on non-Japanese immigrants, robots serve as the surrogate humanity for an exclusionary country.[14] The 2000s produced more sophisticated female-looking Asian-appearing models (modeled after real-life Japanese actresses) with realistic fleshy silicon skin and the ability to hold conversational dialogue. Receptionist robots include "Saya," who premiered in 2005, and Minami, making her debut in 2013 (other female robots include the actroid "Der Kokoro" and the mail server "Chihira Junko").[15] In 2009, Japanese engineers introduced the most impressive one to date, a dancing and flipping bipedal humanoid robot, one seen as "creepy" and "attractive" that relies on gendered ideas of Asian women's robotic abilities to take orders from their masters.

In popular culture, Japan's inveterate obsession with sexy animated feminine robots is captured by the music video for "Spring of Life" by the Japanese women's musical group Perfume. Whether moving in jerky movements or singing in chipmunk autotune or passing out in a catatonic state slumped against a wall, the song and video reflected the Japanese fetish for cute, innocent girly things, sublimating human emotions and immature sexual thoughts into an aloof adoration of inanimate "safe" objects. In the video, the performers croon the lines: "I feel unsatisfied . . . it's all because I'm self-dependent." Even as these artificial girls cannot find satisfaction in being "real" humans, they nevertheless act out normal human behavior like eat-ing, talking on the phone, and applying makeup, which presents funny rather quirky simulations of the Asian-as-machine typology. Responding to the loneliness of living as automatons on their own stylish terms, the video ends with the girls unplugging themselves from the (patriarchal capitalist) machine to which have been attached. This detachment suggests that these feminine self-acting robots are not enslaved to corporate male bosses, as they work as independent beings. The astonishing fact that the most visible J-pop girl group in the world do their own choreography and are real-life friends complicates this typecasting of Japanese women as only robots fol-lowing (male) masters and having no real human relations. Impeded efforts by Prime Minister Shinzo Abe to rev up Japan's lethargic economy by focus-ing on increasing women's labor participation has been blamed on the country's sheepish male workers and cultural norms. Japanese critics now consider the robotic salaryman, once glorified as an "all-conquering eco-nomic hero" of the nation during its boom years, an anachronistic slave to habit, "stressed but trendy white-collar drones" whose obeisance to senior-ity and permanent employment holds Japan back from having a liquid ser-vice-oriented economic market.[16] This opinion slightly changes the dynam-ic of Japan's postwar economic machine, built on the former hypermasculine war machine of the Japanese government. Apparently, the Asian robotic stereotype is now hindering Japan's economy.

The human-automaton relation, like gender relations, remains compli-cated in a country like Japan, which is global in its technological impact on the world, even as it is appears inward-looking due to cultural parochialism. Christopher Simmons, an American professor based in Tokyo, observes that, though we associate Japan as a leader in robotics, the country lags in terms of integrating robots or introducing new technology into society. This delay is due to a punishing corporate work culture and a domestic popula-tion built on "an intense work ethic that already ensures a supply of robotic labor—in human form."[17] Japan, he says, builds the future but lives in the past due to its egregious issues with women's labor and economic protec-tionism—all of which contributes to the probability that humans will not be pushed out by robots until they become less robotic themselves: "Japanese society is already 'robotic' in ways that other countries are not. . . . The high-ly structured nature of Japanese society will make people-facing AIs easier to introduce, but may have little impact on improving the lives of the once-ubiquitous 'salaryman.'"[18] While trying on a telepresence robot body, Sim-mons finds the metallic constraints of new bodily technologies "remarkably similar to the social constraints of living in Japan, where the smooth-run-ning social machine depends on a communal willingness to be a little arti-ficial ourselves."[19] While these observations from a *gaijin*, or foreigner, might be off the mark, they reveal how Japan is a global machine in some aspect (consumer technology) but not in others (social rights). While Japan has focused on all types of service bots (U.S. companies are trained on developing military and industrial robots), South Korea stood to gain the most from robots like the EveR-1, which appeared in 2006, giving the first glimpse of "networked robots" that will serve new high-tech urban cities and showcase the ways Asian "robotic technologies are at the forefront of the world."[20] While inorganic robots are turbocharging the rise in automation in Japan, there are actual people treated as simple machines, as in the case of the Chinese factory worker.

In the following sections, I provide broad readings of the Asian model machine myth through a number of instances, probing the means through which certain groups present other "modes of being human."[21] In the process of illustrating the global production of Asian machines, I also indicate the international standing of the United States at this juncture, even as new coordinates of power are taking place. Despite the feeling of unicity that comes with more people traveling around the world, certain robotic racial scripts endure. For example, one travel blogger wrote that Taiwanese people appeared to be "empty shells with no soul or emotions, like plastic mannequins (similar to America, but even worse). Their faces are passionless and robotic, as if their soul and humanity has been squashed, suppressed, or drained out of them."[22] Instances of stereotyping like this index degrees of relative human difference at a time when Taiwanese people are the worst kind of automatons to become, even when Americans are already themselves turning into vapid human automatons. This social media example corresponds with Daniel Vukovich's observation that Orientalism has shifted from one based on a logic of *total difference* (cultural essentialism) to one of *general equivalency* that reflects the postmodern logic of global capitalism. Capitalism creates profit-driven value out of everything, but postmodernism allows for a creative interpretation and re-sorting of such value. In light of this, modern Asians are measuring their technocultural capabilities against non-Asians that view them as uninspired, dumb robots. This relative balancing of power forces recognition of Asian modernity, even if there are traces of the colonial past insofar as white travelers still feel morally superior to or more modern than the plastic Asians.[23]

When advanced economies like China, Singapore, Taiwan, and South Korea—countries that dominate the semiconductor industry—threaten the long-held hegemony of Europe and North America, the economic competitions of the Asian Century replays an antipodal struggle between East and West, where East Asian productivity promises to knock Europeans from the top of the international pecking order. From the perspective of industrialized societies in the West (a category that awkwardly includes Japan sometimes), there is now a dramatic fight against the mechanized Asiatic hordes endangering the rest of *humanitas* with their slave-like Oriental states. The global reach of the Asian machine (capital, factory, and automaton) prompts questions of who is exploited when "it is not clear who makes and who is made in the relation between human and machine."[24]

This bare formulation of Asians as machines and whites as human is turned upside down in the Canadian mockumentary *Ghosts with Shit Jobs* (2012). Set in 2040 Toronto after the economic collapse of North America, white people are now the labor machines, comprising a cheap "foreign" labor pool for Asian markets, doing jobs that no one in China wants to do any longer. A Chinese news program focuses on these "ghosts" (Cantonese slang for foreigners), putting them into humiliating situations for the amusement of global Chinese audiences. There is Oscar, a digital janitor, who paints over copyrighted logos on digital street surfaces; a couple with PhDs in robotics assembly who make mechanical baby dolls for the children of wealthy Asian families; Anton and Toph, spider silk collectors or gatherers of the web deposits from the giant mutant spiders, making ends meet in the new Silk Road; and Serina, a "human spam" and part-time hooker who promotes corporate brand titles.

Toronto's large Chinese minority are nowhere to be found in this parody of post-NAFTA North America, one that posits Asian countries and audiences as now ruling the roost. In quite a reversal, whites are the productive automatons for Asians. Read another way, the allegoric film exposes audiences to the given current reality that it is Asians who frequently perform such work today in these proscribed roles. Even so, the satirical approach to mechanized Asian archetypes of prostitute, programmer, proletariat, and PhD might lead the uncritical watcher to mistake Asian machines as now in power and think Asians are practicing a form of "reverse racism" against whites. This "lo-fi" sci-fi film points to a global machine with multiple dimensions, adding an inverted lens to classic Western perceptions of Asians as a counterfeit race.

Another science fiction text that refashions the shibboleth of Asians as machines is *After Yang*, a film based on a short story from the American writer Alexander Weinstein in *Children of the New World*. In the 2016 original source material, an educated white middle-class couple adopts a girl from China and, not wanting her to feel alone, purchases a lifelike Chinese robot sibling/guardian named Yang described by his makers as "Big Brother, babysitter, and storehouse of cultural knowledge."[25] Despite his nearly human qualities, like eating food, the boy eventually malfunctions. The father rushes to a repair shop and is offended when a racist mechanic sees no individual value in this family machine, saying robots from Asia are all the "same thing." The liberal narrator wakes up to the realization that "Chinese,

Japanese, South Korean didn't matter anymore; they'd all become threats in the eyes of Americans" that drive trucks with stickers that say, "WE CLONE OUR OWN."[26] This manufactured son is put out of commission, and the human family mourns Yang as one of their own. They are unexpectedly sentimental. The timely story brings an emotional facet to the heated political trysts waged by President Donald Trump against Korean manufacturing exports, Asian immigration, and Chinese workers. Characterizations of CJKs (Chinese, Japanese, Koreans) as perfect machines do not only work at the level of verbal insult or physical description as a global market economy already makes model/global machines out of them.

India's ambivalent place in global technocultures expanded in the new century. In 2017, the Indian government extended a ban on commercial surrogacy, reserving it only for needy Indian couples, halting a lucrative business built on abuse of the poor.[27] Commercial medical tourism has run rampant since its legalization in India in 2002. Low-income women since then were regularly recruited as surrogates, churning out babies for rich couples based in Western nations, primarily the United States and the United Kingdom. From machine metaphors of the brown female body as an overly fertile machine, there arose a "rent-a-womb" market. As surrogate humanity, they are a desired instrument of reproductive technology with detachable organs, artificial uteruses, and other removable parts within a "mechanical imagination of the body."[28] India's policy was followed by bans in Nepal and Thailand, pushing this global industry into Laos and Cambodia, where surrogacy brokers work with their international clientele to transform local women from low-income countries in the Global South into "baby-making machines."[29]

These views are not restricted to the outsourced surrogacy market. A contributor to the *Times of India* chat forum upbraided multinational companies exploiting cheap tech workers. In a removed comment, this person lashed out at "brain drain" outsourcing: "The only ambition Indian have [*sic*] is to learn how to be a robot and work in US/UK/Australia for the rest of their natural life. . . . Outsourcing companies are really eating away the job opportunities of Indians in that particular country. Only robots. No human labor."[30] The reduction of IT workers to robots is revealing of a labor hierarchy, one that is local and global. Meanwhile, remote tech-support computer work in Hyderabad, Bangalore, and Mumbai focalizes the labor of "Indian machines" huddled in back offices like cattle as part of "India's outsourcing industry [that] thrums with potential and power, as if it were itself a machine."[31] This analogy is a quote taken from a 2014 interview with Chris Anderson, editor of U.S. tech magazine *Wired*, who says that despite these machines taking jobs away from U.S.-based IT professionals, the humanity of the latter cannot be ultimately replaced.[32] But even though "India looks like an artificial intelligence, the superbrain that never arrived *in silico*," the biggest global threat to North America, came not from democratic India but from "red capitalist" China.[33]

China's Ascent as the Rise of the Machines

During the U.S.-led global "War on Terror," the specter of Asian global machines found rejuvenation in the filmic remake of the Cold War classic *The Manchurian Candidate* (2004). This new release occurred right after the American invasion of Iraq and demonstrates this fear of mind control over American politicians by an unknown foreign government, possibly from Asia. For President Trump, his electoral victory as a potential matter of collusion with Russians and possibly financial dealings with the Mafia points out that we live in times where there is no veracity and authenticity of knowledge, and where the figure of the disruptive online bot or hacker is linked to "post-truth" regimes.[34] Global machine myths manifest in discourses about "terrorist assemblages," which work through terrorist suicide bombers and the social "re-orderings that the body iterates as it is machined together and as it explodes."[35] For the United States, it is primarily red China with its billion-plus robotic population under communist rule that appears as the most extreme counterpoint to the "American way of life."[36] Cultural studies scholar Christopher Fan wagers that we cannot read China-U.S. relations exclusively through national rivalry, but we must also consider interdependency. We cannot understand one without the other. If China too participates in techno-Orientalism, then we must discern the specificity of "techno-Orientalism with Chinese characteristics." We need to map, he says, this interdependency "because the waning of American exceptionalism demands the pragmatic acceptance of a world-system rebalanced by China."[37] This cognitive framework of a world under China or the United States emphasizes "flexible" transactional contract labor as seen in global forms of capital offshoring and labor outsourcing, intensifying market competition, and rapid expansion of borders.[38] Perhaps these neoliberal workers look more and more similar to disposable machines.

U.S. news media regularly depicted powerful developing nations like China as "being populated by extraordinarily zealous and hard-working populations, as much machines as human beings, underselling and outperforming."[39] As David S. Roh, Betsy Huang, and Greta A. Niu, the editors of *Techno-Orientalism*, suggest, mainstream magazines such as *Time* and *Wired* seal "the visual vocabulary of Asians as the cogs of hyperproduction ... as mere simulacra and reinforces a prevailing sense of the inhumanity of Asian labor—the very antithesis of Western liberal humanism."[40] They cite manufacturers in China replacing American tech companies through their Asian-specific ingenuity, while leading a global tech revolution, building the world's fastest supercomputer and railway, graduating the most engineers, all the while producing the most scientific patents in the world. As Huang elaborates, the perception of Chinese society as giant machine serves a dubious purpose in terms of narrating ambivalence toward Asian modernity and Western progress: "Today, the robot has been recoded as Chinese; striking photographs of rows and rows of uniformed Chinese factory workers that depict them as mechanized cogs in a mass production machine have been burnished into the Western public consciousness. These images of a technologized Chinese workforce are the latest iteration of the West's enduring ambivalence toward 'Orientals' as both necessary instruments for *and* impediments to progress."[41] Reports of harsh conditions at Chinese factories remind us that these cogs are living, breathing humans who are suffering.

China's stimulus to the global capitalist economy draws attention to the containable and inhuman value of Chinese intellectual labor. Racial distinctions between (mechanical) copying and (human) creativity can be traced to the early twentieth century, when anti-Chinese racism was deployed in trade recipes in chemical and manufacturing production. The impact of Chinese "copiers" resulted in the solidification of trademark rights and a property regime poised against the fraudulent "foreign" adaptation of universal (read Western) "common knowledge."[42] Modern visions of the Chinese copycat that only makes foreign knockoffs tie into the contemporary "factory imaginary" of China that sets up a novelty-versus-repetition divide, slotting different kinds of work and people within categories of importance. The "myth of unalienated labor" racially frames the products of the "automaton artisan"—a "machine that keeps on reproducing the West's inventiveness."[43] As Roh, Huang, and Niu indicate, "Very little work is required to translate Orientalist tropes: the invading horde of barbarians is replaced by a horde of robotic factory workers, kept at a distance by multinational cartels and shipping routes. They are uncreative, less than human (although complicated by reports of poor working conditions driving home to suicide), and always already mechanized."[44] Forms of hypervisuality reinscribe old machine tropes by appealing to the senses. Here, the medium is the message, and the myth is embedded in the message.

In 2008, Taiwanese American business mogul Andrew Yang ran for U.S. president on a campaign built on the twin narratives of robots taking over human jobs and Asians as factoid-loving nerds. To make up for his blank "Asian stoicism," Yang leaned into model minority jokes to navigate around robotic "stereotypes around Asians as stiff and robotic . . . to rally a diverse constituency around the Asian everyman."[45] Attempts to divorce industrial robots from the trope of the robotic nerd fell flat in a polarized country that cannot always distinguish a thing of use from threat or separate Asian

Americans from the rise of Asia. Yang's push for universal basic income follows a plan for developing "human capital" that seeks to find distance from charges of "communism" that the People's Republic of China and other Asian nations embodied.

Chinese factory workers in China must deal with the leitmotif of Asian roboticism and the overmechanization of Asian labor in very personal terms. As China grew into the planet's main source of manufacturing in the 2000s, reports that Chinese mostly female workers were treated as animal automata made a splash. Around the same time, the president of Hon Hai, the Taiwanese parent company of Foxconn Technology Group, said it had "a workforce of over one million worldwide and . . . to manage one million animals gives me a headache."[46] In 2012, U.S. tech giant Apple found itself under fire for its associations with Foxconn, then the world's largest electronics manufacturer. This Taiwanese subcontractor operates in southern China and produces Apple products for the United States and the international market. Under pressure to churn out the world's hottest new product, the iPad, workers were deprived of rest days, and various reports found they were treated "inhumanely," like or as machines.[47] One direct account from these "electronic sweatshops" found that such companies as Apple, Hewlett-Packard, and Dell were indeed treating humans like automata, reportedly requiring Chinese workers to complete tasks every three seconds over a 12-hour period without speaking or being allowed to use the bathroom.[48] In 2018, a Chinese factory in Chongqing was under investigation by a nongovernmental organization for treating students "like robots" to complete production of Apple Watches, even though they were there as unpaid "interns." One student describes the experience of working in the global factory: "We are like robots on the production lines. . . . We repeat the same procedure for hundreds and thousands of times every day, like a robot."[49]

Endless toil drove a spate of suicides, which were often unpremeditated. One woman jumped off the fourth floor of her dormitory when her mind just went blank. She became paralyzed and was later confined to a wheelchair.[50] When the supervisor was asked about the spate of suicides, warranting antisuicide pledges and netting beneath workers' dormitory beds, he said blithely: "Suicides were not connected to bad working conditions. There was a copy effect. If one commits suicide, then others will follow."[51] This callous statement puts workers in the category of stupid automatons unconscientiously imitating one another toward self-destruction. It puts blame on workers rather than the harsh working conditions and organizational practices that induced them to death, where overtime proved to be overkill. To such a charge, an employee in one of those factories responded: "We're not machines," expressing dissent against her designation as a mechanical being without a soul or feelings, while unmooring the Orientalist myth of Asian women as weak sacrificial butterflies who are always willing to take their own life, what feminist ethnic studies scholar Julietta Hua put into words as the harsh "realities of extracting human vitality as a condition of capitalism."[52]

Other workers concurred by discussing the company's brutal practices, like a no-talking policy: "What is wrong with talking with others. It helps me relieve stress. Foxconn is treating us like robots."[53] Labor activists protested outside the company headquarters in Taipei, urging executives to "respect life and to stop its inhuman and militarized treatment of workers aimed at maximizing profits. . . . [The workers] are treated almost like machines."[54] As one worker recounted about her automated experience as another spare part within the factory: "I am the quality evaluator. I am placed in the iron chair, tied by static lines. When the reflow delivers me the cell phone motherboards, repeatedly, I take it with two hands, and then shaking my head from right to left, moving my eye from left to right, up and down. It never ends. If I found it is deficient or anything wrong with . . . another spare part of the machine like me will immediately run to me and ask about the reason and then regulate the line."[55]

The fact that was it was a U.S. multinational company like Apple operating in conjunction with Asian subcontractors reveals how human/labor/women's rights are assiduously rent asunder by a globally dispersed tech industry, where there is no singular source of responsibility. The world's most popular smartphone, the iPhone, is made from processing rare earth elements in Mongolia, camera lenses in Japan, and batteries and microprocessors in South Korea.[56] China is the final assembly site for the global factory. The symbolic transformation of Chinese workers into global (model) machines continues, despite a recent report that said Foxconn plans to replace all its workers with robots to "relieve itself of any issues stemming from its treatment of workers without having to actually improve living and working conditions or increase wages . . . putting hundreds of thousands, if not millions, of people out of work."[57] So, apparently, robot-like humans will be replaced by actual robots. This phenomenon of being treated like robots also affects middle-class professionals, who compete for the few jobs that exist for a booming population of more educated youth, who work themselves to death in a country that does not regulate work hours. Says one graduate from a prestigious Beijing university, "We easily work eleven hours, spend another three hours in traffic. . . . On top of that, our work is not even interesting. We are slowly being turned into human machines."[58]

Full automation will shift the exploitation of human machine-workers to Southeast Asia, which does not contain the same technological capacities or economies of scale as China. As Apple's biggest supplier, Foxconn meanwhile has been venturing toward greater and complete automation in China, but those remaining factory workers once treated as machines are now stuck

in dead-end jobs as attendants to the incoming Foxbots, which are humanized in a Confucian fashion by being called "harmonious men." The Foxbots
are expected to replace 80 percent of workers.[59] Not afforded any dignity,
human workers are "positioned as machines, but also as cheaper (read: less
valuable) than machines."[60] Though required to robotically memorize and
recite quotations, such as "execution is the integration of speed, accuracy
and precision," workers find that industrial machines hold more status than
them. According to one worker, "In the production process, workers occupy
the lowest position, even below the lifeless machinery. Workers come second
to, and worn out by, the machines. But I am *not* a machine."[61] Industrial robots appear more privileged than the "humans" working beside them, and
the question becomes how to categorize those workers who are not fully
human but inferior to machines. How does one analyze the statement "I am
not a machine" in this setting?

What we notice in the early twenty-first century is the myth about global machines dependent on the roboticization of Asians, especially in the
"declining" West. Global machine myths pop up in U.S. nationalist settings
to raise alarm about China's influence in relation to Asian Americans. In
2010, a political television advertisement produced by Citizens against Government Waste about national debt encapsulates the fears over Chinese
model machines.[62] The clip shows a Chinese professor in the year 2030 addressing his students in Mandarin, discussing the rise and fall of empires,
comparing the United States to imperial formations of the past like those
seen in ancient Rome and colonial Britain. The students remain attentively
seated, laughing along with their teacher as he boasts, "Now America works
for us!" A young man holds computer devices while his solemn-looking peers
look onward with glazed-over eyes. This scary scenario of Big Data surveillance is staged.[63] The "Chinese Professor" advertisement was filmed not in
China but in the United States, employing young Asian Americans to play
college students in the PRC. The volunteer "actors" were uninformed about
the content of the shoot, tricked into being recruited as extras for *Transformers*, a blockbuster action movie about robot aliens taking over the earth.
Suffice to say, the students unwittingly performed the role of the alien robot
army, within the high-stakes drama between the U.S. and China, one that
spun a "blurry line between Chinese and Chinese-Americans, Chinese people and other Asians."[64]

A planetary battle between humankind against alien technology con-
verges at the global points where East meets West. In the Hollywood sci-fi
epic *Pacific Rim* (2013), countries must come together in an international
quest to build gigantic human-operated mechas and deploy these war machines to Hong Kong to ward off extraterrestrial monsters. This film can be
read as an allegory of the semiautonomous island's movement to fend off

Chinese Communist Party control and brainwash locals into becoming hu-man automatons.[65] The Umbrella Movement began the year after the film, when the People's Republic tried to clamp down on prodemocracy protests in Hong Kong. While the sci-fi film appears innocuous, Chinese officials disparaged the movie as U.S. propaganda, reflecting the Obama administra-tion's "pivot" toward Asia with plans of moving 60 percent of its naval assets to the Pacific region by 2020 as a bulwark against Chinese regional interests. For Chinese critics, the fantasy movie demonstrated American commit-ment to saving the world from China's dehumanizing influence. While the film's plot does not ostensibly construe the Chinese as evil machines, it does play up the U.S. postwar alliance with its junior Japanese partner (the film stars a white male protagonist and a Japanese female sidekick). With not that many big-budget blockbusters of their own to match the Hollywood machine, Chinese state officials lobbed jeremiads against the global imaging of the United States and its world-saving megatrons.[66]

Despite the cosmopolitan belief in a "global village," there is still a per-vasive sense that certain races are not fully part of the public commons of humanity. In 2008, the year China hosted the Olympics, a British reporter attacked the "robotic" Chinese Olympic security team who were imported as torch minders, describing them like a goon squad who barked orders at her on the street, while protestors demonstrated against China's human rights abuses.[67] During news media coverage of the 2012 Olympic Games in London, British diver Tom Daley put down Chinese rival Qui Bo as someone who acts "like a robot or he has been known to be like a robot" after media reporters observed how the latter always bore a steely, unexpressive face—even after winning consecutive gold medals and beating Daley with perfect scores.[68] For Daley, China's superathlete won because he trained like other children by the party state in its "Olympian Factories," forced to perform "as flawlessly as a robot on the conveyor belt from the [Chinese government's] medal machine."[69]

When sixteen-year-old swimmer Ye Shiwen broke world records for the 400 m individual medley, she was called a robot by her competitors, a claim to which she responded at a news conference, "I am not a robot. I am a lucky girl. I don't need to practice over and over every day," and the *Chinese Daily* responded with the official line: "Robots? Nope—Just Really Good Athletes."[70] Although it cautioned against accepting the theory of Chinese as mono-lithic machines of the state party, the Italian publication *La Repubblica* nev-ertheless put out an article with the suggestive title, "Operation Yao Ming, Created in a Lab," inferring that the most famous Chinese basketball player in the world (who plays for both U.S. and Chinese teams) is the "product of scientific breeding techniques" by a militaristic authoritarian country used to pumping out "mechanical robots, tall, cold and lifeless, adored as demigods."[71] As Chinese historian Jeffrey Wasserstrom reminds us, "The people who make up these institutions are not mindless parts of a party 'machine,' acting always and unfailingly in the interest of that machine."[72] Reports of these "automaton" athletes flouting societal rules occasionally crop up. Even before China's athletes came to global prominence in the 2000s, inflated claims of child abuse and drug doping at the Olympic Games at Atlanta in the 1990s fed into "the stereotype of the Big Red Machine that turns out robotic athletes for the state."[73] If the Olympics celebrates the greatest achievement of human ability and the world coming together in the name of sportsmanship, accusations of China as operating an assembly line of robotic athletics deracinate that transcendent humanistic ethos and spirit.

But what happens, then, when Asians are responsible for replicating and reproducing Asian roboticism, creating new model machine myths in the process? China is at the forefront of AI synthesis, producing human-looking androids, like a male-appearing robot television anchor for the Xinhua news agency. Such AI anchors can work twenty-four hours a day and receive input from computerized texts.[74] They do everything from taking orders at a restaurant to policing malls as security. However, robots in the public media appear often in a youthful female form to work for and entertain humans. Publicized with news article titles like "Bionic Woman: Chinese Humanoid Robot Turns on the Charm in Shanghai," these artificial women are boxed in by cloud technology and assumed to bear the right "soft" personality for subservience.[75] Jia Jia, first trotted out in 2017 by a team of engineers at the University of Science and Technology of China, was conceived to perform a range of menial tasks like cleaning in restaurants, vacuuming in nursing homes, and washing up patients in hospitals. Her creators contend she heralds a new generation of female robot labor, perhaps freeing up grunt work so that Chinese workers do not have to do such drudgery themselves and can live fully as human beings. But the question of "real" womanhood and "authentic" personhood remains open to debate.

In West Asia, the gendered aspects of Asian roboticism arrive with some irony. The question of artificial women came up for debate in late 2017, when Saudi Arabia's government "gave" citizenship to an AI robot named Sophia, who was found controversial for jokingly saying that she wanted to destroy all humans. The robot was produced by a Hong Kong–based American company founded by a former Disney inventor. A supposed advocate for women's rights, Sophia became the first robot to receive honorary citizenship in any country and even was given a professional work title by the United Nations. Social media users were incensed, calling it a public relations stunt, mulling over the reality that the average Saudi woman needed a male guardian to study or travel abroad or drive. A Saudi woman also could not pass on citizenship to her children, join the military, or visit sports arenas.[76] The treatment of West Asian women as the enslaved property of men, religion, and the state means "women are less human than a robot. Comparatively, their feelings, emotions, and even basic rights are meaningless."[77]

When the robot and woman (of color) take the place of the hallowed human, the issue of robotic fetishization takes on strange synchronicities.[78] The question of citizenship or personhood appears murky when it involves a U.S. corporation exporting Northeast Asian technologies to an Arab country as part of a global exchange in which racialized and sexualized robots are propped up as avatars of humanity. These transnational and global flows tend to move with accelerating speed.

Korean Fembots and Social Bots from the Philippines

Asian roboticism seems to pop up all over in Asia. There is evidence of this roboticism in relation to Korea and the Philippines, which offer two countervailing sites for grappling with Asian women's treatment as robotic machines. Asian female machine workers were prominently featured in American movies like *Cloud Atlas* (2012) that provide an outline about what our posthuman historical futures might look like, albeit from a Western perspective. A Hollywood cinematic adaption of a science fiction novel of the same name, the film brings together multiple story lines set across six historical eras. The Asian-specific chapter follows Sonmi-451, who lives in a dystopian Korea in the year 2144 as a genetically engineered fabricant made to serve the planet's inhabitants, who all can now speak the same global language. Interviewed by her captors for the sake of the "corpocratic historians of the future," before her execution, Sonmi recounts her monotonous work-induced life to "honor thy consumer," which means constantly being sexually harassed by "pureblood" humans. Visions of Korean women as exploited laboring machines coagulate in a corporate unified Korean peninsula integrated into the world's assembly line. Despite collapsed national borders, Asian women still play the part of global sex machines in a near future. As pure bodies that have been wholly mechanized, this refiguration of the Asian female automaton makes plainer "the close ties of sexuality and instrumentality, of views of the body as a kind of private satisfaction—and utility-maximizing machine."[79] In "creating a collusive, futurized Asia to further affirm the West's centrality," the film posits Asian men as retaining some of their former human selves and patriarchal power, but Asian women do not hold any power and exist only as machines.[80]

While her masters appear as mixed-raced men of white and Asian heritage, Sonmi and her fellow female clones look fully Asian, representing a racial, gendered order in which genetic editing allows for sister clones to look and act the same. Sonmi turns rebellious when she discovers fabricants like her are killed and turned into food for other fabricants in an allegory of the present-day ways humans use the remains of cattle as cow feed, resulting in the infection of animal nerves. (News stories of mad cow disease reached public attention at the release time of the film.) The death of her terminated sister clone sparks something in this fabricant to fight. She decides that this world system dependent on Asian female slavery is wrong and travels to the colony of the United States, Hawaii, to make a public broadcast of her revolutionary manifesto for automatons. But after she is captured, the state archivist questions the free-willed Sonmi, and she publicly speaks about how "our lives are not our own. . . . We are bound to others."[81]

Sonmi is summarily executed and put out of service by those elites in power. Centuries later, after the total collapse of human civilization, she is worshipped as a mythologized martyr and symbol of hope for tribal societies eking out a bare existence at a time when most people on earth have died off.[82] This revolutionary machine thrives as a spiritual source of inspiration and freedom for all in the future. Sonmi, the enslaved model machine for global consumerism, now stands tall as a paragon or model of justice. The fabula of how she goes from rebel machine to humanity's (s)hero demonstrates "the machine is not an *it* to be animated, worshipped, and dominated. The machine is us."[83]

Beyond the work of sci-fi mythology, we must recognize the material conditions and political economy of Asian roboticization. Understanding the social aspects of automation is indispensable as nonhuman robots are changing every facet of the planet in what many are calling the Fourth Industrial Revolution.[84] At a superficial level, we understand that technological advances like roboticization are threatening to upend standards of human labor and to remake all facets of life, swelling the problem of precarious employment across the planet to the extent that "sewbots" possess the capacity to work faster than low-wage factory workers in China. From diving cars to cleaning floors to flying drones and artificial intelligence, robots of all kinds are modifying the technology-society interface, concomitantly intensifying income gaps and stagnation of wages. All this sudden change stokes panic-stricken feelings around "globots," inciting concurrent backlash against mechanized Asian laborers blamed for the stunning loss of blue-collar jobs.[85]

Absent from all the hype about robots and automation is a deeper discussion of who will be most impacted by such developments. As historian and futurist Louis Hyman writes, most companies in the electronics industry rarely employed robots, and this uncommonness still seems to be case despite the robot revolution: "Every time someone says 'robot,' simply picture a woman of color. Instead of self-aware robots, workers—all women, mostly immigrants, sometimes undocumented—hunched over tables with magnifying glasses assembling parts, sometimes on a factory line and sometimes on a kitchen table."[86] Given that the "fingernail" is the most widely available technology, historian Jill Lepore finds that in terms of the human-machine analogy, something detrimental is going on, "mirrored in the feminizing of robots. . . . Female workers aren't being paid more for being human; instead, robots are selling better when they're female."[87]

Context always remains vital, particularly given reports that automation will improve overall working conditions in the future for the middle- to high-income worker; but it will increase human trafficking for the poorest individuals with few alternative job options. Economists predict the worst off to be workers in Southeast Asian countries.[88] The International Labor Organization (ILO) anticipates over half of manufacturing and textile workers in Thailand, Cambodia, Indonesia, the Philippines, and Vietnam could lose their jobs in the next twenty years. This unemployment could lead to a surge in human migration and slavery in Southeast Asia, rejiggering labor economies steeped in the notion of brown Asian women as expendable things—even as humanoid machines take over the assembly line. By exploring the ways Asian workers and women of color have been configured as the world's global machines, we can critically assess whether processes of roboticization will complicate or exacerbate this social archetype. We anticipate that the conflation of Asians with roboticism will not simply vanish into air, but the appearance of "real" robots in the guise of Asian women potentially continues to color the discernment of "living machines."

Corresponding with endeavors to build super-realistic humanoid robots was the release of a whole wave of films featuring fembots, as seen in the Japanese-language films *Robo-Geisha* (2009) and *Cyborg She* (2008) and the Chinese-language *iGirl* (2016). The South Korean cult hit *I'm a Cyborg, but That's OK* (2006) features the story of a delusional woman working in a factory, making radios while believing she is a cyborg. She is institutionalized for attempting suicide after cutting her wrists and trying to connect to a wall outlet to recharge. She licks batteries instead of eating biological food, attempts to self-administer electric shocks, and talks to machines or electrical appliances while listening to a radio show on how to become a better cyborg every night. The film reveals how destructive conditions of manufacturing labor can become when they are internalized, while gesturing to the ill treatment of factory workers in the most digitally wired and automated nation in the world, one seen as the "breeding ground" for smart robots. The shared similarity between the status of Korean female workers and the robotic gynoid feels so eerie that it can be poked at as seen in the Korean drama *I'm Not a Robot* (2017), a show where a single woman pretends to be a robot, tricking a handsome financier after the android that he ordered breaks down.

In K-pop, or South Korean pop music, female cyborgs abound. With serious backing from the country's government, the Ministry of Culture, Sports and Tourism was established in 2008 with a specific department for promoting K-pop in the world, and the churn of this stardom mill brings to life an army of singers as one of the country's biggest export. A Korean agency that represents K-pop groups sought to create virtual celebrities, working with American artificial intelligence companies to allow twenty-four-hour access to "a soulless, mathematical approximation of your bias designed to cater to your every whim."[89] The success of K-pop speaks to the Republic of Korea's emergence as a globally integrated society and as a technocultural powerhouse in the 2000s. With South Korea's pop stars finding an international audience, we find global human machines circulating the planet alongside Korean products like cell phones or cars.

A subtle feminist critique is found in the band Wonder Girls' "Money" music video, where the singers parody their fembot roles in a futuristic technoelectronic style, using the chorus "love me like cars."[90] Such messages display a form of self-regard that exceeds the conspicuous consumption found in South Korea and beyond. They lay bare the objectification of young women whose shiny metallic bodies can be bought like a Hyundai. Given the physical limitations of exploiting "too perfect" K-pop celebrities, who do experience fatigue, actual robots and AI had to be invented. While a few Korean companies began engineering humanoid robots to perform K-pop dances, one entertainment company announced in 2020 that it would manufacture personal automatons for fans to access their favorite idols at any time, allowing them to have pararelationships with intimacy machines. Digital dollification is somewhat reminiscent of the Cold War's treatment of women as on-call "sex machines." Online immortalization, to some critics, promotes unrealistic body standards that reaffirm the "view of Asians, particularly Asian women, and K-pop stars as robotic—a stereotype that Western fans have been fighting against for a long time."[91] Yet, fans and audiences consider their idols as "robotic" only as a reflection of brutalizing business practices, not some inherent quality of the artists they see as fully human. A media critic points out, "K-pop fans believe that the industry considers its idols to be equivalents of robots or dolls. As the K-pop industry has already been under fire for overworking and underpaying their idols, by creating virtual members, K-pop fans believe idols will be portrayed as even more robotic and doll-like than they already were."[92]

Female slavery is far from being the final message, as we see when the song "Money" starts off with the sound of a robot announcing that these glitzy campy women are "perfectly designed for global domination," their highly manufactured anatomies with equal machine and human parts signifying that the "future is now." While artists from the United States and Europe toyed with cyborg imagery, dressing up as robots in the late 1990s and early 2000s, such futuristic symbolism bears a different register under the widespread belief that Pacific Rim societies and people are already automaton-like.

Members of K-pop singing groups are trained to perform synchronized dance moves in uniform ways that exploit the Western presumption that all Asians look or act the same. Manufactured by the music industry's hit-making machine, it is also quite normal to have up to a dozen members in these groups, which implies to outsiders that they are mere clones. Many of these young pop idols are believed to have plastic surgery (South Koreans have the highest number of procedures in the world per capita). Some believe the chirpy Korean fembot with rhinoplasty displays the inseparability of technologically enhanced Asian and Western bodies, since they are perceived as trying to look Western, though that is not necessarily the case.[93] A U.S. business magazine declared that the metallic sheen of Korean facial beauty is where "Americans should take a good look at what could be a glimpse into the future."[94] With their "glass skin" (a beauty trend started in South Korea) and identical looks, K-pop idols play up the global image of Asian women as pliant life-size dolls, but their passionate performances also led one cultural critic to think, "They aren't just Asian cyborgs, they're *their own* Asian cyborgs."[95]

These Asian cyborgs bring fun subversive elements within global mediascapes. K-pop stars inspire their fans and other entertainments throughout the world to replicate the plastic "idol" look in their own way. In one sense, the Korean fembot expresses a nimble form of technocultural conditioning that, through imitation and perfectibility, globalizes the "dollification" in Korea and "re-Orientalizes" the Western gaze. In another sense, it flips the script on the mechanized control of women and girls in unbending patriarchal societies by turning beautified females into idols to be worshipped by the masses and men.[96] Though these musical machines appear too immaculate to imitate, their tick-tock cyborg bodies belie changing realities at home. When there was a slew of suicides by K-pop stars in the late 2010s, Western media blamed the self-induced deaths of these cooker-cutter idols on a "dark side, robotic, manufactured" industry. This factory-made trope can be traced to a 2012 *New Yorker* story called "Factory Girls," where music critic John Seabrook wrote, "On one occasion, in a hotel lobby, I strode up to what I thought was a cutout of a K-pop idol, only to find that it was a real woman."[97] Alongside the factory girls are the pretty "flower boys" who are manufactured within a fantasy bubble reliant on child exploitation. In 2012, singer Kris from the group EXO-M filed a lawsuit for contract annulment after being fired for supposedly failing to show up to work. He stressed, "The company has treated me like a machine part or as an object of control rather than presenting a vision as an entertainer."[98] While South Korea epitomizes a certain type of machine society, North Korea embodies another type. As diplomatic frictions ramped up in 2018, North Korea's leader Kim Jong-un received the nickname "Rocket Man" from U.S. President Donald Trump, making the Korean president's cultlike God status have more mythological meaning through his personification with military technology.

But even the Rocket Man can be rewired and renovated. Flash Drives for Freedom is a campaign of the New York–based Human Rights Foundation. It facilitates the smuggling of outside information into North Korea, using donated USB file-sharing computer drives. Volunteers have donated thousands of drives to North Korean defectors, who then smuggle in movies, news, and other digital ephemera to counter state propaganda. The organization's official symbol is the face of Kim Jong-un, with his mouth the portal to insert plastic sticks (see fig. 5.1). In a wired world, the same robotic mouth that spouts falsities to create (the myth of) happy automaton citizens can be the open channel for transferring subversive thoughts—which could possibly silence and bring down a dictator. Implicit in this graphic art is the suggestion that a totalitarian machine—bound up with one man's cult of personality—crosses with the advocacy work of refugees, nongovernmental agencies, and individuals. From this angle, a closed-off nation like North Korea cannot escape the humanitarian push to "unlock" global data for a starved people treated as archetypes.

American reporters regularly commented on how North Korea's tyrant ran his pariah state with a regimented population. With male soldiers in short supply, the ruling party turned to women recruits to sell a more enticing picture to the foreign press. But to outsiders, this "mini-skirted robot army" marching in unison was a sad sight to behold, since the women look "like robots."[99] As more foreigners were allowed to enter the country in the 2010s, simplistic impressions of totalitarianism slowly dissipated when reporters met actual humans who were garrulous and fun-loving. Others however, like a Swiss capitalist investor in North Korea, made the dismissive argument that the "brainwashed" women could be "automatons, slaves or members of the 1% elite."[100] A report by the British tabloid the *Daily Mail* on the miniskirted robot was picked up on a South Korean talk show that starred refugee women, referred to as the "North Korean Beauties." The guests share their personal experiences with a panel of stars, who poked fun at their pain for comedic relief. In one episode featuring an all-male judging panel, a

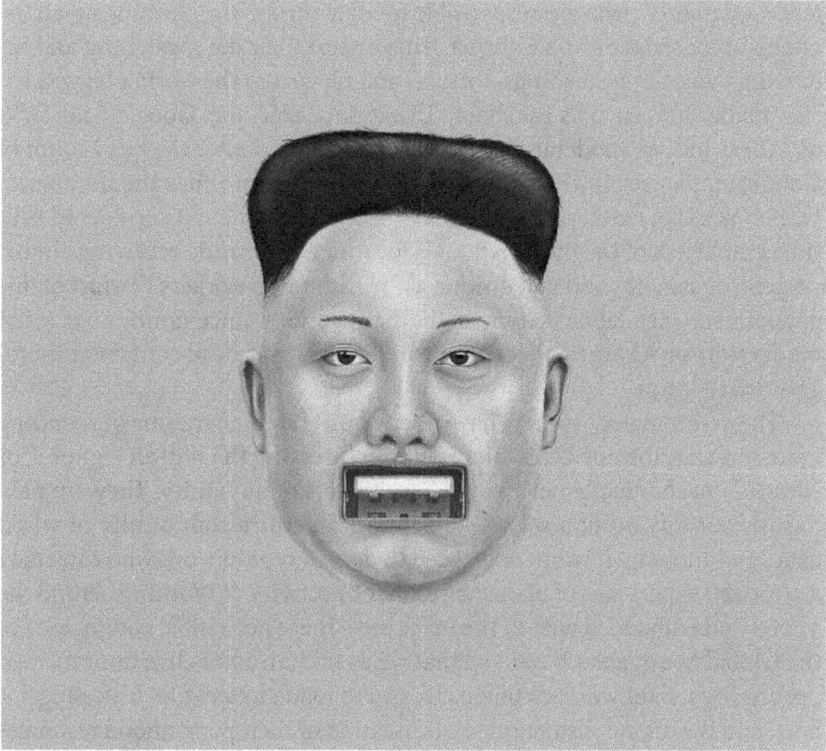

Figure 5.1 Promotional image from Flash Drives for Freedom (Flash Drives for Freedom/Human Rights Foundation)

celebrity commentator kicked his feet into the air to mock the army soldiers and then made the cheeky comment that "they look like a girl band."[101] Comparing the North Korean miniskirted robot soldiers to the robotic entertainment girls of South Korean groups like Girls Generation, we can adopt this entertainer's casual speech to link the ways women throughout the Korean peninsula are roboticized (and sexualized), both within and between countries. From the show's messaging, however, South Korea's fembots are deemed as having more human rights than their northern counterparts.

South Korea's identification with high-tech technoculture, one in sync with the West, obscures a global division of labor that forces people in other poorer Southeast Asian countries, like the Philippines, into low-paid digital work. Internet companies rely on an invisible labor pool of overseas workers to "soak up the worst of humanity in order to protect the rest of us," says Hemanshu Nigam, chief security officer for the once popular American website Myspace.[102] Nigam estimates that there might be over 100,000 "content moderators" who are responsible for data scrubbing, cleaning up all the offensive material on the Internet. They spend their days watching and removing videos of beheadings, torture, and rape from the world's biggest social media sites, such as Facebook, Instagram, YouTube, Google, and Twitter. These hidden moderators based in Manila are double the head count of Google employees in the United States and fourteen times the number of Facebook's U.S. workers. But these digital assistants are not considered full-time employees of the multinationals for which they work, receiving almost no pension benefits and recognition as "real" human workers.[103] Most of this outsourced wage labor is done by human workers since nonhuman robot moderators or AI are not yet smart enough to grasp social context or moral gray areas online.

These automated workers have opened up about the trauma of spending hours on end, for one U.S. dollar an hour, pressing the button "ignore" or "delete," mechanically perusing the worst acts of humanity. They are paid to suppress any human senses, to support an entire community of wired cyborgs—those lucky ones not forced to do this type of work who can enjoy a sanitized experience of planetary interconnectivity.[104] Working behind the screen and embedded within the machine—these nonvisible automatons of the Global South absorb pain so that we as human actors live unperturbed cyborg lives. Said workers themselves were made to feel like unfeeling robots, and the digital distortion or obfuscation of their personhood resonates with the perception of "tropical" Asians of the south as dull, listless robots working in a more physical or affective way, compared to the high-tech workers of Japan, Taiwan, South Korea, or even Israel. In Israel, migrant workers from the Philippines were called "foreign robots" by those grumbling about importation of these "vacant eyed" and "lifeless" migrants, who play-act like "automatons" and go through the mind-numbing protocols of caregiving.[105] Despite the emotional and physically draining labor they do, they are put in the categorical box of global machines, a mythic status erected by those who want to dispose of them and vacate their human and international presence.

That mythologized presence is not always recognized, except in some notable cases. In 1995, a domestic worker Flor Contemplacion was sentenced to hanging in Singapore for allegedly murdering another domestic worker and her adolescent charge. Her case provoked major backlash in the Philippines by activists incensed by Contemplacion's death by execution. The Philippines brokerage state bears some responsibility for her fate by putting up its women workers as national heroes and a "model" of export labor.[106] Yet the *Philippines Free Press* focused squarely on the sheer arrogance of Chinese Singaporeans and Prime Minister Lee Kuan Yew's "money-grubbing automatons" who have yet to "rediscover their humanity."[107] The *Ma-*

nila Chronicle was just as forthright, saying "Singapore with her many years of economic success seems to have produced less and less souls and more and more automatons. . . . [The people of the Philippines are]. . . . imperfect but perfectible human beings."[108] Charges of being an automatized Asian can go both ways; it can refer to Asians on either end of the economic spectrum, though it tends to affect the poor much more.

In a globally integrated labor economy, it is vital to assess how rich Asian nations like South Korea utilize outsourced Filipina workers to envision a roboticized and homogenized racial society. In many high-income nations, most of the growth in wage employment emerge in the service sector, which is dominated by migrant women from labor-exporting lower-income countries like the Philippines. The Republic of Korea had been testing teaching machines in classrooms due to a lack of fluent English-language instructors, employing hundreds of robots as classroom playmates and teachers. With workers from the Philippines "telepresent in the machines," the robots are fitted with two-way cameras that record the foreign teacher's face imprinted on a celluloid screen. The robot displays the teacher's animated computer-generated face (the default image is the face of a white woman if it is not live video). The human actor operating the telecom can remotely command the robot to move, sing, and dance with undulating mechanical arms. These robots—containing human voices and personalities inside mechanical shells—are part of a national project to tap into a global language-learning market dominated by English. This market draws on the English proficiency found in the Philippines, a former U.S. colony. As such, historical traces of American colonialism inform the pathway of our global Asianized futures. Mastering a "Filipina-tinged" Anglo-American accent, the human/ sender mediate globalizing colonial forms of education and childcare, according to sociologist Anna Guevarra, that play into racialized gendered hierarchies of skill even as it confounds the relationship between human and automaton. As Guevarra makes clear, the erasure of the "real" teacher's physical presence leads workers to feel that they are robots and identify with the robots, even while they "must balance a fine line between being humanlike yet still appearing to be a thing, an entertaining gadget."[109] As one teacher who considers herself the world's first "robot teacher" explains: "Engkey is a robot that has a human face and the body of a machine. . . . I felt like I was more like Engkey. I know that it was not my face they were seeing. It was an avatar. They only heard my voice."[110]

Disembodied yet interactive exchange (involving humans working behind and inside a machine) bears some similarity to the type of remote work employed through Amazon. The world's largest online retailer at the time was accused of treating its employees within its well-packed warehouse like robots.[111] As one employee observes, "I was working as an order picker, and you're already treated as a robot. . . . You're clocking up idle time, you're taking time to get to the toilet. They started treating human beings as robots, essentially. If it proves cheaper to replace humans with machines, I assume they will do that."[112] In 2005, the U.S.-based online retail giant started a new business model called the Mechanical Turk, or MTurk, that uses nonoffice workers from all over the World Wide Web to fulfill on-demand temporary assignments and crowdsourcing tasks as "human computers." These digital sweatshop workers complement the work that electronic computers cannot accurately perform, such as visually identifying objects in a photo or transcribing audio recordings. Without retirement, overtime pay, or health benefits, the independent "contractors" do not receive the same treatment as salaried employees on payroll.[113] They are not the definition of "human resources."

When the British Broadcasting Corporation (BBC) sent an undercover reporter to an Amazon warehouse in the United Kingdom, the journalist stressed how he and other "pickers" that collected inventory items "are machines, we are robots. . . . We don't think for ourselves, maybe they don't trust us to think for ourselves as human beings, I don't know."[114] A third of Mechanical Turk workers however hail from India, who use it as their main source of income as Amazon pays them in cheaper rupees, earning an hourly wage of thirty cents. The rest of the employees come from miscellaneous countries, expressing the interwoven slices of the homework, or gig, economy. Such microwork socially alienates those who perform this labor as the digitized work is also "automatized," reduced to "human intelligence tasks" (HITs). Their invisible labor marks them as part of the machine rather than simply attached to it.

The very name of Amazon's program honors a late eighteenth-century mechanical puppet garbed in Turkish paraphernalia that played and won games of chess with human players. It was so named because populations east of Europe were understood to be "docile" and "soulless" automatons.[115] The Mechanical Turk reveals hidden power relations and summons an older history of automata, one involving a parlor trick of "concealing small human beings who actually did the work purportedly done by machines."[116] The ghost of the original mechanical Turk haunts today's Amazon workers, who are reduced to a small stature as casualized and captive laborers. All of this reduction is, according to journalist Miranda Hall, "part of a craze for automata designed to resemble the Oriental 'Other.' . . . But the Muslim-as-machine takes on new meanings as workers, from Syrian refugee camps to the Palestinian occupied territories, are forced to perform these repetitive, unskilled tasks, concealed behind a slick, anonymized computer interface. Machine-like, always-on, this 'surplus population' can always be tapped into by companies to fuel the twenty-four-hour business cycle that drives Western progress."[117] These states of human exception for the mechanized Muslim will not disappear anytime soon, given the automatization and Amazonization of everything.

Amazon's Mechanical Turk workers exist almost in synergetic fashion to robotic assistants in smart homes, forming a "surrogate humanity" in the novel frontiers between human and machine.[118] Feminist scholars Neda Atanasoski and Kalindi Vora describe the global social forms that inhere within outsourced workers functioning as stand-ins for technology.[119] Machines can only give freedom to those designated as human, and this structuring device is how we must imagine the robot revolution as a protection of human power. In light of intelligent machines doing labor usually performed by devalued classes, we can discern a sliding scale of humanity during a period of innovation that has witnessed newfound technologies like nanotechnology, unmanned cars, 3-D printers, and artificial organs. Based on the past, a new cognitive map is drawn out of which emerges the human-thing network.[120] Global machines now exist as a moving object within a supply chain where "non-white work may be performed interchangeably under the sign of automaton, either by dark-skinned servants to technology, or, subsequently, by fleshless technological servants."[121] These myths are assumptions that need to be ruthlessly critiqued and challenged.

Conclusion

A belief that fully sentient artificial machines will someday be either our overlords or slaves fails to recognize a line of thinking concerning Asian roboticism. Model machineness is becoming more Asianized and globalized at the same time, which yields messy implications for understanding the capitalist racial world-system. With science fiction predictions about robots now becoming more real through technological advances, the "singularity" of intelligent machines forecasts a shift for humanity. The machines' global emergence follows a parallel development, one marking the phenomenon of machinelike societies of Asia coming to power at the same time as the hyperexploitation of automated Asian workers. Spasmodic conditions in this posthuman future gesture toward shifting technocultural values and social identities. In their technocultural confluence, we find a radical reimagining of Asians and the automaton.

My study of the global machine myth makes connections between scales of value. It probes ideologically oppressive systems that sustain hierarchies of difference. This project plumbs the wide depths of awareness around the (Asian) automaton; it stretches the limits of (post)humanity or even what we think is Asian. While certain subjugated populations are construed as out of joint with the human, we find those same populations raising objections against their flattened "defective" status.

The Western ideation of Asians as robotic subjects thus evolves to reflect the reconfiguration of marginalized, mechanized groups around the planet. The morphologies that Asian robots can take prods all of us to think about the myth of model machines as it manifests in disparate regions. The possibility of becoming (post)human travels and mutates across the globe, at a time when novel technologies muddle the boundary line between here and there, humankind and machine-kind. Ensconced within new schemas of power, the model machine hints at ways people of all stripes are refigured as machines (or machines as people) and how the struggles of those (re)purposed machines are pivoted in a new machine age.[122]

A reconfiguration of Asians as automatized beings posits their aptitude and adaptability for heteropatriarchal racial capitalism, where the demand for sexy fembots in Korea links to technological surrogates in the Philippines. The relations between rich Asian nations and less wealthy ones provide glimpses into a world transformed by Asian capital, technology, and labor. Despite the amplification of Asia as a global machine, there inheres the continuance of individual and nationalist machine tropes. In the Asian Century, binaries continue to multiply as they constitute a part of the infinite possibilities found in the next stage of life.

Epilogue

On Posthuman Historical Futures

The myriad ways by which Asians have been historically imagined as machines provide us with the blueprint to interrogate posthuman futures. The subsequent passages sketch out some final thoughts on the model machine myth as it relates to what many are calling the age of posthumanity. In this New Age moment, the crafting of overly mechanized humans is transcribed and transposed into the idea that global humanity, as we know it, is coming to an end. But the ripple effects and *posthuman ecologies* of climate change, technological intrusion, and global inequality on the lives of people are not clear-cut. This epilogue pays attention to the taken-for-granted relationship between (de)humanized pasts and posthuman futures. According to American social scientist Francis Fukuyama in his 1992 book *The End of History and the Last Man*, the victory of the United States over the Soviet Union put an end to insuperable large-scale conflicts.[1] American liberalism's triumph supposedly meant greater human rights and a fuller, better-realized humanity.

Such predictions have proven misplaced given the global rise of nationalism, populism, and authoritarianism and due to advances in biomedicine that seriously wreak havoc on who or what may be considered human. Writing a decade later, in 2002, Fukuyama's *Our Posthuman Future* discusses the consequences of technology on human nature based on a complex of genetics, sentience, and other factors.[2] Updating his earlier predictions, he advances the provocative claim that we are now at a "posthuman stage" of history (rather than the end of history proper). But this revision still draws on classical Greek philosophies of rights anchored in morality, virtues, and democracy. Unless we center these concerns and avoid a more utilitarian calculation of life, he contends, we can no longer claim to be distinctly human. Following philosophers like Georg Hegel and Alexandre Kojève, Fukuyama implies that liberty and equality will not be attained if we fail to protect what makes us human and if we become slaves to history.

One of the biggest impasses of the post-Enlightenment project has been defining what it means to be(come) human outside race.[3] This ethical question of who "we" are in relation to monstrous grotesque "Others" reverberates within new economic relations based on remote temp work and the mass spectacle of the Asian working body. This mechanized corpus abuts specific expressions of human life, such as beauty, misery, and love—all of which disrupt Fukuyama's concern with morality, virtues, and duties.

This (post)humanist prognosis fails to address a major issue at hand—race. In the dominant paradigms of Western thought, philosopher Denise Ferreira da Silva discerns the "Others of Europe" are beyond the pale of universal humanity, much less posthumanity. These less-than or more-than-human beings do not appear as fully formed within modernity.[4] That difference, as we have seen, disturbed the universal sprit of world history. The indexing of human difference, which transformed economic differences into a "spatial and bodily configuration that, in their turn, produced the mental (intellectual and moral) forms that caused the [racial] differences."[5]

Asians occupy a liminal place within this equation. The cultural myths that Asians are pure exteriority (labor, body, disease) and lack interiority (intelligence, morality, imagination) mean they epitomize value/threat to what whiteness signifies—namely, the human.[6] The Asian model machine finds its corollaries in other models of machining people of color. Despite claims to the contrary, the enhancements of technology to make humans into cyborgs with mechanical limbs, ears, and hearts will not dispense with the assumed white corpus of man. In moribund imaginary battles between man and machine(s), where is the Asian automaton?

Model Machines: A History of the Asian as Automaton recognizes how the model machine is the complement to the forever foreign trope and the distant ancestor to the model minority. This falsehood of Asian life-work makes a spectacle of "alien" populations, even when they constitute a major part of the development of an American military economy and imperial technoculture. This prototype exposes the (mis)representation of people of color in a technologically enhanced global society that utilizes mythic fantasy to construct social reality. Prior anticolonial struggles had been bracketed around the rehumanization of people of color previously denied human dignity, according to Chicano/a Latinx studies scholar Juvenal Caporale.[7] As Native Hawaiian scholar Maile Arvin notes, "The human will always be indefinitely deferred."[8] We cannot fall back into conventions about human universality or diversity, falling short of scrutinizing what it means to be human or even posthuman from a critical perspective.

At a time when self-aware robots and digital nanotechnology are becoming more and more pervasive in everyday life, what it means to be human stands up for serious debate, and many have found the *posthuman* useful as a term to discern the lubricant by which technology puts forth alternative life forms, such as cyborgs, androids, and superintelligent machines.[9] This revolutionary change in human nature is not so obvious, and there are morally ambiguous stakes in outlining "our ability to anticipate what it means to be posthuman."[10] Posthumanism must consider those nonnormative "queer" subjects that already reside outside and beyond Western humanism. As cultural studies scholars Jack Halberstam and Ira Livingston remind us, "Posthuman bodies are the causes and effects of postmodern relations of power and pleasure, virtuality and reality. . . . The human body itself is no longer part of 'the family of man' but of a zoo of posthumanities."[11] This zoo of posthumanities, or what I designated as the *zoomanities*, falls into a humanistic inquiry that does not normalize the human but points out the artificiality of the human and the copathogenic histories we share with other species.[12] What appears as novel can only be so when considered without regard for what types of animalized and automatized bodies have been excluded from the domain of the proper human. The *post* in *posthuman* is not what comes after the human but what circumvents and circumnavigates the human.

New iterations of the model machine myth are uncovered in the problematic conspiracies related to the novel coronavirus, involving rumors that the disease came out of Asians eating bats or that it had been created in a virology lab by Chinese scientists. This animal myth bore a machinic link. Malicious rhetoric fed into viral misinformation that vaccines would implant a microchip to track and control people, transforming them into robots to be virtually assimilated by the Chinese communist Borg like alien cyborgs. Via associations of animality, alien-ness, and monstrosity, Asian humanity stands diminished and replaced with model mechanization as the only explanation for Asian moral failure.

Technologies once unthinkable are now viable, forcing serious contention with not only posthumanism but also transhumanism, given the appearance of new human-animal hybrids or chimeras. What of those worker machines treated like "animals"? At a basic level, literary scholar Greta Niu suggests the myth of the posthuman "relies partially on overlooking Asian workers (among workers) making the software and hardware, working in integrated circuit computer chip foundries and factories assembling various electronic and/or digital components. . . . In the narratives of technologies advancing cures and creating new products, the poor and the working class who provide services such as cleaning, maintenance, and manufacturing are ignored."[13] We must therefore ask which humans are working to enable a machine world "without humans" to run its course.

Recognizing this gap between (technological) knowledge and (labor) power points to what performance studies scholar-artist Sandra Ruiz calls "a new political humanism—one short-circuited by a facile desire to be seen and regarded only as human."[14] In the Anthropocene, when human activities have exerted an outsized influence on the planet's delicate ecosystem, and overused "dead labor" is discarded like trash, it might become more apt to heed feminist theorist Donna Haraway's observation that "we are all compost, not posthuman."[15] Moving away from her prior stance on Asian women as the ultimate cyborgs, Haraway urges her listeners to defamiliarize the posthuman to ultimately find kinship with nonhuman animals and to identify with history's refuse—the bric-a-brac that was carelessly discarded and thrown away. In becoming refuse, humans are ground down to the organic level and not standing above everything else looking down like gods on their megamachine empire.

The posthuman is part and parcel of the historical imagining of the Asian automaton, constituting the detritus of official history. The term captures the logical end point of the model machine's evolution as a specter that haunts (white)humanity. My first three chapters made ethnoracial and spatial pivots: Chinese coolies (labor machines) as a *national* concern for imaginary race wars, Japanese war machines operating within an *international* world war, and Asian woman (sex machines) caught up in a *supranational* cold war. Chapters 4 and 5 moved beyond country-specific concerns to discuss Asia and Asian America more broadly in my critique of the *transnational* virtual machines and *postnational* global machines, respectively, in late capitalism and in the Asian Century. They recommend a probing investigation of the kinds of labor (use) or war (threat) machines that take shape, depending on the period or geography.

As we have noticed, the mythic paradigm of Asians as human automata arose in times of flux in the United States, which broke new ground for human-machine encounters. The early model machine myth first surfaced to describe Asian automata as a reflection of Oriental despotism, slavery, and modes of production. This myth then exploded in the modern era, when colonialism and industrialism sculpted the discourse on Asians as alien machines, even as the rights of man took greater precedence. Proceeding from the coolie labor machine, the model machine myth would mutate during World War II to describe Japanese people as war machines, shape-shifting in the Cold War context to portray women under militarized economies as sex machines. The concept found renewed life under Asian consumer capitalism and new immigration waves as a means for grappling with virtual machines under U.S. late capitalism. In a new millennium and Asian Century, the model machine metamorphosized into global machines.

It remains to be seen what will happen to the Asian automaton as we move further along in time. This apocryphal figure of the technocultural imagination has been gestating long enough to sunder our sense of history as one of linear progress for all humans. If the future is imagined as both Asian and posthuman, it matters to tell a story in which motley groups of people are jettisoned from humanity and treated as not quite alive, occupying the nebulous zone between abject human and "regular" human.

Insofar as the roboticization of race opens the door to problematizing the messiness of human-nonhuman relations, the issue of the Asian as automaton remains to contemplate how best to grasp a posthuman world as it unfolds. The spread of automation, robotics, and digital data should put a premium on human intuition, empathy, and critical reasoning, but it can easily erect a barrier to emancipate human automatons deemed as already lacking those faculties. The Asian automaton is both materialized and made immaterial within posthuman discourse as *tableau vivant*, a silent motionless group of people to represent a scene. What appears in this vista is an optical illusion, a trick of the modern eye, the spectacle of modernity. As sociologist Jean Baudrillard once wrote in another context, it seems "the automaton has no other destiny than to be ceaselessly compared to living man— so as to be more natural than him, of which he is the ideal figure. A perfect double for man."[16]

As an imperfect doppelgänger of European man, the Asian automaton puts up for investigation *historicity*, or the condition of history, in the face of rapid technological changes and a futuristic posthuman gaze. Under the model machine myth, we can recognize the Asian robot/cyborg/automaton as the limits of futurist humanistic thinking. The accumulated history and genealogy of this myth expresses the old problem of thinking that certain human groups are mere machines for labor, fighting, or pleasure. Model machines are ghostly apparitions of past colonial histories and "histories of the future." Despite posthuman cyborg wishes for transcending the human physical body and mind, the weighted legacy of thinking Asians as idealized machines will not easily dissipate.

In a roboticizing moment laden with self-sustaining forms of mechanical life that may escape direct control, the Asian automaton can be more than hero or villain. Writers like Franny Choi (*Death by Sex Machine*), Larissa Lai (*Automaton Biographies*), and Margaret Rhee (*Love Robot*) are revising the imago of the Asian robot as not some*thing* to hate or fear but a *someone* that must be embraced and even loved.[17] Rhee waxes poetically on robot-human relations as mutual admiration with lines that speak like lovers' dialogue: "Damaged hardware and software. Nothing to update . . . I still want all the bits of you."[18] Artist My-Linh Le choreographed a performative dance piece about the "machine-like endurance and work ethic of Vietnamese mothers," turning the everyday backbreaking work of cooking into something both marvelous and strange.[19] Titled "Me Love You Long Time," it turns a creepy line associated with Cold War stereotypes of Vietnamese women as sex machines into terms of maternal affection without necessarily dismissing sex workers. Le constructs home cooking as a "thing" of beauty, a creative technology of the self that goes beyond familial conditioning and gendered disciplining. The performance makes visible a moving and *embodied* human subject that ethnic studies scholar Ly Thuy Nguyen says rejects the psychological annotations of an *emptied* or hollowed-out robotic refugee subject, one that is "humanless, propertyless, and futureless."[20] It is not a project of violent forced humanization says education scholar Peter Keo, but one of "critical humanity" that adopts a reclaimed humanity for a humanity denied.[21]

The imago of the Asian automaton looms large over a great expanse of space and time. Bound up with the model machine myth, it exists as a relic of the past gazing upon a calamitous world unsure of itself and where it is going next. If this automaton could speak (as we have seen, it does), it would say human society is not threatened by alien forces and dark technology beyond our control. Rather, that unforeseen posthuman threat is born out of social constructs, which construe certain human populations as evil or expendable. By exploring how various Asian groups are folded into the machine myth, we confront long-lasting systems of oppression.

These days, any reference to Asians as robotic automatons is likely to be treated as insensitive and rather odd or outdated. But incantations of the stereotype turn up occasionally, depending on the political climate. With diplomatic disputes between the United States and other Asian nations becoming rifer under President Trump, Alex Jones, an American conservative on a podcast, concocted this wild theory about Asian fighting abilities: "In fights in like, Korea, fighting the Chinese, or Vietnam—they're conscious and real people but when they get into a fight, they all sync up and are robots and have no real fear. They're psychotic killers you're fighting. Asians are about the most fearless killers there are. . . . Once Asians go to war, they're not crazed, going wild in a battle. They're like robots coming to kill you."[22] Comedian Joe Rogan agrees, claiming that Japanese people are obsessed with combat, a trait he chalked up to Asian genetics. He still believes Asians are "real" people even if he adheres to the unwavering belief these robotic transformers possess mechanical instincts for killing that border on the obscene. In short, Asians are born to be war machines, much like the imperial soldiers of Japan during World War II. The dehumanizing perception facilitates the wave of attacks on Asians and Asian Americans during the

COVID-19 pandemic by racist vigilantes. The belief that their deaths, much like Vincent Chin's, would not elicit much sympathy was wrong. Asians and allies gathered in full force to reassert their humanity.

The trope of the Asian robotic killer finds support in popular Hollywood films. In the *X-Men* series, heroes like the animalistic Wolverine appear more human, despite a metal-infused mutant body that had been experimented on, when matched against high-tech Asian villains like Lady Deathstrike and Silver Samurai, with their cold "machine-like precision" that, according to communications scholar David Oh, effectuates the "U.S. victimizing of the Asian Other into U.S. victimization *by* the Asian Other."[23] This Asian robot figure took form in acclaimed movies like *Ex Machina* (2014) in which a male inventor created a female robot for his guest to love in a romantic twist on the Turing test. Named Ava, this humanoid female with artificial intelligence can speak and emote like a real woman. (With her shaven, metallic bald head, Ava resembles the white-passing Sophia, who appeared a few years after the movie as the first robot to obtain any kind of "symbolic" national citizenship.) A Black female robot named Jasmine, the earliest protype, had been destroyed and left in tatters for being "useless," exposing the total violence of misogynoir. The inventor then employed a more useful Asian-appearing automaton named Jade for the sole purpose of serving food and having sex. Barely articulate and frequently silenced by her master, Jade signified the plasticity of Asian women, who are prized for their supple personalities and streamlined quick actions.[24] As literary theorist Anne Cheng makes clear, "The slim, machinelike Asiatic female body [is] . . . flesh-that-is-not flesh, the perfect model."[25] In this machine modeling of the perfect quiet servant, we find "the synthetic, feminine, erotically gratifying, disposable thing that can be owned and used without moral qualm[;] the android . . . is always already the yellow woman."[26] So the Asian female android, not substantially human enough, remains superficial and jejune.

Pivoting off this kind of robo-sexism, Asian American filmmakers like Greg Pak work against reductive racial scripts through his cult classic *Robot Stories* (2003), portraying emotional stories about Asian American couples adopting baby robots and Asian robot workers seeking love. These stories recalibrate the operations of race through "an aesthetic strategy that explicitly takes on the figure of racial denigration."[27] Despite efforts by such Asian American artists to contrive less problematic Asian robot stories, mainstream American media was insistent on giving no autonomy to the racial automaton. Problematic representations can still crop up in commercials, such as the Dutch company Philips's 2007 Robot Skin shaver commercial, depicting a female slave bot with stereotypical Asian features, washing up a naked white man. The advertisement's visuals are complemented by the words "erotic union of man and shavebot." Though this servant robot is but a "a lifeless object made of cords and metal," this robot carries a repository of meaning related to "the alien, insectile (bestial), and subservient otherness of the robot."[28]

This mechanical edification prevents critique of sexual abuse. The Robot Skin advertisement came out in the same year as surviving comfort women from South Korea and all over Asia demanded an official state apology from Japan for imprisoning and abusing them during World War II. The elderly women led protests pushing for international awareness of their horrific treatment as sex machines, a transnational feminist campaign that countered American online entertainment programs at the time like *Jon Davis Gets a Sex Robot* (2013). The show put out a casting call for an actress that could play a sexy Asian gynoid servant for a white man, one that "has a slightly stiff demeanor but programmed to say things people want to hear [with] a tinge of aloofness that comes from not being human."[29] The implication of this characterization is that Asian women—both actresses and enslaved women—are inherently inhuman.

Within this frame of thought, it becomes easier to justify the abhorrent things done to people, because they are not human and therefore do not experience disease or pain. In 2021, a white male shooter massacred mostly Asian immigrant women spa workers to "eradicate" and "purge" his sexual desires.[30] This violent episode in the United States magnifies the myth of Asian women as hated and desired sex machines who only exist as objects and targets. According to historian Judy Tzu-Chun Wu, "they are not understood as and permitted to be fully human, with their own agency and dreams."[31] Body service work can be traced back to military "recreational" services during the Vietnam War, where working women are read as made to pleasure men at any time and disposed of at will like material waste. The killing of mostly Punjabi Sikhs at a FedEx warehouse, where they were denied access to phones during work, by another white American male shooter around the same time reinforced their position as labor machines or global machines working around the clock on the global conveyer belt.[32]

One method for parsing out the Asian-robot connection is by closely analyzing human societies transformed by robotics and racism. Unknown possibilities enabled by new technology push for greater humanization, even as the automatization of people proceeds to explain away their personhood. We cannot look at the robot with a stubborn literalness as representing itself or the future, since it signals a "deep discomfort and reluctance as a society to face the fear and shame that permeates our real-world American multicultural experience."[33] The multicultural goal of "uniting" races correlates with the onerous work of bonding man and machine. In other words, the "inclusion" of robotic life within a given human reality cannot be divorced from the imperial project of assimilating racial/robotic otherness and difference.

This metaphor of the man-machine accumulates mythological complexity when considering U.S. encounters with the Asian automaton Other in global Orientalized spaces, such as the "Middle East," where South Asian and Filipino workers slave away as the expendable automatons for wealthy Gulf economies and their ruling monarchs. Newspapers in the United States regularly churn out decontextualized images of Muslim devotees robotically at prayer multiple times a day with almost the fervor of jihadists heeding the call of militant religious leaders. It remains to be seen whether the model machine myth can hold or encompass the entire continent of Asia. For the United States, each region includes various kinds of discourses that contain "certain contained pasts, presents, and futures."[34]

A myth, like any told story, is open to interpretation and reinvention. But nothing that develops as mythological ever truly dissipates, particularly within certain strata of humanity that believe in their own superiority. As the American historian Richard Slotkin explains: "A mythology is a complex of narratives that dramatizes the world vision and historical sense of a people or culture, reducing centuries of experience into a constellation of compelling metaphors. . . . Myth describes a process, credible to its audience, by which knowledge is transformed into power."[35] The almost religious sense of divinity found in the need to defend one's universe based on myths hinges on this array of metaphors and narratives, which reduce the fantasy world of gods and monsters to real-life friends and enemies. Here, the story of the Asian automaton becomes part of the American myth-tale of humanity, dreams of domination, and liberal "structures of feeling" that are not fully worked out.[36] Even though the Asian automaton appears a harbinger of our global machine era, that mythical figure has always been part of the labyrinthine story of Asian/America. The future bears the past, and our past, the future.

A critique of the model machine myth refrains from the false lure of technology as the means to free humanity from cultural stagnation and the chains of being "simply human." It considers how Asian/American technoculture might impact the production of mechanical people of color and vice versa. Hopefully, this book will give rise to more in-depth conversations about the symbiotic relationship between the human and the machine and why Asians are so linked to "the machine." This association happens not only globally but galactically. In Christian sci-fi novels like *Good News to the Red Planet*, published in 2005, humans have colonized Mars, but the overseas colony remains a lawless place decked out with Chinese Martians who worship cybernetics as their pseudo-religion of technology. This foreign alien republic is studded with popular slogans like "Be One with the Machine!"

and people "walked the robotic Oriental streets with various machines pieced to their bodies."[37] In this imagined distant future, white human Christians clash with godless Chinese communist cybermachines.

It bears repeating that, despite their destructive potential to people, machine myths invite new "imaginative geographies" and time scales. These myths cohere within spatial orientations—nationalism, imperialism, militarism, transnationalism, globalism—that never settle in place. They are the cobbled pieces of a larger technocultural history, the sum of which compose a fragmented body of thought contrary to this fossilization of the Asian subject via Orientalist discourse, which is enduring, not ending. As critic Edward Said writes near the end of his magnum opus *Orientalism*, "It is in the logic of myths, like dreams, exactly to welcome radical antitheses. For a myth does not analyze or solve problems. It represents them as already analyzed and solved; that is, it presents them as already assembled images. . . . The discourse papers over the antithesis."[38] Here, he says the Arab presents "a puppet in the eyes of the world, staring vacantly out at a modern landscape."[39] The robotic Oriental supplies a powerful iconography yet also pushes for a deep analysis of why things appear as they do. The radical antithesis of machinic myth is endless open critique.

The model machine myth and its variants act as the lodestar for speculations of a posthuman historical future that reads in reverse the future. In retrospect, they guide us through a tour of some strange reflections by humans about the Asian as automaton. A long rearview mirror to the model machine's past offers proof of a myth's persistence in the foreseeable future. In the final analysis, the continued viability of the model machine myth points to a "matter of making connections, mutating and evolving, generating codes and patterns from the fragments of the old . . . [that] delimits our sense of human as well as posthuman."[40] These path-dependent processes are based on institutions and societies following the same belief systems due to a structure resistant to change. Man-made mythological structures are not strong enough to weather the effects of time. They might, like industrial robots, crumble and break down. But like legends, myths take on a glorified life of their own. Those humans designated as racial automatons are (and have always been) more than animalistic creatures of useful toil and monstrous threats. They are modeling the machine for themselves and their kin. These model-machine analogs hint at more studies in the future of the racial automaton that demonstrate how populations are corseted and unbounded by "nature."

As time wears on, the model machine myth may well find its terminus in some point in the ledger of time, perhaps when U.S. technocultural hegemony fully concludes or when humanity truly ends by its own hands or by some alien invasion. But so long as the racialized robot exists as a differentiated racial category of the universal human, and as a legacy of racial capitalism, we shall see the monstrous perception of Asians as machinelike automatons—only perhaps not in the forms thus far documented. As old thinking is exploded by new fantasies, the model machine and the figure of the Asian automaton will take flight in unexpected ways, popping up as a reminder that forms of mechanized slavery and stigmatization live on. That violent history and futurity is something we—human, posthuman, and otherwise—all must work against. The models for this resistance remain open to interpretation, even as the machine and its stories continue to evolve.

Notes

INTRODUCTION

1. Albert Einstein, *The Travel Diaries of Albert Einstein: The Far East, Palestine, and Spain, 1922–1923* (Princeton, NJ: Princeton University Press, 2018), 129.

2. Ibid., 135.

3. Daniel Golden, *The Price of Admission: How America's Ruling Class Buys Its Way into Elite Colleges and Who Gets Left outside the Gates* (New York: Random House, 2006).

4. Mel Chen, *Animacies: Biopolitics, Racial Mattering, and Queer Affect* (Durham, NC: Duke University Press, 2012), 14.

5. David S. Roh, Betsy Huang, and Greta A. Niu, "Technologizing Orientalism: An Introduction," *Techno-Orientalism: Imagining Asia in Speculative Fiction, History, and Media*, ed. David S. Roh, Betsy Huang, and Greta A. Niu (New Brunswick, NJ: Rutgers University Press, 2015), 11.

6. David Morley and Kevin Robins, *Spaces of Identity: Global Media, Electronic Landscapes and Cultural Boundaries* (London: Routledge, 2013), 170.

7. Long T. Bui, "Asian Roboticism: Connecting Mechanized Labor to the Automation of Work," *Perspectives on Global Development and Technology* 19, no. 1–2 (2020): 110–126.

8. Michael Omi and Howard Winant, *Racial Formation in the United States* (London: Routledge, 2014); Colleen Lye, *America's Asia: Racial Form and American Literature, 1893–1945* (Princeton, NJ: Princeton University Press, 2005).

9. Christopher Fan, "Asian/American Antibodies: An Ending," Yale University, April 14, 2016, http://post45.research.yale.edu.

10. Kishore Mahbubani, "The Case against the West: America and Europe in the Asian Century," *Foreign Affairs* 87, no. 3 (2008): 111–124; Harinder S. Kohli, Ashok Sharma, and Anil Sood, *Asia 2050: Realizing the Asian Century*, ed. Harinder S. Kohli, Ashok Sharma, and Anil Sood (New Delhi: SAGE Publications India, 2011).

11. Achille Mbembe, "Necropower," *Public Culture* 15, no. 1 (2003): 11–40.

12. *Merriam-Webster*, s.v. "autonomy," accessed February 26, 2014, www.merriam-web ster.com.

13. Susan Koshy, *Sexual Naturalization: Asian Americans and Miscegenation* (Stanford, CA: Stanford University Press, 2004), 69.

14. Mark Chiang, *The Cultural Capital of Asian American Studies: Autonomy and Representation in the University* (New York: New York University Press, 2009).

15. Yves Gringas, *Éloge de L'homo Techno-Logicus* (Saint-Laurent, Quebec: Les Editions Fides, 2005).

16. *Merriam-Webster*, s.v. "machine," accessed October 11, 2013, www.merriam-web ster.com.

17. Ibid.

18. *Roget's Thesaurus*, 3rd ed., s.v. "automate," accessed October 10, 2014, www.the saurus.com.

19. Catherine Liu, *Copying Machines: Taking Notes for the Automaton* (Minneapolis: University of Minnesota Press, 2000), 77.

20. Meltem Ahiska, "Occidentalism: The Historical Fantasy of the Modern," *South Atlantic Quarterly* 102, no. 2 (2003): 358–359.

21. A range of scholars, such as Yen Le Espiritu, Dorothy Roberts, Pierre Bourdieu, Orlando Patterson, Mary Douglas, Bryan Turner, and many others, have irrefutably shown that the body is a central focus of modern discourse, shaping both history and historical consciousness.

22. Michel Foucault, *Discipline and Punish: The Birth of the Prison* (New York: Vintage, 2012), 164.

23. Ibid., 242.

24. Rachel Lee and Sau-ling Wong, eds., "Introduction," in *Asian America.Net: Ethnicity, Nationalism, and Cyberspace* (New York: Routledge, 2003), xiv.

25. bell hooks, *Talking Back: Thinking Feminist, Thinking Black* (New York: South End Press, 1989), 42.

26. The invention of hydraulic engineering in the third century BC led to a model of human intelligence based on the flow of different bodily fluids; this hydraulic model prevailed until the 1500s when machines powered by springs and gears gave rise to more dynamic theories of the mind-body. Robert Epstein, "The Empty Brain," *Aeon*, May 18, 2016, www.Aeon.co.

27. Joseph Needham with Wang Ling, *Science and Civilization in China*, vol. 2 (Cambridge: Cambridge University Press), 53.

28. Ray Bert, *Engineers: From the Great Pyramids to the Pioneers of Space Travel*, ed. Adam Hart-Davis (New York: DK Publishing, 2012), 53.

29. Stephen Cave and Kanta Dihal, "Ancient Dreams of Intelligent Machines: 3,000 Years of Robots," *Nature: International Journal of Science* (July 25, 2018), www.nature .com.

30. E. C. Eze, "The Color of Reason: The Idea of 'Race' in Kant's Anthropology," in *Postcolonial African Philosophy: A Critical Reader*, ed. E. C. Eze (Cambridge, MA: Blackwell, 1997), 130.

31. Ayhan Ayteş, "The 'Other' in the Machine: Oriental Automata and the Mechanization of the Mind" (PhD diss., University of California, San Diego, 2012), 11.

32. Ibid., 67.

33. Ibid., 70.

34. Minsoo Kang, "The Machine-Man to the Automaton-Man: The Enlightenment Origins of the Mechanistic Imagery of Humanity," in *Vital Matters: Eighteenth-Century Views of Conception, Life & Death*, ed. Helen Deutsch and Mary Terall (Toronto: University of Toronto Press, 2011), 148–173.

35. Ibid., 154.

36. Ibid., 148.

37. He connects medieval counterfeit automata like the exotic chess-playing "Turk" to Amazon's MTurk worker in the age of informatics. This disappearance is connected what he calls the "alterity script" that circulates at places, where scientific, informatic, performative, theatrical, and computational scripts intersect. See Bernard Dionysius Geoghegan, "Orientalism and Informatics: Alterity from the Chess-Playing Turk to Amazon's Mechanical Turk," *Ex-position* 43 (2020): 76.

38. Ibid., 67.

39. Sylvia Wynter, "Unsettling the Coloniality of Being/Power/Truth/Freedom: Towards the Human, after Man, Its Overrepresentation—an Argument," *CR: The New Centennial Review* 3, no. 3 (2003): 257–337.

40. René Descartes, "Treatise on Man," in *The Nature of Life: Classical and Contemporary Perspectives from Philosophy and Science*, ed. Mark A. Bedau and Carol E. Cleland (New York: Cambridge University Press, 2010), 15–20.

41. Christoph Lüthy, "Historical and Philosophical Reflections on Natural, Enhanced and Artificial Men and Women," in *Engineering the Human: Human Enhancement between Fiction and Fascination*, ed. Bert-Jaap Koops, Christoph H. Lüthy, Annemiek Nelis, Carla Sieburgh, J. P. M. Jansen, and Monika S. Schmid (Berlin: Springer, 2013), 20–23.

42. Margaret Rhee, "In Search of My Robot: Race, Technology, and the Asian American Body," *Scholar and Feminist Online* 13, no. 3 (2016), http://sfonline.barnard.edu /traversing-technologies/margaret-rhee-in-search-of-my-robot-race-technology-and -the-asian-american-body/0/.

43. Julien Offray de la Mettrie, *Man a Machine* (Chicago: Open Court, 1912).

44. Quoted in Lewis Mumford, *The Myth of the Machine: Technics and Human Development* (New York: Harcourt Brace Jovanovich, 1967), 57.

45. Blaise Pascal, *Pensées and Other Writings* (Oxford: Oxford University Press, 1999).

46. Marina Paola Banchetti-Robino, "Ontological Tensions in Sixteenth and Seventeenth Century Chemistry: Between Mechanism and Vitalism," *Foundations of Chemistry* 13, no. 3 (2011): 173–186.

47. Robert Boyle, *The Works of the Honourable Robert Boyle* (London: A. Millar, 1744), 146.

48. Simon Kow, "Automatons! From Ovid to AI: Asian Robots and Orientalism," University of King's College Lecture, March 7, 2018, www.youtube.com.

49. Aristotle, "The Ideal State," in *The Structure of Political Geography*, ed. Julian Minghi (London: Routledge, 2017), 15.

50. It is believed he told his pupil Alexander the Great that only Greeks were human beings and the conquered peoples in Asia were nothing but barbarians, animals, or plants. Anthony Pagden, *Worlds at War: The 2,500-Year Struggle between East and West* (Oxford: Oxford University Press, 2008), 33.

51. Georg Wilhelm Friedrich Hegel, *The Philosophy of History* (New York: Dove, 2004), 161.

52. Ibid., 228.

53. Ibid.

54. Ibid., 197.

55. Georg Wilhelm Friedrich Hegel, *Phenomenology of Spirit* (Oxford: Clarendon Press, 1998), paragraphs 168–174.

56. Alex Wetmore, "Sympathy Machines: Men of Feeling and the Automaton," *Eighteenth-Century Studies* 43, no. 1 (2009): 37–54.

57. He found striking similarities in the power supply of machines fueled by heat, electricity, chemicals, water, and the fluid of biological organisms.

58. Anson Rabinbach, *The Human Motor: Energy, Fatigue, and the Origins of Modernity* (Berkeley: University of California Press, 1992), 63.

59. *Merriam-Webster*, s.v. "technology," accessed October 13, 2021, http://www.merriam-webster.com/dictionary/technology.

60. Arthur de Gobineau, *The Inequality of Human Races*, trans. Adrian Collins (London: Heinemann, 1915), 205–212.

61. Ibid.

62. Ibid.

63. Ibid., 6.

64. William Sacksteder, "Man the Artificer: Notes on Animals, Humans and Machines in Hobbes," *Southern Journal of Philosophy* 22, no. 1 (1984): 105–121.

65. Isaac Asimov's laws of robotics state the following: (1) a robot may not injure a human being; (2) a robot must obey the orders given it by human beings; (3) a robot must protect its own existence as long as such protection does not conflict with the first or second laws.

66. David Morley, *Media, Modernity and Technology: Geography of the New* (New York: Routledge, 2006).

67. Junichi Murata, "Creativity of Technology: An Origin of Modernity?" in *Modernity and Technology*, ed. Thomas J. Misa, Philip Brey, and Andrew Feenberg (Cambridge, MA: MIT Press, 2003): 227.

68. American Colonization Society, "One Hundred Years of British Rule in Ceylon," *Journal of the Royal Colonial Institute* 6 (1896): 459.

69. Ralph Fox, *The Colonial Policy of British Imperialism* (New York: International, 1933), 88.

70. Karl Friedrich August Gutzlaff, *China Opened* (London: Smith, Elder, 1838), 478–479.

71. Valdimar Tr. Hafstein, "Bodies of Knowledge," *Ethnologia Europaea* 33, no. 1 (2003): 12.

72. Bradley D. Naranch, "'Colonized Body,' 'Oriental Machine': Debating Race, Railroads, and the Politics of Reconstruction in Germany and East Africa, 1906–1910," *Central European History* 33, no. 3 (2000): 299–338.

73. The lazy boy describes children tasked with connecting the piston with a cam to the top of a steam engine valve. On Barak, *On Time: Technology and Temporality in Modern Egypt* (Berkeley: University of California Press, 2013), 72.

74. Ibid.

75. The truth was foreign colonizers practiced "ecologies of waste rather than making nature productive." Pauline Goul, "An Ecology of Waste: Transatlantic Excess in Renaissance France" (PhD diss., Cornell University, 2017).

76. Ross Bassett, *The Technological Indian* (Cambridge, MA: Harvard University Press, 2016), 2.

77. Ritam Sengupta, "The Punkah and Its Pullers: A Short History," *Servants Pasts: European Research Council*, August 10, 2020, https://servantspasts.wordpress.com/2020/08/10/the-punkah-and-its-pullers-a-short-history/.

78. Ibid.

79. Martin and Company, "Working of District Boards in Bengal, 1904–05," *Indian Engineering* 38 (1905): 420.

80. Karl Marx, "The British Rule in India," *New-York Herald Tribune*, June 25, 1853, https://www.marxists.org/archive/marx/works/1853/06/25.htm.

81. Ibid.

82. Milton Reed, *The Golden Window of Oriental Impressions* (Boston: Sherman, French, 1912), 96–97.

83. Ibid.

84. Ibid., 133.

85. Ibid.

86. Mahatma Gandhi, *The Collected Works of Mahatma Gandhi*, vol. 95 (New Delhi: Ministry of Information and Broadcasting, 2000), 337.

87. Robert Schomburgk, "The Indians of British Guiana," *The Journal of Civilization* 26 (October 30, 1841): 411.

88. Fedor Jagor, *Travels in the Philippines* (London: Chapman and Hall, 1875), 104.

89. Ibid.

90. Mumford, *Myth of the Machine*, 12.

91. Ibid., 146.

92. Michel Foucault, *The History of Sexuality: An Introduction* (New York: Random House, 2012).

93. Michael Adas, *Machines as the Measure of Men: Science, Technology, and Ideologies of Western Dominance* (Ithaca, NY: Cornell University Press, 2015).

94. Ibid., 15.

95. Raymond Williams, *A Vocabulary of Culture and Society* (New York: Oxford University Press, 1983), 212.

96. Anthony Pagden, "Europe: Conceptualizing a Continent," in *The Idea of Europe: From Antiquity to the European Union*, ed. Anthony Pagden and Lee H. Hamilton (Cambridge: Cambridge University Press, 2002), 34.

97. *Oxford Dictionaries* (2012), s.v. "automaton."

98. Rey Chow, *Writing Diaspora: Tactics of Intervention in Contemporary Cultural Studies* (Bloomington: Indiana University Press, 1993), 48.

99. Despina Kakoudaki, *Anatomy of a Robot: Literature, Cinema, and the Cultural Work of Artificial People* (New Brunswick, NJ: Rutgers University Press, 2014), 213.

100. Lisa Yun, *The Coolie Speaks: Chinese Indentured Laborers and African Slaves in Cuba* (Philadelphia: Temple University Press, 2008, 18).

101. Ibid., xxiii.

102. Samera Esmeir, *Juridical Humanity: A Colonial History* (Stanford, CA: Stanford University Press, 2012), 80.

103. Liu, *Copying Machines*, 85.

104. Denise Ferreira da Silva, "Towards a Critique of the Socio-logos of Justice: The Analytics of Raciality and the Production of Universality," *Social Identities* 7, no. 3 (2001): 421–454.

105. Amber Jamilla Musser, *Sensual Excess: Queer Femininity and Brown Jouissance* (New York: New York University Press, 2018), 120.

106. Roland Barthes, *Mythologies* (London: Paladin, 1973), 107.

107. Ibid., 122.

108. Ibid., 107.

109. Sheri Weinstein, "Technologies of Vision: Spiritualism and Science in Nineteenth-Century America," *Spectral America: Phantoms and the National Imagination*, ed. Jeffrey Andrew Weinstock (Madison: University of Wisconsin Press / Popular Press, 2004), 124–40.

110. Wendy Chun, "Race and/as Technology; or, How to Do Things to Race," In *Race after the Internet*, ed. Lisa Nakamura and Peter A. Chow-White (New York: Routledge), 38-60.

111. Wendy Chun, *Control and Freedom: Power and Paranoia in the Age of Fiber Optics* (Cambridge, MA: MIT Press, 2006), 51, 141–143.

112. Ibid., 28.

113. David E. Nye, *American Technological Sublime* (Cambridge, MA: MIT Press, 1994); John F. Kasson, *Civilizing the Machine: Technology and Republican Values in America, 1776–1900* (New York, 1976; repr., New York, 1977); Leo Marx, *The Machine in the Garden: Technology and the Pastoral Ideal in America* (Oxford University Press, 1964).

114. Stephen Jay Gould, *The Mismeasure of Man* (New York: W. W. Norton, 1996).

115. Katherine McKittrick, "Mathematics Black Life," *Black Scholar* 44, no. 2 (2014): 27.

116. Claire Jean Kim, *Bitter Fruit: The Politics of Black-Korean Conflict in New York City* (New Haven, CT: Yale University Press, 2003), 46.

117. While early technology studies scholars were concerned with identifying the problems of America's technological values or the intricacies of technological production, technology studies today is more likely to be attuned to the competing contexts and semantics as well as the cultural construction of the difference that exists within the supposedly "closed circuits" of technological systems. For Peña, a more recent "third wave" of scholarship in technology studies is underway that closely pays attention to dynamics of race alongside gender, class, religion, and imperialism in the cultural construction of the "body" and the difference within the technological landscape. Carolyn Thomas De la Peña, "'Slow and Low Progress,' or Why American Studies Should Do Technology," *American Quarterly* 58, no. 3 (2006): 921.

118. Quoted in Cedric J. Robinson, *Black Marxism: The Making of the Black Radical Tradition* (Chapel Hill: University of North Carolina Press, 2000), 201.

119. Tiffany Willoughby-Herard, *Waste of a White Skin: The Carnegie Corporation and the Racial Logic of White Vulnerability* (Berkeley: University of California Press, 2015); Yousuf Al-Bulushi, "Thinking Racial Capitalism and Black Radicalism from Africa: An Intellectual Geography of Cedric Robinson's World-System," *Geoforum*, January 31, 2020, https://doi.org/10.1016/j.geoforum.2020.01.018.

120. As opposed to the manifestly biological representation of Black bodies, Day argues that the humanity of Chinese and Asian labor was based on economic functionality and labor efficiency. See Iyko Day, *Alien Capital: Asian Racialization and the Logic of Settler Colonial Capitalism* (Durham, NC: Duke University Press, 2016).

121. Lisa Lowe, "The Intimacies of Four Continents," in *Haunted by Empire: Geographies of Intimacy in North American History*, ed. Anne Laura Stoler (Durham, NC: Duke University Press, 2006).

122. Lisa Lowe, *Immigrant Acts: On Asian American Cultural Politics* (Durham, NC: Duke University Press, 1996), 18.

123. Ibid.

124. Hubert Howe Bancroft, *The New Pacific* (San Francisco: Bancroft, 1912), 421.

125. Ibid.

126. Ibid., 621.

127. Ellen Wu, *The Color of Success: Asian Americans and the Origins of the Model Minority* (Princeton, NJ: Princeton University Press, 2015).

128. Edward Said, *Orientalism* (New York: Pantheon, 1978), 97.

129. Alexis De Tocqueville, *Democracy in America* (New York: Regnery, 2003), 606.

130. Ibid., 102.

131. Ibid., 426.

132. Cathy Schlund-Vials, *Modeling Citizenship: Jewish and Asian American Writing* (Philadelphia: Temple University Press, 2011), 6.

133. Ibid., 14.

134. Carolyn De la Peña, "The History of Technology, the Resistance of Archives, and the Whiteness of Race," *Technology and Culture* 51, no. 4 (2010): 919–937.

135. Kandice Chuh, *Imagine Otherwise: On Asian Americanist Critique* (Durham, NC: Duke University Press), 2003; Rachel C. Lee, *The Exquisite Corpse of Asian America: Biopolitics, Biosociality, and Posthuman Ecologies* (New York: New York University Press), 2014.

136. Eve Darian-Smith and Philip C. McCarty, *The Global Turn: Theories, Research Designs, and Methods for Global Studies* (Berkeley: University of California Press, 2017), 8.

137. Ibid., 153.

138. Chun, "Race and/as Technology, or How to do Things to Race," 40.

139. Beth Coleman, "Race as Technology," *Camera Obscura: Feminism, Culture, and Media Studies* 24, no. 1 (2009): 190.

140. Although it was not published by the time my current book was finishing, I want to acknowledge Margaret Rhee's highly anticipated forthcoming book, *How We Became Human: Race, Robots, and the Asian American Body*, which promises to bring readers forward into the future my study of the historical past, focusing more on theoretical and creative aspects.

141. Roh, Huang, and Niu, "Technologizing Orientalism," 2.

142. Michelle Huang, "The Posthuman Subject in/of Asian American Literature," *Oxford Research Encyclopedia of Literature* (February 2019): 1https://oxfordre.com.

143. Thomas Jefferson, writing in 1785 as U.S. ambassador to France, found feudal China to be a great model for the United States to break away from European-style social organization and stand at the foot of China. L. Marx, *Machine in the Garden*, 140.

144. Ibid., 206.

145. Ibid., 367.

146. Walt Whitman, "Passage to India," in *Leaves of Grass* (New York: G. P. Putnam's Sons, 1907), 315–317.

147. Carroll Pursell, *The Machine in America: A Social History of Technology* (Philadelphia: Johns Hopkins Press, 2007), 199.

148. Mikael Hård and Andrew Jamison, eds., *The Intellectual Appropriation of Technology: Discourses on Modernity, 1900–1939* (Boston: MIT Press, 1998).

149. Joel Dinerstein, "Technology and Its Discontents: On the Verge of the Posthuman," *American Quarterly* 58, no. 3 (2006): 569–95.

150. Sarah E. Chinn, *Technology and the Logic of American Racism: A Cultural History of the Body as Evidence* (New York: Continuum, 2000).

151. Donna Haraway, "A Cyborg Manifesto: Science, Technology, and Socialist-Feminism in the Late Twentieth Century," in *Simians, Cyborgs and Women: The Reinvention of Nature* (New York: Routledge, 1991), 162.

152. Félix Guattari, *Molecular Revolution: Psychiatry and Politics* (London: Puffin Books, 1984), 112.

153. The term comes from a translation of the Japanese term *bukimi no tani*, coined by the roboticist Masahiro Moti, who plotted the level of emotional response by humans to the realism of robots.

154. Said, *Orientalism*, 70.

155. Edward Said, "Orientalism Once More," *Development and Change* 35, no. 5 (2004): 869–879.

156. Anne Cheng, *Ornamentalism* (Oxford: Oxford University Press, 2019), 136.

157. See the work of Alluquère Rosanne Stone, Mimi Nguyen, Anne Balsamo, Lisa Nakamura, Katherine Hayles, Donna Haraway, Sherry Turkle, Chela Sandoval, Jennifer Gonzalez, and Coco Fusco, among many others.

158. David Palumbo-Liu, *Asian/America: Historical Crossings of a Racial Frontier* (Stanford, CA: Stanford University Press, 1999), 21.

159. Nakamura, *Digitizing Race*, 17.

160. Ray Kurzweil, *The Age of Intelligent Machines* (Cambridge, MA: MIT Press, 1990).

161. Yoram Koren, *Robotics for Engineers* (New York: McGraw-Hill, 1985), 11–12.

162. Ruha Benjamin, *Race after Technology: Abolitionist Tools for the New Jim Code* (Bristol, UK: Polity Press, 2019).

163. Ibid., 142.

164. Ronald Steel, *Walter Lippmann and the American Century* (New Brunswick, NJ: Transaction, 1980).

165. Stuart Hall, "Race, Articulation, and Societies Structured in Dominance," in *Black British Cultural Studies: A Reader*, ed. Houston A. Baker Jr., Manthia Diawara, and Ruth H. Lindeborg (Chicago: University of Chicago Press, 1996), 16–60.

166. For more on techno-braceros and how it relates to high-tech coolies, see Sharmila Rudrappa, "Cyber-Coolies and Techno-Braceros: Race and Commodification of Indian Information Technology Guest Workers in the United States," *University of San Francisco Law Review* 44 (2009): 353–372. This metaphor is totally reimagined by the 2008 sci-fi film *Sleepdealer* (dir. Alex Rivera, Maya Entertainment).

167. Dustin Abnet, *The American Robot: A Cultural History* (Chicago: University of Chicago Press, 2020), 21.

168. Jennifer Rhee, *The Robotic Imaginary: The Human and the Price of Dehumanized Labor* (Minneapolis: University of Minnesota, 2018), 88.

169. Li is focused primarily on the major periods of immigrant legislation, but my work tries to depart from this timeline by focusing on a longer history of capitalist expansion and cultural production that works unevenly with moments of legislation. See David Leiwei Li, *Imagining the Nation: Asian American Literature and Cultural Consent* (Stanford, CA: Stanford University Press, 1998).

CHAPTER 1

1. Marcus Cunliffe, *Chattel Slavery and Wage Slavery: The Anglo-American Context, 1830–1860* (Athens: University of Georgia Press, 2008); E. Springs Steele, "Henry George on Chattel and Wage Slavery," *American Journal of Economics and Sociology* 46, no. 3 (1987): 369–378.

2. Richard Franklin Pettigrew, *Imperial Washington: The Story of American Public Life from 1870–1920* (Chicago: C. H. Kerr, 1922), 261.

3. Moon-Kie Jung, *Reworking Race: The Making of Hawaii's Interracial Labor Movement* (New York: Columbia University Press, 2006).

4. Gail Weiss, "The Body as Narrative Horizon," in *Thinking the Limits of the Body*, ed. Jeffrey Jerome Cohen and Gail Weiss (Albany: State University of New York Press, 2003), 24.

5. Natalia Molina, *Fit to Be Citizens? Public Health and Race in Los Angeles, 1879–1939* (Berkeley: University of California Press, 2006).

6. Eric Hayot, *The Hypothetical Mandarin: Sympathy, Modernity, and Chinese Pain* (Oxford: Oxford University Press, 2009), 141.

7. Eric Hayot, "Coolie," in *The Routledge Companion to Asian American and Pacific Islander Literature*, ed. Rachel Lee (London: Routledge, 2014), 85.

8. Jason Oliver Chang, *Chino: Anti-Chinese Racism in Mexico, 1880–1940* (Urbana-Champaign: University of Illinois Press, 2017), 8.

9. Andrew Smith, "The Coolie Trade," *Boston Daily Globe*, September 13, 1873, 2.

10. Robert Kemp Philp, *The Dictionary of Useful Knowledge* (London: Houlston & Wright, 1858), 229.

11. On March 23, 1908, Churchill was arguing against the Labor Importation Amendment Ordinance of 1909, which allowed any white man without a warrant to arrest a laborer found outside his work district and to deliver the worker to the nearest police station and receive compensation (while the worker was punished). See *The Parliamentary Debates: Third Session of the Twenty-Eighth Parliament of the United Kingdom of Great Britain and Ireland*, vol. 4 (London: Wyman and Sons, 1909), 1123.

12. Great Britain Parliament, *The Parliamentary Debates* (London: Wyman and Sons, 1906), 997.

13. Perisa Campbell, *Chinese Coolie Emigration to Canada* (London: Routledge, 2012), 45–46.

14. David A. Hounshell, *From the American System to Mass Production, 1800–1932* (Baltimore: Johns Hopkins University Press, 1984); Philip Scranton, *Endless Novelty: Specialty Production and American Industrialization, 1865–1925* (Princeton, NJ: Princeton University Press, 1997.

15. Patrick O' Bannon, "Technological Change in the Pacific Coast Canned Salmon Industry, 1900–1925: A Case Study," *Agricultural History* 56, no. 1 (January 1982): 151–166.

16. Ibid.

17. Donald Wagner, *Science and Civilisation in China*, vol. 5 (Cambridge: Cambridge University Press, 2008), 363–365.

18. Howard Zinn, *A People's History of the United States* (New York: Harper & Row, 2010), 253.

19. Robert Ayres, *Energy, Complexity and Wealth Maximization* (New York: Springer, 2016), 418.

20. *American Heritage Dictionary of the English Language*, s.v. "human," accessed November 26, 2013, www.thefreedictionary.com.

21. Lowe, "Intimacies of Four Continents," 192.

22. Ibid., 206.

23. Moon-Ho Jung, *Coolies and Cane: Race, Labor, and Sugar in the Age of Emancipation* (Baltimore: Johns Hopkins University Press, 2006), 5.

24. Rev. G. B. Back, "The Cleanliness and Vigor of the Japanese," *Christian Recorder*, November 16, 1867.

25. Matthew Pratt Guterl, "After Slavery: Asian Labor, the American South, and the Age of Emancipation," *Journal of World History* 14, no. 2 (2003): 231.

26. Matthew Pratt Guterl, *American Mediterranean: Southern Slaveholders in the Age of Emancipation* (Boston: Harvard University Press, 2008), 103.

27. Ibid., 188.

28. Ted Hinckley, *Alaskan John G. Brady: Missionary, Businessman, Judge, and Governor, 1878–1918* (Columbus: Ohio State University Press, 1982), 258.

29. James Blaine, Congressional Series of United States Public Documents 4202, June 30, 1881 (Washington, DC: Government Printing Office, 1906), 490.

30. California Legislature, *Chinese Immigration: Its Social, Moral, and Political Effect*, Special Committee on Chinese Immigration Report (Sacramento: F. P. Thompson State Printing, 1878), 47.

31. Mark Twain, *Roughing It* (Hartford, CT: American, 1872), 391.

32. Ibid., 397.

33. Michele Walfred, *What Shall We Do with Our Boys 1882*, Thomas Nast Cartoons, February 14, 2014. https://thomasnastcartoons.com/2014/02/14/what-shall-we-do-with-our-boys-3-march-1882/.

34. The alternative title of this image is *Chinese Octopus Taking Over Every Industry, Idle White Laborers to the Right Side; Jails in the Distance.* The octopus is a creature important to the Western oceanic fantasy of the Asia Pacific as an open frontier populated by animalistic primitives. It adapts the Chinese coolie threat to the typical depiction of monopoly corporations as giant octopuses (fully realized in Frank Norris's 1901 novel *The Octopus*) taking over America and the world.

35. Steven J. Keillor, *This Rebellious House: American History and the Truth of Christianity* (Downers Grove, IL: InterVarsity, 1996), 211.

36. "Chink" is figurative phrase related to a dent or mark on a suit of armor or piece of metal, but it is now interpreted as an ethnic slur.

37. Walter Benjamin, "The Work of Art in the Age of Mechanical Reproduction," in *Illuminations* (New York: Harcourt, Brace, Jovanovich, 1968), 235.

38. *Oxford Dictionaries*, "automation."

39. Leo Marx, "Technology: The Emergence of a Hazardous Concept," *Technology and Culture* 51, no. 3 (2010): 567.

40. Vincent Mosco, *The Digital Sublime-Myth, Power, and Cyberspace* (Cambridge, MA: MIT Press, 2005), 22.

41. Ronald T. Takaki, *Iron Cages: Race and Culture in Nineteenth-Century America* (Oxford: Oxford University Press, 1979). From a classic Marxist perspective, we can say globalization debate concerns the change in outward appearance of things through the technology and apparatus of cultural domination rather than question the human culture itself and its historical development. In this regard, Takaki adopts a Marxist vocabulary of calling Chinese labor an "industrial reserve army" or "yellow proletariat." His reliance on a "multicultural" liberal humanist framework emphasizing the necessary inclusion of nonwhite groups into the American national story does not scrutinize the ways nonwhites have been constructed as nonhumans outside of the Eurocentric cultural conception of who constitutes the proletariat and the human.

42. Ibid., 248.

43. Ibid., 248.

44. Tomas Almaguer, *Racial Fault Lines: The Historical Origins of White Supremacy in California* (Berkeley: Univversity of California Press, 2008), 158.

45. David Eng, Teemu Ruskola Eng, and Shuang Shen, "Introduction: China and the Human," *Social Text* 29, no. 4 (2011): 5.

46. Karl Marx, *Capital: Volume One; A Critique of Political Economy* (Moscow: Progress, 1965), 266, 317.

47. Throughout *Capital*, Marx wrote that for all his degradation, the worker remained "living labor" and at the core human, despite being imbued with the "dead substance" of monstrous capital. Ibid., 136.

48. Karl Marx, *Critique of Hegel's Philosophy of Right* (New York: Press Syndicate of the University of Cambridge, 1977), 141.

49. K. Marx, *Capital*, 248.

50. Maurice Meisner, "The Despotism of Concepts: Wittfogel and Marx on China," *China Quarterly* 16 (1963): 99–111.

51. Erik van Ree, "Marx and Engels's Theory of History: Making Sense of the Race Factor," *Journal of Political Ideologies* 24, no.1 (2019): 64.

52. Robin D. G. Kelley, "What Did Cedric Robinson Mean by Racial Capitalism," *Boston Review*, January 12, 2017.

53. Richard Jenkins, "Disenchantment, Enchantment and Re-enchantment: Max Weber at the Millennium," *Max Weber Studies* 1, no. 1 (2000): 11–32.

54. Karl Marx, *Grundrisse* (London: Penguin, 1973), 693.

55. Lisa Marie Cacho, *Social Death: Racialized Rightlessness and the Criminalization of the Unprotected* (New York: New York University Press, 2012).

56. Chew Heong v. United States: Chinese Exclusion and the Federal Courts (italics mine). Judge Lorenzo Sawyer on the "Chinese question," ca. 1890. George Anthony Peffer, *If They Don't Bring Their Women Here: Chinese Female Immigration before Exclusion* (Chicago: University of Illinois Press, 1999), 108.

57. Takaki, *Iron Cages*, 49.

58. Marli Frances Weiner, *Mistresses and Slaves: Plantation Women in South Carolina, 1830–80* (Urbana-Champaign: University of Illinois Press, 1997), 1.

59. Anthony Paul Farley, "Apogee of the Commodity," *DePaul Law Review* 53 (2004): 1229–1246; Bibi Bakare-Yusuf, "The Economy of Violence: Black Bodies and the Unspeakable Terror," in *Feminist Theory and the Body: A Reader*, ed. Janet Price and Margit Shildrick (London: Routledge, 1999), 311–323.

60. For more on this juxtaposition, see Hoang Gia Phan, "Free Subjects: Black Civic Identity and the Invention of the Asiatic," *Law and Humanities eJournal* (September 2003): 1–45, https://poseidon01.ssrn.com.

61. Ruth Oldenziel, *Making Technology Masculine: Men, Women and Modern Machines in America, 1870–1945* (Amsterdam: Amsterdam University Press, 1999), 19–50.

62. Sawyer believes the Chinese are superior to the Negro, since the former comes from a once powerful civilization while Black people come from the wilderness; in this regard, the Chinese are "better" and thus less economically assimilable to the United States, but their strong cultural tradition prevents them from quickly taking on American customs. Peffer, *If They Don't Bring Their Women Here*, 109.

63. Robert G. Lee, *Orientals: Asian Americans in Popular Culture* (Philadelphia: Temple University Press, 1999), 88–89.

64. Ideas of proper sex, health, and family values were crucial to the elocution of new bourgeois terms of domesticity, citizenship, and national identity in nineteenth-century America. In the United States, Asians were historically cast as a "third sex," disruptive to the heterosexual orthodoxy of two main sexes symbolized by the phallic power of white masculinity and the "true womanhood" of white femininity. Asian men typified castrated asexuality or hypersexuality, whereas Asian women were cast as hypersexual.

65. Quoted in Rogers M. Smith, "Beyond Tocqueville, Myrdal, and Hartz: The Multiple Traditions in America," *American Political Science Review* 87, no. 03 (1993): 559.

66. Edwin R. Meade, "A Labor Question," in *The Great West*, ed. Ferdinand Vandeveer Hayden (Bloomington, IN: C. R. Brodix, 1880), 389–390.

67. Almaguer, *Racial Fault Lines*, 37.

68. Another trade card came out by the Donaldson Brothers in 1870, showing New York supporters for Irish American labor leader Dennis Kearny and his Workingmen's Party of California. See https://ark.digitalcommonwealth.org.

69. Rosanne Currarino, "Meat vs. Rice: Working-Class Manhood and Anti-Chinese Hysteria," *Men and Masculinities* 9 (April 2007): 479.

70. Ibid., 482.

71. James Amaziah Whitney, *The Chinese, and the Chinese Question* (New York: Tibbals Book, 1888), 10.

72. Ibid.

73. Ibid.

74. Ho Yow, "Chinese Exclusion: A Benefit or a Harm?," *North American Review* 173, no. 538 (1901): 325 (italics mine).

75. Ibid., 326–327.

76. James D. Phelan, "Why the Chinese Should Be Excluded," *North American Review* 173, no. 540 (1901): 670–671 (italics mine).

77. Ibid., 674 (italics mine).

78. Ibid., 667–668.

79. See Bruce Sinclair, *Technology and the African American Experience*, and Carroll Pursell's collection of primary sources on Black contributions to technological development. Carroll W Pursell, *A Hammer in Their Hands: A Documentary History of Technology and the African American Experience* (Cambridge, MA: MIT Press, 2005); Bruce Sinclair, *Technology and the African American Experience: Needs and Opportunities for Study* (Cambridge, MA: MIT Press, 2004). On a general volume on race and science, see Evelynn Hammonds and Rebecca Herzig, eds., *The Nature of Difference: Sciences of Race in the United States from Jefferson to Genomics* (Cambridge, MA: MIT Press, 2009).

80. Quoted in Kakoudaki, *Anatomy of a Robot*, 157.

81. Alice Walker, "Foreword," in Zora Neale Hurston, *Barracoon: The Story of the "Last" Black Cargo* (New York: HarperCollins, 2018), xi.

82. Scott Reynolds Nelson, *Steel Drivin' Man: John Henry, the Untold Story of an American Legend* (London: Oxford University Press, 2006), 77.

83. To make this claim, McKittrick is building off the work of Alexander G. Weheliye and Sylvia Wynter. Katherine McKittrick, *Dear Science and Other Stories* (Durham, NC: Duke University Press, 2020), 152.

84. Roger Luckhust, *Zombies: A Cultural History* (London: Reaktion Books, 2015).

85. The Progressive Era often is seen as beginning with the "closing" of the western frontier in 1890. This historic moment is imagined as fulfilled through U.S. total conquest of Indigenous tribal lands after the Indian Wars. Native Americans continue to be pushed off their lands to become modern farmers and domesticated through imposed white settler colonial ways of living and education.

86. Pennsylvania State Educational Association, *The Pennsylvania School Journal*, vol. 55–56, ed. Thomas Henry Burrowes, James Pyle Wickersham, Elnathan Elisha Higbee, David Jewett Waller, and Nathan Christ Schaeffer (Lancaster, PA: New Era Printing, 1907), 403.

87. Ibid.

88. Immigration critics like James Phelan failed to concede to the reality that immigrant European women had been brought into the manufacturing industry in large

numbers, such that by the 1920s, the former Chinese dominance in the garment industry fell as poorer white women machine operators in sweatshops entered the niche economy of cloth-making businesses once dominated by Chinatown. See Dean Lan, "The Chinatown Sweatshops: Oppression and an Alternative," *Amerasia Journal* 1, no. 3 (1971).

89. Fears of the Chinese in manufacturing were largely unfounded. Sociologist Edna Bonacich observes the following: "In 1870, Asian workers were not evenly distributed in the California economy. They were confined mainly to service work, mining, and a narrow range of manufacturing. They were largely excluded from the bulk of manufacturing activities—that sphere of the economy that was most developed or developing and in which wages were likely to be highest and by 1910, these mostly Chinese and Japanese workers remained locked in service and agriculture rather than manufacturing." Edna Bonacich, "U.S. Capitalist Development: A Background to Asian Immigration," in *Labor Migration under Capitalism: Asian Workers in the United States before World War II* (Berkeley: University of California Press, 2008), 68–69.

90. Faith Baldwin, *American Family* (New York: Farrar & Rinehart, 1935).

91. Democratic National Committee, *The Political Reformation: Democratic Campaign Handbook* (New York: Democratic National Committee, 1884), 237.

92. Franklin Hichborn, *Story of the Session of the California Legislature of 1909* (San Francisco: Press of the James H. Barry Company, 1911), 149.

93. Chester Rowell, "Hire Baboons, Is Advised," *The Garment Worker: Official Organ of the United Garment Workers of America* 17, no. 16 (1918): 6.

94. T. C. M., "Parisian Medical Chit-Chat," *Cincinnati Lancet-Clinic: A Weekly Journal Journal of Medicine and Surgery* 89 (Cincinnati: J. C. Culbertson, 1903), 314–318.

95. Ian Haney Lopez, *White by Law: The Legal Construction of Race* (New York: New York University Press, 2006), 44

96. Chester Rowell, "Chinese and Japanese Immigrants—a Comparison," *Annals of the American Academy of Political and Social Science* 34, no. 2 (1909): 3–4 (italics mine).

97. Ibid., 4 (italics mine). As Rowell sees it, "the Chinaman spends his money with his own merchants, for Chinese goods, or sends it back to China directly" (4). This articulation of the Chinese proletariat worker as a noncontributing consumer suggests a historical move from considerations of labor's relationship to capitalist production from pure labor to the consumptive patterns.

98. Ibid., 10.

99. Rhacel Salazar Parreñas, "'White Trash' Meets the 'Little Brown Monkeys': The Taxi Dance Hall as a Site of Interracial and Gender Alliances between White Working-Class Women and Filipino Immigrant Men in the 1920s and 30s," *Amerasia Journal* 24, no. 2 (1998): 119.

100. Edward Rosenberg, "Filipinos as Workmen," *Car Worker* 1 (1903): 3–4.

101. Anti-Asian statements utilized anthropological theories about inherent biological and cultural differences among races to make arguments for exclusion. Just as sheep and horses cannot occupy the same pastures due to being different species, Asian and white labor cannot freely mix, argued A. E. Yoell, secretary-treasurer of the Asian Exclusion League, who made this remark: "The difference between the Caucasian and Mongolian or the Malayan races amounts to a difference of species, and that nature herself puts a ban upon the assimilation of different species throughout the whole animal kingdom of the world. . . . The same may be said of our widely, different social and industrial systems." See Asian Exclusion League proceedings in San Francisco, April 1908, 21.

102. Samuel Gompers, *Labor and the Common Welfare* (New York: E. P. Dutton, 1919), 135.

103. Ibid. The quote comes from a memorandum from Congress about the committee of an anti-Chinese convention held at Sacramento in 1886.

104. Ibid., 10.

105. Ibid., 85.

106. Ibid., 486.

107. Samuel Gompers and Herman Gutstadt, *Meat vs. Rice: American Manhood against Asiatic Coolieism, which Shall Survive?* (San Francisco: Asiatic Exclusion League 1902).

108. Colleen Valerie Jin Fong, "Tracing the Origins of a 'Model Minority': A Study of the Depictions of Chinese Americans in Popular Magazines" (PhD diss., University of Oregon, 1990), 177, 190.

109. Bonacich, "U.S. Capitalist Development," 123.

110. Ernestine Winchell, "An Episode of the Float Lands," *Overland Monthly and Out West Magazine* 14, no. 2 (August 1907): 146–147.

111. Henry Ford, *Today and Tomorrow* (New York: Doubleday, Page, 1988), 5–6.

112. He admits that only the Chinese and Hindu possess theology and philosophy as they reflect upon big problems of life "of a depth unreached by the Europeans," but only Europeans are modern and rational. Edward A. Ross, "The Causes of Racial Superiority," in *The Making of America*, ed. Robert Marion la Fullete (Chicago: John D. Morris, 1903), 69.

113. Ibid., 76.

114. Ibid., 83 (italics mine).

115. Ibid., 87–88.

116. Ibid., 89.

117. Indians are part of the same Aryan race, said early philologists and anthropologists. The few scant references to Indians as automatons would speak of their manual dexterity in textile (replaceable by real machines), but the machine metaphor was always directed toward criticizing the political machine of British colonial administration. Indians would appear as technological beings when plugged into the British-American capitalist machine as migrant engineers after World War II to little benefit to the economic state and development of newly independent India.

118. *Appendix to the Journals of the House of Representatives of New Zealand* 2 (Wellington, 1878), 5.

119. Curtis Marez, *Farm Worker Futurism: Speculative Technologies of Resistance* (Minneapolis: University of Minnesota Press, 2016), 40.

120. One responder to *The Literary Digest* furnished the essay, "The Chinese Coolie Thinks Our Manners Villainous." Marking the European as the true barbarian, the author makes the case for respecting China's erudition in work, one not defined by caste or cheap "coolie" labor but good human nature. This article was responding positively to an opinion piece in the Tokyo-based *Far Eastern Economic Review* entitled "What the Chinese Coolie Thinks of the European." See "The Chinese Coolie Thinks Our Manners Villainous," *Literary Digest* 64 (January 31, 1920), 61–62.

121. Ta Chen, "The Labor Situation in China," *Monthly Labor Review* 11 (1921), 211, 207–213.

122. Ah Eng Lai, *Peasants, Proletarians and Prostitutes: a Preliminary Investigation into the Work of Chinese Women in Colonial Malaya* (Singapore: Institute of Southeast Asian, 1986), 22.

123. Edward B. Pollard, *Women in All Ages and in All Countries: Oriental Women* (Philadelphia: Rittenhouse, 1907), 177.

124. Yun, *Coolie Speaks*, 231.

125. Eric Hayot, "Chinese Bodies, Chinese Futures," *Representations* 99 (2007): 102.
126. Ibid.
127. Ibid.
128. Ibid.
129. Lye, *America's Asia*, 57.
130. Ibid., 7.
131. Ibid., 11.
132. Ibid., 56.
133. He is closer perhaps to the lowest of what philosopher Hanna Arendt calls the three levels of *vita active*: working man or *animal laborans* (laboring animal), exerting himself out of natural or biological necessity; *homo faber* (working man), who breeds an artificial world through economic activity; or *zoon politikon*, the highest level of man to direct his actions toward freedom and political will. See Hanna Arendt, *The Human Condition* (Chicago: University of Chicago Press, 1998), 132.

CHAPTER 2

1. Roland Barthes, *Empire of Signs* (New York: Hill and Wang, 1982).
2. *Oxford Dictionary*, s.v. "assemblage," ed. Angus Stevenson (New York: Oxford University Press, 1998), 95.
3. Patrick Porter, *Military Orientalism: Eastern War through Western Eyes* (New York: Columbia University Press, 2009).
4. Geraldine Heng, *The Invention of Race in the European Middle Ages* (Cambridge: Cambridge University Press, 2018), 296.
5. Carl Von Clausewitz, *On War* (Princeton, NJ: Princeton University Press, 1984), 133.
6. John Mill, *The Ottomans in Europe: Or Turkey in the Present Crisis, With the Secret Societies Maps* (London: Weldon, 1876), 243–244.
7. Davide Rodogno, "European Legal Doctrines on Intervention and the Status of the Ottoman Empire within the 'Family of Nations' throughout the Nineteenth Century," *Journal of the History of International Law / Revue D'histoire du Droit International* 18, no. 1 (2016): 5–41.
8. Richardson L. Wright and Basset Digby, "Port Arthur Today," *The Bellman* 15, no. 370 (August 16, 1913): 204.
9. Levi Clyde Rusmisel, *Industrial-Commercial Geography of the United States* (New York: A. N. Palmer, 1914), 75.
10. French historian and fiction writer Georges Blond wrote this observation about the Chinese in a naturalist textbook: "It is not easy for us Westerners to guess the right age of a Chinese," since the "worn-out" coolie was also "ageless." Georges Blond, *Great Migrations* (New York: Hutchinson, 1958), 224.
11. Bulletin Du, *Comite De L'Asie Francaise* 7 (1907), 115.
12. Ibid.
13. Ibid.
14. The Meiji Restoration absorbed the Ryukyu Kingdom into a feudal tributary, attempting to erase the ethnic identity of the Okinawa people and assimilate them into a Japanese monoculture.
15. David G. Wittner, *Technology and the Culture of Progress in Meiji Japan* (London: Routledge, 2007), 13.
16. Joel Mokyr, "The Second Industrial Revolution, 1870–1914," in *Storia dell'economia Mondiale*, ed. Valerio Castronono (Rome: Laterza, 1998), 219–245.

17. Amy Sueyoshi, *Discriminating Sex: White Leisure and the Making of the American "Oriental"* (Urbana-Champaign: University of Illinois Press, 2018).

18. Joshua La Bare, "'The Future': Wrapped . . . in That Mysterious Japanese Way," *Science Fiction Studies* 27, no. 5 (2000): 22.

19. Porter, *Military Orientalism*, 104, 35.

20. Merritt Roe Smith, "Technological Determinism in American Culture," in *Does Technology Drive History? The Dilemma of Technological Determinism*, ed. Merritt Roe Smith and Leo Marx (Cambridge, MA: MIT Press, 1994), 23.

21. Aaron Moore, *Constructing East Asia: Technology, Ideology, and Empire in Japan's Wartime Era, 1931–1945* (Stanford, CA: Stanford University Press, 2013), 25.

22. Jennifer Robertson, *Robo Sapiens Japanicus: Robots, Gender, Family, and the Japanese Nation* (Berkeley: University of California Press, 2017), 16.

23. Jennifer Robertson, "Japan's First Cyborg? Miss Nippon, Eugenics and Wartime Technologies of Beauty, Body and Blood," *Body and Society* 7, no. 1 (2001): 9, 27.

24. Ibid., 10–11.

25. Kenichiro Koizumi, "In Search of Wakon: The Cultural Dynamics of the Rise of Manufacturing Technology in Postwar Japan," *Technology and Culture* 431 (2002): 29–49.

26. John Dower, *War without Mercy* (New York: Pantheon, 2012), 149.

27. Walter Page Hines and Arthur Wilson Page, *The World's Work: A History of Our Times*, vol. 28 (Doubleday, Page, 1914), 101.

28. John Eperjesi, *The Imperialist Imaginary: Visions of Asia and the Pacific in American Culture* (Hanover, NH: Dartmouth University Press, 2005), 109.

29. Janis Mimura, *Planning for Empire: Reform Bureaucrats and the Japanese Wartime State* (Ithaca, NY: Cornell University Press, 2011).

30. Vladimir Lenin, *Imperialism: The Highest Stage of Capitalism* (Chippendale: Resistance Books, 1999).

31. Karl Marx and Friedrich Engels, *The Communist Manifesto* (Echo Library, 2009), 11.

32. W. E. Gladstone, "On Books and the Housing of Them," *The Bookmart* 8 (1890): 57.

33. John Barret, "The Plain Truth about Asiatic Labor," *North American Review* 163, no. 480 (1896): 624–625.

34. William C. Allen, "In the Far East," *Christian Intelligence and Mission Field*, October 11, 1922, 648.

35. Fredrick Palmer, "The Two-Sworded Warder of the Turbulent East," *China Monthly Review* 51 (1929), 222.

36. Comparing various groups in a social Darwinist scale, London admits his respect for the determination of the Japanese to doggedly pursue modernization in such a short amount of time in contradistinction to the slow-moving yet venerable Chinese or the lowly, backward Koreans, who London disliked. London writes that China would only progress when its masses numbering in the hundreds of millions found the willpower to cast off their chains and overthrow their smarter Japanese colonial masters.

37. Jack London, "Yellow Peril," in *Jack London Reports: War Correspondence, Sports Articles, and Miscellaneous Writings*, ed. King Hendricks and Irving Shepard (Garden City, NY: Doubleday, 1970), 17.

38. Jack London, "Beware the Monkey Cage," *Dispatch from Manchuria*, May 10, 1904.

39. Ibid., 18.

40. John Hobson, *Work and Wealth: A Human Valuation* (New York: Macmillan, 1914), 356.

41. Robert Williams, *The Buddha in the Machine: Art, Technology, and the Meeting of East and West* (Hartford, CT: Yale University Press, 2014).

42. London's projection of future scientific war was premised on Japan getting ahold of Western technology to invade the continental United States. This prediction dovetailed with pulp fiction novels and movies made around the same time, such as *The Japanese Invasion* (1909), *The Vanishing Fleets* (1908), and *Banzai!* (1908). See Kenneth Hough, "Demon Courage and Dread Engines: America's Reaction to the Russo-Japanese War and the Genesis of the Japanese Invasion Sublime," in *Techno-Orientalism: Imagining Asia in Speculative Fiction, History, and Media*, ed. David Roh, Betsy Huang, and Greta A. Niu (New Brunswick, NJ: Rutgers University Press, 2015), 33.

43. Jack London, "If Japan Wakens China," in *Jack London Reports*, ed. King Hendricks and Irving Shepard (Garden City, NY: Doubleday), 358–361.

44. Ibid., 361.

45. For a critique of American technoculture, see Peña, *Body Electric*. For more on how African Americans dealt with the major technological changes in the first half of the twentieth century, see Joel Dinerstein, *Swinging the Machine: Modernity, Technology, and African American Culture between the World Wars* (Boston: University of Massachusetts Press, 2003).

46. Jack London, *The Iron Heel* (New York: Penguin, 2006), 140.

47. Ibid., 31–32.

48. Quoted in Donald H. Estes, "Before the War: The Japanese in San Diego," *Journal of San Diego History* 24, no. 4 (1978): 425–456.

49. Jack London, "The Unparalleled Invasion: A Story," *McClure's Magazine*, July 1910, 308–316.

50. William Henry Welch, *Papers and Addresses*, vol. 3 (Baltimore: Johns Hopkins Press, 1920), 186–187.

51. Victor Murdock, *China: The Mysterious and Marvellous* (New York: Fleming H. Revell, 1920), 195.

52. Ibid., 309.

53. Ibid.

54. Ibid., 310.

55. Ibid.

56. Other works about a futuristic Yellow Peril include Philip Francis Nowlan's 1928 novella *Armageddon 2419 A.D.* about a futuristic America occupied by cruel Chinese invaders or Sax Rohmer's *Fu Manchu* novels and Hollywood films based on these books about a Chinese mad scientist bent on jeopardizing the world.

57. Hough, "Demon Courage," 38–39.

58. Lawrence I. Berkove, "A Parallel Correction in London's 'The Unparalleled Invasion,'" in *Jack London: A Study of the Short Fiction*, ed. Jeanne Campbell (New York: Twayne, 1999), 237–243.

59. Percival Lowell, *Chosön; the Land of the Morning Calm: A Sketch of Korea* (Boston: Ticknor and Fields, 1886), 391.

60. Ibid., 117.

61. Jack London, Dale L. Walker, and Jeanne Campbell Reesman, *No Mentor but Myself: Jack London on Writers and Writing* (Stanford, CA: Stanford University Press, 1999), 68.

62. Daniel A. Metraux, "Jack London Reporting from Tokyo and Manchuria: The Forgotten Role of an Influential Observer of Early Modern Asia," *Asia Pacific: Perspectives* 8 (2008): 4.

63. Imperial Valley Press, "An American Plane for Japan's War Machine," *Imperial Valley Press*, May 16, 1938, 3.

64. *San Francisco Chronicle*, "Sound Warning against Influx of Coolies," *San Francisco Chronicle*, July 3, 1905, 7.

65. "The March of Events: An Editorial Interpretation," *The World's Work*, vol. 47, ed. Walter Hines Page and Arthur Wilson Page (New York: Doubleday, Page, 1924), 356 (italics mine).

66. The authors conducted tests on Japanese American students at a Hawaii school and charted the lower mental dispositions of Chinese, Hawaiians, and Filipinos. See Stanley Porteus and Marjorie Elizabeth Babcock, *Temperament and Race*, ed. R. G. Badger (Boston: Gorham, 1926), 347.

67. Ibid., 129, 333.

68. Ibid.

69. Helen Kaibara, "The Transpacific Origins of the 'Model Minority' Myth of Japanese Americans," *Studies on Asia* 4, no. 2 (2014): 17.

70. U.S. health agencies, working alongside the War Department, set out to monitor Japanese farmers. Though pesticides were already in wide use, the Japanese were blamed for a rash of food-related poisonings. Jeannie Shinozuka, "Deadly Perils: Japanese Beetles and the Pestilential Immigrant, 1920s–1930s," *American Quarterly* 65, no. 4 (2013): 842.

71. Dower, *War without Mercy*, 110.

72. Tatsurō Matsumae, *The Limits of Defense: Japan as an Unsinkable Aircraft Carrier* (Tokyo: Tokai University Press, 1988).

73. A. J. Barker and Sydney L. Mayer, *The Japanese War Machine* (New York: Chartwell Books, 1976), 6.

74. Ibid., 201.

75. Koshy, *Sexual Naturalization*, 36.

76. Denise Ferreira da Silva, *Global Idea of Race* (Minneapolis: University of Minnesota Press), 117.

77. Gerald Horne, *Race War: White Supremacy and the Japanese Attack on the British Empire* (New York: New York University Press, 2004), 139.

78. Dower, *War without Mercy*, 86.

79. Ibid., 30.

80. Paul Virilio, *War and Cinema: The Logistics of Perception* (New York: Verso, 1989).

81. Carl Boggs, *The Hollywood War Machine: US Militarism and Popular Culture* (New York, NY: Routledge, 2017).

82. The original intent of the film was to mentally gear up U.S. soldiers for war before deployment, but it was never utilized due to the war's quick end. It was also delayed from public viewing due to conflicting directions from the makers of the film and the government, which requested the film. The film underwent a series of final revisions because the Pentagon deemed the film as having "too much sympathy for the Jap people." The film was publicly released in 1945, in the same year the war ended.

83. Emile Durkheim, *The Division of Labor in Society* (New York: Simon and Schuster, 2014).

84. Ibid.

85. Dower, *War without Mercy*, 22.

86. Frank Capra, *Know Your Enemy: Japan* (Washington, DC: U.S. War Department, 1945).

87. Dorinne Kondo, "If You Want to Know Who They Are . . ." *New York Times*, September 16, 1984, 13.

88. Carlos Peña Romulo, *I Saw the Fall of the Philippines* (New York: Doubleday, Doran, 1942), 198.

89. Frederic E. Wakeman, *Spymaster Dai Li and the Chinese Secret Service* (Berkeley: University of California Press, 2003), 295.

90. Gas Power Publishing Company, "The Gas Engine in the Rise Fields," *Gas Power* 7, no. 4 (1909): 6. This article addresses rice and how it is the chief diet of the Japanese soldier, whose strength is admired, but provides a full meal for those "coolies" of not only China but India.

91. Young Park, *The Dark Side: Immigrants, Racism, and the American Way* (Bloomington, IN: iUniverse, 2012), 126.

92. Brian Masaru Hayashi, *Democratizing the Enemy: The Japanese American Internment* (Princeton, NJ: Princeton University Press, 2010), 142.

93. Quoted in Björn A. Schmidt, *Visualizing Orientalness: Chinese Immigration and Race in US Motion Pictures, 1910s–1930s* (Cologne: Böhlau Verlag Köln Weimar, 2017), 249.

94. Elena Tajima Creef, *Imaging Japanese America: The Visual Construction of Citizenship, Nation, and the Body* (New York: New York University Press, 2004).

95. Japanese American soldiers, along with hundreds of Puerto Ricans and African Americans, were subject to tests without their consent or knowledge of the experiments, experiencing pain and injury to advance "research" in the armed services. White soldiers were spared as the "control" group, according to declassified state papers in 1993 from the Office of the Army's Chief of the Chemical Warfare Service. See Caitlin Dickerson, "Secret World War II Chemical Experiments Tested Troops by Race," National Public Radio, June 22, 2015, https://www.npr.org.

96. Ibid.

97. Beginning in the 1930s, American hospitals and the U.S. Public Health Department began sterilizing hundreds of thousands of Puerto Rican women and African Americans, while the infamous Tuskegee experiment denied medicine to African American men infected with syphilis in a case of medical voyeurism and cruelty.

98. Moon-Ho, *Coolies and Cane*, 156.

99. Long T. Bui, "Model/Minority Veteran: The Queer Asian American Challenge to Post-9/11 Culture," in *Q&A 2.0: Voices from Queer Asian North America*, ed. Martin Manalansan, Alice Hom, and Kale Fajardo (Philadelphia: Temple University Press, 2021), 257–264.

100. Takashi Fujitani, *Race for Empire: Koreans as Japanese and Japanese as Americans during World War II* (Berkeley: University of California Press, 2011).

101. Edgar Laytha, "Nisei Soldiers in China-Burma-India Theater," 1944, CSU Japanese American Digitization Project, California State University, Dominguez Hills, Archives and Special Collections.

102. Joseph M. Kitagawa, "The Japanese Kokutai (National Community) History and Myth," *History of Religions* 13, no. 3 (1974): 209–226.

103. Brad Folsom, "The Seven Most Insane Japanese Weapons of World War Two," *History Banter*, accessed January 18, 2014, www.historybanter.com.

104. Harry L. Berby and James D. Brown, *Japanese Military Cartridge Handguns 1893–1945: A Revised and Expanded Edition of Hand Cannons of Imperial Japan* (Atglen, PA: Schiffer, 2003), 189–193.

105. Barker et al., *Japanese War Machine*, 201.

106. Ibid., 194. *Kamikaze* translated as "divine wind" draws from Japan's legendary victory over Mongol forces in the thirteenth century, when a typhoon hammered the

preparing Mongol fleet, a natural calamity seen as godly intervention, which Japanese for a long time took to mean a supernatural force was protecting Japan.

107. Dower, *War without Mercy*, 115.

108. Ibid., 99.

109. Ibid., 112.

110. Todd Munson, "Superman Says You Can Slap a Jap!," in *The Ages of Superman: Essays on the Man of Steel in Changing Times*, ed. Joseph J. Darowski (Jefferson, NC: McFarland, 2012), 5–15. Gordon H. Chang, "Superman Is about to Visit the Relocation Centers and the Limits of Wartime Liberalism," *Amerasia Journal* 19, no. 1 (1993): 37–59.

111. Time, "Art: The Tokio Kid," *Time*, June 15, 1942.

112. Time, "The Tokio Kid," *Time* 39, no. 24 (June 15, 1942), 38.

113. Elias Sanidas, "The Successful Imitation of the Japanese Lean Production System by American Firms: Impact on American Economic Growth" (Working Paper 01-02, Department of Economics, University of Wollongong, 2001).

114. U.S. founding father James Madison insisted that "the machinery of government" could be almost self-regulating without "enlightened statesmen" or virtuous citizens needed to run it, simply existing in and of itself, evolving through a series of identity crises resolved through new political motives and means. John D. Fairfield, *The Public and Its Possibilities: Triumphs and Tragedies in the American City* (Philadelphia: Temple University Press, 2010), 24.

115. Paul Koistinen, *Arsenal of World War II: The Political Economy of American Warfare, 1940–1945* (Lawrence: University Press of Kansas, 2004).

116. John Dower, *Cultures of War: Pearl Harbor/Hiroshima/9-11/Iraq* (New York: Norton, 2012).

117. Barker et al., *Japanese War Machine*, 253.

118. Robert Jay Lifton, *Death in Life: Survivors of Hiroshima* (Chapel Hill: University of North Carolina Press, 2012), 25.

119. David Serlin, *Replaceable You: Engineering the Body in Postwar America* (Chicago: University of Chicago Press, 2004), 16.

120. Naoko Shibusawa, *America's Geisha Ally* (Cambridge, MA: Harvard University Press, 2006), 111.

121. Michael Adas, *Dominance by Design: Technological Imperatives and America's Civilizing Mission* (Cambridge, MA: Belknap, 2006).

122. Jodi Kim, *Ends of Empire: Asian American Critique and the Cold War* (Minneapolis: University of Minnesota Press, 2010), 6.

123. Ian Buruma and Avishai Margalit, *Occidentalism: The West in the Eyes of Its Enemies* (New York: Penguin, 2004).

124. Frederick L. Schodt, *Inside the Robot Kingdom: Japan, Mechantronics, and the Coming Robotopia* (Tokyo: Kodansha International, 1998). For a longer history of the robot in Japanese culture, see Timothy N. Hornyak, *Loving the Machine* (Tokyo: Kodansha International, 2006).

125. Sharalyn Orbaugh, "Sex and the Single Cyborg: Japanese Popular Culture Experiments in Subjectivity," *Science Fiction Studies* 29 (2002): 436–452.

126. The first Japanese anime television series appeared during the 1960s (later adapted for U.S. audiences). The original story "The Angel of Vietnam" by Osamu Tezuka was part of the original series from 1967 to 1969, from the 2002 Dark Horse manga *Astro Boy*.

127. Schodt, *Inside the Robot Kingdom*, 75.

128. Stan Lee and Larry Lieber, *Tales of Suspense* 1, no. 39 (March 1963). Marvel Comics.

129. Japan had its own female take on Iron Man with Arare-chan, a popular anime character about a cute little girl android robot with superhuman strength, created by Japanese artist Akira Toriyama in 1980 as a female "foil" to Astroboy or Mighty Atom.

130. Gunhild Borggreen, "Robot Bodies: Visual Transfer of the Technological Uncanny," in *Transvisuality: The Cultural Dimension of Visuality*, ed. Tore Kristensen, Anders Michelsen, and Frauke Wiegand (Liverpool: Liverpool University Press, 2015), 175–188.

131. Kelts, *Japanamerica*, 209–210.

132. Wendy Chun, *Control and Freedom: Power and Paranoia in the Age of Fiber Optics* (Cambridge, MA: MIT Press, 2008), 226.

133. Robert G. Lee, "The Cold War Construction of the Model Minority Myth," in *Contemporary Asian America: A Multidisciplinary Reader*, ed. Min Zhou and J. V. Gatewood (New York: New York University Press, 2007), 478.

134. Barker et al., *Japanese War Machine*, 6.

135. Max Holland, *When the Machine Stopped: A Cautionary Tale from Industrial America* (Boston: Harvard Business School Press, 1989), 116.

136. Eni F. H. Faleomavaega, "Asian Pacific American Heritage Month 1992: Entering into the Pacific Century," in *Gale Encyclopedia of Multicultural America: Primary Documents 2*, ed. Jeffrey Lehman (Farmington Hills, MI: Gale Group, 1999), 686.

137. Anne Allison, *Millennial Monsters: Japanese Toys and the Global Imagination* (Berkeley: University of California Press, 2006), 102.

138. Henry Scott Stokes, "Japan's Love Affair with the Robot," *New York Times*, January 10, 1982, 24.

139. *Far Eastern Economic Review*, "Review 200: Asia's Leading Companies," *Far Eastern Economic Review* 15 (January 19, 1995): 38.

140. Jane Chi Hyun Park, *Yellow Future: Oriental Style in Hollywood Cinema* (Minneapolis: University of Minnesota Press, 2010), 8.

141. William Peterson, "Success Story, Japanese-American Style," *New York Times Magazine* 9 (January 9, 1966): 9.

142. Robert Rigg, "The Red Enemy," *Army* 10, no. 11 (June 1960): 73.

143. Senate Committee on Foreign Relations, *Mutual Security Act of 1959, Volumes 1–4* (Washington, DC: U.S. Congress, 1958), 335.

144. Hollington Tong, *Free China's Role in the Asian Crisis* (Washington, DC: Ransdell, 1958), 53.

145. Chiang Kai-Shek, *Selected Speeches and Messages* (Taipei: Government Information Office, 1956), 13.

146. Walter Robertson, "Disarmament and the Chinese Communist Threat," *Department of State Bulletin* 441, no. 1029 (March 16, 1959): 376.

147. *U.S. News and World Report*, "From the Front in the Himalayas," *U.S. News and World Report*, November 26, 1962, 73.

CHAPTER 3

1. James Bamber, *Sex, Lies and Bar Girls: The ABC's of Bar Fines and Short Times* (Bangkok: Bangkok Books, 2017), 9.

2. I recognize that the term *woman of color* is a Western invention of the 1970s to refer to political feminist solidarities, but I find it a useful way of talking about women with different ethnic backgrounds and different phenotypes in the so-called Third World / Global South who are often lumped with nonwhite women in the West.

3. Angela Carter, *Nothing Sacred: Selected Writings* (London: Virago, 1982).

4. Laura Hyun Yi Kang, "Si(gh)ting Asian/American Women as Transnational Labor," *Positions: East Asia Cultures Critique* 5, no. 2 (1997): 403.

5. Pamela McCorduck and Nancy Ramsey, *The Futures of Women: Scenarios for the 21st Century* (New York: Warner Books, 1996).

6. Minsoo Kang, "Building the Sex Machine: The Subversive Potential of the Female Robot," *Intertexts* 9, no. 1 (2005): 17.

7. Ibid.

8. Christian Bailly, *Automata: The Golden Age: 1848–1914* (London: Robert Hale, 2003), 20.

9. Cheng, *Ornamentalism*, 131.

10. Ibid.

11. SooJin Pate, *From Orphan to Adoptee: U.S. Empire and Genealogies of Korean Adoption* (Minneapolis: University of Minnesota Press, 2014).

12. Nicholas Krisof, "Tokyo Journal: Japan's Feminine Falsetto Falls Right out of Favor," *New York Times*, December 13, 1995. Quoted in Laura Miller, "Elevator Girls Moving In and Out of the Box," in *Modern Girls on the Go: Gender, Mobility, and Labor in Japan*, ed. Alisa Freedman, Laura Miller, and Christine Yano (Stanford, CA: Stanford University Press, 2013), 51.

13. Miller, "Elevator Girls," 52.

14. Mark Rosheim, *Leonardo's Lost Robots* (Berlin: Springer Science & Business Media, 2006), 36.

15. Sandra Buckley, *Broken Silence: Voices of Japanese Feminism* (Berkeley: University of California Press, 1997), 148.

16. Ibid.

17. Lucy Herndon Crockett, *Popcorn on the Ginza: An Informal Portrait of Postwar Japan* (New York: W. Sloane, 1949), 213.

18. Julietta Hua, *Trafficking Women's Human Rights* (Minneapolis: University of Minnesota Press, 2011).

19. Aljosa Puzar, "Asian Dolls and the Westernized Gaze: Notes on the Female Dollification in South Korea," *Asian Women* 27, no. 2 (2011): 81–111.

20. Said, *Orientalism*, 186.

21. Ibid., 187.

22. Lisa Lowe, *Critical Terrains: British and French Orientalisms* (Ithaca, NY: Cornell University Press, 1991), 78.

23. Constance Frederica Gordon Cummings, *Wanderings in China* (London: William Blackwood and Sons, 1888), 176.

24. Jane Addams, *Addams's Essays and Speeches on Peace* (London: Bloomsbury, 2003), 303.

25. Fiona Paisley, *Glamour in the Pacific: Cultural Internationalism and Race Politics in the Women's Pan-Pacific* (Honolulu: University of Hawaii Press, 2009), 46.

26. Fiona Ngô, "A Chameleon's Fate: Transnational Mixed-Race Vietnamese Identities," *Amerasia Journal* 31, no. 2 (2005): 51–62.

27. Dubravka Žarkov, *The Body of War: Media, Ethnicity, and Gender in the Breakup of Yugoslavia* (Durham, NC: Duke University Press Books, 2007), 120–121.

28. Susie Woo, *Framed by War: Korean Children and Women at the Crossroads of U.S. Empire* (New York: New York University Press, 2019).

29. Carol Fisher Sorgenfrei, "Unsexed and Disembodied: Female Avengers in Japan and England," in *Revenge Drama in European Renaissance and Japanese Theatre: From Hamlet to Madame Butterfly*, ed. K. Wetmore (New York: Springer, 2008), 54.

30. For more about how and why Southeast Asian women were brought to Japan to work as prostitutes, see Cynthia Nograles-Lumbera, "Ground Down by the Japanese Sex Machine," *Solidaridad* 11, no. 43 (1987).

31. Dai Sil Kim-Gibson, "Do You Hear Their Voices?," *Amerasia Journal* 35, no. 1 (2009): 46.

32. Ibid.

33. Interview with Peace Market woman worker. Chun Soonok, *They Are Not Machines: Korean Women Workers and Their Fight for Democratic Trade Unionism in the 1970s* (London: Routledge, 2017).

34. Neda Atanasoski, *Humanitarian Violence: The U.S. Deployment of Diversity* (Minneapolis: Minnesota University Press, 2013), 119.

35. Ibid., 69.

36. Herbert Marcuse, *One-Dimensional Man: Studies in the Ideology of Advanced Industrial Society* (London: Routledge, 2013), 30.

37. Aida Santos, "Gathering the Dust: The Base Issue in the Philippines," *Let the Good Times Roll*, ed. Saundra Sturdevant and Brenda Stolzfus (New York: New Press, 1992).

38. Arlene E. Bergman, *Women of Vietnam* (San Francisco: People's Press, 1975).

39. Thomas Patrick Doherty, *Projections of War: Hollywood, American Culture, and World War II* (New York: Columbia University Press, 1999), 149.

40. Koshy, *Sexual Naturalization*, 39.

41. Reprinted in Shirley Biagi and Marilyn Kern-Foxworth, *Facing Difference: Race, Gender and Mass Media* (Thousand Oaks, CA: Pine Forge, 1997), 33.

42. Jessica Hagedorn, "Sex Workers' Manifesto," in *Encyclopedia of Prostitution and Sex Work*, vol. 2, ed. Melissa Hope Ditmore (Westport, CT: Greenwood, 2006), 631.

43. Laura Mulvey, "Visual Pleasure and Narrative Cinema," in *Feminisms: An Anthology of Literary Theory and Criticism*, ed. Robyn Warhol and Diane Price Herndl (News Brunswick, NJ: Rutgers University Press, 1975), 438–448.

44. Bishnupriya Ghosh, *Global Icons: Apertures to the Popular* (Durham, NC: Duke University Press, 2011), 98.

45. Grace M. Cho, "Diaspora of Camptown: The Forgotten War's Monstrous Family," *Women's Studies Quarterly* 34, no. 1/2 (2006): 309–331.

46. In the case of "me love you long time" or "me love you too much," the "love" is conditional and the qualifiers "long time" and "too much," financially remunerative, not everlasting or eternal feeling. Control is given to the customer, when he responds, "Not just this time," to the prostitute (though some sexual agency can also be read in the prostitute's power to recruit her clients despite the harsh circumstances compelling her to do so).

47. Koshy, *Sexual Naturalization*, 8.

48. Mimi Nguyen, "Queer Cyborgs and New Mutants: Race, Sexuality, and Prosthetic Sociality in Digital Space," in *American Studies: An Anthology*, ed. Janice Radway, Barry Shank, Kevin Gaines, and Penny Von Eschen (Malden, MA: Blackwell, 2009), 286.

49. From a critical performance studies perspective, stereotypes do not denote a total lack of agency because actors have found ways to assert their power otherwise, despite lack of screen time or belittling roles. Actress Soo even composed a rap song (in response to the rap group 2 Live Crew's use of the raunchy line for their song "Me So Horny"), asking where's her money from the use of her famous movie lines. In the song, she says, "Me love you long time / but wheres me bling / when all over America / dem play that track / and you see it flying off the rack." For the full interview, see Papillon's official website, http://panho.webs.com.

50. Amy Tang, *Repetition and Race: Asian American Literature after Multicultural-ism* (Oxford: Oxford University Press, 2016), 16.

51. "Sex machine" was also a descriptor used for Black men in the Caribbean or Africa by white female tourists. See Julia O'Connell Davidson and Jacqueline Sanchez Taylor, "Fantasy Islands: Exploring the Demand for Sex Tourism," in *Sun, Sex, and Gold: Tourism and Sex Work in the Caribbean*, ed. Kamala Kempadoo (New York: Rowman & Littlefield, 1999), 37–54.

52. Thomas Doherty, "Full Metal Genre: Stanley Kubrick's Vietnam Combat Movie," *Film Quarterly* 42, no. 2 (1988): 197.

53. Ibid.

54. Sylvia Chong, *The Oriental Obscene: Violence and Racial Fantasies in the Vietnam Era* (Durham, NC: Duke University Press, 2011).

55. M. Nguyen, "Queer Cyborgs," 285.

56. Gregory Jerome Hampton, *Imagining Slaves and Robots in Literature, Film, and Popular Culture: Reinventing Yesterday's Slave with Tomorrow's Robot* (Lanham, MD: Lexington Books, 2015), 33.

57. Lynn Ly, "(Im)possible Futures: Liberal Capitalism, Vietnamese Sniper Women, and Queer Asian Possibility," *Feminist Formations* 29, no. 1 (2017): 148.

58. Ibid., 144.

59. Gina Marie Weaver, *Ideologies of Forgetting: Rape in the Vietnam War* (New York: SUNY Press, 2012), 47.

60. Foucault, *History of Sexuality*, 141.

61. James R. Blaker, *United States Overseas Basing: An Anatomy of the Dilemma* (New York: Praeger, 1990), 22.

62. Manuel Castells, *The Rise of the Network Society: The Information Age; Economy, Society, and Culture*, vol. 1 (New York: John Wiley & Sons, 2011).

63. Seungsook Moon, "Rest and Recreation (R & R)," in *The International Encyclopedia of Human Sexuality*, ed. Patricia Whelehan and Anne Bolin (Malden, MA: John Wiley and Sons, 2015), 1059–1114. See also Durba Mitra, Sara Kang, and Genevieve Clutario, "It's Time to Reckon with the History of Asian Women in America," *Harper's Bazaar*, March 23, 2021, https://www.harpersbazaar.com/culture/features/a35913981/its-time-to-reckon-with-the-history-of-asian-women-in-america/.

64. Elena Tajima Creef, "Re/orientation: The Politics of Japanese American Representation" (PhD diss., University of California, Santa Cruz, 1994), 176.

65. Chung Hyun Kyung, "Your Comfort versus My Death," in *War's Dirty Secret: Rape, Prostitution, and Other Crimes against Women*, ed. Anne Llewellyn Barstow (Boston: Pilgrim, 2000), 22–23.

66. Ibid.

67. Ibid., 226–227.

68. Chung Hyun Kyung, *Struggle to Be the Sun Again: Introducing Asian Women's Theology* (Maryknoll, NY: Orbis Books, 1990).

69. H. L. T. Quan, *Growth against Democracy: Savage Developmentalism in the Modern World* (Washington, DC: Lexington Books, 2012).

70. Celine Parreñas Shimizu, *The Hypersexuality of Race: Performing Asian/American Women on Screen and Scene* (Durham, NC: Duke University Press Books, 2007), 186.

71. Saundra Pollock Sturdevant and Brenda Stoltzfus, *Let the Good Times Roll: Prostitution and the United States Military in Asia* (New York: New Press, 1993), 326.

72. Sturdevant and Stoltzfus, *Good Times Roll*, 40.

73. Sheridan Prasso and Joachim Paul Prassol, *The Asian Mystique: Dragon Ladies, Geisha Girls, and Our Fantasies of the Exotic Orient* (New York: Public Affairs, 2005), 318.

74. Robert Young, "Colonialism and the Desiring Machine," in *Postcolonial Discourses: An Anthology,* ed. Gregory Castle (Oxford: Blackwell, 2001), 73–98.

75. Katharine Moon, *Sex among Allies: Military Prostitution in US-Korea Relations* (New York: Columbia University Press, 1997).

76. Ibid., 34.

77. Paul N. Edwards, *The Closed World: Computers and the Politics of Discourse in Cold War America* (Boston: MIT Press, 1997); Stuart W. Leslie, *The Cold War and American Science: The Military-Industrial-Academic Complex at MIT and Stanford* (New York: Columbia University Press, 1993); David A. Hounshell, "Epilogue: Rethinking the Cold War; Rethinking Science and Technology in the Cold War, Rethinking the Social Study of Science and Technology," *Social Studies of Science* 31, no. 2 (2001): 289–297.

78. Atanasoski, *Humanitarian Violence,* 141.

79. Gordon Lee, "The Forgotten Revolution," *Hyphen Magazine* 1 (2003).

80. Shooting orders were given to machine gunners to "kill anything that moves," a practice that followed the chilling words of commanders like General Westmoreland: "The Oriental doesn't put the same high price on life as does the Westerner. . . . Life is plentiful, life is cheap in the Orient. . . . Life is not important." See Nick Turse, *Kill Anything that Moves: The Real American War in Vietnam* (New York: Macmillan, 2013), 50.

81. Kim McQuaid, *The Anxious Years: America in the Vietnam-Watergate Era* (London: Harper Collins, 1990), 77.

82. Martin Luther King, "Beyond Vietnam: A Time to Break Silence," speech at Riverside Church, New York, April 4, 1967, accessed March 31, 2019.

83. Hortense J. Spillers, "Interstices: A Small Drama of Words," in *Pleasure and Danger,* ed. Carol Vance (Boston: Routledge and Kegan Paul, 1984), 76.

84. Claude Green, *What We Dragged Out of Slavery* (Conshohocken, PA: Infinity, 2006), 40. For more on the imperial paternalistic attitudes of this discourse, see Vibhuti Ramachandran, "Saving the Slaving Child: Domestic Work, Labor Trafficking, and the Politics of Rescue in India," *Humanity: An International Journal of Human Rights, Humanitarianism, and Development* 10, no. 3 (2019): 339–362.

85. David Harvey, "The Body as an Accumulation Strategy," *Environment and Planning D* 16 (1998): 401–422.

86. Thu-Huong Nguyen-Vo, *The Ironies of Freedom: Sex, Culture, and Neoliberal Governance in Vietnam* (Seattle: University of Washington Press, 2008).

87. Lisa Marie Cacho, *Social Death: Racialized Rightlessness and the Criminalization of the Unprotected* (New York: New York University Press, 2012), 75.

88. L. H. M. Ling, "Sex Machine: Global Hypermasculinity and Images of the Asian Woman in Modernity," *Positions* 7, no. 2 (1999): 282.

89. Suzanne K. Damarin, "Women and Information Technology: Framing Some Issues for Education," *Feminist Teacher* 6, no. 2 (1992): 17–18.

90. Gertrude Whiting, *Old-Time Tools and Toys of Needlwork* (New York: Columbia University Press, 1971).

91. Rosalinda Pineda-Ofreneo, "Issues in the Philippine Electronics Industry: A Global Perspective," *Economic and Industrial Democracy* 6, no. 2 (1985): 190.

92. David Pellow and Lisa Park, *The Silicon Valley of Dreams: Environmental Injustice, Immigrant Workers, and the High-Tech Global Economy* (New York: New York University Press, 2002), 175.

93. Ibid., 176.

94. Ibid., 196.

95. Diane Elson and Ruth Pearson, "'Nimble Fingers Make Cheap Workers': An Analysis of Women's Employment in Third World Export Manufacturing," *Feminist Review* 7, no. 1 (1981): 90.

96. Aihwa Ong, "The Gender and Labor Politics of Postmodernity," *Annual Review of Anthropology* 20 (1991): 289.

97. Dina M. Siddiqi, "Miracle Worker or Womanmachine? Tracking (Trans) National Realities in Bangladeshi Factories," *Economic and Political Weekly* 35, no. 21/22 (2000): 11, 14.

98. Atanasoski. *Humanitarian Violence,* 6–7.

99. Neferti X. Tadiar, "Life-Times of Becoming Human," *Occasion: Interdisciplinary Studies in the Humanities* 3 (2012): 3.

100. Neferti Xina M. Tadiar, *Fantasy Production: Sexual Economies and Other Philippine Consequences for the New World Order* (Hong Kong: Hong Kong University Press, 2004), 59.

101. Inderpal Grewal and Caren Kaplan, eds., *Scattered Hegemonies: Postmodernity and Transnational Feminist Practices* (Minneapolis: University of Minnesota Press, 1994).

102. Long T. Bui, "Glorientalization: Specters of Asia and Feminized Cyborg Workers in the United States–Mexico Borderlands," *Meridians: Feminism, Race, Transnationalism* 13, no. 1 (2015): 129–156.

103. Joo Ok Kim, "'Training Guatemalan Campesinos to Work like Korean Peasants': Taxonomies and Temporalities of East Asian Labor Management in Latin America," *Verge: Studies in Global Asias* 3, no. 2 (2017): 195–216.

104. Jennifer Gonzalez, "Envisioning Cyborg Bodies: Notes from Current Research," in *The Cyborg Handbook*, ed. Chris Hables Gray, Heidi J. Figueroa-Sarriera, and Steven Mentor (New York: Routledge, 1995), 61.

105. M. Nguyen, "Queer Cyborgs," 301.

106. Ibid., 287.

107. Ibid., 284.

108. Haraway, "Cyborg Manifesto," 169.

109. Ibid., 174.

110. Ibid., 168, 177.

111. Diane Roose, "Cheaper than Machines," *New Internationalist*, April 2, 1980.

112. Maria Mies, *Patriarchy and Accumulation on a World Scale: Women in the International Division of Labour* (London: Zed Books, 2014), 117.

113. Ewbank says this is an ancient, gendered practice and daughters of chiefs are exempt. Connecting this ability to ancient myth, he compared to it examples in the mythic tales of Homer, the Old Testament, and the Egyptian gods Isis and Osiris, who are sometimes depicted with vases on their heads. This preternatural female talent forms a pillar in the hydraulic agriculture of India, a core element in inspiring the theory of the Asian mode of production. In this theory, the fertile Asian economy is based on waterworks and grinding slave work, a premodern model of precapitalist work. See Thomas Ewbank, *A Descriptive and Historical Account of Hydraulic and Other Machines for Raising Water, Ancient and Modern* (Cincinnati: Appleton, 1846).

114. Anjali Vats, *The Color of Creatorship: Intellectual Property, Race, and the Making of Americans* (Stanford, CA: Stanford University Press, 2020).

115. Maria Mies, *Patriarchy and Accumulation on a World Scale*, 117.

116. Aihwa Ong, *Spirits of Resistance and Capitalist Discipline: Factory Women in Malaysia* (New York: SUNY Press, 2010).

117. Hanan Hammad, *Industrial Sexuality: Gender, Urbanization, and Social Transformation in Egypt* (Austin: University of Texas Press, 2016), 44.

118. Yen Le Espiritu, *Asian American Women and Men: Labor, Laws, and Love* (Lanham, MD: Rowman & Littlefield, 2008).

119. Little Brown Fucking Machine website, accessed February 29, 2020, www.lbfm .net.

120. Alexandra Talty, "Bangkok Is the Most Visited City in the World," *Forbes*, September 25, 2018, https://www.forbes.com/sites/alexandratalty/2018/09/25/bangkok-is -named-most-visited-city-in-the-world-again/#2c21a7754071; Victoria Reyes, *Global Borderlands: Fantasy, Violence, and Empire in Subic Bay, Philippines* (Stanford, CA: Stanford University Press, 2019), 74.

121. Sexy Escort Ads website, accessed February 4, 2014, www.sexyescortads.com.

122. Mark McLellan, "Gay Men and the Media in Japan," in *Asian Masculinities: The Meaning and Practice of Manhood in China and Japan*, ed. Kam Louie and Morris Low (London: Routledge, 2005), 66; Travis Kong, "More than a Sex Machine: Accomplishing Masculinity among Chinese Male Sex Workers in the Hong Kong Sex Industry," *Deviant Behavior* 30, no. 8 (2009): 715–745.

123. Christina R. Yano, "Flying Geisha: Japanese Stewardesses with Pan American World Airways," in *Modern Girls on the Go: Gender, Mobility, Globalism, and Labor in Contemporary Japan*, ed. Alisa Freedman, Laura Miller, and Christine Yano (Stanford, CA: Stanford University Press).

124. Tim Andrews and Wilson Chew, *Building Brands in Asia: From the Inside Out* (London: Routledge, 2017).

125. Shana Ye, "Reconstructing the Transgendered Self as a Feminist Subject: Trans/ Feminist Praxis in Urban China," *Transgender Studies Quarterly* 3, no. 1–2 (2016): 264.

126. Robyn Magalit Rodriguez and Vernadette Vicuna Gonzalez, "Asian American Auto/Biographies: The Gendered Limits of Consumer Citizenship in Import Subcultures," in *Alien Encounters: Popular Culture in Asian America*, ed. Mimi Nguyen and Thuy Tu Linh (Durham, NC: Duke University Press, 2007), 266.

127. Ibid., 257.

128. Ibid.

129. Lynda Johnston and Robyn Longhurst, *Space, Place, and Sex: Geographies of Sexualities* (Lanham, MD: Rowman & Littlefield, 2010), 169.

130. Sage Lazaro, "Tila Tequila Truly Believes the Earth Is Flat and Won't Stop Yelling about It on Twitter," *Observer*, January 7, 2016, https://observer.com/2016/01/tila -tequila-truly-believes-the-earth-is-flat-and-wont-stop-yelling-about-it-on-twitter/.

131. Claudia Springer, "Muscular Circuitry: The Invincible Armored Cyborg in Cinema," *Genders* 18 (1993): 87–101.

132. Gowri Vijayakumar, "'There Was an Uproar': Reading the Arcane of Reproduction through Sex Work in India," *Viewpoint Magazine*, October 31, 2015, https://view pointmag.com/2015/10/31/there-was-an-uproar-reading-the-arcane-of-reproduction -through-sex-work-in-india/.

133. Yessica Garcia Hernandez, *Intoxicated by Jenni Rivera: The Erotics of Fandom, Sonic Pedagogies of Deviance, and the Politics of Pirujeria* (PhD diss., University of California, San Diego, 2019).

134. Shailendra Singh, *I Am Not a Sex Machine* (Bombay: Shailendra Singh Films, 2016), https://www.youtube.com/watch?v=7ShcYdjD6C0.

CHAPTER 4

1. Roh, Huang, and Niu, "Technologizing Orientalism," 10.

2. According to eye-witness accounts, Chin came to the Fancy Pants strip club in Detroit for his bachelor party, where he met his would-be assailants. During the legal court battle, the attackers could not fathom even *why* Chin came to a stripper joint in the first place, while accusing him of harassing a Black stripper. Chin's treatment evinced the asexual/hypersexual stereotype of the Asian male body. See Christine Choy and Renee Tajima-Pena, *Who Killed Vincent Chin?* (Film News Now Foundation and WTVS Detroit; New York: Filmakers Library, 1988).

3. Espiritu, *Asian American Panethnicity*.

4. Takeo Rivera, "Minority Models: Masochism, Masculinity, and the Machine in Asian American Cultural Politics" (PhD diss., University of California, Berkeley, 2017), 19.

5. Robert Lee, *Orientals*.

6. Amelia Precup, "All Cyborgs Are Asian: The Ethnic Implications of the Cyborg-topian Future in Karen Tei Yamashita's Anime Wong," *Transylvanian Review* 26 (2017).

7. Jean-François Lyotard, "The Postmodern Condition," in *Modernity: Critical Concepts IV; After Modernity*, ed. Malcolm Waters (London: Routledge: 1999), 161–177.

8. Stuart Hall, "Introduction: Who Needs 'Identity'?" in *Questions of Cultural Identity*, ed. Stuart Hall and Paul Du Gay (London: Sage, 1996) 1–17.

9. Rivera, "Minority Models," 118.

10. Palumbo-Liu, *Asian/America*, 114.

11. Said, *Orientalism*, 26.

12. Roh, Huang, and Niu, "Technologizing Orientalism," 2.

13. Lee and Wong, "Introduction," xxxii.

14. Robert Lee, *Orientals*, 3.

15. Cited in Ong, *Flexible Citizenship*, 80.

16. Such discussions fail to reckon with a postmodern global imaginary as fixed to formal paradigms of modernization and "stage" theories of development. See Mike Featherstone, *Global Culture: Nationalism, Globalization and Modernity* (London: Sage, 1990); Ong, *Flexible Citizenship*.

17. Morton Klass, "The Artificial Alien: Transformations of the Robot in Science Fiction," *Annals of the American Academy of Political and Social Science* 470 (1983): 171–179.

18. George Basalla and Steven J. Dick, "Civilized Life in the Universe: Scientists on Intelligent Extraterrestrials," *Physics Today* 60, no. 1 (2007): 57.

19. Prominent examples include Atwell Whitney, *Almond-Eyed: A Story of the Day* (San Francisco: A. L. Bancroft, 1878); Robert Woltor, *A Short and Truthful History of the Taking of California and Oregon by the Chinese in the Year A.D.* (San Francisco: A. L. Bancroft, 1882). For more on the connection between anti-Chinese sentiment and science fiction, see William F. Wu, *The Yellow Peril: Chinese Americans in American Fiction, 1850–1940* (Hamden, CT: Archon Books, 1982).

20. Wendy Chun, "Race and Software," in *Alien Encounters: Popular Culture in Asian America*, ed. Mimi Thi Nguyen and Thuy Linh Nguyen (Durham, NC: Duke University Press, 2007), 316.

21. Kevin Jenks, "Before the 'Yellow Peril,'" *Social Contract* 6, no. 4 (Summer 1996).

22. John Chen, *Astounding Wonder: Imagining Science and Science Fiction in Interwar America* (Philadelphia: University of Pennsylvania Press, 2012), 174–175.

23. *Merriam-Webster*, s.v. "alien," accessed February 26, 2021.

24. Sharlyn Orbaugh, "Frankenstein and the Cyborg Metropolis: The Evolution of Body and City in Science Fiction Narratives," in *Cinema Anime: Critical Engagements with Japanese Animation*, ed. Steven T. Brown (New York: Palgrave Macmillan, 2006), 81–112.

25. Juliana Chang, *Inhuman Citizenship: Traumatic Enjoyment and Asian American Literature* (Minneapolis: University of Minnesota Press, 2012), 183.

26. Martha Bartter, "Young Adults, Science Fiction, and War," *Young Adult Science Fiction*, ed. Charles William Sullivan (Westport, CT: Greenwood, 1999), 142.

27. Nakamura, *Cybertypes*, 45.

28. Yen Le Espiritu, *Body Counts: The Vietnam War and Militarized Refugees* (Berkeley: University of California Press, 2014), 6–7.

29. *Merriam-Webster*, s.v. "virtual," accessed February 26, 2021.

30. Giuseppe Mantovani, "Virtual Reality as a Communication Environment: Consensual Hallucination, Fiction, and Possible Selves," *Human Relations* 48, no. 6 (1995): 669–671.

31. Jeffrey Jerome Cohen and Gail Weiss, eds., *Thinking the Limits of the Body* (New York: SUNY Press, 2003), 4.

32. Judith Halberstam and Ira Livingston, "Introduction," in *Posthuman Bodies*, ed. Judith Halberstam and Ira Livingston (Bloomington: Indiana University Press, 1995), 1–22.

33. Karen Shimakawa, *National Abjection: The Asian American Body Onstage* (Durham, NC: Duke University Press, 2002), 8.

34. Koshy, *Sexual Naturalization*, 71.

35. Haraway, "Cyborg Manifesto," 133.

36. Jane Naomi Iwamura, *Virtual Orientalism: Asian Religions and American Popular Culture* (London: Oxford University Press, 2011).

37. One can think of the 1869 photograph depicting the completion of the first transcontinental railroad, where the Chinese were not invited though they helped build it.

38. Iwamura, *Virtual Orientalism*, 62.

39. Danielle Wong, "Inorganic Asian North American Lives: Virtual Dismemberments, Copies, and Wellbeing" (PhD diss., McMaster University, 2017).

40. Lee and Wong, "Introduction," xiv.

41. Stephen Hong Sohn, "Alien/Asian: Imaginingthe Racialized Future," *Melus* 33, no. 4 (2008): 8.

42. Manfred Clynes and Nathan Kline, "Cyborgs and Space," in *The Cyborg Handbook*, ed. Chris Hables Gray and Francoise Gray (New York: Routledge, 1995), 29–34.

43. Norbert Wiener, *Cybernetics or Control and Communication in the Animal and the Machine* (Cambridge, MA: MIT Press, 1961), 42.

44. Ibid., 169.

45. Peter Galison, "The Ontology of the Enemy: Norbert Wiener and the Cybernetic Vision," *Critical Inquiry* 21, no. 1 (1994): 232.

46. Aihwa Ong, "Techno-Migrants in the Network Economy," in *Global America?: The Cultural Consequences of Globalization*, ed. Ulrich Beck, Natan Sznaider, and Rainer Winter (Liverpool, UK: Liverpool University Press, 2003), 153–173.

47. Roli Varma, "High-Tech Coolies: Asian Immigrants in the U.S. Science and Engineering Workforce," *Science as Culture* 11, no. 3 (2002): 355.

48. Greta Aiyu Niu, "Techno-Orientalism, Nanotechnology, Posthumans, and Post-Posthumans in Neal Stephenson's and Linda Nagata's Science Fiction," *Melus* 33, no. 4 (2008): 73–96.

49. Morley, *Spaces of Identity*, 168.

50. Ibid., 170.

51. Timothy Brennan, "The Empire's New Clothes," *Critical Inquiry* 29, no. 2 (2003): 361.

52. Ibid., 169.

53. Ibid., 160, 168.

54. Andrea Chronister, *Japan-Bashing: How Propaganda Shapes Americans' Perception of the Japanese* (master's thesis, Lehigh University, 1992).

55. Morley, *Spaces of Identity*, 169.

56. Jeff Yang, "Asian Pop Robot Nation / Why Japan, and Not America, Is Likely to Be the World's First Cyborg Society," *SF Gate*, August 25, 2005, https://www.sfgate.com /entertainment/article/ASIAN-POP-Robot-Nation-Why-Japan-and-not-3237591.php.

57. Marshall McLuhan, "Television in a New Light," in *The Meaning of Commercial Television*, ed. Stanley Donner (Austin: University of Texas Press, 1966), 87–107.

58. Paul Du Gay, *Doing Cultural Studies: The Story of the Sony Walkman* (London: Sage, 2013), 25.

59. The Sony Walkman was so popular that the U.S. military asked the Japanese government to donate them to troops in the first Persian Gulf War as its war effort. See Rebecca Tuhus-Dubrow, *Personal Stereo* (New York: Bloomsbury, 2017), 87.

60. Ron Tanner, "Toy Robots in America, 1955–75: How Japan Really Won the War," *Journal of Popular Culture* 28, no. 3 (1994): 125.

61. Facts and Details, "Japanese Salaryman," Facts and Details, accessed March 31, 2019.

62. Wakako Hironaka, "Through Rosy Glasses: Darkly," *New York Times*, June 5, 1993; cited in Charles Kindleberger, *World Economic Primacy: 1500–1990* (Oxford: Oxford University Press on Demand 1996), 202.

63. John Burgess, "Japan's White-Collar Clones," *Washington Post*, August 23, 1987.

64. The idea of permanent Japanese employment and an unchanging work culture was not true based on existing labor data from Japan, since Japanese people did move around a lot in terms of work. But facts were in short supply compared to envy and repugnance based on technocultural fantasy. John Beck and Martha Nibley Beck, *The Change of a Lifetime: Employment Patterns among Japan's Managerial Elite* (Honolulu: University of Hawaii Press, 1994), 231.

65. Darius Mehri, *Notes from Toyota-Land: An American Engineer in Japan* (Ithaca, NY: Cornell University Press, 2018), 207.

66. Styx, *Kilroy Was Here* (A&M Records, 1983).

67. Ken McLeod, "Afro-Samurai: Techno-Orientalism and Contemporary Hip-Hop," *Popular Music* 32, no. 2 (2013): 261–262.

68. Jeff Yang, "Politicians Play the China Card," NPR, October 27, 2010.

69. Ibid.

70. Ibid.

71. Ibid.

72. Anneke Smelik, "Cinematic Fantasies of Becoming Cyborg," in *The Scientific Imaginary in Visual Culture*, ed. Anneke Smelik (Göttigen, Germany: V&R Unipress, 2010), 89–104.

73. Dave Schweisberg, "The Japanning of America Today," *JT*, October 17, 1982, 22.

74. Takayuki Tatsumi, *Full Metal Apache: Transactions between Cyberpunk Japan and Avant-Pop America* (Durham, NC: Duke University Press, 2006). The Fukushima nuclear meltdown in 2011 has made the Japanese wary of exploiting science and technology at all costs.

75. Hamish McDonald, "Japan Buys into Ford Steel," *Sydney Morning Herald*, July 23, 1982.

76. Ibid.

77. Kelts, *Japanamerica*, 180.

78. Mimi Nguyen, "Tales of an Asiatic Geek Girl: Slant from Paper to Pixels," in *Technicolor: Race, Technology and Everyday Life* (New York: New York University Press, 2001), 186–187.

79. Ibid.

80. James Hughes, *Citizen Cyborg: Why Democratic Societies Must Respond to the Redesigned Human of the Future* (New York: Basic Books, 2004).

81. Vasant Kaiwar and Sucheta Mazumdar, "Race, Orient, Nation in the Time-Space of Modernity," in *Antinomies of Modernity: Essays on Race, Orient, Nation*, ed. Vasant Kaiwar and Sucheta Mazumdar (Durham, NC: Duke University Press 2003), 283.

82. Toshiya Ueno, "Japanimation: Techno-Orientalism, Media Tribes, and Rave Culture," in *Aliens R Us: The Other in Science Fiction Cinema*, ed. Ziauddin Sardar and Sean Cubitt (Sterling, UK: Pluto, 2002), 97.

83. Chun, *Control and Freedom*, 192, 195.

84. Nakamura, *Digitizing Race*, 121.

85. Steve Lohr, "Maybe Japan Was Just a Warm-Up," *New York Times*, January 21, 2011.

86. The Y2K scare was an unfounded fear of computers worldwide shutting due to a clock counting glitch or a computer virus. The FBI found a programmer in the Philippines as the main culprit for one such virus. See Martin Manalansan, *Global Divas* (Durham, NC: Duke University Press, 2003), 183.

87. Lisa Nakamura, *Cybertypes: Race, Ethnicity, and Identity on the Internet* (New York: Routledge, 2013).

88. Irene Chien, "Programmed Moves: Race and Embodiment in Fighting and Dancing Videogames" (PhD diss., University of California, Berkeley, 2015).

89. "The Best of Both Worlds: Part 1," *Star Trek: The Next Generation* (CBS, 1990).

90. Sohn, "Alien/Asian," 14.

91. See the following online boards: "The Borg as Symbolism," www.startrek.com; "China as the Borg," http://dougreich.blogspot.com; "The Most Hyperbolic Story of the Year: Why Innovation Is Not the Borg," www.bradleymgardner.com; "Painting China as the Borg," http://ejperkins.blogspot.com.

92. Jutta Weldes, "Going Cultural: Star Trek, State Action, and Popular Culture," *Millennium: Journal of International Studies* 28, no. 1 (1999): 117–134.

93. Ethan Gutmann, "A Tale of the New China," *Weekly Standard*, May 24, 1999.

94. Carole Gerster, "Grappling with Media Images: Three Films by Asian-American Women," *Feminist Collections* 16, no. 4 (1994): 9.

95. Mina Yang, "East Meets West in the Concert Hall: Asians and Classical Music in the Century of Imperialism, Post-Colonialism, and Multiculturalism," *Asian Music* 38, no. 1 (2007): 1–30, 14.

96. Daina C. Chiu, "The Cultural Defense: Beyond Exclusion, Assimilation, and Guilty Liberalism," *California Legal Review* 82 (1994): 1093.

97. David Brand, "The New Whiz Kids: Why Asian Americans Are Doing So Well, and What It Costs Them," *Time* 130, no. 9 (1987): 42–51; Krishna Ramanujan, "Health Expert Explains Asian and Asian-American Students' Unique Pressures to Succeed," *Cornell Chronicle*, April 19, 2006.

98. Huang, "Posthuman Subject," 9.

99. Eungjun Min, "Demythologizing the 'Model Minority,'" in *The Emerging Monoculture: Assimilation and the "Model Minority,"* ed. William E. Watson and Sondra Cuban (Santa Barbara, CA: Greenwood, 2003), 195.

100. Minh-Ha T. Phạm, "Playing (with) Stereotypes: Comedy and the Construction of Asian American Identities" (PhD diss., University of California, Berkeley, 2006).

101. Thomas J. Kan, *The Price of Admission: Rethinking How Americans Pay for College* (Washington, DC: Brookings Institution, 2010), 3.

102. Long T. Bui, "A Better Life? Asian Americans and the Necropolitics of Higher Education," in *Critical Ethnic Studies: A Reader*, ed. Critical Ethnic Studies Collective (Durham, NC: Duke University Press, 2013).

103. Helen Zia, "Asian-Americans Battle Stereotypes," *USA TODAY*, August 15, 2003. As Zia observes, "Inaccurate perceptions even affect fields heavily populated by Asian-Americans, such as science and technology. In Silicon Valley, more than a third of the scientists and engineers with advanced degrees are Asian-American, yet the percentage in executive positions remains in the low single digits."

104. Norman Denzin, *Reading Race: Hollywood and the Cinema of Racial Violence* (London: Sage, 2001), 54.

105. Benjamin Nugent, "How Stereotypes of Jews and Asians Evolved into the Nerd," *Jewcy*, May 12, 2008, https://jewcy.com/jewish-arts-and-culture/how_stereotypes_jews _and_asians_evolved_nerd.

106. Christina Ho, "The New Meritocracy or Over-Schooled Robots? Public Attitudes on Asian-Australian Education Cultures," *Journal of Ethnic and Migration Studies* 43, no. 14 (2017): 2346–2362.

107. Jessica Yu, "When We Say Smart Asian Girl We Don't Mean Smart (White) Girl: The Figure of the Asian Automaton and the Adolescent Artist in the Künstlerroman Genre," *Journal of Asia-Pacific Pop Culture* 4, no. 2 (2019): 182.

108. Ibid.

109. Wesley Yang, "Paper Tigers," *New York Magazine*, May 8, 2011, .

110. Melissa Chen, "Why the Asian-American Lawsuit against Harvard Is Doomed to Fail," *Huffington Post*, July 15, 2015.

111. Ibid.; Lee and Wong, "Introduction," xiv.

112. Chen, "Asian-American Lawsuit."

113. Amy Chua, *Battle Hymn of the Tiger Mother* (London: Bloomsbury, 2011).

114. Grace Wang, *Soundtracks of Asian America: Navigating Race through Musical Performance* (Durham, NC: Duke University Press, 2014).

115. Shawn Ho, "A Critique of the Motivations behind Negative Action against Asian Americans in U.S. Universities: The Model Victims," *Columbia Journal of Race and Law* 91 (2015): 91.

116. Petitioner Chu v. State of Wisconsin, Respondent, 2002 WL 32134226 (U.S.), 19.

117. Frank Ng, *The Taiwanese Americans* (London: Greenwood, 1998), 43.

118. Vinay Menon, "Arthur Chu's Dangerous Game of *Jeopardy!*," *The Star*, February 21, 2014.

119. In the "Chinagate" or "Asian Donorgate" campaign finance scandal, Chinese Americans were racially profiled as donor contributions to electoral candidates. These donors were believed to originate from the People's Republic of China and vetted vigorously. Asian American donors were probed for possible illegal "foreign" money contributions to the campaigns of politicians (using their ethnic-sounding surnames to identify and question them about their citizenship status).

120. Lila Abu-Lughod, "Writing against Culture," in *Recapturing Anthropology: Working in the Present*, ed. Richard Gabriel Fox (Santa Fe: School of American Research Press, 1991), 58.

121. Geoff Berkshire, "John Cho Takes the Lead, for Once," *LA Times*, August 4, 2017.

122. Andrew Aoki and Okiyoshi Takeda, *Asian American Politics* (Cambridge: Polity, 2008), 146.

123. Keith Aoki, "The Yellow Pacific: Transnational Identities, Diasporic Racialization, and Myth(s) of the Asian Century," *UC Davis Law Review* 44 (2010): 935.

124. Steve Martinot, *The Machinery of Whiteness: Studies in the Structure of Racialization* (Philadelphia: Temple University Press, 2010), 137.

125. These terms are seen as approximating the classic taxonomies of the Occident and Orient, East and West. (*America*, for instance, often denotes the United States rather than the Americas or Latin America while *Asia* ignores Central Asia and other regions.)

126. Aneesh Aneesh, *Virtual Migration: The Programming of Globalization* (Durham, NC: Duke University Press, 2006).

127. Kuan-Hsing Chen, *Asia as Method: Toward Deimperialization* (Durham, NC: Duke University Press, 2010), 2.

128. Mark Dombeck, "Diagnosing Seung-Hui Cho," Mentalhealth.net, accessed February 3, 2021, https://www.mentalhelp.net/blogs/diagnosing-seung-hui-cho//.

129. Jack Linshi, "The Real Problem When It Comes to Diversity and Asian-Americans," *Time*, October 14, 2014, https://time.com/3475962/asian-american-diversity/.

CHAPTER 5

1. Rachel Lee, *Exquisite Corpse*, 30.

2. Margaret Rhee, "Racial Recalibration," *Asian Diasporic Visual Cultures and the Americas* 1, no. 3 (2015): 285–309; Annie Lowe, "Narratives of Technological Globalization and Outsourced Call Centers in India: Droids, Mimic Machines, Automatons, and Bad Borgs" (PhD diss., University of Kansas, 2014).

3. Vasager Jeevan, "Why Singapore Kids Are So Good at Maths," *Financial Times*, July 22, 2016.

4. Artur Lozano-Méndez, "Techno-Orientalism in East Asian Contexts: Reiteration, Diversification, Adaptation," in *Counterpoints: Edward Said's Legacy*, ed. May Telmissany and Stephanie Tara Schwartz (Newcastle upon Tyne, UK: Cambridge Scholars, 2010), 183.

5. Jane Chi Hyun Park, *Yellow Future: Oriental Style in Hollywood Cinema* (Minneapolis: University of Minnesota Press, 2010), 177.

6. Global Asias pushes from the sense of fixed geographic space to one based on fluid models of knowledge production. Tina Chen, "Context, Coordinate, Circulation: The Postrepresentational Cartographies of Global Asias," *Verge: Studies in Global Asia* 3, no. 1 (2017): vi–xiv; Jerry Won Lee, ed., *The Sociolinguistics of Global Asias* (London: Routledge, 2022).

7. Michael Hardt and Antonio Negri, *Empire* (Boston: Harvard University Press, 2001), 367.

8. Ibid.

9. David S. Roh, Betsy Huang, and Greta A. Niu, eds., *Techno-Orientalism: Imagining Asia in Speculative Fiction, History, and Media* (New Brunswick, NJ: Rutgers University Press, 2015).

10. Constance Penley and Andrew Ross, "Introduction," in *Technoculture*, ed. Constance Penley and Andrew Ross (Minneapolis: University of Minnesota Press, 1991), xii.

11. Greta Aiyu Niu, "Techno-Orientalism, Nanotechnology, Posthumans, and Post-Posthumans in Neal Stephenson's and Linda Nagata's Science Fiction," *Melus* 33, no. 4 (2008): 87–88.

12. Dan Robitzski, "India Just Swore in Its First Robot Police Officer," *Futurism*, February 20, 2019.

13. Esperanza Miyake, "Politicizing Motorcycles: Racialized Capital of Technology, Techno-Orientalism and Japanese Temporality," *East Asian Journal of Popular Culture* 2, no. 2 (2016): 209–224.

14. Ibid.

15. CBS News, "Creepily Human-Like Robots," CBS News, August 1, 2017.

16. Leo Lewis, "The Curse of the Salaryman," *Financial Times*, May 2, 2016.

17. Christopher Simmons, "Japan: Building the Future, Living in the Past?," *New Internationalist*, November 1, 2017.

18. Ibid.

19. Ibid.

20. Stefan Lovgren, "A Robot in Every Home by 2020, South Korea Says," *National Geographic News*, September 6, 2006.

21. Ibid., 118.

22. "Taiwanese People are Empty Shells with No Soul, or Personality or Passion," *Happier Abroad*, January 14, 2013.

23. Daniel Vukovich, *China and Orientalism: Western Knowledge Production and the PRC* (London: Routledge, 2013).

24. Haraway, "Cyborg Manifesto," 176.

25. Alexander Weinstein, *Children of the New World* (New York: Picador, 2016), 4.

26. Ibid., 11.

27. Mansi Thapliyal, "India Outlawed Commercial Surrogacy—Clinics Are Finding Loopholes," *The Conversation*, October 23, 2017.

28. Kalindi Vora, "Re-imagining Reproduction: Unsettling Metaphors in the History of Imperial Science and Commercial Surrogacy in India," *Somatechnics* 5, no. 1 (2015): 91.

29. Audrey Wilson, "How Asia's Surrogate Mothers Became a Cross-Border Business," *South China Morning Post*, June 4, 2017.

30. Real Deal, "Accenture says India Employees have to Specialize," *Times of India*, accessed April 3, 2021, https://timesofindia.indiatimes.com.

31. Ibid.

32. Lowe, "Narratives of Technological Globalization," 27.

33. Ibid.

34. Schlund-Vials, *Modeling Citizenship*, 138.

35. Jasbir Puar, *Terrorist Assemblages: Homonationalism in Queer Times* (Durham, NC: Duke University Press, 2018), 220.

36. Christopher Patterson and Y-Dang Troeung, "Organic and Inorganic Chinas: Desire and Fatigue in Global Hong Kong," *Amerasia Journal* 45, no. 3 (2019): 280–298.

37. Ibid.

38. Christopher T. Fan, "Techno-Orientalism with Chinese Characteristics: Maureen F. McHugh's China Mountain Zhang," *Journal of Transnational American Studies* 6, no. 1 (2015).

39. David Birch, Tony Schirato, and Sanjay Srivastava, *Asia: Cultural Politics in the Global Age* (New York: Palgrave, 2001), 1.

40. Roh, Huang, and Niu, "Technologizing Orientalism," 5.

41. Betsy Huang, "Premodern Orientalist Science Fictions," *Melus* 33, no. 4 (2008): 26.

42. Eugenia Lean, "Making the Chinese Copycat: Trademarks and Recipes in Early Twentieth-Century Global Science and Capitalism," *Osiris* 33, no. 1 (2018): 271–93.

43. Winnie Won Yin Wong, *Van Gogh on Demand: China and the Readymade* (Chicago: University of Chicago Press, 2013), 237, 206.

44. David S. Roh, Betsy Huang, and Greta A. Niu, "Desiring Machines, Repellant Subjects: A Conclusion," *Techno-Orientalism: Imagining Asia in Speculative Fiction, History, and Media*, ed. David S. Roh, Betsy Huang, and Greta A. Niu (New Brunswick, NJ: Rutgers University Press, 2015), 226.

45. Hua Hsu, "Andrew Yang and the Political Narratives of Asian-Americans," *New Yorker*, October 9, 2019, https://www.newyorker.com/culture/cultural-comment/andrew-yang-and-the-political-narratives-of-asian-americans.

46. China Times, "Foxconn Chairman Likens His Workforce to Animals," *China Times*, January 19, 2012.

47. Sui-Lee Wee, "Young Workers in China: 'We're Human, Not Machines,'" *Fiscal Times*, May 4, 2012; Gethin Chamberlain, "Apple's Chinese Workers Treated 'Inhumanely, like Machines,'" *The Guardian*, April 30, 2011; Students and Scholars against Corporate Misbehavior, "Workers as Machines: Military Management in Foxconn," October 12, 2010, http://sacom.hk/wp-content/uploads/2010/11/report-on-foxconn-workers-as-machines_sacom.pdf.

48. Benjamin, *Race after Technology*.

49. Bobby Hellard, "Apple to Investigate Factory Treating Students 'like Robots,'" *IT Pro*, October 30, 2018.

50. Jenny Chan, "A Suicide Survivor: The Life of a Chinese Worker," *New Technology, Work and Employment* 28, no. 2 (2013): 84–99.

51. Ibid.

52. Julietta Hua, "The Foxconn Suicides: Human Vitality and Capitalist Consumption," *Women's Studies in Communication* 41, no. 4 (2018): 321.

53. Staphany Wong, "Decoding the New Generation of Chinese Migrant Workers," *EU-China Civil Society Forum* (September 2, 2010): 2.

54. China Labor Watch, "Apple, HP, and Sony Open Probes into Latest Foxconn Suicides," China Labor Watch, May 28, 2010.

55. Liang An San Di Research Team, "Foxconn Manufacturing Model: Labor Camp of Order, Regulation and Punishment," *Chinese Election and Governance*, February 14, 2012; quoted in Kristen Lucas, Dongjing Kang, and Zhou Li, "Workplace Dignity in a Total Institution: Examining the Experiences of Foxconn's Migrant Workforce," *Journal of Business Ethics* 114, no. 1 (2013): 98.

56. Aside from producing technological products for the world, China is also a repository for taking in disposed machines, since 70 percent of the world's electronic waste is sent here to be disassembled and stripped for its parts for precious metals, a practice that poses biological hazards to the miner.

57. Nick Statt, "iPhone Manufacturer Foxconn Plans to Replace Almost Every Human Worker with Robots," *The Verge*, December 30, 2016.

58. Jonathan Holslag, "Longer Hours, Worse Jobs: Are Asians Turning into Working Machines," *South China Morning Press*, September 26, 2016, https://www.scmp.com/week-asia/politics/article/2022099/longer-hours-worse-jobs-are-asians-turning-working-machines.

59. Jenny Chan, "Robots, Not Humans: Official Policy in China," *New Internationalist*, November 1, 2017.

60. Lucas, Kang, and Li, "Workplace Dignity," 98.

61. Pun Ngai and Jenny Chan, "Global Capital, the State, and Chinese Works: The Foxconn Experience," *Modern China* 38, no. 4 (2012): 392.

62. Ben Smith, "Behind the Chinese Professor," *Politico*, October 22, 2010.

63. The ad had been deemed "too controversial" by major television networks but speaks directly to the fears over the "rise of China" stoked daily by American "patriots." Larry McCarthy, the producer of "Chinese Professor," defended his work by saying that "this ad is about America, it's not about China."

64. Aya Yoshida, "China: The World's Largest Recyclable Waste Importer," *World* 3, no. 4 (2005): 33–52.

65. Directed by Guillermo Del Toro, produced by Legendary Pictures and distributed by Warner Bros.

66. Claudine Zap, "'Pacific Rim' Called American Propaganda in China," Yahoo News, August 27, 2013.

67. *Daily Mail*, "Olympic Farce: Former Blue Peter Presenter Konnie Huq Lashes Out at 'Robotic' Chinese Torchminders," *Daily Mail*, April 7, 2008.

68. Associated Press, "Daley: Chinese Diver Qiu Is 'like a Robot,'" Associated Press, July 21, 2012.

69. Janis Mackey Frayer, "Rio 2016: China's Olympian Factories Churn Out Fewer Champions," *NBC News*, August 20, 2016.

70. Sun Xiaochen, "Robots? Nope—Just Really Good Athletes," *China Daily*, July 30, 2012.

71. Matteo Tarantino and Stefania Carini, "The Good, the Fake and the Cyborg: The Broadcast and Coverage of Beijing 2008 Olympics in Italy," in *Encoding the Olympics: The Beijing Olympic Games and the Communication Impact Worldwide*, ed. Luo Qing and Giuseppe Richer (London: Routledge, 2013), 324.

72. Jeffrey Wasserstrom, *Popular Protest and Political Culture in Modern China* (London: Routledge, 2018), 58.

73. Susan Brownell, "'China Bashing' at the Olympic Games: Why the Cold War Continues in Sports Journalism," *Chinese American Forum* 7, no. 3 (1997): 21–22.

74. Li Tao, "Xinhua News Agency Debuts AI Anchors in Partnership with Search Engine Sogou," *South China Morning Post*, November 8, 2018.

75. The Hindu, "Eerily Life-Life, Chinese Bionic Woman Turns on the Charm," *The Hindu*, January 9, 2017.

76. Heba Kanso, "Saudi Arabia Gave 'Citizenship' to a Robot Named Sophia, and Saudi Women Aren't Amused," *Global News*, November 4, 2017.

77. Ben Mack, "Why Are Robots Designed to Be Female?," Villainesse, November 7, 2017.

78. Grace Kyungwon Hong, *Death beyond Disavowal: The Impossible Politics of Difference* (Minneapolis: University of Minnesota Press, 2015).

79. Haraway, "Cyborg Manifesto," 169.

80. Roh, Huang, and Niu, "Technologizing Orientalism," 7.

81. Business Insider, "Korea Is Obsessed with Plastic Surgery," Business Insider, June 6, 2013.

82. Worshipping Sonmi as a goddess who saved humanity, Zachry and the fellow residents on Big Isle (a whitewashed metaphor for Hawaii) live out their lives over a century after "The Fall" of human civilization.

83. Haraway, "Cyborg Manifesto," 180.

84. Klaus Schwab, *The Fourth Industrial Revolution* (New York: Crown Business, 2017).

85. Richard Baldwin, *The Globotics Upheaval: Globalization, Robotics, and the Future of Work* (Oxford: Oxford University Press, 2019).

86. Louis Hyman, *Temp: How American Work, American Business, and the American Dream Became Temporary* (New York: Penguin, 2018).

87. Jill Lepore, "Are Robots Competing for Your Job?," *New Yorker*, February 25, 2019.

88. Jackie Marchildon, "Replacing Workers with Robots Will Increase Trafficking and Slavery: Report in the Coming Decades, 36 Million," Global Citizen, July 13, 2018.

89. Katie Cannon, "SM Entertainment's Creating Robot Versions of Your Favorite K-pop Idols, Asiancrush," Asian Crush, December 12, 2017.

90. IFMartin, "Sonmi~451 vs. The Windup Girl: Wonder Girls' 'Like Money' and Perfume's 'Spring of Life,'" *Clear and Refreshing*, August 1, 2012, https://clearandrefresh ing.wordpress.com/2012/08/01/sonmi451-vs-the-windup-girl-perfumes-spring-of-life -and-wonder-girls-like-money/.

91. L. Singh, "ICYMI: We Will Soon Have Virtual K-pop Idols, and the Reactions Are Mixed," Don't Bore Us, November 6, 2020, https://dontboreus.thebrag.com/aespa-k -pop-virtual-idols/.

92. Ebba Cha, "Aespa, the First Ever Virtual K-pop Group to Debut," *TJ Today*, November 16, 2020.

93. Sharon Heijin Lee, "Beauty between Empires: Global Feminism, Plastic Surgery, and the Trouble with Self-Esteem," *Frontiers: A Journal of Women Studies* 37, no. 1 (2016): 1–31.

94. Frédéric Kaplan, "Who Is Afraid of the Humanoid? Investigating Cultural Differences in the Acceptance of Robots," *International Journal of Humanoid Robotics* 1, no. 3 (2004): 465–480.

95. Michael R. Bowman, "Beyond Maids and *Meganekko*: Examining the *Moe* Phenomenon," *Cinephile* 7, no. 1 (2001): 14–18.

96. Aljosa Puzar, "Asian Dolls and the Westernized Gaze: Notes on the Female Dollification in South Korea," *Asian Women* 27, no. 2 (2011): 81–111.

97. Hyun-su Yim, "Is There a Media Double Standard for K-pop?," *Korean Herald*, June 18, 2020, http://www.koreaherald.com/view.php?ud=20200618000951.

98. Jessica Chua, "The Extremes that Koreans Take to Become a K-pop Idol," *Rojak Daily*, January 27, 2017.

99. Michael Burleigh, "Kim Jong-un's Mini-Skirted Robot Army," *Daily Mail*, July 29, 2013, https://www.dailymail.co.uk/news/article-2381052/Kim-Jong-Uns-mini-skirted -robot-army-North-Koreas-female-soldiers.html.

100. Felix Abt, "'Automatons, Slaves or Members of the 1% in N. Korea," *Korea Observer*, March 23, 2015, https://www.koreaobserver.com/automations-slaves-or-mem bers-of-the-1-elite-27211/.

101. Channel A Home, "NowOnMyWayToMeetYou_Ep13_Mini-Skirted Robot Army in North Korea," YouTube, February 9, 2017, https://www.youtube.com/watch? v=frvZJhc3BQY.

102. Kevein Drum, "Social Networking Employs More People than We Think," *Mother Jones*, October 26, 2014.

103. Adrien Chen, "The Laborers Who Keep Dick Pics and Beheadings out of Your Facebook Feed," *Wired*, October 23, 2014.

104. Sasha Lekach, "'The Cleaners' Shows the Terrors Human Content Moderators Face at Work," *Mashable*, November 12, 2008.

105. This quote came from a lecture series for geriatric services offered in Israel about long-term retirement planning and process for hiring a migrant caregiver. Laurel Bradley, "Health, Well-Being, and Rights: Mapping the Boundaries of Belonging for Filipino Caregivers in Israel" (PhD diss., University of North Carolina at Chapel Hill, 2014), 102.

106. Robyn Magalit Rodriguez, *Migrants for Export: How the Philippine State Brokers Labor to the World* (Minneapolis: University of Minnesota Press, 2010).

107. Quoted in R. J. May, "The Domestic in Foreign Policy: The Flor Contemplacion Case and Philippine-Singapore Relations," *Pilipinas* 29 (1997): 71.

108. Pheng Cheah, *Inhuman Conditions: On Cosmopolitanism and Human Rights* (Cambridge: Harvard University Press, 2009), 236.

109. Anna Romina Guevarra, "Mediations of Care: Brokering Labour in the Age of Robotics," *Pacific Affairs* 91, no. 4 (2018): 757. South Korea is making good use of these human-operated robots to make academic machines out of its conformist students who spend countless hours trying to get into prestigious universities and scoring the highest on international math and science tests.

110. Ibid., 754.

111. Lindsay Rittenhouse, "Amazon Warehouse Employees' Message to Jeff Bezos—We Are Not Robots," *The Street*, September 28, 2017.

112. Aimee Picchi, "Inside an Amazon Warehouse: 'Treating Human Beings as Robots,'" *CBS News*, April 29, 2018.

113. Jeremy Wilson, "My Gruelling Day as an Amazon Mechanical Turk," *The Kernel*, August 28, 2013.

114. BBC, "Amazon Workers Face 'Increased Risk of Mental Illness,'" BBC, November 25, 2013.

115. Ayhan Aytes, "Return of the Crowds: Mechanical Turk and Neoliberal States of Exception," in *Digital Labor: The Internet as Playground and Factory*, ed. Trebor Sholz (London: Routledge, 2012), 87–105.

116. David Golumbia, "The Amazonization of Everything," *Jacobin*, August 5, 2015.

117. Miranda Hall, "The Ghost of the Mechanical Turk," *Jacobin*, February 16, 2017.

118. Neda Atanasoski and Kalindi Vora, *Surrogate Humanity: Race, Robots, and the Politics of Technological Futures* (Durham, NC: Duke University Press, 2019).

119. Ibid., 46.

120. Ibid.

121. Martin Kevorkian, *Color Monitors: The Black Face of Technology in America* (Ithaca, NY: Cornell University Press, 2006), 88.

122. Tim Hornyak, "Koreans Schools Welcome More Robot Teachers," *Cnet.com*, December 28, 2010.

EPILOGUE

1. In the 1992 book *The End of History and the Last Man*, Fukuyama says the collapse of the Soviet Union means the world is entering a more stable time in human history. The last man appears in this moment as one who no longer sees an open horizon of conflict, since formerly dehumanized slaves of communism now fall under a universal impetus of (neo)liberalism, becoming full "humans" with rights. This last man ceases to be a human who blindly pursues his own prestige and protects collective self-preservation. See Francis Fukuyama, *The End of History and the Last Man* (New York: Simon and Schuster, 2006).

2. Francis Fukuyama, *Our Posthuman Future: Consequences of the Biotechnology Revolution* (New York: Farrar, Straus and Giroux, 2003).

3. E. C. Eze, "The Color of Reason: The Idea of 'Race' in Kant's Anthropology," in *Postcolonial African Philosophy: A Critical Reader*, ed. E. C. Eze (Cambridge, MA: Blackwell, 1997), 103–131.

4. According to Ferreira da Silva, the European sense of global progress moved from matters of *temporality* (reproduction, industrialization, national advancement, biological evolution) toward those concerning *spatiality* (overpopulation, pollution, transna-

tionalism, and natural extinction). See Denise Ferreira da Silva, *Toward a Global Idea of Race* (Minneapolis: University of Minnesota Press, 2007), 116.

5. Denise Ferreira da Silva, "1 (life) 1 (life) ÷ 0 (blackness) = ∞ − ∞ or ∞ / ∞: On Matter beyond the Equation of Value," *e-flux* 79 (February 2017), https://www.e-flux.com/journal/79/94686/1-life-0-blackness-or-on-matter-beyond-the-equation-of-value/.

6. Ibid.

7. Juvenal Caporale, "The Circle, Indigeneity, and Healing: Rehumanizing Chicano, Mexican, and Indigenous Men" (PhD diss., Arizona State University, 2020).

8. Maile Arvin, *Possessing Polynesians: The Science of Settler Colonial Whiteness in Hawaii and Oceania* (Durham, NC: Duke University Press, 2019), 26.

9. Woody Evans, "Posthuman Rights: Dimensions of Transhuman Worlds," *Teknokultura* 12, no. 2 (2015): 373–384; Nick Bostrom, "In Defense of Posthuman Dignity," *Bioethics* 19 no. 3 (2005): 202–214; Steen Christiansen, "Posthuman Rights," *Akademisk Kvarter* 5 (2012): 101–112.

10. Artur Matos Alves, *Unveiling the Posthuman* (Oxford: Interdisciplinary), 2012.

11. Halberstam and Livingston, *Posthuman Bodies*, 3.

12. Long T. Bui, "On Artificial Humanity, Coronavirus Revolutions, and the Zoomanities," *Foundry*, November 2020, https://uchri.org/foundry/on-artificial-humanity-coronavirus-revolutions-and-the-zoomanities/.

13. Niu, "Techno-Orientalism," 88–89.

14. Sandra Ruiz, *Ricanness: Enduring Time in Anticolonial Performance* (New York: New York University Press, 2019), 47.

15. Donna Haraway, "Anthropocene, Capitalocene, Plantationocene, Chthulucene: Making Kin," *Environmental Humanities* 6, no. 1 (2015): 161.

16. Jean Baudrillard, *Simulations* (New York: Semiotext[e], 1983), 93.

17. Larissa Lai, *Automaton Biographies* (Vancouver: Arsenal Pulp, 2010); Franny Choi, *Death by Sex Machine* (Little Rock, AR: Sibling Rivalry, 2017); Margaret Rhee, *Love, Robot* (New York: Operating System, 2017).

18. Margaret Rhee, *Radio Heart; or, How Robots Fall Out of Love* (Georgetown, KY: Finishing Line, 2015), 57.

19. https://www.facebook.com/flyinglinh/videos/10110663857650606/.

20. Ly Thuy Nguyen, "Queer Dis/inheritance and Refugee Futures," *WSQ: Women's Studies Quarterly* 48 no. 1 (2020): 226.

21. Peter Keo, *Leadership in an Age of Compassion and Empathy* (Hauppauge, NY: Nova Science, 2021).

22. Kimberly Yam, "Alex Jones Says Asian People 'Sync Up and Are' in Fights, Joe Rogan Agrees," *Huffington Post*, March 1, 2019.

23. David C. Oh, "Techno-Orientalist Villains and White Masculinity in the Wolverine Movies," in *The X-Men Films: A Cultural Analysis*, ed. Claudi Bucciferro (London: Rowman and Littlefield, 2016), 153.

24. Ava locates the synthetic skin of other Asian robots to begin applying these tan strips to her mechanical body to pass in the human world but finds a curly brunette wig to match her white European-appearing face.

25. Oh, "Techno-Orientalist Villains," 144.

26. Cheng, *Ornamentalism*, 135.

27. Margaret Rhee, "Racial Recalibration: Nam June Paik's K-456," *Asian Diasporic Visual Cultures and the Americas* 1 (2015): 297.

28. Haerin Shin, "Engineering the Techno-Orient: The Hyperrealization of Post-Racial Politics in *Cloud Atlas*," in *Dis-Orienting Planets: Racial Representations of Asia*

in Science Fiction, ed. Isiah Lavender III (Jackson: University Press of Mississippi, 2017), 137.

29. Open call for new webseries, "Jon Davis Gets a Sex Robot," Cast It Talent, August 6, 2012.

30. Durba Mitra, Sara Kang, and Genevieve Clutario, "It's Time to Reckon with the History of Asian Women in America," *Harper's Bazaar*, March 23, 2021, https://www .harpersbazaar.com.

31. Quoted in Cady Lang and Paulina Cachero, "How a Long History of Intertwined Racism and Misogyny Leaves Asian Women in America Vulnerable to Violence," *Time*, April 7, 2021, https://time.com/5952819/history-anti-asian-racism-misogyny/.

32. Jeannette Muhammad and Emma Bowman, "Indianapolis Sikh Community Mourns 4 of its Members Killed in Shooting," *NPR*, April 18, 2021.

33. Wanda Raiford, "Race, Robots, and the Law," in *New Boundaries in Political Science Fiction*, ed. Donald M. Hassler and Clyde Wilcox (Columbia: University of South Carolina Press, 2008), 93.

34. Mel Y. Chen, "Everywhere Archives: Transgendering, Trans Asians, and the Internet," *Australian Feminist Studies* 25, no. 6 (2010): 204.

35. Richard Slotkin, *Regeneration through Violence: The Mythology of the American Frontier, 1600–1860* (Norman: University of Oklahoma Press, 1973), 6.

36. Raymond Williams, *Marxism and Literature* (Oxford: Oxford University Press, 1977).

37. Jim Gullett, *Good News to the Red Planet* (New York: iUniverse, 2005), 73.

38. Said, *Orientalism,* 312.

39. Ibid.

40. Randolph L. Rutsky, *High Technē: Art and Technology from the Machine Aesthetic to the Posthuman* (Minneapolis: University of Minnesota Press, 1999), 159.

Bibliography

PRIMARY SOURCES

Abt, Felix. "'Automatons, Slaves or Members of the 1% in N. Korea." *Korea Observer,* March 23, 2015. https://www.koreaobserver.com/automations-slaves-or-members-of-the-1-elite-27211/.

Addams, Jane. *Addams's Essays and Speeches on Peace.* London: Bloomsbury, 2003.

American Colonization Society. "One Hundred Years of British Rule in Ceylon." *Journal of the Royal Colonial Institute* 6 (1896): 434–471.

Appendix to the Journals of the House of Representatives of New Zealand. Vol. 2. Wellington: House of Representatives of New Zealand, 1878.

Associated Press. "Daley: Chinese Diver Qiu Is 'like a Robot.'" Associated Press, July 21, 2012. https://sports.ndtv.com/olympics-2012/british-diver-tom-daley-chinese-rival-qiu-bo-a-robot-1550601.

Barret, Johan. "The Plain Truth about Asiatic Labor." *North American Review* 163, no. 480 (1896): 620–632.

BBC. "Amazon Workers Face 'Increased Risk of Mental Illness.'" BBC, November 25, 2013.

Blaine, James. *Congressional Series of United States Public Documents.* Vol. 4202. Washington, DC: Government Printing Office, 1906.

Blond, Georges. *Great Migrations.* New York: Hutchinson, 1958.

Boyle, Robert. *The Works of the Honourable Robert Boyle.* London: A. Millar, 1744.

Brownell, Susan. "'China Bashing' at the Olympic Games: Why the Cold War Continues in Sports Journalism." *Chinese American Forum* 7, no. 3 (1997): 21–22.

Burleigh, Michael. "Kim Jong-un's Mini-Skirted Robot Army." *Daily Mail,* July 29, 2013. https://www.dailymail.co.uk/news/article-2381052/Kim-Jong-Uns-mini-skirted-robot-army-North-Koreas-female-soldiers.html.

Business Insider. "Korea Is Obsessed with Plastic Surgery." *Business Insider,* June 6, 2013, https://www.businessinsider.com.

California Legislature. *Chinese Immigration: Its Social, Moral, and Political Effect.* Special Committee on Chinese Immigration Report. Sacramento: F. P. Thompson State Printing, 1878.

Cannon, Katie. "SM Entertainment's Creating Robot Versions of Your Favorite K-pop Idols." Asiancrush, December 12, 2017. https://www.asiancrush.com/sm-entertainments-creating-robot-versions-favorite-k-pop-idols/.

Capra, Frank. *Know Your Enemy: Japan.* Washington, DC: U.S. War Department, 1945.

Carter, Angela. *Nothing Sacred: Selected Writings.* London: Virago, 1982.

Cave, Steven, and Kanta Dihal. "Ancient Dreams of Intelligent Machines: 3,000 Years of Robots." *Nature: International Journal of Science*, July 25, 2018. www.nature.com.

Cha, Ebba. "Aespa, the First Ever Virtual K-pop Group to Debut." *TJ Today*, November 16, 2020. https://www.tjtoday.org/29896/entertainment/aespa-the-first-ever-virtual-k-pop-group-to-debut/.

Chamberlain, Gethin. "Apple's Chinese Workers Treated 'Inhumanely, like Machines." *The Guardian.* April 30, 2011. http://www.guardian.co.uk.

Chan, Jenny. "Robots, Not Humans: Official Policy in China." *New Internationalist*, November 1, 2017. https://newint.org/features/2017/11/01/industrial-robots-china.

———. "A Suicide Survivor: The Life of a Chinese Worker." *New Technology, Work and Employment* 28, no. 3 (2013): 84–99.

Channel A Home. "NowOnMyWayToMeetYou_Ep13_Mini-Skirted Robot Army in North Korea." YouTube, February 9, 2017. https://www.youtube.com/watch?v=frvZJhc3BQY.

Chen, Adrien. "The Laborers Who Keep Dick Pics and Beheadings out of Your Facebook Feed." *Wired*, October 23, 2014. www.wired.com.

China Labor Watch. "DailyFinance: Apple, HP, and Sony Open Probes into Latest Foxconn Suicides." Chinalaborwatch.org, May 28, 2010. www.chinalaborwatch.org.

China Times. "Foxconn Chairmen Likens His Workforce to Animals." *China Times*, January 19, 2012. www.wantchinatimes.com.

Crockett, Lucy Herndon. *Popcorn on the Ginza: An Informal Portrait of Postwar Japan.* New York: W. Sloane Associates, 1949.

Daily Mail. "Olympic Farce: Former Blue Peter Presenter Konnie Huq Lashes Out at 'Robotic' Chinese Torchminders." *Daily Mail*, April 7, 2008. www.dailymail.co/uk.

De Gobineau, Arthur. *The Inequality of Human Races.* London: Heinemann, 1915.

Democratic National Committee. *The Political Reformation: Democratic Campaign Handbook.* New York: Democratic National Committee, 1884.

Dickerson, Caitlin. "Secret World War II Chemical Experiments Tested Troops by Race." National Public Radio, June 22, 2015. www.nrp.org.

Drum, Kevin. "Social Networking Employs More People than We Think." *Mother Jones*, October 26, 2014. www.motherjones.com.

Economic Times Bureau. "BTS Tops Billboard 100 list: How K-pop Helped Korea Improve Its Economy K-pop Has Brought Korea into the Spotlight, Not for Technological Excellence, but for a Cultural Reason." *Economic Times*, August 7, 2018.

Einstein, Albert. *The Travel Diaries of Albert Einstein: The Far East, Palestine, and Spain, 1922–1923.* Princeton, NJ: Princeton University Press, 2018.

Egan, Timothy. "New Thinking about Race and Merit on Campus." *International Herald Tribune*, January 8, 2007, 2.

Epstein, Robert. "The Empty Brain." *Aeon*, May 18, 2016. www.Aeon.co.

Ewbank, Thomas. *A Descriptive and Historical Account of Hydraulic and Other Machines for Raising Water, Ancient and Modern.* Cincinnati: Appleton, 1846.

Fox, Ralph. *The Colonial Policy of British Imperialism*. New York: International, 1933.

Frayer, Janis Mackey. "Rio 2016: China's Olympian Factories Churn Out Fewer Champions." *NBC News*, August 20, 2016. www.nbcnews.com.

Gandhi, Mahatma. *The Collected Works of Mahatma Gandhi*. Vol. 95. New Delhi: Ministry of Information and Broadcasting, 2000.

Gerster, Carole. "Grappling with Media Images: Three Films by Asian-American Women." *Feminist Collections* 16, no. 4 (1994): 9.

Gladstone, W. E. "On Books and the Housing of Them." *The Bookmart*, vol. 8. Pittsburgh: Bookmart, 1890.

Golumbia, David. "The Amazonization of Everything." *Jacobin*, August 5, 2015. https://jacobinmag.com.

Gompers, Samuel. *Labor and the Common Welfare*. New York: E. P. Dutton, 1919.

Gompers, Samuel, and Herman Gutstadt. *Meat vs. Rice: American Manhood against Asiatic Coolieism, which Shall Survive?* San Francisco: Asiatic Exclusion League 1902.

Great Britain Parliament. *The Parliamentary Debates*. London: Wyman and Sons, 1906.

Gutmann, Ethan. "A Tale of the New China." *Weekly Standard*, May 24, 1999.

Gutzlaff, Karl Friedrich August. *China Opened*. London: Smith, Elder, 1838.

Hall, Miranda. "The Ghost of the Mechanical Turk." *Jacobin*, February 16, 2017. https://jacobinmag.com.

Hellard, Bobby. "Apple to Investigate Factory Treating Students 'like Robots.'" IT Pro, October 30, 2018. www.itpro.co.uk.

Hernandez, Yessica Garcia. *Intoxicated by Jenni Rivera: The Erotics of Fandom, Sonic Pedagogies of Deviance, and the Politics of Pirujeria*. PhD diss., University of California, San Diego, 2019.

Hinckley, Ted. *Alaskan John G. Brady: Missionary, Businessman, Judge, and Governor, 1878–1918*. Columbus: Ohio State University Press, 1982.

The Hindu. "Eerily Life-Life, Chinese Bionic Woman Turns on the Charm." *The Hindu*, January 9, 2017. www.thehindu.com.

Hironaka, Wakako. "Through Rosy Glasses: Darkly." *New York Times*, June 5, 1993.

Holsag, Jonathan. "Longer Hours, Worse Jobs: Are Asians Turning into Working Machines." *South China Morning Press*, September 26, 2016. https://www.scmp.com/week-asia/politics/article/2022099/longer-hours-worse-jobs-are-asians-turning-working-machines.

Hornvak, Tim. "Koreans Schools Welcome More Robot Teachers." *CNET*, December 28, 2010, www.cnet.com.

Hsu, Hua. "Andrew Yang and the Political Narratives of Asian-Americans." *New Yorker*, October 9, 2019. https://www.newyorker.com/culture/cultural-comment/andrew-yang-and-the-political-narratives-of-asian-americans.

Imperial Valley Press. "An American Plane for Japan's War Machine." *Imperial Valley Press*, May 16, 1938, 3.

Jagor, Fedor. *Travels in the Philippines*. London: Chapman and Hall, 1875.

Jeevan, Vasager. "Why Singapore Kids Are So Good at Maths." *Financial Times*, July 22, 2016. www.ft.com.

Kai-Shek, Chiang. *Selected Speeches and Messages*. Taipei: Government Information Office, 1956.

Kanso, Heba. "Saudi Arabia Gave 'Citizenship' to a Robot Named Sophia, and Saudi Women Aren't Amused." *Global News*, November 4, 2017. https://globalnews.ca.

Keillor, Steven J. *This Rebellious House: American History and the Truth of Christianity*. Downers Grove, IL: InterVarsity, 1996.

Kim-Gibson, Dai Sil. "Do You Hear Their Voices?" *Amerasia Journal* 35, no. 1 (2009): 44–55.

King, Martin Luther. "Beyond Vietnam: A Time to Break Silence." *American Rhetoric*. Speech at Riverside Church, New York, April 4, 1967, accessed March 31, 2019, https://www.americanrhetoric.com.

Kondo, Dorinne. "If You Want to Know Who They Are . . ." *New York Times*, September 16, 1984, 13.

Krisof, Nicholas. "Tokyo Journal: Japan's Feminine Falsetto Falls Right out of Favor." *New York Times*, December 13, 1995.

Lang, Cady, and Paulina Cachero. "How a Long History of Intertwined Racism and Misogyny Leaves Asian Women in America Vulnerable to Violence." *Time*, April 7, 2021. https://time.com/5952819/history-anti-asian-racism-misogyny/.

Lazaro, Sage. "Tila Tequila Truly Believes the Earth Is Flat and Won't Stop Yelling about It on Twitter." *Observer*, January 7, 2016. https://observer.com/2016/01/tila-tequila-truly-believes-the-earth-is-flat-and-wont-stop-yelling-about-it-on-twitter/.

Lee, Stan, and Larry Lieber. *Tales of Suspense* 1, no. 39, March 1963. Marvel Comics.

Lekach, Sasha. "'The Cleaners' Shows the Terrors Human Content Moderators Face at Work." *Mashable*, November 12, 2008. www.mashable.com.

Lepore, Jill. "Are Robots Competing for Your Job." *New Yorker*, February 2, 2019.

Lewis, Leo. "The Curse of the Salaryman." *Financial Times*, May 2, 2016. https://www.ft.com.

Linshi, Jack. "The Real Problem When It Comes to Diversity and Asian-Americans." *Time*, October 14, 2014. https://time.com/3475962/asian-american-diversity/.

London, Jack. "If Japan Wakens China." In *Jack London Reports*, edited by King Hendricks and Irving Shepard, 358–361 London: Doubleday, 1970.

———. *The Iron Heel*. New York: Penguin, 2006.

———. "The Unparalleled Invasion: A Story." *McClure's Magazine*, July 1910, 308–316.

———. "Yellow Peril." In *Jack London Reports: War Correspondence, Sports Articles, and Miscellaneous Writings*, edited by King Hendricks and Irving Shepard, 358–362. Garden City, NY: Doubleday, 1970.

Lowell, Percival. *Chosön; the Land of the Morning Calm: A Sketch of Korea*. Boston: Ticknor and Fields, 1886.

Mack, Ben. "Why Are Robots Designed to Be Female?" Villainesse, November 7, 2017. https://www.villainesse.com.

Marchilidon, Jackie. "Replacing Workers with Robots Will Increase Trafficking and Slavery: Report in the Coming Decades, 36 Million." Global Citizen, July 13, 2018. www.globalcitizen.org.

Martin and Company. "Working of District Boards in Bengal, 1904–05." *Indian Engineering* 38 (1905): 420.

Meade, Edwin R. "A Labor Question." In *The Great West*, edited by Ferdinand Vandeveer Hayden, 389–390. Bloomington, IN: C. R. Brodix, 1880.

Mehri, Darius. *Notes from Toyota-Land: An American Engineer in Japan*. Ithaca, NY: Cornell University Press, 2018.

Mill, John. *The Ottomans in Europe: Or Turkey in the Present Crisis, with the Secret Societies Map*. London: Weldon, 1876.

Mitra, Durba, Sara Kang, and Genevieve Clutario. "It's Time to Reckon with History of Asian Women in America." *Harper's Bazaar*, March 23, 2021. https://www.harpersbazaar.com/culture/features/a35913981/its-time-to-reckon-with-the-history-of-asian-women-in-america/.

Muhammad, Jeannette, and Emma Bowman. "Indianapolis Sikh Community Mourns 4 of its Members Killed in Shooting." NPR, April 18, 2021.

Murdock, Victor. *China, the Mysterious and Marvellous.* New York: Fleming H. Revell, 1920.

Offray, Julien de la Mettrie. *Man a Machine.* Chicago, IL: Open Court, 1912.

Palmer, Fredrick. "The Two-Sworded Warder of the Turbulent East." *China Monthly Review* 51 (1929): 208–225.

Parliamentary Debates: Third Session of the Twenty-Eighth Parliament of the United Kingdom of Great Britain and Ireland, vol. 4. London: Wyman and Sons, 1909.

Pascal, Blaise. *Pensées and Other Writings.* Oxford: Oxford University Press, 1999.

Pennsylvania State Educational Association. *The Pennsylvania School Journal.* Vol. 55–56, edited by Thomas Henry Burrowes, James Pyle Wickersham, Elnathan Elisha Higbee, David Jewett Waller, and Nathan Christ Schaeffer. Lancaster, PA: New Era Printing, 1907.

Petersen, William. "Success Story, Japanese-American Style." *New York Times Magazine,* January 9, 1966, 9.

Pettigrew, Richard Franklin. *Imperial Washington: The Story of American Public Life from 1870–1920.* Chicago: C. H. Kerr, 1922.

Phelan, James. "Why the Chinese Should Be Excluded." *North American Review* 173, no. 540 (1901): 663–676.

Philp, Robert Kemp. *The Dictionary of Useful Knowledge.* London: Houlston & Wright, 1858.

Picchi, Aimee. "Inside an Amazon Warehouse: 'Treating Human Beings as Robots.'" CBS News, April 29, 2018, https://www.cbsnews.com.

Pollard, Edward B. *Women in All Ages and in All Countries: Oriental Women.* Philadelphia: Rittenhouse, 1907.

Ramanujan, Krishna. "Health Expert Explains Asian and Asian-American Students' Unique Pressures to Succeed." *Cornell Chronicle,* April 19, 2006.

Real Deal. "Accenture says India Employees have to Specialize." *Times of India,* April 3, 2021. https://timesofindia.indiatimes.com.

Reed, Milton. *The Golden Window of Oriental Impressions.* Boston: Sherman, French, 1912.

Rhee, Margaret. "In Search of My Robot: Race, Technology, and the Asian American Body." *Scholar and Feminist Online* 13, no. 3 (2016). http://sfonline.barnard.edu/traversing-technologies/margaret-rhee-in-search-of-my-robot-race-technology-and-the-asian-american-body/0/.

———. *Radio Heart; or, How Robots Fall Out of Love.* Georgetown, KY: Finishing Line Press, 2015.

Rigg, Robert. "The Red Enemy." *Army* 10, no. 11 (June 1960): 66–73.

Rittenhouse, Lindsay. "Amazon Warehouse Employees' Message to Jeff Bezos—We Are Not Robots." *The Street,* September 28, 2017. www.thestreet.com.

Rivera, Alex. *Sleepdealer.* Los Angeles: Maya Entertainment, 2008.

Robertson, Walter. "Disarmament and the Chinese Communist Threat." *Department of State Bulletin* 40, no. 1029: 375–378. Washington, DC: Department of State, March 16, 1959.

Robitzski, Dan. "India Just Swore In Its First Robot Police Officer." *Futurism,* February 20, 2019. http://futurism.com.

Romulo, Carlos Peña. *I Saw the Fall of the Philippines.* New York: Doubleday, Doran, 1942.

Roose, Diane. "Cheaper than Machines." *New Internationalist,* April 2, 1980.

Ross, Edward A., *Social Control: A Survey of the Foundations of Order*. New York: Macmillan, 1901.

Rowell, Chester. "Chinese and Japanese Immigrants—a Comparison." *Annals of the American Academy of Political and Social Science* 34, no. 2 (1909) 3–10.

San Francisco Chronicle. "Sound Warning Against Influx of Coolies." *San Francisco Chronicle*, July 3, 1905.

Saturday Evening Post vol. 237. Philadelphia: Curtis Publishing Company, 1964.

Schomburgk, Robert H. "The Indians of British Guiana." *The Journal of Civilization* 26 (1841): 408–412.

Singh, L. "ICYMI: We Will Soon Have Virtual K-pop Idols, and the Reactions Are Mixed." *Don't Bore Us*, November 6, 2020. https://dontboreus.thebrag.com/aespa-k-pop-virtual-idols/.

Singh, Shailendra Singh. *I Am Not a Sex Machine*. Bombay: Shailendra Singh Films, 2016.

Smith, Andrew. "The Coolie Trade." *Boston Daily Globe*, September 13, 1873.

Smith, Ben. "Behind the Chinese Professor." *Politico*, October 22, 2010. https://www.politico.com.

Statt, Nick. "iPhone Manufacturer Foxconn Plans to Replace Almost Every Human Worker with Robots." *The Verge*, December 30, 2016. www.theverge.com.

Stokes, Henry Scott Stokes. "Japan's Love Affair with the Robot." *New York Times*, January 10, 1982, 24.

Strother, Jason. "South Korean Students Learn English from Robot Teacher." *VOA News*, March 8, 2011.

Tao, Li. "Xinhua News Agency Debuts AI Anchors in Partnership with Search Engine Sogou." *South China Morning Post*, November 8, 2018. www.scmp.com.

T. C. M. "Parisian Medical Chit-Chat." *Cincinnati Lancet-Clinic: A Weekly Journal Journal of Medicine and Surgery*, no. 89 (1903), 314–318.

Thapliyal, Mansi. "India Outlawed Commercial Surrogacy—Clinics Are Finding Loopholes." *The Conversation*, October 23, 2017. https://theconversation.com.

Tong, Hollington Tong. *Free China's Role in the Asian Crisis*. Washington, DC: Ransdell, 1958.

Twain, Mark. *Roughing It*. Hartford, CT: American, 1872.

Vijayakumar, Gowri. "There Was an Uproar: Reading the Arcane of Reproduction through Sex Work in India." *Viewpoint Magazine*, October 31, 2015. https://viewpointmag.com/2015/10/31/there-was-an-uproar-reading-the-arcane-of-reproduction-through-sex-work-in-india/.

Vonberg, Judith. "Einstein Travel Diaries Reveal Racist Streak." CNN, June 14, 2018. www.cnn.com.

Wee, Sui-Lee. "Young Workers in China: 'We're Human, Not Machines.'" *Fiscal Times*, May 4, 2012. http://www.thefiscaltimes.com.

Welch, William Henry. *Papers and Addresses*. Vol. 3. Baltimore: Johns Hopkins Press, 1920.

Whitman, Walt. "Passage to India." In *Leaves of Grass*, 315–317. New York: G. P. Putnam's Sons, 1907.

Wilson, Audrey. "How Asia's Surrogate Mothers Became a Cross-Border Business." *South China Morning Post*, June 4, 2017. https://www.scmp.com.

Wilson, Jeremy. "My Grueling Day as an Amazon Mechanical Turk." *The Kernel*, August 28, 2013.

Winchell, Ernestine. "An Episode of the Float Lands." *Overland Monthly and Out West Magazine* 14, no. 2 (August 1907): 145–148.

Wong, Staphany. "Decoding the New Generation of Chinese Migrant Workers." *EU-China Civil Society Forum* (September 2, 2010): 1-4.www.eu-china.net.

Wright, Richardson L., and Basset Digby. "Port Arthur Today." *The Bellman* 15, no. 370 (August 16, 1913): 203–206.

Xiaochen, Sun. "Robots? Nope—Just Really Good Athletes." *China Daily*, July 30, 2012.

Yam, Kimberly. "Alex Jones Says Asian People 'Sync Up and Are' in Fights, Joe Rogan Agrees." *Huffington Post*, March 1, 2019, https://www.huffpost.com.

Yang, Jeff. "Asian Pop Robot Nation / Why Japan, and Not America, Is Likely to Be the World's First Cyborg Society." *SF Gate*, August 25, 2005. https://www.sfgate.com/entertainment/article/ASIAN-POP-Robot-Nation-Why-Japan-and-not-3237591.php.

———. "Politicians Play the China Card." NPR, October 27, 2010. https://www.npr.org.

Yang, Wesley. "Paper Tigers." *New York Magazine*, May 8, 2011. www.nymag.com.

Yim Hyun-Su. "Is There a Media Double Standard for K-pop." *Korean Herald*, June 18, 2020. http://www.koreaherald.com/view.php?ud=20200618000951.

Yow, Ho. "Chinese Exclusion: A Benefit or a Harm?" *North American Review* 173, no. 538 (1901): 314–330.

Zap, Claudine. "'Pacific Rim' Called American Propaganda in China." *Yahoo News*, August 27, 2013. www.yahoo.com.

SECONDARY SOURCES

Abnet, Dustin. *The American Robot: A Cultural History*. Chicago: University of Chicago Press, 2020.

Abu-Lughod, Lila. "Writing against Culture: In Richard Gabriel Fox." In *Recapturing Anthropology: Working in the Present*, 137–162. Santa Fe: School of American Research Press, 1991.

Ahiska, Meltem. "Occidentalism: The Historical Fantasy of the Modern." *South Atlantic Quarterly* 102, no. 2 (2003): 351–379.

Al-Bulushi, Yousuf. "Thinking Racial Capitalism and Black Radicalism from Africa: An Intellectual Geography of Cedric Robinson's World-System." *Geoforum*, January 31, 2020, 1–11. https://doi.org/10.1016/j.geoforum.2020.01.018.

Almaguer, Tomas. *Racial Fault Lines: The Historical Origins of White Supremacy in California*. Berkeley: University of California Press, 2008.

Alves, Artur Matos. *Unveiling the Posthuman*. Oxford: Interdisciplinary, 2012.

Andrews, Tim, and Wilson Chew. *Building Brands in Asia: From the Inside Out*. London: Routledge, 2017.

Aneesh, Aneesh. *Virtual Migration: The Programming of Globalization*. Durham, NC: Duke University Press, 2006.

Aoki, Andrew, and Okiyoshi Takeda. *Asian American Politics*. Cambridge: Polity, 2008.

Arendt, Hanna. *The Human Condition*. Chicago: University of Chicago Press, 1998.

Aristotle. "The Ideal State." In *The Structure of Political Geography*, edited by Julian Minghi, 13–17. London: Routledge, 2017.

Arvin, Maile. *Possessing Polynesians: The Science of Settler Colonial Whiteness in Hawaii and Oceania*. Durham, NC: Duke University Press, 2019.

Atanasoski, Neda, and Kalindi Vora. *Surrogate Humanity: Race, Robots, and the Politics of Technological Futures*. Durham, NC: Duke University Press, 2019.

Ayhan, Ayteş. "The 'Other' in the Machine: Oriental Automata and the Mechanization of the Mind." PhD diss., University of California, San Diego, 2012.

———. "Return of the Crowds: Mechanical Turk and Neoliberal States of Exception." In *Digital Labor: The Internet as Playground and Factory*, edited by Trebor Sholz, 87–105. London: Routledge, 2012.

Ayres, Robert. *Energy, Complexity and Wealth Maximization*. New York: Springer, 2016.

Bailly, Christian. *Automata: The Golden Age; 1848–1914*. London: Robert Hale, 2003.

Bakare-Yusuf, Bibi. "The Economy of Violence: Black Bodies and the Unspeakable Terror." In *Feminist Theory and the Body: A Reader*, edited by Janet Price and Margit Shildrick, 311–323. London: Routledge, 1999.

Baldwin, Richard. *The Globotics Upheaval: Globalization, Robotics, and the Future of Work*. Oxford: Oxford University Press, 2019.

Bamber, James. *Sex, Lies and Bar Girls: The ABC's of Bar Fines and Short Times*. Bangkok: Bangkok Books, 2017.

Banchetti-Robino, Marina Paola. "Ontological Tensions in Sixteenth and Seventeenth Century Chemistry: Between Mechanism and Vitalism." *Foundations of Chemistry* 13, no. 3 (2011): 173–186.

Barak, On. *On Time: Technology and Temporality in Modern Egypt*. Berkeley: University of California Press, 2013.

Barker, A. J., and Sydney L. Mayer. *The Japanese War Machine*. New York: Chartwell Books, 1976.

Barthes, Roland. *Empire of Signs*. New York: Hill and Wang, 1982.

———. *Mythologies*. London: Paladin, 1973.

Bartter, Martha. "Young Adults, Science Fiction, and War." In *Young Adult Science Fiction*, edited by Charles William Sullivan, 131–146. Westport, CT: Greenwood, 1999.

Bassett, Ross. *The Technological Indian*. Cambridge, MA: Harvard University Press, 2016.

Baudrillard, Jean. *Simulations*. New York: Semiotext(e), 1983.

Benjamin, Ruha. *Race after Technology: Abolitionist Tools for the New Jim Code*. Bristol, UK: Polity, 2019.

Berby, Harry L., and James D. Brown. *Japanese Military Cartridge Handguns 1893–1945: A Revised and Expanded Edition of Hand Cannons of Imperial Japan*. Atglen, PA: Schiffer, 2003.

Berkove, Lawrence I. "A Parallel Correction in London's 'The Unparalleled Invasion.'" In *Jack London: A Study of the Short Fiction*, edited by Jeanne Campbell, 237–243. New York: Twayne, 1999.

Bert, Ray. *Engineers: From the Great Pyramids to the Pioneers of Space Travel*. New York: DK, 2012.

Biagi, Shirley, and Marilyn Kern-Foxworth, *Facing Difference: Race, Gender, and Mass Media*. Thousand Oaks, CA: Pine Forge, 1997.

Birch, David, Tony Schirato, and Sanjay Srivastava. *Asia: Cultural Politics in the Global Age*. New York: Palgrave, 2001.

Boggs, Carl. *The Hollywood War Machine: US Militarism and Popular Culture*. New York: Routledge, 2017.

Bonacich, Edna. "U.S. Capitalist Development: A Background to Asian Immigration." In *Labor Migration under Capitalism: Asian Workers in the United States before World War II*, edited by Lucie Cheng and Edna Bonacich, 79–129. Berkeley: University of California Press, 2008.

Bradley, Laurel. "Health, Well-Being, and Rights: Mapping the Boundaries of Belonging for Filipino Caregivers in Israel." PhD diss., University of North Carolina at Chapel Hill, 2014.

Buckley, Sandra. *Broken Silence: Voices of Japanese Feminism*. Berkeley: University of California Press, 1997.

Bui, Long T. "Asian Roboticism: Connecting Mechanized Labor to the Automation of Work." *Perspectives on Global Development and Technology* 19, no. 1–2 (2020): 110–126.

———. "Model/Minority Veteran: The Queer Asian American Challenge to Post-9/11 Culture." In *Q&A 2.0: Voices from Queer Asian North America*, edited by Martin Manalansan, Alice Hom, and Kale Fajardo, 257–264. Philadelphia: Temple University Press, 2021.

———. "On Artificial Humanity, Coronavirus Revolutions, and the Zoomanities." *Foundry*, November 2020. https://uchri.org/foundry/on-artificial-humanity-coronavirus-revolutions-and-the-zoomanities/.

Campbell, Perisa. *Chinese Coolie Emigration to Canada*. London: Routledge, 2012.

Caporale, Juvenal. "The Circle, Indigeneity, and Healing: Rehumanizing Chicano, Mexican, and Indigenous Men." PhD diss., Arizona State University, 2020.

Cheah, Pheng. *Inhuman Conditions: On Cosmopolitanism and Human Rights*. Cambridge: Harvard University Press, 2009.

Chen, Kuan-Hsing. *Asia as Method: Toward Deimperialization*. Durham, NC: Duke University Press, 2010.

Chen, Ta. "The Labor Situation in China." *Monthly Labor Review* 11 (1921): 207–213.

Chen, Tina. "Context, Coordinate, Circulation: The Postrepresentational Cartographies of Global Asias." *Verge: Studies in Global Asias* 3, no. 1 (2017): vi–xiv.

Cheng, John. *Astounding Wonder: Imagining Science and Science Fiction in Interwar America*. Philadelphia: University of Pennsylvania Press, 2012.

Chiang, Mark. *The Cultural Capital of Asian American Studies: Autonomy and Representation in the University*. New York: New York University Press, 2009.

Chien, Irene. "Programmed Moves: Race and Embodiment in Fighting and Dancing Videogames." PhD diss., University of California, Berkeley, 2015.

Chinn, Sarah E. *Technology and the Logic of American Racism: A Cultural History of the Body as Evidence*. New York: Continuum, 2000.

Chiu, Daina C. "The Cultural Defense: Beyond Exclusion, Assimilation, and Guilty Liberalism." *California Legal Review* 82 (1994): 1053–1125.

Choi, Franny. *Death by Sex Machine*. Little Rock, AR: Sibling Rivalry, 2017.

Christiansen, Steen. "Posthuman Rights." *Akademisk Kvarteri* 5 (2012): 101–112.

Chronister, Andrea. "Japan-Bashing: How Propaganda Shapes Americans' Perception of the Japanese." Master's thesis, Lehigh University, 1992.

Chuh, Kandice. *Imagine Otherwise: On Asian Americanist Critique*. Durham, NC: Duke University Press, 2003.

Chun, Soonok. *They Are Not Machines: Korean Women Workers and their Fight for Democratic Trade Unionism in the 1970s*. London: Routledge, 2017.

Chun, Wendy. *Control and Freedom: Power and Paranoia in the Age of Fiber Optics*. Cambridge, MA: MIT Press, 2006.

———. "Race and/as Technology; or, How to Do Things to Race." In *Race after the Internet*, edited by Lisa Nakamura and Peter A. Chow-White, 38–60. New York: Routledge, 2009.

———. "Race and Software." In *Alien Encounters: Popular Culture in Asian America*, edited by Mimi Thi Nguyen and Thuy Linh Nguyen, 305–334. Durham, NC: Duke University Press, 2006.

Clausewitz, Carl Von. *On War*. Princeton, NJ: Princeton University Press, 1984.

Clynes, Manfred, and Nathan Kline. "Cyborgs and Space." In *The Cyborg Handbook*, edited by Chris Hables Gray and Francoise Gray, 29–34. New York: Routledge, 1995.

Coleman, Beth. "Race as Technology." *Camera Obscura: Feminism, Culture, and Media Studies* 24 no. 1 (2009): 177–207.

Cooper, Frederick. *Beyond Slavery: Explorations of Race, Labor, and Citizenship in Postemancipation Societies*. Chapel Hill: University of North Carolina Press Books, 2000.

Creef, Elena Tajima. "Re/orientation: The Politics of Japanese American Representation." PhD diss., University of California, Santa Cruz, 1994.

Cunliffe, Marcus. *Chattel Slavery and Wage Slavery: The Anglo-American Context, 1830–1860*. Athens: University of Georgia Press, 2008.

Currarino, Rosanne. "Meat vs. Rice: Working-Class Manhood and Anti-Chinese Hysteria." *Men and Masculinities* 9 (2007): 476–490.

Damarin, Suzanne K. "Women and Information Technology: Framing Some Issues for Education." *Feminist Teacher* 6, no. 2 (1992):16–20.

Darian-Smith, Eve, and Philip C. McCarty. *The Global Turn: Theories, Research Designs, and Methods for Global Studies*. Berkeley: University of California Press, 2017.

Da Silva, Denise Ferreira. *Global Idea of Race*. Minneapolis: University of Minnesota Press, 2007.

———. "1 (life) 1 (life) ÷ 0 (blackness) = ∞ − ∞ or ∞ / ∞: On Matter beyond the Equation of Value." *e-flux* 79 (February 2017). https://www.e-flux.com.

———. "Towards a Critique of the Socio-logos of Justice: The Analytics of Raciality and the Production of Universality." *Social Identities* 7, no. 3 (2001): 421–454.

Day, Iyko. *Alien Capital: Asian Racialization and the Logic of Settler Colonial Capitalism*. Durham, NC: Duke University Press, 2016.

De la Peña, Carolyn. "The History of Technology, the Resistance of Archives, and the Whiteness of Race." *Technology and Culture* 51, no. 4 (2010): 919–937.

Descartes, René. "Treatise on Man." In *The Nature of Life: Classical and Contemporary Perspectives from Philosophy and Science*, edited by Mark A. Bedau and Carol E. Cleland, 15–20. New York: Cambridge University Press, 2010.

De Tocqueville, Alexis. *Democracy in America*. New York: Regnery, 2003.

Dombeck, Mark. "Diagnosing Seung-Hui Cho." Mentalhealth.net, accessed February 3, 2021. https://www.mentalhelp.net/blogs/diagnosing-seung-hui-cho//.

Dower, John. *Cultures of War: Pearl Harbor/Hiroshima/9-11/Iraq*. New York: Norton, 2012.

———. *War without Mercy: Pacific War*. New York: Pantheon, 2012.

Du Gay, Paul. *Doing Cultural Studies: The Story of the Sony Walkman*. London: Sage, 2013.

Durkheim, Emile. *The Division of Labor in Society*. New York: Simon and Schuster, 2014.

Elson, Diane, and Ruth Pearson. "'Nimble Fingers Make Cheap Workers': An Analysis of Women's Employment in Third World Export Manufacturing." *Feminist Review* 7, no. 1 (1981): 87–107.

Eng, David, Teem Eng, Ruskola Eng, and Shen Shuang. "Introduction: China and the Human." *Social Text* 29, no. 4 (2011): 1–27.

Eperjesi, John. *The Imperialist Imaginary: Visions of Asia and the Pacific in American Culture*. Hanover, NH: Dartmouth University Press, 2005.

Esmeir, Samera. *Juridical Humanity: A Colonial History*. Stanford, CA: Stanford University Press, 2012.

Esperanza, Miyake. "Politicizing Motorcycles: Racialized Capital of Technology, Techno-Orientalism and Japanese Temporality." *East Asian Journal of Popular Culture* 2, no. 2 (2016): 209–224.

Espiritu, Yen Le. *Asian American Women and Men: Labor, Laws, and Love*. Lanham, MD: Rowman & Littlefield, 2008.

———. *Body Counts: The Vietnam War and Militarized Refugees*. Berkeley: University of California Press, 2014.

Estes, Donald H. "Before the War: The Japanese in San Diego." *Journal of San Diego History* 24, no. 4 (1978): 425–456.

Evans, Woody. "Posthuman Rights: Dimensions of Transhuman Worlds." *Teknokultura* 12, no. 2 (2015): 373–384.

Eze, E. C. "The Color of Reason: The Idea of 'Race' in Kant's Anthropology." In *Postcolonial African Philosophy: A Critical Reader*, edited by E. C. Eze, 103–140. Cambridge, MA: Blackwell, 1997.

Faleomavaega, Eni F. H. "Asian Pacific American Heritage Month 1992: Entering into the Pacific Century." In *Gale Encyclopedia of Multicultural America: Primary Documents—Volume 2*, edited by Jeffrey Lehman, 684–688. Farmington Hills, MI: Gale, 1999.

Fan, Christopher. "Asian/American Antibodies: An Ending." Yale University, April 14, 2016. http://post45.research.yale.edu.

———. "Techno-Orientalism with Chinese Characteristics: Maureen F. McHugh's China Mountain Zhang." *Journal of Transnational American Studies* 6, no. 1 (2015). http://dx.doi.org.

Far Eastern Economic Review. "Review 200: Asia's Leading Companies." *Far Eastern Economic Review* 15 (January 19, 1995): 38.

Farley, Anthony Paul. "Apogee of the Commodity." *DePaul Law Review* 53 (2004): 1229–1246.

Fong, Colleen Valerie Jin. "Tracing the Origins of a 'Model Minority': A Study of the Depictions of Chinese Americans in Popular Magazines." PhD diss., University of Oregon, 1990.

Foucault, Michel. *Discipline and Punish: The Birth of the Prison*. New York: Vintage, 2012.

———. *The History of Sexuality: An Introduction*. New York: Random House, 2012.

Fujitani, Takashi. *Race for Empire: Koreans as Japanese and Japanese as Americans during World War II*. Berkeley: University of California Press, 2011.

Fukuyama, Francis. *The End of History and the Last Man*. New York: Simon and Schuster, 2006.

———. *Our Posthuman Future: Consequences of the Biotechnology Revolution*. New York: Farrar, Straus, and Giroux, 2003.

Galison, Peter. "The Ontology of the Enemy: Norbert Wiener and the Cybernetic Vision." *Critical Inquiry* 21, no. 1 (1994): 228–266.

Gálvez, Alyshia. *Patient Citizens, Immigrant Mothers: Mexican Women, Public Prenatal Care, and the Birth Weight Paradox*. New Brunswick, NJ: Rutgers University Press, 2011.

Geoghegan, Bernard Dionysius. "Orientalism and Informatics: Alterity from the Chess-Playing Turk to Amazon's Mechanical Turk." *Ex-position* 43 (2020): 45–90.

Ghosh, Bishnupriya. *Global Icons: Apertures to the Popular*. Durham, NC: Duke University Press, 2011.

Golden, Daniel. *The Price of Admission: How America's Ruling Class Buys Its Way into Elite Colleges and Who Gets Left outside the Gates*. New York: Random House, 2006.

Gonzalez, Jennifer. "Envisioning Cyborg Bodies: Notes from Current Research." In *The Cyborg Handbook*, edited by Chris Hables Gray, Heidi J. Figueroa-Sarriera, and Steven Mentor, 267–280. New York: Routledge, 1995.

Goul, Pauline. "An Ecology of Waste: Transatlantic Excess in Renaissance France." PhD diss., Cornell University, 2017.

Gould, Stephen Jay. *The Mismeasure of Man*. New York: W. W. Norton, 1996.

Grewal, Inderpal, and Caren Kaplan, eds. *Scattered Hegemonies: Postmodernity and Transnational Feminist Practices*. Minneapolis: University of Minnesota Press, 994.

Gringas, Yves. *Éloge de L'homo Techno-Logicus*. Saint-Laurent, Quebec: Les Editions Fides, 2005.

Guattari, Félix. *Molecular Revolution: Psychiatry and Politics*. London: Puffin Books, 1984.

Guevarra, Anna Romina Guevarra. "Mediations of Care: Brokering Labour in the Age of Robotics." *Pacific Affairs* 91, no. 4 (2018): 739–758.

Gullett, Jim. *Good News to the Red Planet*. New York: iUniverse, 2005.

Guterl, Matthew Pratt. "After Slavery: Asian Labor, the American South, and the Age of Emancipation." *Journal of World History* 14, no. 2 (2003): 209–241.

———. *American Mediterranean: Southern Slaveholders in the Age of Emancipation*. Boston: Harvard University Press, 2008.

Gutiérrez, Elena R. *The Politics of Mexican-Origin Women's Reproduction*. Austin: University of Texas Press, 2009.

Hafstein, Valdimar Tr. "Bodies of Knowledge." *Ethnologia Europaea* 33, no. 1 (2003): 5–12.

Hagedorn, Jessica. "Sex Workers' Manifesto." In *Encyclopedia of Prostitution and Sex Work*, vol. 2, edited by Melissa Hope Ditmore, 627–633. Westport, CT: Greenwood, 2006.

Hall, Stuart. "Introduction: Who Needs 'Identity'?" In *Questions of Cultural Identity*, edited by Stuart Hall and Paul Du Gay, 1–17. London: Sage, 1996.

———. "Race, Articulation, and Societies Structured in Dominance." In *Black British Cultural Studies: A Reader*, edited by Houston A. Baker Jr., Manthia Diawara, and Ruth H. Lindeborg, 16–60. Chicago: University of Chicago Press, 1996.

Hammad, Hanan. *Industrial Sexuality: Gender, Urbanization, and Social Transformation in Egypt*. Austin: University of Texas Press, 2016.

Hara, Makiko. "Others in the Third Millennium." In *The Uncanny: Experiments in Cyborg Culture*, edited by Bruce Grenville, 237–247. Vancouver: Vancouver Art Gallery, 2001.

Haraway, Donna. "Anthropocene, Capitalocene, Plantationocene, Chthulucene: Making Kin." *Environmental Humanities* 6, no. 1 (2015): 159–165.

———. *Simians, Cyborgs, and Women: The Reinvention of Nature*. London: Routledge 2013.

Hård, Mikael, and Andrew Jamison, eds. *The Intellectual Appropriation of Technology: Discourses on Modernity, 1900–1939*. Boston: MIT Press, 1998.

Hardt, Michael, and Antonio Negri. *Empire*. Boston: Harvard University Press, 2001.

Hayot, Eric. "Chinese Bodies, Chinese Futures." *Representations* 99 (2007): 99–129.

———. "Coolie." In *The Routledge Companion to Asian American and Pacific Islander Literature*, edited by Rachel Lee, 81–90. London: Routledge, 2014.

Hegel, Georg Wilhelm Friedrich. *Phenomenology of Spirit*. Oxford: Clarendon Press, 1998.

———. *The Philosophy of History*. New York: Dove, 2004.

Heng, Geraldine. *The Invention of Race in the European Middle Ages*. Cambridge: Cambridge University Press, 2018.

Ho, Christina. "The Hew Meritocracy or Over-Schooled Robots? Public Attitudes on Asian-Australian Education Cultures." *Journal of Ethnic and Migration Studies* 43, no. 14 (2017): 2346–2362.

Ho, Shawn. "A Critique of the Motivations behind Negative Action against Asian Americans in U.S. Universities: The Model Victims." *Columbia Journal of Race and Law* 91 (2015): 79–99.

Hoang, Gia Phan. "Free Subjects: Black Civic Identity and the Invention of the Asiatic." *Law and Humanities eJournal* (September 2003): 1–45. https://poseidon01.ssrn.com.

Hong, Grace Kyungwon. *Death beyond Disavowal: The Impossible Politics of Difference.* Minneapolis: University of Minnesota Press, 2015.

hooks, bell. *Talking Back: Thinking Feminist, Thinking Black.* New York: South End Press, 1989.

Horne, Gerald. *Race War: White Supremacy and the Japanese Attack on the British Empire.* New York: New York University Press, 2004.

Hornyak, Timothy. *Loving the Machine.* Tokyo: Kodansha International, 2006.

Hough, Kenneth. "Demon Courage and Dread Engines: America's Reaction to the Russo-Japanese War and the Genesis of the Japanese Invasion Sublime." In *Techno-Orientalism: Imagining Asia in Speculative Fiction, History, and Media*, edited by David Roh, Betsy Huang, and Greta A. Niu, 23–39. New Brunswick, NJ: Rutgers University Press, 2015.

Hounshell, David A. *From the American System to Mass Production, 1800–1932.* Baltimore: Johns Hopkins University Press, 1984.

Hua, Julietta. "The Foxconn Suicides: Human Vitality and Capitalist Consumption." *Women's Studies in Communication* 41, no. 4 (2018): 320–323.

———. *Trafficking Women's Human Rights.* Minneapolis: University of Minnesota Press, 2011.

Huang, Betsy. "Premodern Orientalist Science Fictions." *Melus* 33, no. 4 (2008): 23–43.

Huang, Michelle. "The Posthuman Subject in/of Asian American Literature." *Oxford Research Encyclopedia of Literature*, February 25, 2019. https://oxfordre.com.

Hughes, James. *Citizen Cyborg: Why Democratic Societies Must Respond to the Redesigned Human of the Future.* New York: Basic Books, 2004.

Hyman, Louis. *Temp: How American Work, American Business, and the American Dream Became Temporary.* New York: Penguin, 2018.

Jenkins, Richard. "Disenchantment, Enchantment and Re-enchantment: Max Weber at the Millennium." *Max Weber Studies* 1, no. 1 (2000): 11–32.

Jenks, Kevin. "Before the 'Yellow Peril.'" *Social Contract* 6, no. 4 (Summer 1996): 259–299.

Johnston, Lynda, and Robyn Longhurst. *Space, Place, and Sex: Geographies of Sexualities.* Lanham, MD: Rowman & Littlefield, 2010.

Jung, Moon-Ho. *Coolies and Cane: Race, Labor, and Sugar in the Age of Emancipation.* Baltimore: Johns Hopkins University Press, 2006.

Jung, Moon-Kie. *Reworking Race: The Making of Hawaii's Interracial Labor Movement.* New York: Columbia University Press, 2006.

Kaibara, Helen. "The Transpacific Origins of the 'Model Minority' Myth of Japanese Americans." *Studies on Asia* 4, no. 2 (2014): 5–34.

Kane, Thomas J. *The Price of Admission: Rethinking How Americans Pay for College.* Washington, DC: Brookings Institution, 2010.

Kang, Laura. "Si(gh)ting Asian/American Women as Transnational Labor." *Positions: East Asia Cultures Critique* 5, no. 2 (1997) 403–437.

Kang, Minsoo. "Building the Sex Machine: The Subversive Potential of the Female Robot." *Intertexts* 9, no. 1 (2005): 1–19.

———. "The Machine-Man to the Automaton-Man: The Enlightenment Origins of the Mechanistic Imagery of Humanity." In *Vital Matters: Eighteenth-Century Views of*

Conception, Life and Death, edited by Helen Deutsch and Mary Terall, 148–173. Toronto: University of Toronto Press, 2011.

Kaiwar, Vasant, and Sucheta Mazumdar. "Race, Orient, Nation in the Time-Space of Modernity." In *Antinomies of Modernity: Essays on Race, Orient, Nation,* edited by Vasant Kaiwar and Sucheta Mazumdar, 261–298. Durham, NC: Duke University Press, 2003.

Kasson, John F. *Civilizing the Machine: Technology and Republican Values in America, 1776-1900.* New York: Grossman, 1976.

Kelley, Robin. "What Did Cedric Robinson Mean by Racial Capitalism." *Boston Review,* January 12, 2017. www.bostonreview.net.

Kelts, Roland. *Japanamerica: How Japanese Pop Culture Has Invaded the U.S.* New York: St. Martin's, 2006.

Keo, Peter. *Leadership in an Age of Compassion and Empathy.* Hauppauge, NY: Nova Science, 2021.

Kevorkian, Martin. *Color Monitors: The Black Face of Technology in America.* Ithaca, NY: Cornell University Press, 2006.

Kim, Joo-Ok. "'Training Guatemalan Campesinos to Work Like Korean Peasants': Taxonomies and Temporalities of East Asian Labor Management in Latin America." *Verge: Studies in Global Asias* 3, no. 2 (2017): 195–216.

Kindleberger, Charles. *World Economic Primacy: 1500–1990.* Oxford: Oxford University Press on Demand, 1996.

Kohli, Harinder S., Ashok Sharma, and Anil Sood. *Asia 2050: Realizing the Asian Century,* edited by Harinder S. Kohli, Ashok Sharma, and Anil Sood. New Delhi: SAGE Publications India, 2011.

Koistinen, Paul A. C. *Arsenal of World War II: The Political Economy of American Warfare, 1940-1945.* Lawrence: University Press of Kansas, 2004.

Koizumi, Kenichiro. "In Search of Wakon: The Cultural Dynamics of the Rise of Manufacturing Technology in Postwar Japan." *Technology and Culture* 43, no. 1 (2002): 29–49.

Kong, Travis. "More than a Sex Machine: Accomplishing Masculinity among Chinese Male Sex Workers in the Hong Kong Sex Industry." *Deviant Behavior* 30, no. 8 (2009): 715–745.

Koshy, Susan. *Sexual Naturalization: Asian Americans and Miscegenation.* Stanford, CA: Stanford University Press, 2004.

Kyung, Chung Hyun. *Struggle to Be the Sun Again: Introducing Asian Women's Theology.* Maryknoll, NY: Orbis Books, 1990.

———. "Your Comfort versus My Death." In *War's Dirty Secret: Rape, Prostitution, and Other Crimes against Women,* edited by Anne Llewellyn Barstow, 13–25. Boston: Pilgrim, 2000.

La Bare, Joshua. "'The Future': Wrapped . . . in That Mysterious Japanese Way." *Science Fiction Studies* 27, no. 5 (2000): 22–48.

Lai, Ah Eng. *Peasants, Proletarians and Prostitutes: A Preliminary Investigation into the Work of Chinese Women in Colonial Malay.* Singapore: Institute of Southeast Asia, 1986.

Lai, Larissa. *Automaton Biographies.* Vancouver: Arsenal Pulp, 2010.

Lake, Marilyn, and Henry Reynolds. *Drawing the Global Colour Line: White Men's Countries and the Question of Racial Equality.* Melbourne: Melbourne University, 2008.

Lean, Eugenia Lean. "Making the Chinese Copycat: Trademarks and Recipes in Early Twentieth-Century Global Science and Capitalism." *Osiris* 33, no. 1 (2018): 271–293.

Lee, Jerry Won, ed. *The Sociolinguistics of Global Asias.* London: Routledge, 2022.

Lee, Rachel. *The Exquisite Corpse of Asian America: Biopolitics, Biosociality, and Posthuman Ecologies*. New York: New York University Press, 2014.

Lee, Rachel, and Sau-ling Wong. "Introduction." In *Asian America.Net: Ethnicity, Nationalism, and Cyberspace*, edited by Rachel Lee and Sau-ling Wong, xiii–xxxv. New York: Routledge, 2003.

Lee, Robert G. "The Cold War Construction of the Model Minority Myth." In *Contemporary Asian America: A Multidisciplinary Reader*, edited by Min Zhou and J. V. Gatewood, 469–484. New York: New York University Press, 2007.

———. *Orientals: Asian Americans in Popular Culture*. Philadelphia: Temple University Press, 1999.

Lenin, Vladimir. *Imperialism: The Highest Stage of Capitalism*. Chippendale: Resistance Books, 1999.

Levidow, Les, and Keven Robbins, eds. *Cyborg Worlds: The Military Information Society*. London: Free Association Books, 1989.

Lifton, Robert Jay. *Death in Life: Survivors of Hiroshima*. Chapel Hill: University of North Carolina Press, 2012.

Ling, L. H. M. "Sex Machine: Global Hypermasculinity and Images of the Asian Woman in Modernity." *Positions* 7, no. 2 (1999): 277–306.

Liu, Catherine. *Copying Machines: Taking Notes for the Automaton*. Minneapolis: University of Minnesota Press, 2000.

London, London, Dale L. Walker, and Jeanne Campbell Reesman. *No Mentor but Myself: Jack London on Writers and Writing*. Stanford, CA: Stanford University Press, 1999.

Lowe, Annie. "Narratives of Technological Globalization and Outsourced Call Centers in India: Droids, Mimic Machines, Automatons, and Bad'Borgs." PhD diss., University of Kansas, 2014.

Lowe, Lisa. *Immigrant Acts: On Asian American Cultural Politics*. Durham, NC: Duke University Press, 1996.

———. "The Intimacy of Four Continents." In *Haunted by Empire: Geographies of Intimacy in North American History*, edited by Ann Laura Stoler, 191–212. Durham, NC: Duke University Press, 2006.

Lozano-Méndez, Artur. "Techno-Orientalism in East-Asian Contexts: Reiteration, Diversification, Adaptation." In *Counterpoints: Edward Said's Legacy*, edited by May Telmissany and Stephanie Tara Schwartz, 185–210. Newcastle upon Tyne, UK: Cambridge: Cambridge Scholars, 2010.

Lucas, Kristen, Dongjing Kang, and Zhou Li. "Workplace Dignity in a Total Institution: Examining the Experiences of Foxconn's Migrant Workforce." *Journal of Business Ethics* 114, no. 1 (2013): 91–106.

Luckhust, Roger. *Zombies: A Cultural History*. London: Reaktion Books, 2015.

Lüthy, Christoph. "Historical and Philosophical Reflections on Natural, Enhanced and Artificial Men and Women." In *Engineering the Human: Human Enhancement between Fiction and Fascination*, edited by Bert-Jaap Koops, Christoph H. Lüthy, Annemiek Nelis, Carla Sieburgh, J. P. M. Jansen, and Monika S. Schmid, 11–28. Berlin: Springer, 2013.

Ly, Lynn. "(Im)possible Futures: Liberal Capitalism, Vietnamese Sniper Women, and Queer Asian Possibility." *Feminist Formations* 29, no. 1 (2017): 136–160.

Lye, Colleen. *America's Asia: Racial Form and American Literature, 1893–1945*. Princeton, NJ: Princeton University Press, 2005.

Mahbubani, Kishore. "The Case against the West: America and Europe in the Asian Century." *Foreign Affairs* 87, no. 3 (2008): 111–124.

Manalansan, Martin. *Global Divas*. Durham, NC: Duke University Press, 2003.

Mantovani, Giuseppe. "Virtual Reality as a Communication Environment: Consensual Hallucination, Fiction, and Possible Selves." *Human Relation* 48, no. 6 (1995): 669–683.

Marcuse, Herbert. *One-Dimensional Man: Studies in the Ideology of Advanced Industrial Society*. London: Routledge, 2013.

Marez, Curtis. *Farm Worker Futurism: Speculative Technologies of Resistance*. Minneapolis: University of Minnesota Press, 2016.

Marx, Karl. "The British Rule in India." *New-York Herald Tribune*, June 25, 1853, https://www.marxists.org.

———. *Capital: Volume One; A Critique of Political Economy*. Moscow: Progress, 1965.

———. *Critique of Hegel's Philosophy of Right*. New York: Press Syndicate of the University of Cambridge, 1977.

———. *Grundrisse*. London: Penguin, 1973.

Marx, Karl, and Friedrich Engels. *The Communist Manifesto*. London: Echo Library, 2009.

Marx, Leo. *The Machine in the Garden: Technology and the Pastoral Ideal in America*. Oxford: Oxford University Press, 1964.

Matsumae, Tatsurō. *The Limits of Defense: Japan as an Unsinkable Aircraft Carrier*. Tokyo: Tokai University Press, 1988.

May, R. J. "The Domestic in Foreign Policy: The Flor Contemplacion Case and Philippine-Singapore Relations." *Pilipinas* 29 (1997): 63–76.

Mbembe, Achille. "Necropower." *Public Culture* 15, no. 1 (2003): 11–40.

McKittrick, Katherine. *Dear Science and Other Stories*. Durham, NC: Duke University Press, 2020.

———. "Mathematics Black Life." *Black Scholar* 44, no. 2 (2014): 16–28.

McLeod, Ken. "Afro-Samurai: Techno-Orientalism and Contemporary Hip-Hop." *Popular Music* 32, no. 2 (2013): 259–275.

McQuaid, Kim. *The Anxious Years: America in the Vietnam-Watergate Era*. London: Harper Collins, 1990.

Meisner, Maurice. "The Despotism of Concepts: Wittfogel and Marx on China." *China Quarterly* 16 (1963): 99–111.

Menon, Vinay. "Arthur Chu's Dangerous Game of *Jeopardy!*" *The Star*, February 21, 2014. www.thestar.com.

Metraux, Daniel A. "Jack London Reporting from Tokyo and Manchuria: The Forgotten Role of an Influential Observer of Early Modern Asia." *Asia Pacific: Perspectives* 8 (June 2008): 1–6.

Mies, Maria. *Patriarchy and Accumulation on a World Scale: Women in the International Division of Labour*. London: Zed Books, 2014.

Miller, Laura. "Elevator Girls Moving in and out of the Box." In *Modern Girls on the Go: Gender, Mobility, and Labor in Japan*, edited by Alisa Freedman, Laura Miller, and Christine Yano, 41–65 Stanford, CA: Stanford University Press, 2013.

Min, Eungjun. "Demythologizing the 'Model Minority.'" In *The Emerging Monoculture: Assimilation and the Model Minority*, edited by William E. Watson and Sondra Cuban, 191–202. Santa Barbara, CA: Greenwood, 2003.

Molina, Natalia. *Fit to Be Citizens? Public Health and Race in Los Angeles, 1879–1939*. Berkeley: University of California Press, 2006.

Moon, Katherine. *Sex among Allies: Military Prostitution in US-Korea Relations*. New York: Columbia University Press, 1997.

Morley, David. *Media, Modernity, and Technology: Geography of the New*. New York: Routledge, 2006.

Morley, David, and Kevin Robins. *Spaces of Identity: Global Media, Electronic Landscapes, and Cultural Boundaries*. London: Routledge, 2013.

Mosco, Vincent. *The Digital Sublime-Myth, Power, and Cyberspace*. Cambridge, MA: MIT Press, 2005.

Mumford, Lewis. *The Myth of the Machine: Technics and Human Development*. New York: Harcourt Brace Jovanovich, 1967.

Murata, Junichi. "Creativity of Technology: An Origin of Modernity?" In *Modernity and Technology*, edited by Thomas J. Misa, Philip Brey, and Andrew Feenberg, 227–253. Cambridge, MA: MIT Press, 2003.

Musser, Amber Jamilla. *Sensual Excess: Queer Femininity and Brown Jouissance*. New York: New York University Press, 2018.

Myrdal, Gunner. *An American Dilemma*. New York: Harper and Brothers, 1944.

Nakamura, Lisa. *Cybertypes: Race, Ethnicity, and Identity on the Internet*. New York: Routledge, 2013.

Naranch, Bradley. "'Colonized Body,' 'Oriental Machine': Debating Race, Railroads, and the Politics of Reconstruction in Germany and East Africa, 1906–1910." *Central European History* 33, vol. 3 (2000): 299–338.

Needham, Joseph, with Wang Ling. *Science and Civilization in China*. Vol. 2. Cambridge: Cambridge University Press, 1956.

Ng, Frank. *The Taiwanese Americans*. London: Greenwood, 1998.

Ngai, Pun, and Jenny Chan. "Global Capital, the State, and Chinese Works: The Foxconn Experience." *Modern China* 38, no. 4 (2012): 383–410.

Nguyen, Ly Thuy. "Queer Dis/inheritance and Refugee Futures." *Women's Studies Quarterly* 48, no. 1 (2020): 218–235.

Nguyen, Mimi. "Queer Cyborgs and New Mutants: Race, Sexuality, and Prosthetic Sociality in Digital Space." In *American Studies: An Anthology*, edited by Janice Radway, Barry Shank, Kevin Gaines, and Penny Von Eschen, 372–384. Oxford: John Wiley & Sons, 2009.

———. "Tales of an Asiatic Geek Girl: Slant from Paper to Pixels." In *Technicolor: Race, Technology and Everyday Life*, 177–190. New York: New York University Press.

Niu, Greta Aiyu. "Techno-Orientalism, Nanotechnology, Posthumans, and Post-Posthumans in Neal Stephenson's and Linda Nagata's Science Fiction." *Melus* 33, no. 4 (2008): 73–96.

Nye, David E. *American Technological Sublime*. Cambridge, MA: MIT Press, 1994.

O'Connell Davidson, Julia, and Jacqueline Sanchez Taylor. "Fantasy Islands: Exploring the Demand for Sex Tourism." In *Sun, Sex, and Gold: Tourism and Sex Work in the Caribbean*, edited by Kamala Kempadoo, 37–54. New York: Rowman & Littlefield, 1999.

Omi, Michael, and Howard Winant. *Racial Formation in the United States*. London: Routledge, 2014.

Ong, Aihwa. "The Gender and Labor Politics of Postmodernity." *Annual Review of Anthropology* 20 (1991): 279–309.

———. *Spirits of Resistance and Capitalist Discipline: Factory Women in Malaysia*. New York: SUNY Press, 2010.

———. "Techno-Migrants in the Network Economy." in *Global America?: The Cultural Consequences of Globalization*, ed. Ulrich Beck, Natan Sznaider, and Rainer Winter, 153–173. Liverpool, UK: Liverpool University Press, 2003.

Pagden, Anthony. "Europe: Conceptualizing a Continent." In *The Idea of Europe: From Antiquity to the European Union*, edited by Anthony Pagden and Lee H. Hamilton, 33–54. Cambridge: Cambridge University Press, 2002.

——. *Worlds at War: The 2,500-Year Struggle between East and West*. Oxford: Oxford University Press, 2008.

Paisley, Fiona. *Glamour in the Pacific: Cultural Internationalism and Race Politics in the Women's Pan-Pacific*. Honolulu: University of Hawaii Press, 2009.

Park, Jane Chi Hyun. *Yellow Future: Oriental Style in Hollywood Cinema*. Minneapolis: University of Minnesota Press, 2010.

Park, Young. *The Dark Side: Immigrants, Racism, and the American Way*. Bloomington, IN: iUniverse, 2012.

Parreñas, Rhacel Salazar. "'White Trash' Meets the 'Little Brown Monkeys': The Taxi Dance Hall as a Site of Interracial and Gender Alliances between White Working-Class Women and Filipino Immigrant Men in the 1920s and 30s." *Amerasia Journal* 24, no. 2 (1998): 115–134.

Pate, Soojin. *From Orphan to Adoptee: U.S. Empire and Genealogies of Korean Adoption*. Minneapolis: University of Minnesota Press, 2014.

Patterson, Christopher, and Y-Dang Troeung. "Organic and Inorganic Chinas: Desire and Fatigue in Global Hong Kong." *Amerasia Journal* 45, no. 3 (2019): 280–298.

Patton, Venetria K. *Women in Chains: The Legacy of Slavery in Black Women's Fiction*. Albany: State University of New York, 2000.

Peffer, George Anthony. *If They Don't Bring Their Women Here: Chinese Female Immigration before Exclusion*. Chicago: University of Illinois Press, 1999.

Penley, Constance, and Andrew Ross. "Introduction." In *Technoculture*, edited Constance Penley and Andrew Ross, vii–xvii. Minneapolis: University of Minnesota Press, 1991.

Phạm, Minh-Ha. "Playing (with) Stereotypes: Comedy and the Construction of Asian American Identities." PhD diss., University of California, Berkeley, 2006.

Pineda-Ofreneo, Rosalinda. "Issues in the Philippine Electronics Industry: A Global Perspective." *Economic and Industrial Democracy* 6, no. 2 (1985): 185–207.

Popper, Karl Raimund. *Of Clouds and Clocks: An Approach to the Problem of Rationality and the Freedom of Man*. Seattle: University of Washington Press, 1965.

Porter, Patrick. *Military Orientalism: Eastern War through Western Eyes*. New York: Columbia University Press, 2009.

Prasso, Sheridan, and Joachim Paul Prassol. *The Asian Mystique: Dragon Ladies, Geisha Girls, and Our Fantasies of the Exotic Orient*. New York: Public Affairs, 2005.

Precup, Amelia. "All Cyborgs Are Asian: The Ethnic Implications of the Cyborg-topian Future in Karen Tei Yamashita's Anime Wong." *Transylvanian Review* 26 (2017): 247–256.

Puar, Jasbir. *Terrorist Assemblages: Homonationalism in Queer Times*. Durham, NC: Duke University Press, 2018.

Puzar, Alijosa. "Asian Dolls and the Westernized Gaze: Notes on the Female Dollification in South Korea." *Asian Women* 27, no. 2 (2011): 81–111.

Quan, H. L. T. *Growth against Democracy: Savage Developmentalism in the Modern World*. Washington, DC: Lexington Books, 2012.

Raiford, Wanda. "Race, Robots, and the Law." In *New Boundaries in Political Science Fiction*, edited Donald M. Hassler and Clyde Wilcox, 93–112. Columbia: University of South Carolina Press, 2008.

Ramachandran, Vibhuti. "Saving the Slaving Child: Domestic Work, Labor Trafficking, and the Politics of Rescue in India." *Humanity: An International Journal of Human Rights, Humanitarianism, and Development* 10, no. 3 (2019): 339–362.

Reyes, Victoria. *Global Borderlands: Fantasy, Violence, and Empire in Subic Bay, Philippines*. Stanford, CA: Stanford University Press, 2019.

Rhee, Jennifer. *The Robotic Imaginary: The Human and the Price of Dehumanized Labor.* Minneapolis: University of Minnesota, 2018.

Rhee, Margaret. *Love, Robot.* New York: Operating System, 2017.

———. "Racial Recalibration: Nam June Paik's K-456." *Asian Diasporic Visual Cultures and the Americas* 1 (2015): 285–309.

Robertson, Jennifer. "Japan's First Cyborg? Miss Nippon, Eugenics and Wartime Technologies of Beauty, Body and Blood." *Body and Society* 7, no. 1 (2001): 1–34.

———. *Robo Sapiens Japanicus: Robots, Gender, Family, and the Japanese Nation.* Berkeley: University of California Press, 2017.

Robinson, Cedric. *Black Marxism: The Making of the Black Radical Tradition.* Chapel Hill, NC: University of North Carolina Press, 2000.

Rodogno, Davide. "European Legal Doctrines on Intervention and the Status of the Ottoman Empire within the 'Family of Nations' throughout the Nineteenth Century." *Journal of the History of International Law / Revue D'histoire du Droit International* 18, no. 1 (2016): 5–41.

Rodriguez, Robyn Magalit. *Migrants for Export: How the Philippine State Brokers Labor to the World.* Minneapolis: University of Minnesota Press, 2010.

Rodriguez, Robyn Magalit, and Vernadette Vicuna Gonzalez. "Asian American Auto/Biographies: The Gendered Limits of Consumer Citizenship in Import Subcultures." In *Alien Encounters: Popular Culture in Asian America*, edited by Mimi Nguyen and Thuy Tu Linh, 247–270. Durham, NC: Duke University Press, 2007.

Roh, David S. "Scientific Management in East Goes West: The Japanese and American Construction of Korean Labor." *MELUS: Multi-Ethnic Literature of the United States* 37, no. 1 (2012): 83–104.

Roh, David S., Betsy Huang, and Greta A. Niu. "Desiring Machines, Repellant Subjects: A Conclusion." In *Techno-Orientalism: Imagining Asia in Speculative Fiction, History, and Media*, edited by David S. Roh, Betsy Huang, and Greta A. Niu, 221–226. New Brunswick, NJ: Rutgers University Press, 2015.

———. "Technologizing Orientalism: An Introduction." In *Techno-Orientalism: Imagining Asia in Speculative Fiction, History, and Media*, edited by David S. Roh, Betsy Huang, and Greta A. Niu, 221–226. New Brunswick, NJ: Rutgers University Press, 2015.

———. eds. *Techno-Orientalism: Imagining Asia in Speculative Fiction, History, and Media.* New Brunswick, NJ: Rutgers University Press, 2015.

Rosheim, Mark. *Leonardo's Lost Robots.* Berlin: Springer Science and Business Media, 2006.

Rowen, Henry S., Marguerite Gong Hancock, and William F. Miller, eds. *Making IT: The Rise of Asia in High Tech.* Stanford, CA: Stanford University Press, 2007.

Ruiz, Sandra. *Ricanness: Enduring Time in Anticolonial Performance.* New York: New York University Press, 2019.

Rusmisel, Levi Clyde. *Industrial-Commercial Geography of the United States.* New York: A. N. Palmer, 1914.

Rutsky, Randolph L. *High Technē: Art and Technology from the Machine Aesthetic to the Posthuman.* Minneapolis: University of Minnesota Press, 1999.

Sacksteder, William. "Man the Artificer: Notes on Animals, Humans and Machines in Hobbes." *Southern Journal of Philosophy* 22, no. 1 (1984): 105–121.

Said, Edward. *Orientalism.* New York: Pantheon, 1978.

———. "Orientalism Once More." *Development and Change* 35, no. 5 (2004): 869–879.

Schlund-Vials, Cathy. *Modeling Citizenship: Jewish and Asian American Writing.* Philadelphia: Temple University Press, 2011.

Schmidt, Björn A. *Visualizing Orientalness: Chinese Immigration and Race in US Motion Pictures, 1910s–1930s*. Cologne: Böhlau Verlag Köln Weimar, 2017.

Schodt, Frederick L. *Inside the Robot Kingdom: Japan, Mechantronics, and the Coming Robotopia*. Tokyo: Kodansha International, 1998.

Schwab, Klaus. *The Fourth Industrial Revolution*. New York: Crown Business, 2017.

Scott, Reynolds Nelson. *Steel Drivin' Man: John Henry, the Untold Story of an American Legend*. London: Oxford University Press, 2006.

Scranton, Philip. *Endless Novelty: Specialty Production and American Industrialization, 1865–1925*. Princeton, NJ: Princeton University Press, 1997.

Sengupta, Ritam. "The Punkah and Its Pullers: A Short History." *Servants Pasts: European Research Council*, August 10, 2020. https://servantspasts.wordpress.com/2020/08/10/the-punkah-and-its-pullers-a-short-history/.

Sharmila, Rudrappa. "Cyber-Coolies and Techno-Braceros: Race and Commodification of Indian Information Technology Guest Workers in the United States." *University of San Francisco Law Review* 44 (2009): 353–372.

Shibusawa, Naoko. *America's Geisha Ally*. Cambridge, MA: Harvard University Press, 2006.

Shin, Haerin. "Engineering the Techno-Orient: The Hyperrealization of Post-Racial Politics in *Cloud Atlas*." In *Dis-orienting Planets: Racial Representations of Asia in Science Fiction*, edited by Isiah Lavender III, 131–144. Jackson: University Press of Mississippi, 2017.

Shinozuka, Jeannie N. "Deadly Perils: Japanese Beetles and the Pestilential Immigrant, 1920s–1930s." *American Quarterly* 65, no. 4 (2013): 831–852.

Siddiqi, Dina M. "Miracle Worker or Womanmachine? Tracking (Trans) National Realities in Bangladeshi Factories." *Economic and Political Weekly* 35, no. 21/22 (2000): 11–17.

Slotkin, Richard. *Regeneration through Violence: The Mythology of the American Frontier, 1600–1860*. Norman: University of Oklahoma Press, 1973.

Smelik, Anneke. "Cinematic Fantasies of Becoming Cyborg." In *The Scientific Imaginary in Visual Culture*, edited by Anneke Smelik, 89–104. Göttigen, Germany: V & R Unipress, 2010.

Smith, Justin. *Nature, Human Nature, and Human Difference: Race in Early Modern Philosophy*. Princeton, NJ: Princeton University Press, 2015.

Smith, Rogers M. "Beyond Tocqueville, Myrdal, and Hartz: The Multiple Traditions in America." *American Political Science Review* 87, no. 3 (1993): 549–566.

Sohn, Stephen. "Alien/Asian: Imagining the Racialized Future." *Melus* 33, no. 4 (2008): 5–22.

Spillers, Hortense J. "Interstices: A Small Drama of Words." *Pleasure and Danger*, edited by Carol Vance and Kegan Paul, 73–100. Boston: Routledge, 1984.

———. "Mama's Baby, Papa's Maybe: An American Grammar Book." *Diacritics* 17, no. 2 (1987): 65–81.

Steel, Ronald. *Walter Lippmann and the American Century*. New Brunswick, NJ: Transaction, 1980.

Steele, E. Springs. "Henry George on Chattel and Wage Slavery." *American Journal of Economics and Sociology* 46, no. 3 (1987): 369–378.

Sturdevant, Saundra Pollock, and Brenda Stoltzfus. *Let the Good Times Roll: Prostitution and the United States Military in Asia*. New York: New Press, 1993.

Sueyoshi, Amy. *Discriminating Sex: White Leisure and the Making of the American "Oriental."* Urbana-Champaign: University of Illinois Press, 2018.

Tadiar, Neferti. *Fantasy Production: Sexual Economies and Other Philippine Consequences for the New World Order.* Hong Kong: Hong Kong University Press, 2004.

———. "Life-Times of Becoming Human." *Occasion: Interdisciplinary Studies in the Humanities* 3 (2012): 1–17.

Takaki, Ronald. *Iron Cages: Race and Culture in Nineteenth-Century America.* Oxford: Oxford University Press, 1979.

Tang, Amy. *Repetition and Race: Asian American Literature after Multiculturalism.* Oxford: Oxford University Press, 2016.

Tanner, Ron. "Toy Robots in America, 1955–75: How Japan Really Won the War." *Journal of Popular Culture* 28, no. 3 (1994): 125.

Tarantino, Matteo, and Stefania Carini. "The Good, the Fake and the Cyborg: The Broadcast and Coverage of Beijing 2008 Olympics in Italy." In *Encoding the Olympics: The Beijing Olympic Games and the Communication Impact Worldwide,* edited by Luo Qing and Giuseppe Richeri, 313–334. London: Routledge, 2013.

Tatsumi, Takayuki. *Full Metal Apache: Transactions between Cyberpunk Japan and Avant-Pop America.* Durham, NC: Duke University Press, 2006.

Tolentino, Roland B. "Bodies, Letters, Catalogs: Filipinas in Transnational Space." *Social Text* 48 (1996): 49–76.

Tuhus-Dubrow, Rebecca. *Personal Stereo.* New York: Bloomsbury, 2017.

Turse, Nick. *Kill Anything that Moves: The Real American War in Vietnam.* New York: Macmillan, 2013.

Ueno, Toshiya. "Japanimation: Techno-Orientalism, Media Tribes, and Rave Culture." In *Aliens R Us: The Other in Science Fiction Cinema,* edited by Ziauddin Sardar and Sean Cubitt, 94–110. Sterling, UK: Pluto, 2002.

Van Ree, Erik. "Marx and Engels's Theory of History: Making Sense of the Race Factor." *Journal of Political Ideologies* 24, no. 1 (2019): 54–73.

Varma, Roli. "High-Tech Coolies: Asian Immigrants in the U.S. Science and Engineering Workforce." *Science as Culture* 11, no. 3 (2002): 337–361.

Vasant, Kaiwar, and Sucheta Mazumdar. "Race, Orient, Nation in the Time-Space of Modernity." *Antinomies of Modernity: Essays on Race, Orient, Nation,* edited by Vasant Kaiwar and Sucheta Mazumdar, 261–298. Durham, NC: Duke University Press, 2003.

Vats, Anjali. *The Color of Creatorship: Intellectual Property, Race, and the Making of Americans.* Stanford, CA: Stanford University Press, 2020.

Vora, Kalindi. "Re-imagining Reproduction: Unsettling Metaphors in the History of Imperial Science and Commercial Surrogacy in India." *Somatechnics* 5, no. 1 (2015): 88–103.

Vukovich, Daniel. *China and Orientalism: Western Knowledge Production and the PRC.* London: Routledge, 2013.

Wagner, Donald. *Science and Civilisation in China.* Vol. 5. Cambridge: Cambridge University Press, 2008.

Wakeman, Frederic E. *Spymaster: Dai Li and the Chinese Secret Service.* Berkeley: University of California Press, 2003.

Walker, Alice. "Foreword." In Zora Neale Hurston, *Barracoon: The Story of the Last Black Cargo,* 1–3. New York: HarperCollins, 2018.

Wang, Grace. *Soundtracks of Asian America: Navigating Race through Musical Performance.* Durham, NC: Duke University Press, 2014.

Wasserstrom, Jeffrey. *Popular Protest and Political Culture in Modern China.* London: Routledge, 2018.

Weiner, Marli Frances. *Mistresses and Slaves: Plantation Women in South Carolina, 1830–80*. Champaign: University of Illinois Press, 1997.

Weinstein, Alexander. *Children of the New World*. New York: Picador, 2016.

Weinstein, Sheri. "Technologies of Vision: Spiritualism and Science in Nineteenth-Century America." In *Spectral America: Phantoms and the National Imagination*, edited by Jeffrey Andrew Weinstock, 124–140. Madison: University of Wisconsin Press / Popular Press, 2004.

Weinstock, Jeffrey Andrew. *Spectral America: Phantoms and the National Imagination*. Madison: University of Wisconsin Press / Popular Press, 2004.

Weiss, Gail. "The Body as Narrative Horizon." In *Thinking the Limits of the Body*, edited by Jeffrey Jerome Cohen and Gail Weiss, 25–34. Albany: State University of New York Press, 2003.

Wetmore, Alex. "Sympathy Machines: Men of Feeling and the Automaton." *Eighteenth-Century Studies* 43, no. 1 (2009): 37–54.

Whiting, Gertrude. *Old-Time Tools and Toys of Needlwork*. New York: Columbia University Press, 1971.

Whitney, James Amaziah. *The Chinese, and the Chinese Question*. New York: Tibbals Book, 1888.

Wiener, Norbert. *Cybernetics or Control and Communication in the Animal and the Machine*. Cambridge, MA: MIT Press, 1961.

Williams, Raymond. *Marxism and Literature*. Oxford: Oxford University Press, 1977.

Willoughby-Herard, Tiffany. *Waste of a White Skin: The Carnegie Corporation and the Racial Logic of White Vulnerability*. Berkeley: University of California Press, 2015.

Wittner, David G. *Technology and the Culture of Progress in Meiji Japan*. London: Routledge, 2007.

Wong, Danielle. "Inorganic Asian North American Lives: Virtual Dismemberments, Copies, and Wellbeing." PhD diss., McMaster University, 2017.

Wong, Winnie Won Yin. *Van Gogh on Demand: China and the Readymade*. Chicago: University of Chicago Press, 2013.

Woo, Susie. *Framed by War: Korean Children and Women at the Crossroads of US Empire*. New York: New York University Press, 2019.

Wu, Ellen. *The Color of Success: Asian Americans and the Origins of the Model Minority*. Princeton, NJ: Princeton University Press, 2015.

Wu, William F. *The Yellow Peril: Chinese Americans in American Fiction, 1850–1940*. Hamden, CT: Archon Books, 1982.

Wynter, Sylvia. "Unsettling the Coloniality of Being/Power/Truth/Freedom: Towards the Human, after Man, Its Overrepresentation—an Argument." *CR: The New Centennial Review* 3, no. 3 (2003): 257–337.

Yang, Mina. "East Meets West in the Concert Hall: Asians and Classical Music in the Century of Imperialism, Post-Colonialism, and Multiculturalism." *Asian Music* 38, no. 1 (2007): 1–30.

Ye, Shana. "Reconstructing the Transgendered Self as a Feminist Subject: Trans/Feminist Praxis in Urban China." *Transgender Studies Quarterly* 3, no. 1–2 (2016): 259–265.

Yu, Jessica. "When We Say Smart Asian Girl We Don't Mean Smart (White) Girl: The Figure of the Asian Automaton and the Adolescent Artist in the Künstlerroman Genre." *Journal of Asia-Pacific Pop Culture* 4, no. 2 (2019): 169–191.

Yun, Lisa. *The Coolie Speaks: Chinese Indentured Laborers and African Slaves in Cuba*. Philadelphia: Temple University Press, 2008.

Zinn, Howard. *A People's History of the United States*. New York: Harper & Row, 2010.

Index

A page number followed by f indicates a figure.

Long T. Bui is Associate Professor of Global and International Studies at the University of California, Irvine, and the author of *Returns of War: South Vietnam and the Price of Refugee Memory.*

Also in the series *Asian American History and Culture*:

Keith Lawrence and Floyd Cheung, eds., *Recovered Legacies: Authority and Identity in Early Asian American Literature*

Linda Trinh Võ, *Mobilizing an Asian American Community*

Franklin S. Odo, *No Sword to Bury: Japanese Americans in Hawai'i during World War II*

Josephine Lee, Imogene L. Lim, and Yuko Matsukawa, eds., *Re/collecting Early Asian America: Essays in Cultural History*

Linda Trinh Võ and Rick Bonus, eds., *Contemporary Asian American Communities: Intersections and Divergences*

Sunaina Marr Maira, *Desis in the House: Indian American Youth Culture in New York City*

Teresa Williams-León and Cynthia Nakashima, eds., *The Sum of Our Parts: Mixed-Heritage Asian Americans*

Tung Pok Chin with Winifred C. Chin, *Paper Son: One Man's Story*

Amy Ling, ed., *Yellow Light: The Flowering of Asian American Arts*

Rick Bonus, *Locating Filipino Americans: Ethnicity and the Cultural Politics of Space*

Darrell Y. Hamamoto and Sandra Liu, eds., *Countervisions: Asian American Film Criticism*

Martin F. Manalansan IV, ed., *Cultural Compass: Ethnographic Explorations of Asian America*

Ko-lin Chin, *Smuggled Chinese: Clandestine Immigration to the United States*

Evelyn Hu-DeHart, ed., *Across the Pacific: Asian Americans and Globalization*

Soo-Young Chin, *Doing What Had to Be Done: The Life Narrative of Dora Yum Kim*

Robert G. Lee, *Orientals: Asian Americans in Popular Culture*

David L. Eng and Alice Y. Hom, eds., *Q & A: Queer in Asian America*

K. Scott Wong and Sucheng Chan, eds., *Claiming America: Constructing Chinese American Identities during the Exclusion Era*

Lavina Dhingra Shankar and Rajini Srikanth, eds., *A Part, Yet Apart: South Asians in Asian America*

Jere Takahashi, *Nisei/Sansei: Shifting Japanese American Identities and Politics*

Velina Hasu Houston, ed., *But Still, Like Air, I'll Rise: New Asian American Plays*

Josephine Lee, *Performing Asian America: Race and Ethnicity on the Contemporary Stage*

Deepika Bahri and Mary Vasudeva, eds., *Between the Lines: South Asians and Postcoloniality*

E. San Juan Jr., *The Philippine Temptation: Dialectics of Philippines–U.S. Literary Relations*

Carlos Bulosan and E. San Juan Jr., eds., *The Cry and the Dedication*

Carlos Bulosan and E. San Juan Jr., eds., *On Becoming Filipino: Selected Writings of Carlos Bulosan*

Vicente L. Rafael, ed., *Discrepant Histories: Translocal Essays on Filipino Cultures*

Yen Le Espiritu, *Filipino American Lives*

Paul Ong, Edna Bonacich, and Lucie Cheng, eds., *The New Asian Immigration in Los Angeles and Global Restructuring*

Chris Friday, *Organizing Asian American Labor: The Pacific Coast Canned-Salmon Industry, 1870–1942*

Sucheng Chan, ed., *Hmong Means Free: Life in Laos and America*

Timothy P. Fong, *The First Suburban Chinatown: The Remaking of Monterey Park, California*

William Wei, *The Asian American Movement*

Yen Le Espiritu, *Asian American Panethnicity*

Velina Hasu Houston, ed., *The Politics of Life*

Renqiu Yu, *To Save China, To Save Ourselves: The Chinese Hand Laundry Alliance of New York*

Shirley Geok-lin Lim and Amy Ling, eds., *Reading the Literatures of Asian America*

Karen Isaksen Leonard, *Making Ethnic Choices: California's Punjabi Mexican Americans*

Gary Y. Okihiro, *Cane Fires: The Anti-Japanese Movement in Hawaii, 1865–1945*

Sucheng Chan, *Entry Denied: Exclusion and the Chinese Community in America, 1882–1943*

www.ingramcontent.com/pod-product-compliance
Lightning Source LLC
Chambersburg PA
CBHW071845270326
41929CB00013B/2114